THE FATHERS OF THE CHURCH

A NEW TRANSLATION

VOLUME 4

THE FATHERS OF THE CHURCH

A NEW TRANSLATION

SAINT AUGUSTINE

THE IMMORTALITY OF THE SOUL
translated by
Ludwig Schopp

THE MAGNITUDE OF THE SOUL
translated by
John J. McMahon, S.J.

ON MUSIC
translated by
Robert Catesby Taliaferro

THE ADVANTAGE OF BELIEVING
translated by
Luanne Meagher, O.S.B.

ON FAITH IN THINGS UNSEEN
translated by
Roy Joseph Deferrari
and
Mary Francis McDonald, O.P.

THE CATHOLIC UNIVERSITY OF AMERICA PRESS
Washington, D.C.

NIHIL OBSTAT:

JOHN M. FEARNS, S.T.D.

Censor Librorum

IMPRIMATUR:

✠ FRANCIS CARDINAL SPELLMAN

Archbishop of New York

October, 1, 1947

The *nihil obstat* and *imprimatur* are official declarations that a book or pamphlet is free of doctrinal or moral error. No implication is contained therein that those who have granted the *nihil obstat* and *imprimatur* agree with the content, opinions, or statements expressed.

Library of Congress Catalog Card No. 77 -081336
ISBN 0-8132-1319-3
ISBN **978-0-8132-1319-4** (pbk.)

Reprinted 1977, 1984, 1992
First paperback reprint 2002

CONTENTS

THE IMMORTALITY OF THE SOUL

(*De immortalitate animae*)

Translated

by

LUDWIG SCHOPP, Ph.D.

INTRODUCTION

THE PROBLEM of the soul's immortality has ever arrested the attention of serious thinkers.[1] The very hours before his death, Socrates, 'the best, the wisest and the noblest man,' spent with his friend Crito in discussing this persistent and fascinating subject. To Augustine of Hippo belongs the distinction of having been the first philosopher in the Christian Tradition of the West to compose a formal treatise on the immortality of the soul.[2] In his *Soliloquia* the young Augustine had already exclaimed: 'First of all I should like to know if I am immortal.'[3]

Some authors[4] do not seem to appreciate the originality of Augustine's thought on this problem and present his solution simply as a mere imitation of the Greek philosophers, especially Plato. On the other hand, among those who discuss more thoroughly Augustine's teachings on the survival of the soul and who acknowledge its distinctive merits in the history of philosophy may be included M. Kreutle, G. von Hertling,[5] W. P. O'Connor,[6] and M. Grabmann.[7]

1 Cf. Roy W. Sellars, *The Principles and Problems of Philosophy* (New York 1926) 472.

2 Cf. M. Kreutle, 'Die Unsterblichkeitslehre in der Scholastik von Alkuin bis Thomas von Aquin' 341: 'Der erste Denker, der sich im Abendland mit der Unsterblichkeit der Seele beschäftigte, war Augustinus, dessen feuriger Geist unwiderstehlich nach der Erkenntnis des eigenen Ich verlangte und sich vor allem für das Schicksal desselben nach dem Tode des Leibes interessierte.'

3 *Soliloquia* 2.1.1.

4 J. F. Nourrisson, W. Heinzelmann, F. Wörter, A. Stöckl, W. Turner, G. Papini, and others.

5 G. von Hertling: *Augustin* (Mainz 1902).

6 W. P. O'Connor, *The Concept of the Human Soul according to St. Augustine* (Cath. Univ. of America Diss. 1921) 57-66.

7 M. Grabmann, *Grundgedanken des Heiligen Augustinus über Seele und Gott* (Köln 1929) 52-66.

Augustine's reasons for the immortality of the soul are basically rooted first, in the human mind, and second, in Christian teaching. While his psychological[8] and theological reasons were to be developed and perfected in some of his later writings, such as *De civitate Dei* and *De Trinitate,*[9] the rational demonstration is stressed in the prime of his intellectual and spiritual awakening. His fifth work, *De immortalitate animae,* is devoted expressly to the solution of this problem.

When Augustine, in later years, describes[10] this treatise as an imperfect and 'obscure' draft that, without his knowledge and intention, had come into the hands of others, it is more the form than the content that receives his censure. Although medieval and modern scholarship has done a great deal for the development of psychology, the science of the soul, Augustine's *De immortalitate animae* has lost nothing of its peculiar value and charm in the course of time.[11] In spite of its aphoristic and unpolished form, it is, for the spontaneity and the philosophical spirit of the young author, appraised by some[12] as the most interesting work Augustine wrote in his youth. Medieval thinkers[13] were attracted by its precious and timeless thoughts on *being, life, substance, thinking, truth, virtue, eternity,* and *time.* Its careful perusal will afford also to the modern reader, who is fond of dialectics, psychology, or even psychoanalysis, hours of delight and inspiration. E. Gilson[14] refers to it quite frequently, and

---

8 The desire to survive is fundamental and common to all men. Cf. *De civ. dei* 11, 27, 1.

9 Cf. *De civ. dei* 10, 29.1 and *De Trin.* 13.4.7 ff.

10 *Retractationes* 1.5.1. The *Retractationes* contain Augustine's own record and a personal review of his prolific literary career.

11 J. McCabe, *Saint Augustine and His Age* (London 1910) 164.

12 W. Heinzelmann, *Augustins Lehre von der Unsterblichkeit* 31 n. 20.

13 Cf. P. Pomponazzi, *De immortalitate animae* (Messina-Roma 1925) 122.

14 E. Gilson, *Introduction à l'Etude de Saint Augustin* 65ff. and *passim* (Paris 1943).

scholars like J. Barion, E. Przywara, and others regard it as a valuable source.

The *Immortality of the Soul* is also of great interest for an understanding and an evaluation of Augustine's personal development. Augustine's philosophical progress is closely connected with his personal experience; his philosophy grows and develops in the same rhythm as his restless mind strives for the truth, and as his heart, with an ever increasing flame, burns for happiness.

This short work was written at Milan shortly after Augustine's return from Cassiciacum, where he had written the following books:[15] *Contra Academicos* (Answer to Skeptics), *De beata vita* (The Happy Life), *De ordine* (Divine Providence and the Problem of Evil) and *Soliloquia* (Soliloquies). In *Contra Academicos* he refutes skepticism and proves the existence of an incontestable truth; *De beata vita* deals with the longing for happiness in everyone's soul, that happiness which finds its fulfillment only in the possession of God, the highest Truth and supreme Good; in *De ordine* he praises this God, the *Ordo Ipse,* who in His love has created and well ordered the world and everything in the world, from the brook that flows with an ever changing rhythm, up to man, the most perfect creature on earth. Each man, as an *animal rationale mortale*, is endowed[16] with the faculty of reasoning (*ratione uti*). He is made in the image of God, and thus, by a sacred indissoluble bond, united with his Creator and the soul of his fellow man. In *De ordine*[17] Augustine has

15 The translations of these four books are contained in the first volume of St. Augustine's works in this series.

16 *De ordine* 2.11.32. For the difference between rational and 'rationable,' cf. L. Schopp, *The Happy Life* 9. In *De moribus ecclesiae Catholicae* 1.27.52 we find the definition: 'Man is a rational soul using a mortal and earthly body,' which later (*De Trinitate* 15.7.11) was replaced by: 'Man is a rational substance consisting of soul and body.'

17 *De ordine* 2.18.47.

already come to the conclusion that there are only two worthwhile questions in the realm of philosophy: 'one about the soul, the other about God.' Consequently, in his *Soliloquia* the knowledge of 'God and soul'[18] becomes the final goal of his ardent prayers and search. Here, he speaks of the immortality of the soul and promises another volume devoted to a more careful investigation of this question, a promise he kept in writing *De immortalitate animae.*

The peaceful days of physical relaxation, the delightful hours of philosophical discussions and of spiritual meditation and practice, which Augustine had enjoyed during his stay on the estate of Verecundus in Cassiciacum, have gone. He has returned with his companions to Milan and is now expecting to be officially received into the Church of Christ.[19] Yet, before bowing his head in the baptismal font,[20] he wishes to follow his inner urge to investigate the problem of the immortality of his soul. Here, again, we see how closely and realistically Augustine's thinking is interwoven with his life. He is not so much interested either in the general qualities[21] or in the origin[22] of the soul; primarily, it is the question

18 *Soliloquia 1.2.7.*

19 Augustine was baptized by St. Ambrose, Bishop of Milan, on Holy Saturday, in the year 387, with his son Adeodatus and 'the brother of his heart,' Alypius.

20 H. H. Lesaar's opinion, in *Saint Augustine,* trans. from the German by T. Pope Arkell (London 1931) 130, that *De immortalitate animae* was written after Augustine's baptism, is contradicted by Augustine's *Retractationes* 1.5.7. O'Connor's statement (*op. cit.* 12) that the work was written after Augustine's baptism 'at Cassiciacum shortly after his return from Milan' is, of course, erroneous.

21 This question is treated in *De quantitate animae,* written at Rome in 388.

22 Augustine speaks of the origin of the soul in the beginning of *De quantitate animae* and also, much later (419), in *De anima et eius origine;* see also the tenth book of *De genesi ad litteram* (413). Augustine later (*Retractationes* 1.8.2, 1.4.4, and *De Trinitate* 12.15.24) refutes his previous assumption of the pre-existence of the soul in the Platonic sense, without, however, giving any clear opinion as

of the ultimate end of his soul that stirs his mind and makes him search for a philosophical justification before he takes the decisive step. Not that Augustine is not deeply convinced of the immortality of the soul in accordance with the Christian faith (*auctoritas*), which he already had rated higher than *ratio,* in *Contra Academicos.*[23]However, if neither the name of Christ nor any of those genuinely Christian[24] elements which appear in the four writings mentioned above is found in this treatise, this is to be explained from Augustine's intention to study here the problem of immortality from the rational point of view only.

How does Augustine proceed, to prove the immortality of the soul?

First, as in his earlier *Soliloquia,*[25] he establishes the fact that the soul, because it knows most certainly of its own faculty of reasoning[26] must exist, must be a reality. This reality must be a living substance, since only a living substance is able to reason.[27] In examing more thoroughly the essence, qualities, and faculties of different substances—for instance, all corporeal substances are changeable, occupy space, and can be cut endlessly into parts—Augustine concludes that the soul cannot be corporeal, but must necessarily be an

---

to his view of the soul's origin. As to the four hypotheses mentioned in this connection, see E. Gilson, *op. cit.*, and Bourke, *Augustine's Quest of Wisdom.*

---

23 3.20.43.

24 Cf. A. Dyroff, *Über Form und Begriffsgehalt der augustinischen Schrift. De ordine,* called 'the most important article on the Augustinian dialogues' by E. T. Silk, 'Boethius' *Consolatio philosophiae as a* Sequel to Augustine's Dialogues and *Soliloquia,' Harvard Theological Review* 32 (1939). Cf. also L. Schopp, *The Happy Life* (Introduction); and A. C. Pegis, 'The Mind of St. Augustine.'

25 2.1.1.

26 *De immortalitate animae* 1.1.

27 *Ibid.* 2.2.

incorporeal substance. Although this incorporeal substance is an independent entity,[28] and distinct from its psychical[29] actions it is the seat of science, the principles and contents of which are true; for 'the sum of two and two is four'[30] as well as 'a straight line drawn through the center of a circle is longer than any other line not drawn through the center,'[31] are statements based upon true principles that are immutable. They are true only through the truth. Since there is no interruption[32] in the existence of the truth, it must be everlasting; since the truth can only exist in an incorporeal substance that is alive, and is inseparably connected with it as with its subject, this incorporeal substance, i.e., the soul, must everlastingly live. Thus, the soul is immortal.

Without examining Augustine's dependence[33] upon the Greeks, it will suffice for our purpose to point out that before his baptism he speaks, in a truly Christian spirit, of an incorporeal, individual-substantial human soul and furnishes

---

28 Augustine (*ibid.*) shows the continuity of one's own self and its difference from subsequent psychical occurrences within it, by stating that someone (e.g. the artist) is able to execute an idea that he holds presently in his mind and expects to materialize in the course of time, only through keeping the idea unchanged in his mind, i.e., through his memory.

29 *Ibid.* 4.6.

30 *Ibid.* 2.2.

31 *Ibid.* 1.1.

32 *Ibid.* 4.5.

33 Although Augustine's philosophy basically follows Plato more than Aristotle (see *De civitate Dei* 8.12.), we have already pointed out that Augustine, through a Neo-Pythagorean (probably Nicomachus of Gerasa), was more familiar with the doctrine of Aristotle than generally assumed (see L. Schopp, 'Der Wahrheitsbegriff'; Dyroff, *op. cit.;* and Schopp, *The Happy Life*). *De immortalitate animae* contains Aristotelian as well as Platonic elements. We here would differ from first, Wörter (*op. cit.* 14) who finds only Neo-Platonic ideas, and, second, Nourrisson (*op. cit.* II, 308), who asserts that the Augustinian teaching of the soul is a direct imitation of the Aristotelian doctrine. See also O'Connor, *op. cit.* 27, and W. Thimme, *Augustins erster Entwurf einer metaphysischen Seelenlehre* (Berlin 1908.

rational arguments for its survival after the death of the body; furthermore, that he does not understand this survival in the sense of the Platonic or Plotinian doctrine of reincarnation in beasts,[34] or, like Porphyry, as the rebirth of the soul in other human beings.

De immortalitate animae was written between March 10 (Ash Wednesday) and April (Easter Sunday), 387, since those who wanted to receive baptism had to register as *electi* or *competentes* at the beginning of the Lenten season. Aurelius was at that time in his thirty-third year. This treatise differs in some respect from Augustine's earlier writings. It does not have the form of a dialogue and, as the *Soliloquia*, is without dedication.[35] It gives the impression of being a mere set of premises and conclusions, that sometimes are not fully developed.

This translation is based on the text of Migne, *PL* 32 1021 ff., and all relevant supplementary material has been used.

The task of the translator has not been an easy one, which will be no surprise in the light of Augustine's own words in his *Retractationes*:[36] "The reasoning is involved and too briefly expressed and its resultant obscurity was such that my attention flagged as I read it, and I could hardly understand it myself."

---

34 Augustine, *De civitate Dei* 10.30. For Augustine's dependence upon Plato and Plotin see Kreutle, *op. cit.* 346.

35 *Contra Academicos* was dedicated to his friend and protector Romanianus, *De beata vita* to his friend Theodorus, *De ordine* to his friend Zenobius.

36 *Retractationes* 1.5,1.

SELECT BIBLIOGRAPHY

Texts:

J. P. Migne, *Patrologia Latina* 32 1021 ff. (Paris 1861).

G. G. Leckie, *On The Immortality Of The Soul (De immortalitate animae) by St. Aurelius Augustinus* (New York & London 1938).

F. E. Tourscher, *Saint Augustine, De Immortalitate Animae, The Immortality of the Soul* (Philadelphia 1937).

Secondary Works:

J. Barion, *Plotin und Augustinus* (Berlin 1935).

V. J. Bourke, *Augustine's Quest of Wisdom* (Milwaukee 1945).

Boyer, S.J., *L'Idée de vérité dans la philosophie de Saint Augustin* (Paris 1941).

———, *Christianisme et néo-platonisme dans la formation de Saint Augustin* (Paris 1920).

E. Bréhier, *La philosophie de Plotin* (Paris 1928).

A. Dupont, *La Philosophie de Saint Augustin* (Louvain 1881).

A. Dyroff, *Über Form und Begriffsgehalt der augustinischen Schrift De ordine,* in Grabmann-Mausbach, *Aurelius Augustinus* (Köln 1930).

J. Geyser, *Die erkenntnistheoretischen Anschauungen Augustins zu Beginn seiner schriftstellerichen Tätigkeit,* in Grabmann-Mausbach, *Aurelius Augustinus* (Köln, 1930).

E. Gilson, *Introduction à l'étude de Saint Augustin* (Paris 1943).

M. Grabmann, *Der göttliche Grund menschlicher Wahrheitserkenntnis nach Augustinus und Thomas Aquin* (Münster 1924).

———, *Grundgedanken des Heiligen Augustinus über Seele und Gott* (Köln 1929).

———, *Augustins Lehre vom Glauben und Wissen,* Grabmann-Mausbach, *Aurelius Augustinus* (Köln 1930).

W. Heinzelmann, *Über Augustinus Lehre vom Wesen und Ursprung der menschlichen Seele* (Halberstadt 1868).

———*Augustins Lehre von der Unsterblichkeit und Immaterialität der menschlichen Seele* (Jena 1874).

G. von Hertling, *Augustin* (Mainz 1902).

J. Hessen, *Die Begründung der Erkenntnis nach dem hl. Augustinus* (Münster 1916).

P. B. Jansen, S.J., *Zur Lehre des hl. Augustinus von dem Erkennen der Rationes Aeternae,* in Grabmann-Mausbach, *Aurelius Augustinus* (Köln 1930).

M. Kreutle, '*Die Unsterblichkeitslehre in der Scholastik von Alkuin bis Thomas von Aquin'* in *Philos. Jahrbuch der Görresgesellschaft* (Fulda 1918).

H. H. Lesaar, *Saint Augustine,* trans. by T. Pope Arkell (London 1931).

J. Mausbach, *Wesen und Stufung des Lebens nach dem heiligen Augustinus, in Grabmann-Mausbach, Aurelius Augustinus,* (Köln 1930).

J. McCabe, *Saint Augustine and His Age* (London 1910).

W. Montgomery, 'Saint Augustine's Attitude to Psychic Phenomena,' in *Hibbert Journal* (Oct. 1927).

J. F. Nourrisson, *La philosophie de Saint Augustin* (Paris 1866).

W. P. O'Connor, *The Concept of the Human Soul according to Saint Augustine* (Washington D. C. 1921).

G. Papini, *Saint Augustine,* trans. by M. Prichard Agnetti (New York 1930).

A. C. Pegis, 'The Mind of Saint Augustine' in *Mediaeval Studies* VI (1944) 1-61.

A. Schmitt, *Mathematik und Zahlenmystik,* in Grabmann-Mausbach, *Aurelius Augustinus* (Köln 1930).

H. Schöler, *Augustins Verhältnis zu Plato* (Diss. Jena 1897).

L. Schopp, 'Der Wahrheitsbegriff des Boethius und seine Beziehungen zu dem des hl. Augustinus,' in *Philos. Jahrbuch der Universität Bonn,* (1. Jahrgang 1924).

———, *Aurelius Augustinus Selbstgespräche, Die echten Selbstgespräche ins Deutsche übertragen* (München 1938).

———, *The Happy Life (De beata vita) by Aurelius Augustinus* (St. Louis & London 1939).

W. Schulten, *Augustins Lehre von Summe esse und esse creatum* (Würzburg 1935).

W. Thimme, *Augustins erster Entwurf einer metaphysischen Seelenlehre* (Berlin 1908).

F. Wörter, *Die Unsterblichkeitslehre in den philosophischen Schriften des Aurelius Augustinus mit besonderer Rücksicht auf den Platonismus* (Freiburg 1880).

———, *Die Geistesentwicklung des hl. Augustinus bis zu seiner Taufe* (Paderborn 1892).

S. Zimmermann, *Die Unsterblichkeit der Seele in Platons Phaedo* (Leipzig 1869).

CONTENTS

THE IMMORTALITY OF THE SOUL

Chapter 1

If science[1] exists anywhere, and if it can exist only in the realm of that which lives and always is, and if anything, in which something else dwells forever, must itself always be, then that must live forever in which science exists.

If we who reason exist, that is, if our mind[2] does, and if correct reasoning[3] without science is impossible—and only a

1 *Disciplina* is here translated as 'science.' Augustine (*Soliloquia* 2.11.19) says: 'The word *disciplina* derives from *discere* (to learn).' It signifies the knowledge that can be learned: hence (in *De immortalitate animae* 1.1.) the definition: 'Est enim disciplina quarumcumque rerum scientia.' In the text of the *Soliloquia,* dialectics is called '*disciplina disciplinarum.*' As for the Augustinian concept of science, cf. J. Geyser, *op. cit.* 80 ff. E Gilson, *op. cit.* 18f. and 150 ff. and M. Grabmann, Grundgedanken 91, 102ff. For *scientia and sapientia,* cf. Schopp, 'Der Wahrheitsbegriff.'

2 Augustine gives a definition of *animus* in *De quantitate animae* 13.22: '[the soul] apparently is a certain substance participating in reason adapted to the ruling of the body.' In *De genesi ad litteram* 7. 21, Augustine considers himself unable to give a single adequate term for the human soul. Therefore, one usually finds in his writings the following three terms: *anima, animus* (borrowed from Varro's *De diis selectis;* cf. *De civitate Dei* 7.23.1) and *spiritus* (taken from Porphyry —cf. *De civitate Dei* 10.9.2.—and from Holy Scriptures). Cf. also W. O'Connor, *op. cit.* 38 ff. and Gilson *op. cit.* 56 n.1.

3 The relation of *ratio* to *ratiocinatio* is that of a permanent faculty to its actual use (*De quantitate animae* 27.52). *Ratio* means a certain vision of the mind; *ratiocinato,* a movement of that vision, a search for that which is to be looked upon (*De quantitate animae* 27.53). Cf. also *Soliloquia* 1.6.13; 'Aspectus animae ratio est.' For the term *ratio* in its relation to *mens* and *intelligentia,* cf. also E. Gilson, *op. cit.*

mind in which science does not exist can be without science —then science exists in the mind of man.

Moreover, science is somewhere, for it exists, and whatever exists cannot be nowhere. Again, science can exist only in that which lives. For nothing that does not live learns anything, and science cannot possibly exist in something that does not learn.[4]

Again, science exists always. For whatever exists and is immutable must necessarily exist always. On the other hand nobody denies that science exists. And whoever asserts that only the straight line drawn through the center of a circle is longer than any other line not drawn through the center,[5] and that this statement belongs in the realm of science, as much as admits that there is an immutable science.

Also, nothing in which something else exists always, cannot be but always. Nothing, however, that always is ever suffers the loss from itself of that in which it always exists.

And, when we reason, it is an act of our mind; for only that reason which understands can reason. Neither the body understands, nor the mind, aided by the body, understands, because, when the mind wishes to understand, it is turned away from the body.[6] That which is understood is so always; nothing, however, pertaining to the body is so always.[7] Truly, the body is not able to be of aid to the soul in its striving toward understanding, since it cannot even be of hindrance.

---

4 Cf. *Retractationes* 1.5.2.

5 Schmitt, *op. cit.* 359 f., made a good use of this text. Cf. A. Dyroff *op. cit.* 23, who adduces the geometrical example in *De ordine* 1.2.3.

6 Augustine is here under the strong influence of the reality of the Platonic *mundus intelligibilis* (cf. *De beata vita* 2.8, where he enumerates the particular characteristics of reality). Cf. *Soliloquia* 2.2.3. Wörter here points to Augustine's dependence on Plotinus (*Enneades* 4.7.8). But that Augustine, in later years, recognizes a sound sensual realism, can be drawn from *De Trinitate* 15.12.21.

7 Cf. *Retractationes* 1.5.2.

Moreover, no one reasons correctly without science.[8] Correct reasoning, of course, is the cogitation [the way of thinking] that advances, to the investigation of things not certain, from principles that are certain; nothing is certain in the mind of which it has no knowledge.

But, all that the mind knows it possesses within itself; knowledge does not encompass anything except those things that pertain to some branch of science.[9] For, science is the knowledge of all things.[10]

The human mind, therefore, lives always.

Chapter 2

(2) Reason, certainly, is either the mind or it is in the mind. Our reason, to be sure, is of better quality than our body; our body, in turn, is some kind of a substance,[1] and it is better to be a substance than nothing. Therefore, reason is not nothing. Again, whatever the harmonic structure of a body is, it is by necessity inseparably present in the body as

8 *Cf. Soliloquia* 2.11.20.
9 Cf. *Retractationes* 1.5.2.
10 The *artes liberales* enumerated by him in *De ordine* 2.12.38.

1 Hence, a substance is a something, i.e., the contrary to nothing. In *De beata vita* Augustine has several times opposed *esse* ('being') to *non-esse,* ('not-being'). In *Enarrationes in psalmos* 68.2.5, Augustine gives the following definition: 'Substance is something that is; . . . whatever is no substance is nothing at all.' This text contains Aristotle's definition (with which he was familiar—cf. *Confessiones 4.16.28*), to which he later on gave a more precise wording: 'Substance is the term for a being that can exist in and by itself without being in need of a subject of its being' (*De Trinitate* 3.5.10). *Although, according* to *De Trinitate* 7.6.11, a juxtaposition *of substantia, essentia, natura* seems to be justified in Augustine's writings, he nevertheless does not always identify them (cf. *De civitate Dei.* 12.2; *De Trinitate* 7.4.8). Speaking of God, Augustine usually applies the term *essentia,* e.g., in *De immortalitate animae* 12.19. Cf. also *De Trinitate* 7.1.2. In *De civitate Dei* 12.2, *essentia* is derived from *esse,* in order to have a word for the Greek term *ousía.*

in a subject; nothing else can be believed to be in that structure which is not with equal necessity in that respective body, in which also the structure itself is not less inseparably present.[2]

The human body, however, is subject to change, and reason is immutable.[3] For, all is subject to change that does not exist always in the same way. It is always in the same way that two and four make six. In the same way, it is always true that four is the sum of two and two; this [four], however, is not two; and two, naturally, is not four. Such reasoning is not subject to change;[4] therefore reason exists.

In no way, on the other hand, can that which is inseparably in a subject[5] remain unchanged, after the subject itself is changed. The mind, in turn, is not the structure of the body. Nor can death occur to things not subject to change. The mind, therefore, always lives, whether it itself is reason, or whether reason is inseparably attached to it.

Chapter 3

(3) Constancy possesses some power [*virtus*], and all that is constant is not subject to change. Every power is able to perform some act, being a power even when not[1] in

---

2 Like Aristotle, Augustine distinguishes in man: *vita seminalis, vita sensualis, vita intellectualis* (cf. *De civitate Dei* 5.11). Here 'soul' represents the life principle of man, i.e., the source of his physical unity, which hinders physical dissolution and regulates the vegetative functions of nutrition, growth and procreation. Cf. also Mausbach, *op. cit.*

3 In this chapter Augustine uses *ratio* also for 'idea.' For the concept of *rationes;* see P. Bernhard Jansen, S.J., 'Zur Lehre des hl. Augustinus von dem Erkennen der Rationes Aeternae.'

4 Cf. Schmitt, *op. cit.*

5 For the concept *subjectum,* cf. *Selections from Medieval Philosophers,* ed. Richard McKeon (New York) 499.

---

1 Reading *cum non agit,* from the Louvain edition.

action. Every action,[2] in turn, is moved, or causes moving. Hence, not all that is moved, and certainly not all that causes moving, is subject to change.[3] Moreover, all that is moved by another and does not cause its own moving is something mortal. But, whatever is mortal is subject to change. Consequently, one may quite surely and without opposition conclude that not all that causes moving is subject to change.

There is no motion without substance; each substance either lives or does not live. But, all that does not live is without soul,[4] and no action occurs without soul. Therefore, anything that causes moving in such a way that it does not undergo any change can only be a living substance. But, as a whole, this moves the body gradually. Hence, not everything that moves the body is mutable.

The body, however, is moved only in time, for which reason it is moved more slowly or more quickly; consequently there is something that, while it causes moving in time, is yet not changed itself.[5]

---

2 *Actio* is the actuality of a force, as being is the actuality of a substance or an essence. Cf. also McKeon, *op. cit.* 425.

3 Cf. Plato's *Phaedo* 245 C-E; Plotinus, *Enneades* 4.7.9.

4 The human soul is not only a living substance, but also a vivifying principle. Augustine confirms this (*De quantitate animae* 33.70): '[The soul], through its presence, gives life to this earthly and mortal body.' Cf. also *De agone Christiano* 20.22, and *De civitate Dei* 13.12. In the definition mentioned above (Note 1.2) of the soul as 'substantia quaedam rationis particeps regendo corpori accomodata,' Augustine called this *substantia a 'quaedam,'* whose essence he cannot explain more in detail: '*Substantiam* vero eius nominare non possum' (*De quantitate animae* 1.2). Likewise, the quality of the union of soul and body remained a mystery all his life for Augustine as well as for the philosophers after him; cf. *De civitate Dei* 21.10, where he confesses: 'Quia et iste alius modus, quo corporibus adhaerent spiritus, et animalia fiunt, omnino mirus est, nec comprehendi ab homine potest, et hoc ipse homo est.'

5 From this text it clearly results that an identification of time and movement is not permitted. Movement is measured by time and is, therefore, something different from the measuring time. Time and movements are not the same. Cf. *Confessiones* 11.24.31; Gilson, *op. cit.* 251 ff, and also, for the concept of time, Dyroff, *op. cit.* 43.

But, all that moves the body in time, no matter how it may tend toward one end, is still unable to do all at the same time. It can do only several things; for, that which can be cut into parts is unable to be perfectly one,[6] irrespective of the aid engaged. Nor is any body without parts, nor time without different intervals, nor may the shortest syllable be pronounced in such a way that you hear its end when still hearing its beginning. Morevoer, what is done in this manner must be accompanied once by the expectation that it can be completed and also by memory, in order to comprehend the measure of its capacity. Expectation[7] has to do with the things of the future; memory, with those of the past. The intention to act lies in the present through which the future lapses into the past, and the outcome of the motion of a body, once started, cannot be expected without any memory. For, how could one expect something to cease that never either had a start or has, in no way, been moved. Again, the intention that is present of bringing something to an end cannot be carried out without expectation that belongs to the future; further, that is not, which is either not as yet, or is not any more. Hence, in the one who intends to carry out something, there can exist something that really [still] belongs in the realm of things not yet in existence. For, several things can be simultaneously in the one who acts,[8] although the several things that are being done cannot

6 'Unity' is one of the three transcendental qualities of all being in the Augustinian philosophy. 'Everything is created by the One, everything is striving back to the One' (*De vera religione* 55. 133). But 'although every body is a true body, it is a false unity since it is not a unity in the highest sense' (*De vera religione* 34) and this quotation reproduces the idea of our text.

7 Cf. Gilson, *op. cit.* 85 f.

8 The three extensions, past, present, and future, can be reduced to the present with the help of memory. A detailed analysis of the power of memory is given by Augustine, especially in the tenth book of his *Confessiones*.

exist at the same time. Thus, in the one who moves there can exist things, although they cannot be in that which is moved. But, whatever things cannot be at the same time and which, nevertheless, are passing from the future into the past, are of necessity subject to change.

(4) Hence, we now gather that there can be something that remains unchanged, even though it moves things that are subject to change. For, when the mover's intention, to bring the body that is moved to a desired end, is not changed; and when the body, out of which something is made, is changed, movement after movement, through this same motion; and when the very intention of carrying out, which evidently remains unchanged, moves the very members of the workman,[9] and the wood or the stone used by the workman—who would doubt that the foregoing is not a correct conclusion?

Therefore, no one should think, if some change of bodies is effected, that the mind, being the moving agent, necessarily is changed or on account of this perhaps would die, no matter how great its intention was in the change. For, it is able to hold simultaneously in this intention the memory of the past, as well as the expectation of things to come—all of which cannot be without life.[10]

Although there is no destruction without change and no change without motion, nevertheless, not every change effects destruction and not every motion effects change. For, one

9 This image of artist and matter was transmitted by Augustine and Boethius (*Isagoge in Porphyrium*) to the Middle Ages.

10 This is the *vita intellectualis* of the human soul, including its three main faculties, memory, intelligence, and will. These are not separated essences, but participate in the substantiality of the soul. This idea is later expressed more clearly: 'These three, therefore, memory, intelligence, will are not lives, but one life; not three souls, but one soul; and, consequently, not three substances, but one substance' (*De Trinitate* 10.11.18.). Cf. *ibid.* 15.22,42.

may rightly state that our own body is moved in many ways, by all kinds of actions, and certainly is changed by growing older, but not that it has undergone destruction, meaning that it is without life. Accordingly, one may forthwith believe that the mind is not deprived of life, even though, through motion, some change may, perhaps, affect it.

Chapter 4

(5) If, therefore, something changeless, which cannot be without life, remains in the mind, it necessarily follows, then, that life everlasting remains in the mind. For, it really is so that, if the former statement is [correct], the second must also be correct. And the former is correct.

Who, indeed, would dare to say, passing over other instances, either that the principle [*ratio*] of numbers is mutable; or that there exists any art[1] which is not based on this principle [*ratio*]; or that the art is not in the artist, even though he is not presently practicing it; or that he possesses the art, without its being in his mind; or that it could be where life is not; or that, what is immutable can at any time not be; or that art is one thing and its underlying principle [*ratio*] *another.* For, even if art as a whole may be called a certain collection of principles [*rationum*], it can almost truly be called one principle, and be understood as such. But, whether this is the one way or the other, as a matter of fact art is none the less immutable. It is evident, however, not only that art is in the mind of the artist, but also that it cannot be but in his mind, and inseparable from it. For, if art is separated from the mind, it will be either

1 Regarding the Augustinian concept of art (*ars*), we refer to *De immortalitate animae* 4.6, but also to *De genesi contra Manichaeos* 1.7.13, *De vera religione* 30.56. and *De musica* 1.4.6; 6.12.35.

outside the mind, or nowhere; or it will pass continuously from mind to mind.

But, since there is no place for art without life, so life with reason belongs to nothing but the mind.[2] Moreover, what exists cannot be nowhere, nor can what is immutable at any time not exist. However, if art passes from mind to mind, leaving the one, in order to dwell in the other, then nobody teaches art without losing it, or, again, nobody becomes educated but by the forgetting or the death of his teacher.[3] If these statements are most absurd and false, as they really are, then the human mind is immortal.

(6) If, indeed, art exists at one time in the mind and at another time does not, a state sufficiently known through forgetting and ignorance, the logic of this argument in no way supports the immortality of the mind, unless the antecedent is invalidated in the following manner: Either there is something in the mind that is not actual in present thought, or the art of music is not in a trained mind while, and as long as, it is concerned only with geometry. This latter statement, however, is false; hence, the former is true. But, the mind is not aware that it possesses something, except what has entered its thought. Therefore, something may be in the mind of whose presence there the mind itself is not aware. How long this unawareness persists is of no importance. For, if the mind has concerned itself for so long a time with other things that it is unable readily to pay attention to things previously thought of, such a state of mind is called forgetting[4] or ignorance.[5]

---

2 Cf. *Retractationes* 1.5.2.

3 Cf. *De magistro* 11.40 and 12.41; also *Confessiones* 10.11.

4 What is probably meant is the forgetting of empirical knowledge previously acquired.

5 Inexperience (*imperitia*) also may be interpreted merely empirically. The proof is that Augustine also calls the soul, which (in a figurative

But when, either reasoning with ourselves or being cleverly questioned by another about certain liberal arts, we discover[6] that those things we have found are nowhere else but in our mind, and since discovering [*invenire*] is not the same as making [*facere*] or causing [*gignere*]—otherwise the mind would bring forth eternal things by means of temporal discovery, for it often does discover eternal things; (what, for instance, is so eternal as the principle [*ratio*] of a circle or anything else in arts of this kind, and is it not understood that they always have been and always will be?)—then it is evident that the human mind is immortal, and that all true principles are in its innermost regions,[7] even though it may appear as if, through want of actual knowledge or through forgetting, it either does not possess them or has lost them.

Chapter 5

(7) Now, let us see to what extent we are able to accept a change of the mind. For, granting that the mind is the subject in which art exists and that the subject cannot undergo any change unless that which is in the subject also be changed, who of us can hold that art and principle [*ratio*] are unchangeable in the mind, if the mind in which they exist is proved changeable? Again, what change is greater than that into contraries? And who denies that the mind—let alone, other examples—sometimes is stupid and at other times wise?

---

sense) increases and decreases, *peritior* and *imperitior* (*De quantitate animae* 18-19).

6 'Discover' is not necessarily to be understood as (*reminiscense*) in the Platonic sense. For in *Soliloquia* 1.8..15 Augustine clearly states the doctrine of divine enlightening

7 This text is *usually* quoted in favor of Platonic innatism and of pre-existence as being parts of Augustinian philosophy, but in Augustinian philosophy in its final shape the Platonic remembering is completely separated from the hypothesis of pre-existence.

Therefore, let us first examine in how many ways that which is called a change of the mind may be accepted. In my opinion, these ways, quite evident and clear to us, are two with regard to *genus* [kind], but manifold with regard to *species.* For, the mind is changed, so to speak, either according to the passions of the body or its own passions;[1] according to the passions of the body, by age, sickness, pain, work, injury, and carnal desire; according to its own passions, in turn, through desire, joy, fear, worry, zeal, and study.

(8) Since a combination of all these changes furnishes no conclusive argument that the mind is mortal, there is certainly no need to be afraid of any of them alone. However, it still remains to be seen that they do not contradict our former conclusion, namely, that by changing the subject everything in the subject necessarily be changed.

But, they furnish no contradiction. For, our conclusion refers only to such a change of a subject as that through which the subject is forced entirely to change its name. If, for example, wax somehow changes from a white to a black color, it remains, none the less, wax. It is also the same if it changes to a round form from a square, or from soft to hard, or from warm to cold. All these changes are within the subject, and wax is the subject. And wax remains no more and no less wax, even though these qualities are changed. Therefore, a change of those qualities can occur in the subject, while the subject itself, in regard to its essence and its name, is not changed.[2]

1 *Passiones* (affections) of the body, as well as of the soul, have subdivisions. Among the latter he first mentions the four sensual impulses of the soul in the traditional order: concupiscence (*cupiditas*), joy (*laetitia*), fear (*metus*), sadness (*aegritudo* or *tristitia*), and then *studere* and *discere,* the two last belonging to the order of will and knowledge.

2 Difference between substance (essence which bears the name of a

If, however, the change of those qualities in the subject be so great that that which was said to be subject can no longer be called so at all—as when, for instance, the wax through the heat of fire dissolves into the air and undergoes this change in such a manner that we rightly conceive the subject to be changed, because it was wax, and is wax no longer—then in no way could anyone logically believe that there remains any of those qualities which were in that subject in so far as it was this subject.

(9) Therefore, if the soul, as stated above, is the subject in which reason is inseparably present, then, by the same logical necessity with which reason being in the soul is proved, reason is immortal; so the soul, since the soul can be only a living soul, and reason within the soul cannot be without life. For, indeed, reason would remain under no circumstances immutable, if its subject did not exist. This however, would actually occur if the soul underwent such a change that it would make the soul a *no-soul,* i.e., would compel the soul to die.

But, none of these changes, effected either by the body or by the soul itself (although it is not an unimportant question whether some of these changes are effected by the soul itself, i.e., so that the soul itself is their cause), has the effect of making the soul a *no-soul.* Therefore, we do not have to fear these changes, neither in themselves, nor, certainly, with regard to our conclusions.

'something') and accident. These correspond, to the *formae substantiales* and *accidentales* in Boethius (*Isagoge in Porphyrium*) which have their origin in Aristotle and were later through Boethius taken up by Gilbertus Porretanus, John of Salisbury, Alanus de Insulis, and others.

Chapter 6

(10) Hence, I see that we have to devote all our reasoning power to the task of knowing what reason is, and in how many ways it may be defined, so that the immortality of the soul may be established according to all these ways. Reason is [*a*] the vision of the mind by means of which it beholds the true, by itself and without the help of the body; or [*b*] the contemplation itself of the true, without the aid of the body; or (*c*) the true itself, which it beholds.

As to the first, no one will doubt that reason is in the mind; about the second and third there may be some question. But, the second, also, cannot be without the mind. With regard to the third, the important question arises whether the true itself, which the mind beholds without the aid of the body, exists by itself and is not in the mind, or whether it can exist without the mind.

But, howsoever this may be, the mind could not by itself behold it, except through some kind of connection with the true. For, all we contemplate[1] we grasp by cogitation or pereive through sense or intellect.[2] And, all things that are perceived through one of the senses are sensed as existing outside of us and are contained in space, which, we affirm, makes possible their perception.[3] Those things that are comprehended by the intellect, however, are comprehended as existing nowhere else but in the comprehending mind itself and, at the same time, as not contained in space.

---

1 *Contemplari* is to be understood in a broader sense; it includes the whole of thinking, based upon sensual and intellectual perception.

2 Cf. the treatment of *sentire* and *pati* in connection with sense perception and sensation, in *De quantitate animae* 23-25.

3 Reading *unde percipi quidem posse affirmantur* (instead of *unde nec . . .*, as in Migne). The *nec* is also lacking in the text used by Tourscher.

(11) Evidently, this connection of the beholding mind and the true which it beholds is such that: either the mind is the subject and the true inherent in the subject; or, contrariwise, the true is the subject and the mind is inherent in the subject; or, both are substances.

However, if of the three the first holds true, the mind is immortal as well as reason, because—according to our previous argumentation—reason can only exist in something that is alive. The same logic is also valid in the second instance. For, if that true which is called reason does not contain anything changeable, as it appears, then nothing can be changed which is contained in the true as in a subject. Thus, the entire struggle centers around the third hypothesis. For, if the mind is a substance and if reason [the true] with which the mind is connected is likewise a substance, one would not absurdly believe that reason [the true] may remain, while the mind could cease to exist. It is manifest, however, that the mind, as long as it is not separated, but connected with reason [the true], necessarily remains and lives.

By what force, then, can the mind be separated? Could it be a corporeal force whose power is weaker, whose origin is lower, and whose order[4] is less unified? Not at all. Could it be by an animal force? But again, how could it work? Is it so that a more powerful mind cannot contemplate reason [the true] unless it has another mind separated from it? However, reason [the true] would not be wanting to a single one, even if all minds together would contemplate it. And, because nothing is more powerful than reason [the true] itself, than which nothing is less changeable, the mind not yet connected with reason [the true] can by no means be more powerful than the one already connected with it.

---

4 Cf. above, 3.3 n.6.

It remains that either reason [the true] itself separates from itself the mind, or the mind by its own volition is separated from [the true]. However, there is no trace of envy in the nature of reason [the true] to prevent it from offering itself to the enjoyment of the mind. Then, everything, to the extent of its higher level of being, is the cause of being to whatever is connected with it, which is just the opposite of destruction. But, the mind by its own will, one may say without too great absurdity, may be separated from reason [the true]—provided that an individual separation between things not contained in space is possible at all.[5] This latter statement, indeed, can be directed against all the points above, against which we have furnished other objections.

What then? May we conclude already that the mind is immortal? Or that it can be extinguished, although it cannot be separated from [the true]? However, if this force of reason [the true], through its very connection, affects the mind—for it cannot but affect it—it affects it certainly only in such a way that it gives it its being. And reason [the true] itself is there in the highest degree where changelessness is conceived in the highest degree.[6] Therefore, reason [the true] forces that mind somehow to be, which it, from its own being, affects. Thus, without separation from reason [the true], the mind cannot be extinguished. But, a separation is impossible, as we have reasoned above. Therefore, the mind cannot perish.

Chapter 7

(12) On the other hand, the mind cannot turn away from

5 Cf. *Retractationes* 1.5.2.

6 Whatever is immutable is eternal and true according to Augustine. Since truth exists only in reason, he concludes that reason in its highest degree is to be found only where highest immutability is, namely, in God.

reason [the true]—in doing so it falls into foolishness—without suffering a defect; for, just as the mind enjoys a more perfect being when turned toward reason [the true] and adhering to it—because it adheres to something unchangeable which is the truth[1] that is in the highest degree and primordial—so, when turned away from reason [the true], the mind has a less perfect being—and this means a defect. But, every defect is tending toward nothing, and no destruction can be more properly conceived than if that which has been something becomes nothing. Wherefore, a trend toward nothing is a trend toward destruction. Why this [destruction] does not fall upon the mind, although it is subject to defect, is hard to say.

While we may concede here the foregoing premises, we deny the conclusion that that which is tending toward nothing perishes, i.e., that it actually reaches nothing. The correctness of our denial may also be observed in the body.

Since each body is a part of the sensible world, the closer it approaches the volume of the universe, the larger it is and the more space it occupies; the more the body does this, the larger is the body. For, the whole is larger than the part. Wherefore, it is necessarily smaller when it is reduced. It suffers a defect, then, when it is reduced. A body is naturally reduced if something is taken away from it by way of cutting off. From this it follows that through such taking away it tends to nothing. But, no cutting off actually leads the body to nothing. For, each part that remains is a body and occupies, to the extent of its quantity, some space. This is only

1 Only God is the immutable Being, Truth itself; therefore, He is in the highest degree and from the very beginning. He also is the highest Reason, and man can avoid foolishness and recognize truth only if turned toward that Reason. This idea runs through the whole of Augustine's philosophy and is, therefore, the foundation of his concept of truth, upon which his metaphysical-intellectual voluntarism is based.

possible for the reason that it has parts, into which it may repeatedly be cut. Thus, there is no limit for a body being reduced by means of unlimited cuttings; hence it can suffer defects and tend toward nothing, though it is never able to reach nothing.[2]

This can likewise be stated and conceived with regard to space itself and to any interval whatever. For, if one takes away, let us say, a half of such defined divisions, and again the half of the remainder, and so forth, the interval will more and more decrease, advancing toward a limit which, however, it will by no means reach.

How much less, then, have we to fear this in regard to the mind. For, the mind is certainly better and more alive than the body, since it is the mind that gives life to the body.

Chapter 8

(13) However, if not the material mass, but its form, gives to the body its being[1]—a statement proved by invincible logic—then the body is the more perfect, the better formed and the more beautiful it is,[2] just as it is so much the less perfect, the uglier and the more deformed it is.[3] The latter defect occurs to the body, not through cutting off some of its mass—about which enough has been said already—but by taking away its form.

---

2 Cf. *Confessiones* 12.11.14 and 19.28, where it is said that no creature can sink back into nothingness.

---

1 For Augustinian doctrine of matter and form cf. Schopp, 'Der Wahrheitsbegriff' 1. Here matter is the *capacitas formarum* and comes very close to the conception of Aristotle, who imputes to matter only *potential being* and *being-different*.

2 *Species* is found in Augustine more often than *forma*; therefore here, *speciosius* for 'better formed.'

3 'Deformed' (*deformis*) signifies loss of form. Schulten, *op cit.* 86, calls attention to the difference between *deformitas* and *informitas*.

This point has to be carefully investigated and discussed so that no one may venture the thought that the mind perishes by such a defect. Furthermore, when the mind, while being unwise, is deprived somewhat of its form, the belief may arise that this privation can go so far that it despoils the mind entirely of its form and, by this destruction, reduces it to nothing and forces it to perish.

Therefore, if we would show that this [destruction into nothing] cannot even befall the body—namely, that it is deprived of that form through which it is body—we can rightly demonstrate how much less the mind can be deprived of that [form] through which it is mind. To be sure, no one who has carefully examined himself will contest that any mind whatever has to be given preference to any kind of body.

(14) Thus, our reasoning may start with the proposition that nothing makes or begets itself; otherwise, it would have been before it was. If the latter is untrue, the former is true. Likewise, what has been neither made nor originated and yet exists, must, by necessity, be eternal. Whosoever attributes such a nature and excellence to any body commits a grave error. But, why quarrel? To a far greater extent we are forced to attribute such a nature to the mind. Thus, in the case that a body is eternal, then certainly every mind is eternal, because any mind is to be preferred to any body, as are all eternal things to things not eternal.

Again, if—as correctly stated—the body is made, it is made by the act of someone who is not inferior to the body; otherwise, he would not have had the power to give to the product that, whatever it is, in which the being of the product consists. Nor could the maker have given this to a product that is equal. For, the maker must have something for the making which is of a higher degree than what he makes. For, it is not absurdly said of a begetter that he is [in some way] identical with what is begotten by him.

Hence, the whole body has been made by some force and nature more powerful and more excellent, at least not corporeal. If body was made by body, the whole body could not have come into existence. For, our statement at the outset of our reasoning, namely, that nothing could by itself come into being, is indeed true. This force and incorporeal nature which effected the whole body, however, preserves the whole by its ever-present power. For, after the making, it did not vanish and did not desert the thing made.

This substance, now, which is not a body, is—so to speak—not moved in space, so that it cannot be separated from that substance existing in space. Neither can that effective power vanish so as not to hold together its product or to let it ever lack its form, by which it is insofar it is at all.[4] For, what does not exist through itself will certainly not exist if deserted by that through which it exists. We cannot say, however, that when the body was made it received also the gift of being self-sufficient and self-supporting, in case it should be deserted by its creator.

(15) If this is so, the mind, which evidently surpasses the body, has this ability to a higher degree. Thus the mind's immortality is immediately proved, in case it can exist through itself. For, that which has this quality is by necessity incorruptible and, therefore, cannot perish, because nothing deserts itself. But, the mutability of the body is evident, as the whole motion of the entire body sufficiently indicates. Hence, it becomes clear to those who investigate carefully—as far as

---

4 In contradiction to the Epicureans and Stoics, Augustine again denies the extension in space of the soul.

such a nature can be investigated—that, through ordered mutability,[5] the immutable is imitated. However, that which exists through itself is not even in need of any motion, since with the utmost abundance it exists for itself; every motion is directed at another thing which is lacked by what is moved.

Thus, a form is present in the whole body, because a more excellent nature supplies and conserves the things it has made. This change, naturally, does not deprive the body of being a body, but lets it pass from one form to another by a well-ordered movement. For, not a single part of the whole can be reduced to nothing, because that effecting force comprises the whole and, through its power, that neither works nor is inactive, gives existence to everything that exists through it insofar as it does exist.

Consequently, no one should deviate from reason to such an extent as not to be certain that the mind surpasses the body, or—if this is conceded—as to believe that the body never could not be a body, but that the mind could not be mind. Because this never happens to the mind, and the mind cannot exist without life, the mind surely never dies.

Chapter 9

(16) If someone declares the mind should not fear that destruction which effects a thing, which had being before, to become nothing, but the kind of destruction that makes us call those things dead that are wanting life, he should be aware of the fact that no thing lacks itself.

But, mind is a certain principle of life. Thus, it is understood that everything animated is alive, while all that is inanimated, but can be animated, is dead, i.e., deprived of life. Therefore, the mind cannot die. Moreover, if the mind

5 Cf. *Confessiones* 12.11.14.

could ever be in need of life, it would not be mind, but something animated. If the latter is absurd, the mind has far less to fear this kind of destruction, that even life in no way has to fear.

Hence, to be sure, if the mind dies at the moment when that life deserts it, the life itself that deserts the mind is more correctly understood as being the mind, so that whatsoever is deserted by life is not so much the mind as the deserting life itself. For, if anything is considered deserted by life and dead, it is understood that it is deserted by the soul; however, this life deserting the things that die, is itself the mind, and does not desert itself. Thus, the mind does not die.[1]

Chapter 10

(17) Or perhaps we ought to believe—as some have done—that life is some kind of organization [*temperatio*] of the body. Of course, this thought would never have occurred to them, if by means of the same mind—withdrawn from the habit of bodies and purified—they had been able to see those things that have true[1] being and remain changeless.

Who, indeed, in the pursuit of a thorough self-introspection, has not experienced that his understanding of things became more adequate to the extent of his ability to withdraw and remove his mental intention from the senses of the body? If the mind were an organization of the body, this would have been impossible.

---

1 Cf. also J. Mausbach, 'Wesen und Stufung des Lebens nach dem heiligen Augustinus.'

---

1 Augustine's term for unchangeable things, as used here, namely, *vere esse,* contradicts the opinion expressed by Schulten (*op. cit.* 16) that Augustine calls God alone *vere esse.* Schulten refers probably to a text of the *Confessiones* (7.11.17, analyzed by Barion, *op. cit. 45*), where, with regard to God, it is stated: 'Id enim vere est, quod incommutabiliter manet.'

For, a thing which had no nature of its own and was not a substance, but, as with color and shape, was present in a body inseparably, would in no wise try to turn away from that body toward the perception of intellectual things, and would, so far as possible, be able to behold them and, through this vision, become better and more excellent.[2] In no way, indeed, can shape, or color, or even that very organization of the body—being a certain mixture of the four elements of which the body is composed—turn away itself from that body, in which it is as in a subject inseparably inherent.

Moreover, those things understood by the mind, when the latter turns away from the body, are surely not corporeal—and still they *are* and exist in the highest degree because they keep themselves always unchanged.

Nothing could be more absurd[3] than to say that the objects seen by our eyes have being, while those things which we discern with our intellect do not; since only a fool would doubt the fact that the intellect has an incomparably higher rank than our eyes.

However, when the mind sees those things which it perceives as keeping themselves unchanged, it shows sufficiently that it is associated with them in a marvelous, though not corporeal, way, i.e., not in space. For, either they are in the mind, or the mind itself is in them. Regardless of which one of these statements is correct, either [*a*] one is in the other as in a subject or else [*b*] either one is a substance.

---

2 'Understanding' and 'becoming-better,' truth and virtue, are the solid and immovable pillars of the Augustinian philosophy.

3 This reproach of absurdity concerns the materialistic psychology of the Epicureans and Stoics (cf. E. Zeller, *Die Philosophie der Griechen* 3.1;2. Ed. p. 385 f.). With regard to them, Augustine has already declared (4,5) that the soul possesses a being, and even a better one than the body, without having length, breadth and height in space.

But, if the first [*a*] is correct, then the mind is not in the body as in its subject, as color and shape are, because mind is either itself a substance or it inheres in the subject of another substance that is not a body.[4] But if the second [*b*] is true, the mind does not inhere in the body as in its subject, as color, because it is a substance. Yet, the organization of the body inheres in the body as in its subject, as color does. The mind, therefore, is not the organization of the body, but the mind is life. Again, no thing abandons itself, and only that dies which is abandoned by life. Therefore, the mind does not die.[5]

Chapter 11

(18) Again, the only thing to be feared is that the mind perish by defect, i.e., that it may be deprived of the form that gives it existence.[1] Although, as I think, enough has been said about this matter and although it has been demonstrated by sure reasoning that this is impossible, nevertheless, attention should be paid to the point that the only cause for fear lies in the undeniable fact that a foolish mind is in some state of defect, while the wise enjoys a more stable and fuller being.

4 Therefore the human soul is neither an accident of the body nor in any way qualitatively linked with it. Cf. also *De Trinitate* 9.4.4ff. and 10.10.15.

5 Cf. Zimmerman, *Die Unsterblichkeit der Seele in Platons Phaedo* 66. It was reproduced by Plotinus (*Enneades* 4.7.11).

1 Since Augustine's philosophy is built upon metaphysics, he likes to apply metaphysical notions also in the fields of epistemology (truth) and ethics (virtue); cf. Schopp, *The Happy Life*. In his earlier period this inclination sometimes brings him into difficulties, e.g., *De immortalitate animae* 7.12. Cf. also Thimme. With what mastery the older Augustine explains this defect, which, though leading the soul to its destruction, i.e., to its *dissimilitudo Dei*, does not affect its mode of being and its substance, has been shown (with reference to sources) by Schulten, *op. cit.* 51f.

But if, as cannot be doubted, the mind is then most wise when it sees the truth that is always and without change, and, joined by a divine love, inheres in the truth immovably,[2] and if all that exists in any manner exists by the power of that essence which exists in the highest and most sublime degree, then, also, the mind, insofar as it exists, either derives its being from that essence, or it exists through itself. Now, if it exists through itself, it never abandons itself, because it is its own cause of existence, and it never perishes, as we have shown above. If, however, it derives its being from that essence, we must carefully investigate what could be so contrary to it as to take away from the mind that *being-mind* which is accorded by that essence.

What, then, is this contrary? Perhaps falsity, since that essence is truth? It is clear, and beyond any doubt how much falsity can harm the mind. Can it do more than deceive? But, only a living person is deceived. Hence, falsity cannot destroy the mind.

If, then, falsity, which is contrary to truth, cannot deprive mind of *being-mind,* the gift of truth (for that is the way of invincible truth), what else could be found capable of taking away from mind *being-mind*? Truly, nothing; for nothing is more powerful than its contrary [the truth] to take that away which derives its existence from this contrary [the truth].

Chapter 12

(19) If we are thus searching for that which is contrary to the truth, not in so far as it is truth, but in so far as it exists in the highest and most perfect degree—although this very being exists to the extent of its truth; because we say that

2 The moral element is time and again combined with the intellectual one: truth-virtue.

truth is that by which all things are true as far as they exist: and they exist only as far as they are true—in no way, then, should I like to pass over the point which rather clearly supports my position.

Since no being, in so far as it is a being, has a contrary, how far less has that first being, called the truth, a contrary in so far as it is a being.[1]

The first statement is true. For, all being is a being only for the reason that it is. Being, however, has, its only contrary, non-being:[2] wherefore, nothing is the contrary of being. In no manner, therefore, can anything be contrary to that substance that is in the highest degree and from the very beginning. Hence, if the mind has its very being from this being—the mind must have it from another source, since it has it not from itself except from that being more excellent than the mind—then there is nothing through which it loses it, because no thing is contrary to the thing through which the mind has its being. Therefore, it cannot perish.

Of course, the mind can possess wisdom in turning toward the source of its being, and can lose it by turning away from it. Now, turning away is the contrary to turning toward. But, the mind cannot lose that which it has from that source to which no thing is contrary. Therefore, the mind cannot perish.

---

1 It would be unjustified to interpret (with F. Wörter, *op. cit.* 108) the *summa essentia* here, as well as in 15.24, as *nous* in the Plotinian sense; this essence actually is God, just as in the preceding chapter Augustine speaks of the 'divine love,' and in 13.22 he emphasizes that 'only God is better than the soul—God who cares for the soul.' Schulten (*op. cit.* 16) and Gilson (*op. cit.*) agree with this interpretation of the present text.

2 This opposition of 'being' and 'not-being', which so often appears (cf. 2.1. n.1) and which in *De beata vita* was also transferred by Augustine into the field of ethics, probably is an after effect of the Manichaean doctrine of the principles of light and darkness in the field of physics and ethics (cf. Mausbach, *op. cit.* 137).

Chapter 13

(20) Here, perhaps, the important question arises: Whether the mind, though it does not perish, may not be transformed into a substance of lower degree. The thought may occur to someone and not without justification, that this is effected by the following reasoning, that the mind will never arrive at nothing, yet it could, perhaps, be changed into a body. For, if that which was first mind became a body, it will not altogether not be.

This [transformation] is impossible however, unless either the mind itself wills it, or it be forced by another; yet, mind can never be a body, either by reason of its own will or that of force. The statement above implies that the mind, *if* it becomes body, does so either by its own desire or by force, but it does not imply that it becomes body either by its own desire or by force. Never, however, will the mind have such a desire.

For, all the desire the mind has toward the body is either to possess it, or to vivify it, or to build it up somehow, or in some form to advise it. None of these is possible, unless the mind is better than the body. Of course, if the mind becomes body, it will not be better than the body. Thus, the mind will not desire to be body. There is no better proof for this conclusion that when the mind investigates itself regarding this point. In such manner, the mind readily discovers that its only desire is to act, to know, to feel something, or just to live, as far as it has power over the body.

(21) But, if the mind is forced to be body, by what, after all, is it forced? Certainly, from something more powerful. Hence, it cannot be forced by the body itself. For, in no way is any body more powerful than any mind. But, a more

powerful mind exercises force only upon something subject to its authority. In no wise is a mind under the authority of another, except by its own desires. That mind, therefore, exercises force only to the extent to which the desires of the other, that is forced, permit.

It has been stated, however, that the mind does not desire to be body. It is further evident that the mind does not arrive at the full enjoyment of its desire by losing all desires, and it would lose them by becoming a body. The mind cannot be forced to become a body by some other mind, which has no right to force it, except through the desires of the subjugated mind.[1] Furthermore, the mind that has authority over another mind necessarily prefers to have authority over a mind than over a body, in order either to give it good advice or to rule it with malice. Therefore, the mind will not desire to be a body.

(22) Finally, this mind which exercises force is either a body invested with life or is without a body.[2] If it is without a body, it is not in this world. And if this is so, it is the supremely Good and cannot wish such an ignominious transformation for another mind.

But, if it is a body invested with life, then the other upon which it exercises force is either something invested with life or it is not. In the latter case it cannot be forced to anything by another. For, no one is more powerful than the one who exists in the highest degree. Again, the mind is in the body; it is forced to whatever it is forced by something in the body. Who, after all, doubts that the mind in no way can undergo such a great change through a body?

This would be possible if the body were to be more power-

1 Points to the freedom of the will.
2 Cf. *Retractationes* 1.5.3.

ful than the mind. Whatever that may be to which the mind is forced through the body, it certainly is not forced through [its own] body, but through its own desires, as has been already explained sufficiently.

However, more excellent than the rational soul—as all agree—is God. Yet, He surely takes care of the soul, and thus the soul cannot be forced by Him to be changed into a body.

Chapter 14

(23) If the mind, therefore, neither through its own will nor through an outside force, suffers such a transformation, from what source, then, can it suffer it? Should one perhaps fear, because sleep, frequently against our will, overpowers us, that the mind, through such a defect, be changed into a body—as though our mind in any part whatever would become weaker simply because our members become languid through sleep. But what the mind does not feel are only material objects, since sleep, whatever its cause may be, derives from the body and is working within the body.

Sleep somehow deprives the senses of feeling and in some way closes them off, so that the soul gladly yields to such a change of the body. This change is quite natural, since it restores the body from the strain of labor, yet this change does not deprive the mind either of the power of feeling or of understanding. Hence, the mind has the images of sensible things present with such an exact similarity that, at that very time [of sleep], they cannot be distinguished from the objects of which they are images, and, if the mind conceives something, it is equally true for it whether it sleeps or is awake.

If, for instance, someone during a dream has appeared to himself to be engaged in a discussion and, pursuing true principles, has learned something in this discussion, then these true principles also remain the same and unchangeable after his awakening. Yet, other circumstances may be found untrue, such as the place of the discussion, or the person with whom he seemed to have the discussion, and—as far as their sound is concerned—even the words seemingly used in the discussion, and other things of such kind as are to be perceived, or acted upon, through the senses by awakened persons. Yet, these things pass away and in no way reach the level of everlasting presence of true principles. From this, one may conclude that, through a bodily change such as sleep, the soul's use of the same body can be reduced, but not the soul's proper life.

Chapter 15

(24) Finally, united with the body (and this not in space, although the body occupies space) the soul is affected[1] prior to the body by those highest and eternal principles, changeless and not contained in space, and not only prior, but also to a greater extent. For, the prior affect in the soul occurs to the extent that the soul is nearer to these principles, and, by the same token, the soul is more greatly affected in proportion to the superiority over the body. This nearness is not one in space, but in the order of nature. In this order, then, it is understood that a form is given by the highest Being through the soul to the body—the form whereby the latter exists, in so far as it exists.

Hence, the body subsists through the soul and exists by the very fact that it is animated, whether universally, as is

1 By speaking here of '*affici*' of the soul by the eternal principles, Augustine transfers the concept which was held by Plato (*Theaetetus* 151 E; 163 A) in respect to sense perception to the field of purely intellectual knowledge.

the world,[2] or individually, as is each and everything that has life within the world.

This yields the conclusion that the soul, through the soul, could become a body, and that this would be possible in no other way at all. Because this does not happen—as the soul remains soul in that through which it is soul, and the body subsists through the soul, which gives, but does not take away, its form—the soul cannot be changed into a body.

For, if the soul does not give the form which in turn it receives from the supreme Good, the body is not formed by it, and, if the body is not formed by it, it is either not formed at all, or it assumes a form as close[to the supreme Good] as the soul. However, the body is formed, and, if it would assume a form as close [to thesupreme Good as the soul], it would be like the soul. But the important point here is: The soul is the more excellent the closer [to the supreme Good] the form is which it assumes. But, the body also would have assumed a form close [to the Highest] if it had not received its form from the soul. For, if there were not an intermediate cause,

2 Wörter (*op. cit.* 71) sees in this text a distinction, made by Augustine on the pattern of Plotinus (Enneades 4.7.12), between the general world-soul and the individual souls. Gilson (op. cit. 274) declares: 'A maintes reprises, au cours de sa longue carrière, saint Augustin s'est demandé si l'âme de l'homme était la plus haute des âmes créés par Dieu, ou s'il ne faudrait pas admettre, au-dessus d'elle, l'existence d'une âme du monde qui servirait à Dieu d'instrument dans l'administration de l'univers? Platon le croyait; pour lui, Augustin estime surtout que c'est là une grande et difficile question, qu'il se reconnaît incapable de résoudre soit par l'autorité de l'Écriture, soit par l'évidence de la raison.' Dyroff (*op. cit.* 36) has already stated in his discussion with Wörter that Augustine's 'Anima quae usquequaque est' (De ordine 2.11.30) was not necessarily influenced by Plotinus' world soul; he thinks that this statement can be interpreted, if not as the divine Logos, as 'the *pneuma* of Aristotle that is spread all over the world,' Augustine was familiar with this Aristotelian idea through the Neo-Pythagorean Nicomachus of Gerasa. Augustine himself (*Retractationes* 1.5.3.) reports that this statement of his was said *temere*.

the body would have assumed a form quite as close as the soul.

There is nothing between the supreme Life, which is immutable Wisdom and Truth, and that which is brought to life as the last one, i.e., the body, except the vivifying soul.[3] If the soul gives a form to the body so that the latter is body in so far as it exists, it does not, through this transfer, take away the form; however, by a transformation of the soul into a body the soul would lose its form.

Hence, the soul does not become body: neither by itself, because the body is only made by the soul when the soul remains soul; nor by another soul, because the body is made by the soul only through transfer of a form, and only by privation of its form would the soul be converted into body, if it were converted.

Chapter 16

(25) This can be said, also, of the irrational soul or life, that the rational soul cannot be converted into the irrational. If the irrational soul itself were not subjected to the rational by reason of its inferior rank, it would assume a form in an equal way and be like the latter. In natural order, the more powerful beings transmit to the lower ones the form which they have received from the supreme Beauty. And, surely, if they give, they do not take away. The things of inferior rank, in so far as they are, are for the very reason that the more powerful beings transmit to them the form by which they are; these are by reason of their power more excellent. To these natures it is given that they have greater power, not for the reason that they are heavier than those of lighter weight, but for the reason that without large extension in

3 This recalls *De vera religione* 53.113.

space they are more powerful because of the very form that makes them more excellent. In this way the soul is more powerful and excellent than the body. Hence, since the body subsists by the soul, as has been said, the soul itself can in no way be transformed into a body. For no body is made unless it receives its form from the soul. Again, in order that the soul become a body, it could do so only by losing, but not by receiving a form; this is impossible for the reason that the soul is not contained in space and is not united in space with the body. For, if this could be so, perhaps a larger mass could through a *form* turn the soul, in spite of the soul's higher rank, into its own of lower rank—as with the larger air and the smaller fire. But, that is not so. Each mass that occupies space is not in its entirety in each of its single parts, but only in all taken together. Hence, one part is in one place; another in another.

The soul, however, is present at the same time and entire, not only in the entire mass of its body, but also in each of its individual parts.[1] For, it is the entire soul that feels the pain of a part of the body, yet it does not feel it in the entire body. When, for instance, there is an ache in the foot, the eye looks at it, the mouth speaks of it, and the hand reaches for it. This, of course, would be impossible, if what of the soul is in these parts did not also experience a sensation in the foot; if the soul were not present, it would be unable to feel what has happened there. For, it would be incredible of a mes-

---

1 While according to Aristotle and Plato—cf. H. Schöler, *Augustinus Verhältnis* zu Platon 91.3—the soul's faculty of thinking had its seat in the head; Plotinus (*Enneades* 4.3.3) was of the opinion that the whole soul was in each part of the body. This doctrine is also found in Boethius (*De persona et duabus naturis Christi* 4.6). Whether Boethius drew from Augustine or both from Plotinus, or all three, independently of one another, from a common source, is not to be decided here.

senger to announce a fact, the occurrence of which he had not experienced. The sensation which occurs does not run through the mass of the body by continuation in such fashion as not to remain unnoticed by other parts of the soul which are elsewhere, but the entire soul feels what is going on in the particular part of the foot and feels it only there where it occurs. Hence, the entire soul is present, at one and the same time, in the single parts, and it experiences sensation as a whole, at one and the same time, in the single parts.

And yet, it is not present as a whole in such a manner as the whiteness or any other quality of this kind is present as a whole in each single part of the body. For, what the body, through a change of this whiteness, experiences in one part cannot be extended to the whiteness in the other part. Hence the result that, since the parts of the mass are distant from each other [in space], the mass itself is distant from itself. That this, however, does not apply to the soul is proved by the sense experience [in the foot] mentioned above.

THE MAGNITUDE OF THE SOUL

(De quantitate animae)

Translated

by

JOHN J. McMAHON, S.J.
Fordham University

IMPRIMI POTEST:

F. A. McQUADE, S.J., Praep. Prov.

Neo Eboraci

die 24 Oct., 1946

INTRODUCTION

AUGUSTINE wrote *De quantitate animae* in Rome, sometime during 387 or 388.[1] In his *Retractationes* he states:[2] 'In the same city I wrote a dialogue in which there is a lengthy treatment and discussion of the soul.' He adds that the treatise has been so entitled, since the question of the soul's magnitude was therein submitted to a careful and searching examination for the purpose of showing, if possible, that the soul lacks corporeal quantity, but is nevertheless a great reality (*tamen magnum aliquid esse*).

The dialogue in which St. Augustine and his friend Evodius participate is divided into six unequal parts, according to the questions that Evodius proposes for discussion: (1) the origin of the soul; (2) the nature of the soul; (3) the magnitude of the soul; (4) the reason for its union with the body; (5) the nature of this union; (6) the nature of the soul separated from the body.

The last three topics are touched on very briefly (Ch.36). A slightly less brief treatment is given to the first two questions (1-2). The main part of the dialogue, then, is devoted to the discussion of the soul's magnitude (3-35).

Augustine's title is somewhat puzzling, at first. It is necessary to remember his own distinction between magnitude of extent and magnitude of power. When we speak of the height of Hercules, we are considering his magnitude of extent; when we talk of his valor and brave deeds as a hero, we are describing his magnitude of power (3.4; 17.30).

1 V. J. Bourke, *Augustine's Quest of Wisdom* 90, 105.
2 1, 8 (PL 32.594).

Augustine denies that the soul has magnitude of extent, in the real sense: 'But I can say this: that it [the soul] is not long, or wide, or strong, or any of those things that one usually looks for in measuring bodies. . . . And, far from concluding that the soul is nothing because you cannot find length in it or any such thing, you should rather deem it all the more precious precisely because it has none of these things' (3.4). He will allow a metaphorical sense in which we speak of the enlargement of the soul that comes from 'studies of the moral good that are calculated to promote the good and happy life' (19.33).

In excluding all magnitude of extent from the soul, Augustine mentions justice as an example of a reality that is neither long, nor wide nor strong (4.5); he would rather have Evodius think of the soul as something like justice than as something like the wind. Evodius wonders how the soul can picture to itself worlds as great as this and without number and in what space the soul can keep all these images (5.9). To answer this difficulty, Augustine turns the discussion to a consideration of geometrical figures (6.10-12.22). The conclusion is reached that it is because of the soul's power that it is able to hold in its memory the great spaces of sky, earth and sea (14.23).

Evodius goes on to offer two main difficulties: one derived from the fact that the body grows and becomes stronger; the other from the fact that we feel anything pricking us at any part of the body. These facts seem to show that the soul grows with the body and that the soul is physically extended throughout the body in such a way that it has quantity (15.26). The first difficulty is answered in seven chapters (16-22); the second, in ten chapters (23-32).

The soul does not become greater by reason of a growing body; the soul's greatness is not extent, but virtue. If virtue results from the size of the body, then, the taller or stronger a man is, the more prudent he should be (16.28). But, Augustine drily remarks, the truth is quite different. Nor does the mere lapse of time increase the size of the soul. Why should it, when bodies themselves often get smaller, the older they become? (17.29) The power to speak is no proof that the soul grows in a real sense, for this absurdity would result: that, every time a man would acquire a new skill, his soul would really grow; and every time he would forget anything, his soul would shrink (18.33). However, one may speak of enlargement of the soul in a metaphorical sense (19.33). But, it is important to notice that the kind of subjects that one studies has a decisive influence on this kind of spiritual growth. Some studies enrich and enlarge. These are 'studies of the moral good that are calculated to promote the good and happy life.' Other studies merely dissipate the mind; others, again, are injurious, 'inflicting on the soul a grievous wound' (19.33). In these last two categories he would place flute-playing and the dainty appraisal of food, the ability 'to tell from what lake a fish was hooked or from what vintage a wine was made.' Evodius thinks he finds in physical strength a reason for holding that the soul really grows (21.35). Augustine replies that mere size is no guarantee of physical strength (21.36-22.40).

The soul feels anything that pricks the surface of the body. This fact seems to prove that the soul is extended through the body, like the blood, in such a way as to have quantity. To this second of the main difficulties of Evodius, Augustine proposes a lengthy discussion of sensation, with special reference to the sense of sight (23.41-29.61). The main point of his peculiar and unsatisfactory account of sensation seems to be this: if the eye, or rather the soul through the eye, sees an object, without being actually present at the place where the object is, why cannot the soul through the sense of touch perceive anything pricking the body, without being physically extended? (29,59) As for the curious fact that a worm may be cut in two and both parts live and move as though they always had been two worms. Augustine fails to see how this phenomenon can alter the clear conclusion of previous arguments that the soul lacks quantity. He urges Evodius to study 'whether what very learned men say is the objective truth or not, namely, that the soul can in no way be divided in itself, but only by reason of the body' (32.68.).

After he answers the objections of Evodius, Augustine proceeds, in what is the most exalted section of the dialogue (33-36), to a positive exposition of the 'magnitude of the soul, not in extent of space or time, but in force and power,' (33.69). There are, he points out, seven degrees or levels of the soul's power: Animation, Sensation, Art, Virtue, Tranquillity, Approach and Contemplation (35.79). The first three reveal the soul's power in the body; the next two, its power in itself; the last two, its power before God. The soul thus passes through three stages: matter, spirit, and God. By its power it gives life to matter, sensation to the body, and art or reasoning to man, in an ascending order of importance (33.70-72). At the fourth level the soul withdraws from baser things to itself and cleanses itself with the help of God from all defilement: On this level moral goodness begins and all true worth resides (33.73). Finally cleansed of all stains and established in virtue, the soul possesses itself in tranquillity and fears nothing whatever for itself. This is the fifth stage. In the next stage the soul learns 'to direct a calm and steady gaze towards that which is to be seen' (33.75). It yearns to see God. Finally after great labors, it comes through God to the last level, or rather a 'mansion' (33.76), where it enjoys the Supreme and True Good, the Unchanging

Source, the Unchanging Wisdom, the Unchanging Love, the One, True, and Perfect God (34.77).

The translation is based on the text of Migne (PL 32. 1035-1080). The English version by Reverend Francis E. Tourscher, O.S.A., has proved helpful. The translation of the title *The Magnitude of the Soul* has been adopted from A. C. Pegis: 'The Mind of St. Augustine' (*Mediaeval Studies* VI [1944] 6).

SELECT BIBLIOGRAPHY

Vernon J. Bourke, *Augustine's Quest of Wisdom* (Milwaukee 1945).

Mary P. Garvey, *Saint Augustine: Christian or Neo-Platonist?* (Milwaukee 1939).

Edward K. Rand, *Founders of the Middle Ages* (Cambridge 1928) 259-266.

Francis E. Tourscher, *St. Augustine, De Quantitate Animae, The Measure of the Soul* (Philadelphia 1933).

CONTENTS

THE MAGNITUDE OF THE SOUL

Chapter 1

EVODIUS. I see that you have plenty of time on your hands; please tell me how you would answer some questions of mine which, I believe, are not foolish or out of order. For, more than once when I brought some problems for you to solve, you decided to put me off by quoting some Greek proverb or other which forbids us to pursue that which is over our heads. But, in my problem, I am sure, I am not reaching beyond myself. And so, if I ask you about the soul, I hope that you will not reply: 'What have we to do with what is above us?' Rather, [you may conclude that] I may deserve to learn what we are in ourselves.

AUGUSTINE. State briefly what you want to hear about the soul.

E. I will do so, for I have mulled over this so much that I have the points at my fingertips. My questions are: (1) What is the origin of the soul? (2) What is its nature? (3) What is its magnitude? (4) What is the reason for its union with the body? (5) What is the effect of this union? (6) What is the effect of its separation from the body?

(2) *A.* Your question about the origin of the soul brings to my mind two interpretations. It is one thing to say: Whence is man? If what we want to know is the land of his birth. It is quite another thing to ask: What is he composed of, that

is, of what elements and realities is he made? Which of these do you expect to hear mentioned, when you ask: What is the origin of the soul? Do you want to know the district, if I may express it that way, or the country from which it came, or are you asking about its very substance?

E. As a matter of fact, I should like to know about both of these, but I prefer to leave it to you to decide which of the two I am to hear about first.

A. I believe that God, its Creator, is, so to speak, the soul's proper habitation and its home. As for its substance, I really cannot find a name. I certainly do not think that it belongs to those ordinary and familiar things of which we are aware through our senses. I do not think that the soul is composed either of earth or water or air or fire, or of all of these together, or of any combination of them. Now, if you were to ask me: What is a tree composed of?—I should mention those four well-known elements[1] of which such things are supposed to consist. But, if you go on to ask: What does earth consist of or water or fire or air?—I should have no answer to make. In the same way, when you ask: What does man consist of?—I can reply: Of body and soul. If you were to ask further about the body, I shall fall back on those same four elements. However, since your question is about the soul, which appears to be simple and with a substance of its own, I am just as puzzled as though you were asking the previous question: What is earth composed of?

E. But I do not understand why you want to say that the soul has a substance of its own, since you said it was created by God.

---

1 The Greek 'Physicists' of the Fifth Century B. C. taught that the universe is composed of four material principles, earth, air, fire and water. Cf. Aristotle, *Metaphysics* I iii. At the time of Augustine this doctrine was still in vogue; cf., *De genesi ad litteram* 2.

A. Just as I cannot deny that earth was made by God and still I cannot say of what other elements, so to speak, earth is composed; for earth lacks parts in so far is it is earth,[2] and for that reason is said to be an element of all those bodies that are formed from the four elements. Therefore, there is no contradiction in my statement that the soul is made by God and has its own proper nature. God Himself is the author of the soul's peculiar nature, just as He is the maker of fire, air, water, and earth—the elements that make up all other things.

Chapter 2

(3) *E*. For the present I accept your explanation that the soul comes from God. I shall think it over carefully and, if I have any difficulty, I shall bring it up later. Now, please explain the nature of the soul.

A. It seems to me that the soul is like to God. For your question is about the human soul, if I mistake not.

E. That is exactly what I should like you to explain: how the human soul is like to God. For, although we believe that God has been made by no one, you said previously that the soul is made by God Himself.

A. Do you really think it difficult for God to make something like Himself, when you see from the great variety of images that such power has been granted even to us?

E. But, it seems that our creations some day come to an end, whereas God made the soul immortal, as I believe, unless, possibly, you have a different view.

A. Do you mean, therefore, that man's creations should have the same quality as those of God?

2 As a primary element of bodies, earth, in the doctrine mentioned above, was regarded as not having parts.

E. Certainly I should not say that. But just as He, being immortal, makes something immortal in His own likeness, so we, being immortal, having been made so by God, in making something in our own likeness ought to make something immortal also.

A. You would be correct if you could paint a picture in the likeness of what you believe is immortal in you, but now your painting discloses the likeness of the body, which is certainly mortal.

E. How, then, am I like to God, when I cannot make anything immortal, as He can?

A. Just as it is impossible for an image of your body to do what your body can, so it should be no cause for wonder that your soul has not the same power as He in whose likeness it has been made .

Chapter 3

(4) *E*. Your explanation of that point is enough for the present. Now tell me. What is the magnitude of the soul?

A. What do you mean by magnitude? For I do not understand whether you are asking about the extent, as it were, of its width, or length, or strength, or of all these taken together, or whether you desire to know what the soul can do. For, we are wont to inquire: How great is Hercules?—meaning, How many feet tall is he? And again: How great a hero is he?—meaning, What is his valor or prowess?

E. I desire to know how great is the soul in both senses of the word.

A. The first sense of greatness cannot be mentioned, cannot even be thought of, in connection with the soul. The soul must not be regarded in any way as either long, or wide, or strong. Such qualities, in my opinion, are attributes of bodies; thus we are merely applying to the soul our ideas about bodies. The liturgy[1] of the Church has, therefore, a wise precept that whoever would restore himself to the condition of man as created by God, namely, to the likeness of God, must despise all corporeal things and renounce the entire world, which we see is corporeal, for that is the only way of accomplishing the soul's salvation, or of renovation, or reconciliation with its Maker. And so, to your query: How great is the soul?—I am unable to give an answer. However, I can say this, that it is not long, or wide, or strong, or any of those things that one usually looks for in measuring bodies. And I shall give you the reason for my view, if you like.

E. Of course I do, and I am all ears to hear it. For, if the soul is none of these things, it seems to me to be, as it were, nothing.

A. First of all, if you agree, I shall show you that there are many things which you cannot say are nothing; yet in them you cannot find anything like the measurements that you are looking for in the soul. And, far from concluding that the soul is nothing because you cannot find length in it or any such thing, you should rather deem it all the more precious precisely because it has none of these things. In the second place, we shall see whether it actually has any dimensions.

E. Use whatever order and method you wish. I am all prepared to listen and to learn.

Chapter 4

(5) *A.* That is fine! But I should like you to answer this question, for possibly you already know what I am trying

1 There seems to be reference here to the instructions the catechumens received before being baptised, perhaps to the Lenten Scrutinies at which Augustine had been present in Milan during the Lent of 387.

to teach you. You do not doubt, I am sure, that this tree is not absolutely nothing?

E. Of course not. No one doubts that.

A. You do not doubt, do you, that justice is much more excellent than this tree?

E. That surely is an absurd supposition—as if there were any comparison at all!

A. You are very gracious. But now to this point. Since it is evident that this tree is of so little value in comparison with justice that in your opinion there is hardly any ground for comparison, and since you admit that this wood is certainly something, would you support the belief that justice itself is nothing?

E. Only a fool would believe that!

A. You are certainly right. But, perhaps you think that this tree is a reality because it is tall in its own way, and wide, and strong, and that if you should take away these properties, it will be nothing.

E. So it seems.

A. But, what about justice? You have admitted that it is a reality, that it is more divine and more noble, in fact, than this tree. Does it seem to you, then, to have length?

E. Not at all. Justice is neither long, nor wide, nor anything I can think of like that.

A. If justice, therefore, is not any of these things, and yet is not nothing, why do you think that the soul is nothing, if it has no length?

E. Well, now I see that it does not follow that the soul is nothing, if it is neither long, nor wide, nor strong. But, you know that you have not yet stated whether it really is something. It can happen that many things which lack these dimensions are to be reckoned of great value, but I do not think it is immediately evident from your argument that the soul belongs to this category.

(6) *A.* I know that we still have to unravel that question, and I promised that I would explain it later on. But, because the question is very difficult and requires deeper insight than one is accustomed to use in the ordinary affairs of daily life, I warn you to be alert in following the thread of our argument, and neither to be vexed at the weariness you will feel in making the required steps, nor put out at the slow pace at which you will finally arrive at the conclusion you desire to reach. My first question is: Do you think that there is any body that does not have some length and depth and height, according to its size?

E. I don't understand what you mean by height.

A. I mean the dimension which makes it possible for the interior of a body to be an object of thought, or, if the body is transparent as glass, the object of sense perception. In my opinion, at least, if you take this dimension away, bodies can neither be perceived by the senses nor be thought of at all as bodies. On this point I want you to open up your mind to me.

E. Undoubtedly my view is that it is impossible for bodies to be without these three dimensions.

A. What is that? Can you think of these three dimensions existing anywhere except in bodies?

E. I do not see how they can be elsewhere .

A. Therefore, you think that the soul is simply a body?

E. If we admit that even the wind is a body, I cannot deny that the soul seems to be a body, for I think it is something like the wind.

A. The wind, I grant, is as much a body as a current of air, if you were to ask me about that. For we perceive that the wind is merely this air in a state of agitation. The truth of this can be confirmed in a quiet place, sheltered from all winds, where, by waving away flies with a small fan, we move the air and feel its breath. Now, when the motion of the air is caused by the less evident movement of heavenly or earthly bodies through the great space of the universe, it is called the wind and gets a different name according to the different corners of the sky from which it comes. Or, don't you think so?

E. Yes; and I take as likely what you say. However, I did not say that the soul is the wind, but something like it.

A. Tell me, first of all, do you think this wind, about which you are talking, has any length or breadth or height? Then we shall see whether the soul is some such thing and we can investigate, also, how great it is.

E. What can be easily found to have greater length or width or height than the air which in a state of agitation is the wind, as you have just convinced me?

Chapter 5

(7) *A*. You are right. Now, you do not think your soul exists anywhere except in your body, do you?

E. No, I don't.

A. Is the soul inside the body only, like the contents of a bottle, so to say, or only on the outside, like a covering, or do you think it is both inside and outside?

E. I think it is both inside and outside. For, unless it were inside, there would be no life inside of us, and unless it were on the outside, it could not feel a slight prick on the skin.

A. Why, then, do you question further about the magnitude of the soul, since you see that it is as large as the spaces of the body allow?

E. If reason teaches this, I shall seek no further.

A. You are right not to go beyond what reason tells us. But does this explanation seem to you to be very cogent?

E. Yes, since I do not find any other. I shall ask at the proper time a question that bothers me, namely: Does the soul's shape remain the same when it has left the body? I recall that I placed this last on the list of the questions to be asked. I thought I should mention it here, because a question about the number of souls seems to belong to a discussion of quantity.

A. Yes, there is a connection, but first let us finish our discussion about the extension of the soul, for I am not yet satisfied on that point, so that, in resolving your doubts, I hope to discover some new light for myself.

E. Ask as you wish. For, your pretended doubt now makes me really question what I had presumed was already settled.

(8) *A.* Tell me, please, does not what we call memory seem to you to be a mere word?

E. No one would say that.

A. Does memory, in your opinion, belong to the soul or the body?

E. It would be absurd to doubt about that. Can we believe or imagine that a lifeless body remembers?

A. Do you still remember the city of Milan?

E. Very much so.

A. Now that mention has been made of it, do you recall its size and character?

E. Yes I do, and nothing more vividly and completely.

A. Now, although you do not behold it with your eyes, you see it in your mind.

E. That is so.

A. You also remember, I believe, how distant it is from us at this moment.

E. Yes, I recall also that.

A. Therefore, you also see in your mind the intervening space.

E. Yes, I do.

A. Since your soul is here where your body is, and does not extend beyond the space of the body, as the previous proof made clear, how is it that it sees all these things?

E. It is done through memory, I believe; not because the soul is present to those places.

A. The impressions of those places, then, are stored in the memory.

E. I think so, for I have no idea what is going on in those places at this moment. Certainly I would be aware of it, if my mind actually reached those places and perceived what is being done there now.

A. What you say seems to me to be true. But certainly, these impressions are of bodies.

(9) *E.* Necessarily so, for cities and climes are nothing else than bodies.

A. Have you ever looked into a tiny mirror or have you ever seen your face reflected in the pupil of another person's eye?

E. Often indeed.

A. Why does the face appear smaller than it really is?

E. How could you wish anything different than that the image be in keeping with the size of the mirror?

A. The images of bodies must be small, therefore, if the bodies in which they are reflected are small.

E. Necessarily so.

A. Why, then, since the soul is in so small a space as its body, can so great images be reflected in it, as cities, and the width of the earth, and any other immense object that can be imagined? I wish you to consider somewhat more carefully how great and how many objects our memory contains; all of these, of course, are contained in the soul. How great therefore, the depth, the width, the immensity of the soul that can hold all these things, although our previous proof seems to show that the soul is only as great as the body.

E. I cannot find anything to reply, nor can I explain enough how much I am disturbed. And I laugh at myself for having been taken in so quickly by my earlier argument that I should want to confine the magnitude of the soul within the boundaries of the body.

A. Does the soul seem to you now to be some such thing as the wind?

E. Not at all. For, even if this air, whose flow in all probability is believed to be the wind, could fill this entire world, the soul can picture to itself worlds as great as this without number, and in what space the soul would keep all these images is beyond my power to surmise.

A. See, then, how much better it is to believe, as I said earlier, that the soul is neither long, nor wide, nor high, as you admitted regarding justice.

E. I should easily agree if I were not more at a loss than before how the soul, without any length, or width, or height of its own, can hold images without number of such great spaces.

Chapter 6

(10) *A.* A careful discussion of these three topics—length, width and height—may possibly furnish a solution to your difficulty, so far as a solution may be found. Make an effort, therefore, to think of length which has not yet taken on any width.

E. I cannot think of anything like that. A spider's thread is one of the most tenuous things we are wont to see, and yet, if I place that before my mind's eye, the length is there *per se,* and also width and height. No matter how slight these last two are, at least I cannot deny their existence.

A. Your answer is not entirely absurd; surely, when you think of these three dimensions in a spider's thread, you see them clearly and you know that one is not the other.

E. How could I help knowing that there is a difference; for how else could I see that not one of them is wanting to this thread?

A. As your mind grasped the distinction between them, so, too, it has the power to think of length alone, apart from the other two dimensions, provided you do not imagine a particular body. For, no matter what shape this may be, it will not be without these three dimensions. Now, it is an incorporeal reality that I wish you to understand. Indeed, length alone cannot be found in a body; it can be understood only by the mind.

E. Now I see what you mean.

A. As for this length, then, you see surely that it allows no cutting lengthwise, even in thought; if it did, it would also have width.

E. That is evident.

A. This length, then, pure and simple, if you will, we shall call a line. That is the name many learned men give it.

E. Call it what you please. I am not one to bother about names when the reality itself is clear.

(11) *A.* You do well. Not only do I approve, but I counsel you always to make it your delight to have more care for reality than for words. But this line, which I think you now understand correctly, if it is extended from one end or from both ends as far as possible, will have no end, as you see.

Or is it too much for the keenness of your mind to see that?

E. I see it clearly and without any trouble.

A. You see, then, that a figure will never be formed simply by prolonging that line.

E. I do not understand what you mean by figure.

Chapter 7

A. For the present I call a figure that in which any space is enclosed by a line or lines. For example, suppose you are to draw a circle or four lines meeting at their extremes; you would draw in such a way that the end of one line would not fail to unite with the end of the other line.

E. Now I think I know what you mean by a figure. But I wish I could see as well the drift of all this and how you will use this to let me know what I seek about the soul.

(12) *A.* At the start I warned you about this and I asked you to be patient with our roundabout method. And now I repeat the request. Our search is not for a trifle. Its object is not readily discerned, for we want to know this subject distinctly and hold on to it, if possible. To trust the word of another is one thing; to trust our own reason is a different thing; to take something on authority is a great timesaver and involves no toil. If this way has any attraction for you, you may read in the extensive writings of great and good men what they thought should be said about these subjects as a safe and easy guide for the unlearned; and these men aimed at securing the confidence of persons whose minds, being either

too slow or too occupied, could find no other safe road to truth. Such persons, whose number is very great, if they wish to grasp the truth by reason, are easily taken in by sophisms that land them in the swamp of error from which they never or only with difficulty succeed in emerging and extricating themselves. For these, then, it is a decided advantage to trust a most reliable authority and to shape their conduct according to it. If you think that such a way is safer, I shall not only offer no resistance, but shall thoroughly approve. But, if you cannot bridle your eager conviction of coming to the truth by reason, you must be prepared for long, hard, and circuitous riding, pursuing the path where reason beckons—that reason alone which is worthy of the name, that is, right reason. Not only is it right, but it is also sure and free from every semblance of falsehood, if man can ever attain to that state where no false argument or specious pretext can make him betray the truth.

E. I shall desire nothing more eagerly. Let reason guide and lead me where it will; only let it bring me to the goal.

Chapter 8

(13) *A.* God will do this, and we should implore His help exclusively—especially, at least in such matters. But let us return to the discussion I began. Since you know what a line is and what a figure is, my question is this: Can any figure be made if a line should be extended from either end or from one end to infinity?

E. Certainly not.

A. What, then, must one do to make a figure?

E. Make the line finite, and extend it in the form of a circle until both ends meet. I do not see any other method of enclosing a space with one line. This is the only way of making a figure according to your definition.

A. Suppose I want to make a figure with straight lines. Can this be done with one line?

E. Not at all.

A. With two?

E. Not with two, either.

A. With three?

E. Yes, you can.

A. Very good. You perceive clearly and hold that, to make a figure with straight lines, you cannot do it with less than three. If any reasoning process opposed this, would it change you from your opinion?

E. Really, if anyone should prove to me that this is false, I would lose all confidence in my ability to know anything.

A. Well, then, tell me how you make a figure with three lines.

E. By joining their ends one to the other.

A. Is not an angle made at the joining?

E. That is right.

A. How many angles in this figure?

E. As many as there are lines.

A. Are the lines equal or unequal?

E. Equal.

A. Are the angles all equal or is one more acute or more obtuse than the other?

E. The angles are also equal.

A. In a figure whose three sides are equal, are the angles necessarily equal also?

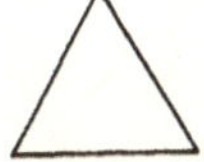

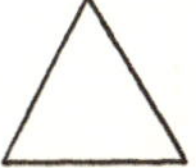

E. They must be equal.

A. Now, suppose that the three sides of the figure are unequal, is there any possibility of the angles being equal?

E. None whatever.

A. Correct. Now, another question. Which figure has the more beautiful and striking proportions—the one whose sides are equal or unequal?

E. Undoubtedly the one that excels in equality is more perfect.

Chapter 9

(14) *A*. So you prefer equality to the lack of it.

E. Certainly, like everyone else.

A. Now notice, in the figure whose three angles are equal, which part is opposite an angle, a line or an angle?

E. A line, as I see it.

A. Now, suppose you have a figure in which an angle is opposite an angle, and a side opposite a side, would you not admit that such a figure has more equality?

E. I grant you that, but I do not see how you can make such a figure out of three lines.

A. Out of four, then?

E. Yes, out of four.

A. Then a better figure results from four equal lines than from three?

E. I would say so, since it has greater equality.

A. Another point. Can a figure of four equal lines be made in such a way that the angles are not all equal?

E. I think it is possible.

A. How?

E. By widening two angles and by closing up the other two.

A. Do you notice that the wider angles face each other and the same is true of the smaller ones?

E. That is absolutely true.

A. You notice that here, too, equality obtains as far as possible. Once you make a figure of four equal lines, either all four angles are exactly equal or at least are equal in pairs, and the pairs are opposite each other.

E. I notice that and hold it as correct.

(15) *A.* Does it not strike you that these figures in their own way reveal unmistakably a kind of unfailing justice?

E. What do you mean?

A. Because we say, I believe, that justice is equity, and equity seems to be derived from equality. Now, the virtue of equity certainly requires that each man be given what is his. This 'to each his own' implies a definite distinction of persons. Do you not think so?

E. That is evident and I agree entirely.

A. Do you think there is any distinction, if all things are equal without any difference whatever between them?

E. None whatever.

A. Therefore, justice cannot be maintained unless there is some inequality, if I may use the word, in the things in which it[justice] is maintained, and some unlikeness.

E. I understand.

A. Since, therefore, we admit a dissimilarity between those figures under discussion, for, although both are composed of equal sides, yet one has three and the other four angles—do you not perceive a certain closeness to justice in this: that the figure which cannot admit equality of opposite parts maintains invariably an equality of angles, while in the other figure, which has complete equality of opposites, the law of angles permits inequality up to a point? Since I was excited over this fact, I cannot help but put the question to you whether this truth, this equity, this equality, would be a source of any delight to you.

E. I see now what you mean and I am indeed filled with wonder.

A. Another point. You have good reason to prefer equality to inequality; in fact, I think there is no human being who would not make the same choice. Well, then, let us look for the figure, if you will, that has the greatest equality. For, whatever it be, we shall certainly prefer it to all others.

E. Let us do so; I desire to know what it is.

Chapter 10

(16) *A.* My first question: Of those two figures about which we have surely talked enough, does that one seem to you to excel which is composed of four equal sides and of as many equal angles? As you notice, it has equality both of sides and of angles. While we could not find this equality in the figure that is enclosed by three equal sides, yet this figure has an equality of opposites, for a side is opposite an angle and an angle opposite a side.

E. It is just as you say.

A. Has this figure, then, the greatest equality, or do you think differently? If it has, it will be superfluous to continue our search; if it has not, I should like you to prove it to me.

E. I think it has, for I cannot detect any inequality where the lines and the angles are both equal.

A. I disagree, for a straight line has the greatest equality until it comes to angles. But when it joins another line from the opposite side and makes an angle, do you not see that this is something unequal? Does that part of the figure which is closed by a side seem to you to coincide in equality or in likeness with that part which is enclosed by an angle?

E. In no way. I am ashamed of my hasty answer. I was led astray by the equality I observed between the sides and between the angles themselves. It is quite evident, however, that the sides differ greatly from the angles.

A. Take another clear proof of inequality. You surely notice that there is a center point in each of these two figures, namely, the triangle with equal sides and the square.

E. I see that plainly.

A. Now, when we draw lines from this same center to the sides of the figures, will the lines drawn be all equal or unequal?

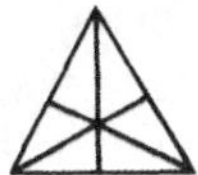

E. Unequal, of course, for the lines we draw to the angles will necessarily be somewhat longer.

A. How many in the square; how many in the triangle?

E. Four here, and three there.

A. Again, of all the lines, which are the shortest and how many are there in each figure?

E. The same, namely, those drawn to the middle of the sides.

A. Your answers are perfectly correct and there is no

need of our dwelling on this point. It is enough for our purpose to see that, while great equality obtains in these figures, it is not yet perfect in every respect.

E. I see that clearly and what that figure is that has the greatest equality I am very anxious to know.

Chapter 11

(17) *A.* What else can it be, do you think, except the figure whose boundary is everywhere consistent, with no angle breaking up its equality and from whose center equal lines can be drawn to every part of the boundary.

E. Now I believe I understand, for I think you are describing the figure which is enclosed by one line drawn in a circle.

A. You understand rightly. Now, then, consider this. Since the previous reasoning has shown that a line is understood only in length, and assumes no width, and, therefore, cannot be divided lengthwise in the direction of its extent, do you think that any figure can be found without width?

E. None.

A. Is there any possibility of width being without length, even though it be width alone, in the same way as we earlier understood length to be without width. Or is this impossible?

E. I see that it is impossible.

A. You also see, unless I am mistaken, that width can be divided in all directions, whereas a line cannot be divided lengthwise.

E. That is evident.

A. Which do you consider of greater value: what is divisible or indivisible?

E. What is indivisible, certainly.

A. You prefer, therefore, a line to width. For, if what is indivisible is to be preferred, we must necessarily prefer what is less divisible. But, width can suffer division in all directions, whereas length can be divided only crosswise, for it does not allow division lengthwise. It is, therefore, of greater value. Or is your thought different?

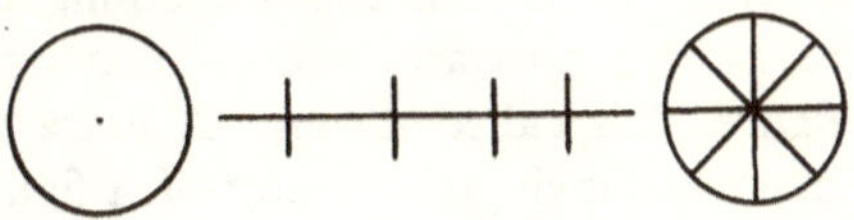

E. Reason compels me to admit completely what you say.

(18) *A.* Let us now investigate this problem, if you will, whether there is anything in keeping with this line of thought that is completely indivisible. It will then be so much better than even a line. For, you observe, a line can be divided innumerable times crosswise. So I now pass on to you the task of discovering this by yourself.

E. I think that what we were placing in the figure as the center, from which lines are drawn to the boundary, is indivisible. For, if it is divided, it certainly cannot lack length or even width. If it has only length, it is not the starting place from which lines are drawn, but is itself a line. And if, moreover, it is wide, then a further center must be sought, from which lines are drawn to the boundary of the width. But, reason rejects both suppositions. Hence, this will be something that is indivisible.

A. Your statement is correct. But does it not seem to you that the same holds true of the starting place of a line, even though a figure is not yet formed for our mind to locate its center. I say that the origin of a line where length begins to exist is something I want you to understand as having no length whatever. For, if you take it as having length, you fail completely to understand that a point is where length begins.

E. I agree entirely.

A. This, then, which I see you now understand, is the most excellent of all our findings, since it completely excludes division. It is called a point when it occupies the center of a figure. But, if it is the beginning of a line, or even lines or their end, or even when it marks something that must be understood as having no parts without having become the center of a figure, it is called a sign. A mark without parts is a sign; a mark occupying the center of a figure is a point. Thus, every point is also a sign, but not every sign is a point. Mutual agreement on these terms is something I wish to have, in order to lessen our talking around the topic under discussion. While many would reserve the term 'point' for the center not of any figure, but only of a circle or a sphere, we need not labor too much over words.

E. I agree.

Chapter 12

A. You surely also see how many functions it has. For, from a point a line takes its origin and in a point it ends. No figure can be made of straight lines unless the angle is closed by a point, and, wherever a line can be cut, it is cut through a point, although a point itself cannot be cut. It is required for the joining of every two lines. Finally, although reason has shown that the circle, because of its equality, surpasses all other plane figures (for we have said nothing yet of solids), what else is the regulator of this symmetry than the point placed in the center? Much can be said of the function of the point, but I use restraint and leave further considerations to you.

E. You are undoubtedly right. If any difficulty arises I shall not be slow to ask. I do see fairly well, I think, the marvelous function of this sign.

(20) *A.* Now, then, turn your attention to this question. Since you clearly understand what a sign is, what length is, and what width is, which one of these seems to have need of another and in such a way that without the other it cannot exist?

E. I see that width needs length; otherwise it could not be understood. I notice further that length does not need width for its existence, but without a sign it could not exist. The sign, however, clearly stands by itself and needs none of these.

A. It is as you state, but consider carefully whether width can be bisected from every side or whether, although it allows more division than a line, it cannot allow division from one side.

E. I do not know why it cannot.

A. I believe your memory is faulty, for you cannot be ignorant of this. I shall remind you of it in this way. Certainly your conception of width is such that no notion of height intrudes into it.

E. That is entirely correct.

A. Now, to this width let height be added, and answer me whether this addition does not increase the possibility of further division on every side.

E. You have given me a very good hint. Now I see that not only from above or from below, but also from the sides, division can be made. In fact, there is no part remaining that cannot be bisected. Hence, it is clear that one cannot cut width on those sides where height is to be erected.

(21) *A.* Since, therefore, you have a true concept of length and width and height, I ask whether you can have height without the other two dimensions.

E. I see that you cannot have height without length, but you can have height without width.

A. Go back, then, to your conception of width. If you imagine it to be lying flat, as it were, now turn it upright on any side, as if you were, let us suppose, to put it through the narrowest crack between two closed doors. Do you understand yet what I mean?

E. I understand what you say, but not yet, perhaps, what you mean.

A. Simply this, that you answer whether width now placed in an upright position seems to you to have converted itself into height and to have forfeited the name and description of width, or whether it still remains width, notwithstanding its position.

E. I think it has become height.

A. Please recall our definition of height.[1]

E. I recall it now and I am ashamed of my answer. Width raised even in this position allows no vertical division lengthwise from top to bottom. Wherefore, the concept of width rules out any interior, although it does allow a center and boundaries. But, in your previous demonstration about height, it was said, I recall, that there is no height where the mind cannot perceive something inside.

A. You are correct and I was hoping that you would recall that. I want you to answer now whether you prefer what is true to what is false.

E. If I had any doubt, I would be unbelievably stupid.

A. Is that a true line, then, that can be cut lengthwise? A truc sign that can be divided in some way? A true width which, when turned upright, allows vertical division lengthwise from top to bottom?

E. Nothing is less true.

1 See p. 65.

Chapter 13

(22) *A.* Did you ever see with the eyes of the body a point or a line or width as we have been describing it?

E. Never, indeed. These things are not corporeal.

A. But, if corporeal things are seen with the eyes of the body, in accordance with certain marvelous affinity of natures, should not the soul by which we see these incorporeal things be itself neither a body nor in any way like a body? Or have you a different opinion?

E. Well, I admit now that the soul is not a body or anything like a body, but please tell me what it is.

A. Consider, for the present, whether we have proved that it lacks entirely all quantity, for this is the question we are discussing now. For, what is the soul was the earlier topic of our discussion. That you have forgotten surprises me. You remember that you asked first: Whence is the soul? which, I recall, we handled in two ways: one, in which we inquired about its place of origin, as it were; the other, in which we considered whether it was composed of earth, or fire or any other of these elements, or of all together, or of a combination of some of them. And we agreed on this conclusion, that an answer to this question is as much beyond us as the answer to the question: Whence is earth or any other one of the elements? For, it must be understood that, although God made the soul, it has a definite substance which is neither of earth, nor of fire, nor of air, nor of water, unless, perchance, one should think that God gave to earth a nature that is exclusively its own and did not give to the soul a nature that is proper to it. If you wish a definition of what the soul is, I have a ready answer. It seems to me to be a certain kind of substance, sharing in reason, fitted to rule the body.[1]

1 For the significance of this definition, cf. E. Gilson, *The Spirit of Medieval Philosophy* (New York 1936) 174.

Chapter 14

(23) And now, focus your attention on the problem of whether the soul has a kind of quantity and local extension, if I may use such terms. Now, because it is not a body—otherwise it could not understand anything incorporeal, as the previous reasoning proved—it undoubtedly lacks space by which bodies are measured. For this reason, it is beyond the possibility of belief or understanding that any such quantity should be in the soul. If you wonder why the soul, which has no quantity, holds in its memory the great spaces of sky and earth and sea, it is because of its amazing power, some notion of which our previous discussions should have brought within the focus of your mind's eye, more or less depending on its ability to grasp these things. For, if whatever lacks length, width, and height is not a body, as reason has demonstrated; if one of these dimensions cannot be in a body without the other two; if, nevertheless, we have granted that the interior eye of the soul, that is to say, the intelligence, has the power to see even a mere line—then I think that our premises warrant the conclusion that the soul is not only not a body, but that it is superior to a body. Granting that, I think there can be no doubt that it is superior to a line, for it is absurd to say that what is superior to a body is not superior to the dimensions without which a body cannot exist, namely, length, width, and height. But, the line itself, which is inferior to the soul, is superior to the other two dimensions, because it allows less division than they. Moreover, the further these two dimensions are extended in space, the more they outstrip a line in regard to division. A line has no other extension than that of length. Now, if you take away the only extension a line has, namely length, nothing of extension remains. Therefore, whatever is superior to a line is necessarily without extent and

admits no division or cutting whatever. Therefore, all for naught is our labor in seeking after the soul's magnitude; there is no such thing, since the soul, we grant, is superior to a line. And, if a circle is the best of all plane figures, and if in a circle nothing is more excellent or more important than a point, which beyond all doubt is without any parts—why should anyone be astonished that the soul, which is neither a body, nor extended in length, nor spread out in width, nor massed in depth, has, nevertheless, such power that it rules all the members of the body and presides over all the motions of the body for all the world as the director of its activity?

(24) Moreover, since the center of the eye, which is called the pupil, is simply a certain point and, despite that, has so much power that from a somewhat elevated spot it can take in and survey half the sky, whose space is beyond words to describe—why should it be so strange that the soul should be without any bodily magnitude composed of those three dimensions, even though it can represent any bodily magnitude whatever? But, to few men is it allowed to discern the soul by the soul, that is, so that the soul sees itself.[1] It sees, moreover, through the intelligence, which alone has the power to see that nothing is more powerful and more majestic in reality than those natures which the mind understands to be, so to say, without bulk. The magnitude of a body is not without reason called its bulk, and, if bulk is to be reckoned of great value, then elephants would be wiser than we. If someone, knowing their ways, should say that elephants are wise

1 From the context the thought does not seem to be that the soul has a direct intuition of its own nature, but, rather, that the soul must use its 'sight' or reason, a task that is difficult for most men when there is question of investigating the nature of the soul. In this connection, Augustine's earlier remarks on authority and reason should be read again.

(I myself was astonished when I watched them and I have observed that men are often in doubt about this point), at least he will grant, I believe, that a little bee knows more than an ass; certainly, to compare their size would be more than ridiculous. Or, again, in connection with what we were saying about the eye, who does not see that the eye of the eagle is much smaller than ours. Yet, the eagle, flying so high that it is lost to view in the clear light, can easily see a hare in a thicket and a fish beneath the waves. But, if the size of the body counts for nothing, as regards the power of perception in the senses themselves which can perceive only corporeal things, is there any ground for fearing that the human soul is nothing? Does not the soul's far superior and almost only sight, reason itself,[2] by which it strives even to find itself—does not reason, that is, the soul itself, prove that it lacks every kind of magnitude by which space is occupied? We must regard the soul as great, great indeed, but not great with any material bulk. That way of thinking comes more easily to those who are well trained and approach these questions not from a desire of empty glory, but from a divine love of truth; or, though less equipped for subtle investigation, come to seek out the answer with patience, docility, and trust in the guidance of good men, with the determination to turn themselves away, as far as is permitted in this life, from the tyranny of the senses. In divine Providence it cannot happen that the pious, chaste, and diligent quest of religious souls for themselves and their God, that is, for truth, should go unrequited.

---

2 For Augustine, reason is the sight of the soul; reasoning is the moving of this sight over the things that are to be seen. This distinction is explained below on p. 119 f.

Chapter 15

(25) But, let us now leave this question, unless you have a difficulty, and go on to another. Perhaps our discussion of those figures dragged on longer than you liked. However, you will see how much bearing it has on other points, if you grant that it sheds some light on the present inquiry. Studies like this train the mind to look at rather subtle points, lest, dazed by their light and unable to bear it, the soul seek willing refuge in the darkness from which it desired to escape. This study is also, as far as man is given to investigate these matters, the source of most certain arguments for settling doubts about established conclusions. As for myself, I have fewer doubts about these things than about the things we see with our eyes. To me it is an intolerable offense against logic to admit that we excel the animals in intelligence and that the object we see with our bodily eyes is a thing which even some animals see better, and, at the same time, to insist that what we see with our mind is nothing. If it were said that the mind is of the same nature as the object of bodily vision, no more unwarranted statement would seem to be uttered.

(26) *E.* I am very happy to follow your thoughts and I agree. Yet I wonder about this: while it is so clear to me that the soul has no corporeal quantity that I show not the slightest resistance to those arguments, and while I am entirely unaware of any point which I cannot grant, why is it that, as the body grows with age, the soul grows, too, or at least, would seem to grow? Who would deny that small children are not to be compared in cleverness to some animals? Who would doubt that as they grow older their soul also seems to grow? Then, if the soul is extended through the space of

the body, why does it not have quantity? If, however, it is not extended, how does it feel all over anything that strikes it?

A. These points that you bring up have often caused me to wonder, too; therefore, I have an answer ready for you that I am wont to give myself. How good it is, your reason will lead you to decide; yet, such as it is, it is an answer I certainly cannot improve upon, unless perchance, God should suggest something better to my mind during the course of our discussion. But, let us follow our usual procedure, if you please; that is, you reply to your own questions, as reason suggests. First of all, let this be our point of inquiry: Whether this is certain proof of the simultaneous growth of body and soul that, with the approach of age, man becomes fit for human association and becomes more and more skilled in it?

E. Let us proceed as you wish, for I like very much this method of teaching and learning. I do not know why it is, but, when I arrive at the answer to a question that my ignorance led me to ask, the discovery is not only satisfying but stimulating.

Chapter 16

(27) *A.* Tell me whether 'greater' and 'better' seem to you to be two distinct things or one and the same thing called by two different names.

E. I know that we say that one thing is greater and another is better.

A. Which of these two do you think connotes quantity?

E. That which we say is greater.

A. When we admitted that the round figure is better than the square, was it quantity that made the difference or something else?

E. It was not quantity by any means; as we decided earlier, the cause of this excellence is equality.

A. Now, then, focus your attention on this question: Would it seem to you that virtue is a certain equality of a life completely in harmony with reason? For, if in life conduct is at variance with right principles, we are more offended, if I mistake not, than when some part of a circle is more or less distant from the center than the other parts. Or do you have a different opinion?

E. Rather, I agree entirely and I think your description of virtue is correct. For, only that should be called or regarded as reason which is true. Surely, only he whose whole life corrresponds to the truth—only he, or certainly he above all—lives well and uprightly. Only the man who is so minded must be judged to have virtue and to live it.

A. Your statement is correct. But, surely you see that a circle is more like virtue than any other plane figure. For that reason we are wont to give high praise to the line of Horace[1] in which he says, when describing the wise man, 'His strength is in himself; all smooth and round, his ego is a little world'—and with good reason. For, you will not find in the endowments of the soul anything that is more harmonious with itself in every way than virtue; nor in plane figures anything more symmetrical than a circle. Wherefore, if a circle not by the greatness of space, but by a certain uniform design, excels other figures, how much more should our esteem of virtue be, which surpasses all the other affections of the soul not by occupying greater space, but by conforming to reason in a certain Godlike harmony.

(28) Now, when a child is praised for growing up, what

1 *Satires* II, vii, 86.

is said to be the goal of that growing, if not virtue? Is that not so?

E. Obviously.

A. You should not think, therefore, that the soul grows by increasing its size with age as the body does. For, by growing, the soul comes to virtue, which, we admit, derives all its beauty and perfection not from any greatness of space, but from the great power of consistency. And if greater is one thing and better is another, as you already admitted, the soul should not be called greater but better by reason of its advancing with age and becoming subject to reason. But, if this results from the size of the members, the taller or stronger a man is, the more prudent he should be. That the truth is quite different I feel you will not deny.

E. No one would deny it. Still, since you yourself admit that the soul grows with age, I wonder how it happens that, being without any quantity, a soul is helped by the space of time, even though not by the size of the members.

Chapter 17

(29) *A.* Cease to wonder, because my answer to you here will be along similar lines. Just as the size of the members furnishes no basis for arguing that the soul is helped because many men of rather slight and small build are found to be wiser than some others who have a large frame, so, because we see that some young men are more given to labor and exertion than older men, I do not see why any one should entertain the view that the passing of years adds growth to souls in the same way as it does to bodies. Even bodies—which admittedly are supposed to grow in time and become larger with the years—often enough, the older they get, the smaller they are; not only bodies of the aged, which

shrink and grow smaller with the lapse of time, but even in the bodies of boys we observe that some, although older in years than others, are shorter in size. If, then, the accumulation of years is not a cause of size even of bodies themselves, but all this growth is to be attributed to the action of the seed and of certain elements embedded in nature which are somewhat hidden and hard to recognize, how much less ground is there for the view that the soul becomes longer with length of years, merely because we observe that it has learned much from habit and long experience?

(30) If you are surprised at our usual rendering of the Greek word *makrothumían* by long suffering, I beg you to notice that we apply to the soul metaphors taken from the body, and vice versa. For, if Virgil[1] spoke of a 'wicked' mountain and of a most 'fair' land—which words, you notice, are transferred from the soul to a body—what wonders, then, if we reverse the process and speak of 'longanimity.' since strictly speaking only bodies can be long? Indeed, the virtue called greatness of soul is correctly understood to refer not to any space but to a certain strength, that is, to a power and force in the soul, a virtue, in fact, that is the more esteemed, the more it despises material things. But we shall speak of this later, when we bring up the question how great is the soul, as one is wont to ask how great was Hercules in his mighty deeds and not in the weight of his body. For, so we made our division above. You ought now to recall what we have already said about the point, namely that reason declared that it is important enough to be the main element in all geometrical figures. Does not this importance and main role seem to show a certain magnitude? Yet in a point we find no dimensions? Therefore, when we hear and speak of a

1 *Aeneid* XII 687; *Georgics* II 460.

great and strong soul, we ought not to think of its size, but of its power. Therefore, if we have now spent enough time on your first argument in support of your view that the soul seems to grow with the age of the body, we may pass to the next.

Chapter 18

(31) *E.* I don't know whether we have tracked down all the doubts that cause me real worry; perhaps some elude my memory at present. However, one does come to mind and let us see what there is to it; a very young child does not speak, and yet acquires that power as it grows older.

A. That is easily answered. I believe you understand that each one speaks the language of the people among whom he was born and brought up.

E. Everyone knows that.

A. Suppose, then, that some one was born and brought up among people who do not talk, but by nods and gestures express the thoughts they have to communicate. Do you not think that he would do the same and would not speak, since he never heard anyone speaking?

E. Please do not ask me that, since the supposition is absurd. How can I imagine such men or anyone being born among them?

A. But surely, did you not see at Milan a young man of excellent physique and refined manners, yet so mute and deaf that he understood others only by means of signs and that only in the same way could he express what he wished? This man is very well known. I also knew a farmer and his wife who could speak, yet they had four sons and daughters, or perhaps more (I do not recall exactly how many), who were deaf and dumb: dumb, because they couldn't speak; deaf, because they could take in signs only through their eyes.

E. I knew the first man also, but the second I did not; yet I believe you. But what is the point?

A. You said you could not imagine anyone being born among such people.

E. And I say the same thing now. The persons you mentioned were born of parents who could speak. I believe you admitted that.

A. Yes, I did. Then, since it is clear that some such persons can exist, I ask you to consider, if such a man and woman should marry and should be carried off by some chance to a place remote from civilization, but not incompatible with human living, and if they should have a son who is not deaf, how could he speak with his parents?

E. How do you think, except that his parents would give him signs which he should make back to them? But a small child would not be able to do even this. Hence, my contention remains. Anyhow, what difference does it make whether he acquires the ability to speak or to make signs by growing older, since both belong to the soul which we are loath to admit undergoes any growth.

(32) *A.* You seem to hold that the man who walks a rope has a larger soul than those who cannot do this.

E. That is different, for who does not see that rope-walking is an art.

A. Why, I ask, an art? Is it because he has learned it?

E. That is right.

A. Then, if someone learns something else, do you not hold that this is an art also?

E. Whatever is learned clearly belongs to art; this I do not deny.

A. Did not this boy then learn to make a gesture from his parents?

E. He surely did.

A. You should attribute it to some art of mimicry, therefore, and not to any increase in the soul as it grew older.

E. But I cannot grant that.

A. Therefore, not everything that is learned comes under art, as you just now admitted.

E. It does come under art.

A. Hence, he did not learn the gesture, which you likewise had granted .

E. He did learn it, but it does not come under art.

A. Just a little while before you said that whatever is learned comes under art.

E. I admit that to speak and to make a gesture come under art in so far as we have learned them. But there are some arts which we learn while we watch others, and there are other arts which are taught us by teachers.

A. Which kind does the soul take in by becoming larger? Both kinds?

E. Not both; the former.

A. Do you not think that to walk a rope belongs to that class? It would seem that it is by seeing it done that the skill is acquired.

E. I think so; yet not every spectator who watches carefully how it is done can acquire this skill, but only those who submit to instruction.

A. You are correct. And I would give the same answer about learning to speak, for many Greeks and those of other nationalities often hear us speaking as they might watch a rope walker, but really to learn our language they entrust themselves to teachers, just as we do when we wish to learn theirs. Since such is the case, I wonder why you wish to attribute to the soul's growth the ability to speak, but not the ability to walk a rope.

E. I don't know how you come to mix up these two things. The man who entrusts himself to a teacher to learn our language already knows his own, which I maintain he learned through the soul's growth; when he learns a foreign language, I attribute that to art and not to a larger soul.

A. But, if that boy who was born and bred among mutes, later on and as a young man, by coming across other people, should have learned to speak, when he had known no other language, would you hold the view that at the moment he learned to speak his soul had undergone an increase in size?

E. I would never dare to say that, and I yield to reason. I no longer regard the ability to speak as an argument for holding that the soul is larger, lest I be forced to admit that the soul acquires all the other arts by growing larger; for, if I should say that, this absurdity would follow, that the soul shrinks whenever it forgets anything.

Chapter 19

(33) *A.* You reveal a good grasp of the question. To let you hear the truth, the soul is rightly said to be enlarged, as it were, by learning and to grow smaller by unlearning, but in a metaphorical sense, as we have discussed. You must avoid this misconception that the growth of the soul means that it fills out, as it were, a larger space, whereas in fact a more skillful soul has a greater power to act than a less skillful one. It is important to notice, however, that the kind of subjects that make up its diet of learning has a decisive influence on the soul's girth, to use this expression. Consider: physical growth is of three kinds. One is necessary for the healthy and harmonious development of the different parts of the body. A second is abnormal, that which retards the healthy growth of some parts of the body, as sometimes

happens when a baby is born with six fingers, or in other cases when deviation from the normal is so pronounced that babies are called monstrosities. The third kind of growth is injurious and is what we call a tumor. In this condition the bodily part does indeed grow larger and occupies greater space, but only at the expense of good health. So, too, growth in the soul is normal when its increased size, so to speak, results from studies of the moral good that are calculated to promote the good and happy life. Studies that are taken up with things that are more curious than solidly worthwhile—granted even that on occasion they are not entirely useless—dissipate the mind and hence must be put in our second category. Just because one flute player so delighted the ears of the populace, according to Varro, that they made him a king is no reason for supposing that we can effect enlargment of the mind by flute playing; any more than, if we had heard that a man, endowed with abnormally large teeth, killed an enemy with a bite, we should wish to have the same kind of teeth. There is, finally, a third class of studies that enfeebles the soul, inflicting on it a grievous wound; for to employ the sense of smell and taste in the dainty appraisal of food, to know how to tell from what lake a fish was hooked or from what vintage a wine was made, is surely a deplorable cultivation of the soul. Such training, while appearing to enlarge the soul, merely shrivels the mind and dilates the senses, and must be said, therefore, to produce in the soul nothing else than a tumor or a case of mental rickets.

Chapter 20

(34) *E.* The point you make is well taken and I agree entirely with you. Yet I am not a little puzzled by the fact that, no matter how closely we look at it, the soul of a new-

born child is altogether untrained and unskilled. Why does it not bring with it some art, if it is eternal?

A. You raise a very important question; in fact, I do not know of one more important on which our views are so diametrically opposed. For, while in your view the soul has brought no art with it, in mine, on the other hand, it has brought every art; for to learn is nothing else than to recall and remember.[1] But, do you not see that this is not the right place to investigate that point. Our concern now is evidently with the problem whether the soul is called large or small according to the extent of space. Whether it is eternal, if it is, will be conveniently examined with the question you asked fourth: Why it was given to the body— a question we shall begin to discuss as soon as it is proper to do so. Whether the soul always was or not, whether it will always be, or whether it is at one time uncultivated, at another cultivated— these questions have nothing to do with its magnitude, since we have proved earlier that the duration of time is not the cause even of bodily growth, and since it is evident that lack of skill is compatible with bodily growth and that mental alertness is often the ornament of physical decline. These and many other arguments suffice to prove that the soul does not grow larger in proportion to the greater bulk that the body takes on with the passing years.

1 In his *Retractationes* 1.8 Augustine writes: 'My statement that learing is simply remembering and recalling is not to be taken as if I approved the doctrine that the soul had sometimes existed in another body, here or elsewhere, or in its own body or out of it . . . Surely the soul does not bring with it all the arts nor does it possess them in the same way. For, as regards the arts that pertain to the senses of the body—many branches of medicine and all of astrology—unless a man learns them, he cannot say that he has them. But, those arts which pertain to the understanding alone, these he masters for the reason I mentioned, when he has been wisely questioned and reminded either by himself or another, and thus brings forth the right answer.'

Chapter 21

(35) Let us examine, therefore, if you wish, the force of that other argument of yours, namely, that the soul, which we would find to be without any material extension, feels the sensation of touch over the entire surface of the body.

E. My inclination would be to pass on to that question, were it not that a difficulty remains in connection with strength. How is it that bodily development confers greater strength on the soul, if it does not enlarge the soul? Although the seat of virtue is the soul and of strength, the body, according to the common opinion, nevertheless, I would never separate strength from the soul, since, when the soul leaves the body, so, too, does strength. It is through the body, of course, that the soul uses its strength, as it does the senses. Yet, because these are the operations proper only to a living person, who can doubt that bodily strength also really belongs to the soul? Since we see, therefore, that growing boys have more strength than infants and that the vigor of young men surpasses that of boys, until finally, as the body grows old, its strength wanes, this to me is no slight indication that the soul grows larger with the body and again ages with it.

(36) *A.* Your statement is not altogether absurd. But, as I see it, strength results not so much from the bulk of the body and growth in years as from a certain training and formation of the members. To prove this to you, I ask you this question: Would you say that a man who outstrips another in walking, and is less tired, has the greater strength?

E. I think so.

A. Why, then, as a boy could I cover more ground in hunting birds without getting tired than when, as a young man, I devoted myself to other studies that required a more sedentary life, if greater strength is to be attributed to growth in years and consequent enlargment of soul? Again, it is not the weight and size of the body that wrestling trainers are keen to look for in wrestlers, but the knots of their muscles, the shape of their biceps and the general posture and carriage of the body; from these points they make a good estimate of the man's strength. These physical traits are not worth much in themselves unless accompanied by technique and training. It is not an uncommon sight to see fellows of massive frame beaten by small and slight men in moving and in lifting weights and even in wrestling. Who does not know that an Olympic star is more quickly worn out on a journey than a pack peddler who could be knocked down by one of the other fellow's fingers? Hence, if we do not speak of all strength in the same way, but qualify it as more fitted now for one task, again for another; and if the form and figure of the body count more for strength than its size; and if training is so important that it is commonly believed that the man, who has lifted every day a little calf, could easily lift and hold up the calf when it has grown to be a bull, without feeling the greater weight that it took on little by little—if all this be so, then the greater strength of age does not mean at all that the soul has grown with the body.

Chapter 22

(37) If the larger bodies of animals possess greater strength because they are larger, the reason is that, by the law of nature, what is lighter yields to what is heavier. This is so not only when the force of gravity carries them to their proper place, as moist and earthy bodies fall toward the center of the earth, which is the lowest point downward,

and, to the contrary, aery bodies and bodies of fire go upwards, but also when some mechanical thrust, or impulse, or rebound forces them to follow a course quite different from one they follow of their own natural inclination. When you drop two stones of unequal size from a height at the same time, the larger stone reaches the ground sooner,[1] but, if the smaller is placed under the larger and securely held in that position, the smaller yields and is brought to the ground at the same time as the larger. Likewise, if the heavier stone is thrown down from above and the lighter is hurled upwards against it, at the point of contact the lighter will of necessity be forced back and down. Lest you think that this happens because the lighter stone was being forced against its nature to go upwards, whereas the other was seeking its natural place with greater speed, suppose that the heavier stone is hurled upwards and it meets the lighter stone on the way down. You will see in this case that the lighter stone is stopped and forced upwards, but, on the rebound, falls to a different spot from the one to which its unimpeded fall would carry it. Again, if both, not by natural motion but, so to say, like two men in combat on a field, are thrown one against the other and crash together in mid-air, who would doubt that the smaller will give way to the larger in that direction to which the larger was moving? Since these facts are so, namely, that lighter weights yield to heavier weights, another important factor is the force with which they are put in motion. If the lighter be hurled with greater force, as by some powerful machine, and flung against a heavier body that was thrown with less force, or is already losing its momentum, though the lighter weight may rebound, still

---

1 Augustine is following the common misconception that was not corrected until the time of Galileo (1564-1642).

it lessens the speed of the heavier or even drives it back, depending upon the relation of impact and weight.

(38) With this knowledge in mind, as far as the present discussion demands, see now whether those forces which are called strength in animals harmonize with this reasoning; for who will deny that the bodies of all animals are possessed of weight? Now, an animal moves its weight wherever it wishes by an impulse of its soul, and, of course, the amount of weight the animal has is not a negligible factor. But the soul's impulse makes use of the sinews as ropes to move the weight of the body. Now, moderate dryness and heat nourish the sinews and make them more ready, whereas damp rigidity relaxes and weakens them. Sleep, therefore, makes the members languid, because, according to the physicians, it is cooling and dampening; and men just roused from sleep have little or no energy. Therefore, nothing is more pliable and nerveless than men in a state of lethargy. And it is evident that the influence of wine or of a high fever unbalances the mind of some men and by generating heat so molds and hardens their sinews that they can struggle and perform greater feats of strength than they could in a normal condition, even though their bodily frame is quite reduced and weakened by illness. If what we call strength, therefore, is made up of an impulse from the soul, the mechanism of nerve sinews and the weight of the body, it is the will that supplies the impulse which is considerably stimulated by hope or courage, but retarded through fear and much more through desperation (for fear, provided there be some hope, usually increases strength). The harmonious development of the body perfects the mechanism; moderate health keeps it in order and regular exercise hardens it; weight is supplied by the mass of the members which age and nourishment build up, but

which nutrition alone restores. The man who is equally superior in all of these is a marvel of strength; in proportion to their absence one man is less strong than another. Again, it often happens that the combination of persevering will power and better muscular development makes up for slight weight and in the test proves superior against the odds of sheer weight. Yet again, sometimes the size is so great that even with slight exertion it may crush the supreme effort of a smaller adversary. When, however, through no lack of physical weight or muscular training or will power (which is the soul), a stronger man is beaten by a weaker and a craven soul is worsted by a bolder spirit, I do not know whether this is attributed to strength—unless one is to hold that the soul has its own resources, bringing forth of itself an abundance of daring and confidence. These qualities one man has; another has not. Hence it is understood how far superior the soul is to its own body, even in performing actions that are done through the body.

(39) Wherefore, since the impulses of a young child are fully developed only to pull or push, and its sinews lack strength because of their recent and imperfect formation, lack endurance because of the natural softness of the immature body, and lack hardness because of no exercise; since, moreover, its weight is so slight that it hardly exerts any pressure in colliding with another body and is more liable to be hurt itself than to do harm—who will not think it a sound and prudent inference to hold that the soul has actually grown larger when he sees and knows that the passing years have remedied all these deficiencies and supplied strength which, increasing day by day, is at the service and command of the soul? Such a man would be inclined to conclude that, if he sees little, light darts issuing from a lax bow, which a

youth, hidden from view by a curtain, is using with all his might, and sees these darts make rather short flights and soon drop to the ground; and, if, a little later, he sees full-fledged arrows, weighted with iron, flung high into the sky from a strong bow; and, then, if he is informed that both performances are the result of equal exertion by one and the same archer—such a man, I say, would be inclined to conclude that the archer had grown and increased his strength in that short interval. And what conclusion could be more at variance with the truth than this?

(40) Then again, if the soul does grow, see how foolish it is to infer its growth from the vigor of the body, and not from the fullness of its knowledge, since the former it merely directs; the latter it possesses as its very own. Moreover, if we think that the soul grows larger by the addition of strength, we must admit that loss of strength reduces its stature. But strength is diminished in old age and also by the labor of study, but during those periods knowledge is gathered and built up. And it is impossible for anything to be both increased and diminished at one and the same time. Greater strength in greater age, therefore, is no proof that the soul grows. Many more comments can be made, but, if you are now satisfied, I draw the line so that we may pass on to other questions.

E. I am quite convinced that greater physical strength is not the result of the soul's physical growth; for, to pass over other keen observations of yours, not even a crazy man would say that the soul grows in a fit of insanity or during illness that reduces the body, although everyone knows that insanity and fever usually make the victim more violent than does health. Therefore, please take up now the question which I am all attention to hear: Why the soul feels where-ever the body is touched, if the soul's magnitude has not the same spatial extent as that of the body.

Chapter 23

(41) *A*. Go ahead, then. Let us proceed, as you wish, but you will have to follow me more closely, perhaps, than you think. Therefore give me your best attention and answer me what sort of a reality you think a sense is which the soul uses through the body. For it is called sense by its proper name.

E. I usually hear the senses spoken of as five: seeing, hearing smelling, tasting, and touching. I do not know what more to answer.

A. That division is very ancient and commonly used by the old masters of rhetoric. But I would have you define sense for me, so as to take in all five in one definition and not to take in anything that is not sense. If you cannot do this, it is all right. At least you can do this—and it will be enough—you can either reject or support my definition.

E. Possibly I shall not fail you in that, as far as I can, but even that is not always easy.

A. Listen carefully, then, for I think that sensation is 'a bodily experience of which the soul is not unaware.'[1]

E. This definition satisfies me.

A. Stand by it as your own, then, and defend it while I demolish it bit by bit.

E. I will, indeed, defend it with your help; otherwise, no. Already I find it unsatisfactory; you have good reason for wishing to refute it.

1 Literally, 'sensation is a passion of the body, which [passion] does not escape the notice of the soul.' Augustine's account of sensation is quite unsatisfactory. For an excellent summary and criticism of his theory, cf. V. Bourke, *Augustine's Quest of Wisdom* 111-12.

A. Do not rely too much on authority, especially mine, which is zero. And, as Horace says,[2] 'Dare to have a mind of your own,' lest fear guide you sooner than reason.

E. I have no fear at all, no matter how the problem may turn out, for you check me from going wrong. But begin, if you have anything to say, lest I be worn out by the delay, not by the defense.

(42) *A.* Tell me now, what does your body experience when you see me?

E. It experiences something, to be sure, for my eyes are part of my body, if I mistake not; and if they experience nothing, how could I see you?

A. But it is not enough for you to show that your eyes experience something, unless you indicate also what they experience.

E. What, then, do they experience except sight, for they see? If you were to ask me what a sick man experiences, I should answer: sickness; what a sensuous man: sensuality; what a fearful man: fear; what a joyful man: joy. Why, therefore, not answer your question thus: that a seeing man experiences sight?

A. But, a joyful man feels joy—or will you deny that?

E. On the contrary, I am agreed.

A. I should say the same of the other emotions.

E. I hold the same.

A. But, whatever the eyes perceive, that they see.

E. I should not say that at all. Who sees pain, which the eyes often feel?

A. It is clear that you are thinking about eyes; you are wide awake. Now, then, see whether, just as the joyful man

2 *Epistles* I ii 40.

feels joy by being joyful, the man who sees experiences sight by seeing.

E. Can it be otherwise?

A. Whatever the man who sees feels by seeing, that he must necessarily see.

E. No, not necessarily; for, if he feels love by seeing, does he then see love?

A. Very guardedly and shrewdly said. I am happy that you are not easily deceived. But now, mark this. Since we are agreed that not everything that the eye feels is seen and, again, that not everything that is felt by seeing is seen, do you think that this at least is true—everything that is seen is also perceived?

E. Unless I admit that, I do not see how seeing can be called sensation.

A. But, do we not experience everything that we perceive?

E. That is so.

A. Therefore, if we perceive everything we see and if we experience everything we perceive, then we experience everything we see.

E. I make no objection to that. .

A. Therefore, when we see each other, you experience me and, conversely, I experience you.

E. So I think. Reason forces me to this conclusion at once.

(43) *A*. Take the rest, for I believe it would appear very absurd and stupid to you, if anyone should declare that you there experience a body, where the body itself which you experience is not.

E. It does seem absurd, and I think your statement is correct.

A. Now, is it not evident that my body is in one place; yours, in another?

E. Of course.

A. But, your eyes perceive my body and, if they perceive, they certainly experience. Again they cannot there experience, where what they experience is not. Yet, your eyes are not there where my body is. Therefore, they experience where they are not.

E. Of course I granted all those statements because I thought it unreasonable not to grant them. But this last statement, which is the conclusion of the previous statements, is altogether so foolish that I prefer to admit that some one of my former admissions is unwarranted rather than that this conclusion is true. I should not dare to say even in my dreams that my eyes perceive where they are not.

A. Look, then, where you have dozed off. How could anything take you so badly off guard, if you were as wide awake as you were a while ago?

E. I am going over the argument in my mind very carefully and slowly. Still, it is not sufficiently clear what statement I regret having granted, unless possibly it may be this: that our eyes perceive when we see. Perhaps it is sight that perceives.

A. And so it is, for sight goes forth and through the eyes shines far to light up what we see. Hence it follows that there it sees where the object is which it sees, and not at the point where it goes out to see. It is not you, then, that see, when you see me.

E. Who would be so mad as to say that? Of course I see, but I see by means of sight sent forth through the eyes.

A. But, if you see, you perceive; if you perceive, you are acted upon; and you cannot there be acted upon where you are not. But you see me where I am; therefore, you are acted upon where I am. But, if you are not there where I am, I know not how you dare say that I am seen by you.

E. By means of sight, I say, reaching out to that place where you are, I see you where you are. That I am not there I admit. But, just as though I were to touch you with a rod, I would be the one touching you and I would perceive it; yet I would not be there where I would be touching you. So it is when I say that I see you by means of sight, although I am not there where you are; I am not by this forced to admit that it is not I who see.

(44) *A.* Therefore, you have admitted nothing rashly; for your eyes can be defended in this way, too. Their sight is like a rod, as you say, and that conclusion, therefore, is not unreasonable that your eyes see where they are not. Or have you a different view?

E. It is just as you say. Moreover, I observe this, now, that if the eyes did see there where they are, they would also see themselves.

A. You would be more accurate if you said not that they would see themselves *also,* but that they would see themselves *only*. For, where they are, that is the place which they occupy and occupy alone, and the nose is not there where they are, nor anything else near them. Otherwise, you also would be here where I am, because we are so close together. Therefore, if the eyes were to see only there where they are, they would see only themselves and nothing else. But, since they do not see themselves, we must agree not only that they can see there where they are not, but that they can see only where they are not.

E. Nothing shakes my certainty on this point.

A. You are certain, then, that the eyes are there acted upon where they are not, for, where they see, there they perceive; for seeing is perceiving and perceiving is being acted upon. Therefore, where they perceive, there they are acted upon. But, they see in a different place from where they are. Therefore, they are acted upon there where they are not.

E. It is marvelous how I judge these conclusions to be true.

Chapter 24

(45) *A.* Perhaps your judgment is correct. But now, answer this question: Do we see everything that we know by means of sight?

E. I believe so.

A. You also believe, then, that what we know by seeing, we know by means of sight?

E. I believe that, also.

A. Why, then, when we see only smoke, do we generally know that there is hidden beneath it a fire which we do not see?

E. What you say is true. And now I think that we do not see whatever we know by means of sight; for we can, as you have pointed out, by seeing one thing, know another that sight has not reached.

A. What of this? Is it possible for us not to see the object that we perceive by means of sight?

E. No, it is not possible.

A. Therefore, to perceive with the sense is one thing; to know is another.

E. Altogether different; for we perceive the smoke that we see, and from that we know the presence of the fire which we do not see.

A. You understand rightly. But you certainly see that when this happens, our body, that is, our eyes, have no experience of the fire, but only of the smoke, which is all that they see. For, we have agreed before that to see is to perceive and to perceive is to be acted upon.

E. I hold that and I am agreed.

A. When, therefore, there occurs a bodily experience which makes the soul aware of something, the phenomenon is not for that reason called an activity of one of the five senses, but only when the soul is aware of the bodily experience itself. For, that fire is not seen, or heard or smelled or tasted or touched by us, yet, through the sight of smoke, the soul becomes aware of the fire. While, therefore, this awareness of the soul may not be called an activity of sense, because the body has no experience of the fire, yet it is called knowledge through sense, because the presence of the fire was suspected and established from an experience which the body had, even though it was an experience of something different, that is to say, from seeing something other than the fire.

E. I understand and I see very well that this squares with and supports that definition of yours which you gave me to defend, for so I recall your definition of sensation as 'a bodily experience of which the soul is not unaware.' Therefore, the seeing of smoke we call a sensation, for the eyes experienced that by seeing, and the eyes are parts of the body and corporeal, but the fire, of which the body had no experience, although the presence of the fire is known, we do not call an object of sensation.

(46) *A.* I am delighted with your memory and your ability to follow the argument, but your defense of this definition begins to crumble.

E. Why, I ask.

A. Because you admit, I believe, that, when we are growing or when we grow old, the body is being acted upon. Yet it is clear that we do not perceive this action by any one of the senses, and still the soul is not unaware of it. Therefore, there is one bodily experience of which the soul is not unaware, and yet it cannot be called sensation. For, seeing things become larger, which formerly we had seen smaller, and seeing men grown old who once were certainly youths and boys, we conclude that our bodies, too, even now while we are talking, undergo some such change. And in this way I think we are not deceived. I am more inclined to state that I am deceived in what I see than in what I understand, namely, that my hair is growing now or that the body undergoes constant change. If this change, then, is an action upon the body, which no one denies, and if it is not perceived by our senses, and yet the soul is not unaware of it, this, then, is a bodily experience of which the soul is not unaware, and it is not sensation. Hence, that definition which should include nothing that is not sensation is surely deficient, since it includes this.

E. Nothing remains for me, I see, but to ask you to construct another definition or to correct this one, if you can, for I cannot deny that it is defective for the compelling reason you pointed out.

A. It is a simple matter to correct this, and I would like you to try. If you understand where it errs, you will do so, believe me.

E. Does it err in any other point than in including what is outside its scope?

A. In what way, then?

E. Because even the body of a young man grows old; hence it cannot be denied that it is being acted upon. Since we know this, here is bodily experience of which the soul is aware. Yet, that experience is not perceived by any sense, for I see that I am now growing old and I do not perceive it by hearing, smell, taste, or touch.

A. How, then, do you know it?

E. I gather it from reason.

A. On what grounds does your reason rest?

E. The fact that I see other men old, who, as I now am, were once young.

A. Does not that perception come to us through one of the five senses?

E. Who denies that? But, from the fact that I see them I conclude that I, too, am growing old, a fact which I do not see.

A. What word, then, do you think must be added to this definition to make it perfect? Is it not rather this way, that sensation is a bodily experience of which the soul is not unaware, but such an experience that the soul does not come to know it through a different experience or through anything else.

E. Please state that a little more clearly, I beg you.

Chapter 25

(47) *A.* I will satisfy you, and all the more willingly, if you go slowly rather than hurry. See that you pay strict attention, for, what I shall say will be useful also for other points. A definition contains nothing less, nothing more, than that which it undertakes to explain; otherwise, it is a bad definition. Now, whether a definition is free of such faults is discovered by inversion. A few examples will make this clearer to you. If you were to ask me: What is man?—and if I were to define him this way: Man is a mortal animal—you should not be satisfied with the definition because it contains some modicum of truth. By adding one little word, namely, 'every,' and by inverting the definition, you should see whether the definition will also be true, when inverted; that is to say, you should see whether, just as 'every man is a mortal animal' is true, so would it be true that 'every mortal animal is a man.'

And, this being found to be false, you should reject the definition, because it includes what does not belong to it. For, not only man, but every brute beast is mortal. This definition of man is usually completed by adding 'rational.' Just as every man is a rational animal subject to death, so every rational animal subject to death is a man. The previous definition erred by including too much, for it included brute beasts with man; the present definition is correct, because it includes every man, and only man, and nothing else besides. A definition is likewise faulty by taking in too little, as, for example, if you add 'grammarian': for, although every rational, mortal, grammarian animal is a man, many men who are not grammarians are not included in this definition. Therefore, this definition in its first statement is false, but, when inverted, is true. That every man is a mortal, grammarian animal is untrue, but, it is true that every mortal, grammarian animal is a man. When a definition is false both in its first expression and when inverted, it is surely more defective than either of these, as for example, these two: Man is a white animal or man is a four-footed animal. For, if you say every man is a white animal or every man is a quadruped, the statement is false, and it is false if you invert it. But, there is this difference, that some men come under the former, for most men are white, but the latter applies to none, for not a single man is a quadruped. For the present, this instruction on sounding out definition shows you how they may be tested by direct expression or by inversion. There are many other lessons of this kind, abounding in verbiage and vagueness, which, little by little, as the occasion warrants, I shall try to teach you.

(48) For the present, turn your attention to our definition and now, with your greater knowledge, after studying

it, correct it, for we discovered that the supposed definition of sensation contained something that was not sensation and, therefore, was not true when inverted. It is possibly true that every bodily experience of which the soul is not unaware is sensation—just as it is true that every man is a mortal animal, but false that every mortal animal is a man, because the brute beast is also that. So it is untrue that every bodily experience of which the soul is not unaware is sensation, because our fingernails are growing now and the soul is not unaware of that fact, for we know it; yet we do not perceive it by the senses but by reasoning. Just in the same way, therefore, as 'rational' was added to the definition of man to make it correct, thereby ruling out the brute beasts that had been included—and hence our definition now includes every man and nothing but a man—what word, do you think, must be added to our definition so as to eliminate what is extraneous and to include only sensation and everything that is sensation?

E. I think that something must be added, but, what the word is I do not know.

A. Surely, sensation is always a bodily experience of which the soul is not unaware, but this proposition cannot be inverted, because there is the experience of the body in growing or shrinking that we know and of which the soul, therefore, is not unaware.

E. That is true.

A. How, then, is this experience revealed to the soul: by the experience itself or by something else?

E. By something else, of course, for it is one thing to see the fingernails grown larger; another thing to know that they grow.

A. Since, then, growing is itself an experience of the body which none of the senses perceives, and this growth which we see results from the experience and is not the experience itself, it is clear that we do not know the experience itself directly, but through something else. For, if it were not revealed to the soul by something else, would we not perceive it instead of concluding that it exists?

E. I understand.

A. Why, then, do you hesitate as to what word should be added to the definition?

E. I see now that the definition must be formulated in such a way that sensation will be a bodily experience of which the soul is aware directly, for I believe that every sensation is that and that all that is likewise sensation.

(49) *A.* If that is true, I acknowledge the definition to be complete. But, let us make a test, if you will, to see whether the definition is not tottering from the second fault, like the definition of man to which the term 'grammarian' was added. You recall that we said that man is a rational, mortal, grammarian animal, and that this definition is wrong, because, while inverted it is true, as it stands it is untrue. For, that every man is a rational, mortal, grammarian animal is untrue, although it is true that every rational, mortal, grammarian animal is a man. Therefore, that definition falls down because it includes only man, but not every man. Now, perhaps the same is true of this definition which we are priding ourselves is perfect. For, although every direct awareness in the soul of a bodily experience is sensation, not every sensation is that. And you may understand this from the following: Brute animals, for example have sensations, and nearly all animals have these five senses in their vigor, as far as nature has endowed them. Or will you deny this?

E. Not at all.

Chapter 26

A. Do you grant this: that knowledge exists only when something is perceived and known by certain reason?

E. I grant that.

A. But, brute animals do not use reason.

E. I grant that, too.

A. Knowledge, therefore, does not exist in the brute animal. But, when something is not hidden, it is certainly known. Therefore, brute animals have no sense perceptions, if every sensation includes a direct experience of the body of which the soul is aware. But, they do have sense perceptions, as was granted a little while ago. Why, then, do we hesitate to reject this definition which cannot include every sensation, since, of course, it excludes the sensation of brute animals?

(50) *E*. I confess that I was deceived when I granted to you that knowledge exists only when something is perceived by certain reason. When you asked that, I was thinking only of men, and, of course, I cannot say that brute animals use reason and I cannot deny them knowledge. For, as I think, the dog knew his master,[1] whom he is recounted as recognizing after twenty years, not to speak of other innumerable facts.

A. Tell me, now, if two things were placed before you —one as the goal which you are to reach, the other as the means by which you can reach the goal—which of these two will you rate higher, and which prefer to the other?

E. Who would hestitate to say that the goal rates higher?

A. Therefore, as knowledge and reason are two distinct

1 *Odyssey* XVII 292.

realities, do we arrive at reason by knowledge, or at knowledge by reason?

E. These two are so connected, as I think, that one can be acquired by means of the other, and vice versa. We should not come to exercise reason, unless we knew that we could. Knowledge, therefore, preceded, so that through it we have come to use reason.

A. What is that? Would we ever come without reason to knowledge, which you say precedes?

E. Never would I say that, for it is the height of rashness.

A. By reason, then, we come to knowledge?

E. That is not so.

A. Then, by lack of reason?

E. Who would say that?

A. By what means, then?

E. By no means; knowledge is born in us.

(51) *A.* You seem to forget our previous agreement when I asked you whether you thought that knowledge implies the perception of something with certainty. For you answered, I believe, that such appears to you to be human knowledge. Now you say that man can have some knowledge without reason perceiving anything. Who does not see that nothing can be more contradictory than these two statements: that there is no knowledge unless reason perceives something with certainty, and that there is some knowledge when reason perceives nothing? Therefore, I desire to know which of these two you select; clearly, both cannot be true by any manner of means.

E. I select the latter statement. Indeed, I confess that I granted the former without thinking. For, in our present pursuit of truth by question and answer, how could reason come to a conclusion, unless something has been granted beforehand? Moreover, how could one reasonably grant what he doesn't know? So, then, unless this reason found in me something known as a starting point for leading me on to what is unknown, I would never learn anything by reason and I would never call it reason. Therefore, you have no leg to stand on in disagreeing with me that, prior to reason, there must be some knowledge in us which reason itself uses as a starting point.

A. I grant what you say and, as often as you acknowledge your mistake in making an admission, I will allow you to correct yourself. But do not abuse this privilege, I beg you, by paying scant attention to my questions, lest the habit of making unwarranted conclusions compel you to deny what you ought to admit.

E. Proceed rather to the remaining points, for, although I will do everything possible to increase my vigilance (for I am indeed ashamed of blundering so often in my judgment), yet I will never allow my embarrassment to overwhelm me and prevent me from correcting a blunder, especially if you lend me a helping hand. Stubbornness is surely not a treasure because consistency is a jewel.

Chapter 27

(52) *A*. May that bright jewel be yours as soon as possible: your pithy saying pleases me very much. Now, pay strict attention to what I wish to say. My question is: What do you think is the difference between reason [*ratio*] and reasoning [*raticinatio*]?

E. I fail to see any clear distinction.

A. Look at this, then. See whether you think that in a youth, or a man, or (to remove any ground for doubt) anyone capable of thinking, provided he has a sound mind, reason is inherent, in the same way that health is inherent in the body as long as it is free of disease and wounds. Or is it sometimes present, sometimes absent, as walking, sitting down, talking?

E. In the sound mind, I think reason is always inherent.

A. What of this? If you define reasoning as when we learn something from premises that are granted or are clear in themselves, either by questioning someone else or by linking up things for ourselves, would you say that we or all thinking men are doing this always?

E. No, not always, for no man or no thinking man, as I believe, is always seeking for something by arguing either with himself or someone else. For, he who is seeking has not yet found; if he is always seeking, he never finds. The thinking man, however, has already found (to say nothing more) at least the thought he lacked and was seeking to discover, possibly by discussion or some other means.

A. Your statement is correct. I want you to understand therefore, that the process of being led on to something unknown from premises that are granted or evident is not reason itself. This process is not always present in the sound mind, but reason is.

(53) *E.* I understand, but what is the point of all this?

A. Because a little while ago you said that I ought to agree with you that we have knowledge before reason, on the ground that reason rests upon the knowledge of something in leading us to something unknown. But now we have found that when this leading is done, it is not to be called reason, for the sound mind is not always reasoning, even though it always has reason. Quite properly, this process is called reasoning. So that reason, you might say, is the sight of the mind, but reasoning is reason's search, that is, the actual moving of the sight of the mind over the things that are to be seen. Hence, by reasoning, we search; by reason we see. Further, when this sight of the mind, which we call reason, sees some reality upon which it is focused, we call that knowledge, but when the mind does not see, though it focuses its sight, that is called not-knowing or ignorance. For, not everyone who looks with his bodily eyes sees—an observation we can readily verify by looking in the dark. From this it is evident, I believe, that looking is one thing; seeing, quite another. Applying this distinction to the mind we call one thing reason, the other, knowledge—unless, of course, something prompts you to reject this explanation, or you think the distinction is not clear.

E. The distinction pleases me very much indeed and I am in hearty agreement.

A. See, therefore, whether you think that we look in order to see, or see in order to look.

E. On this point not even a blind man would hesitate to say that looking is for seeing, not seeing for looking.

A. It must be granted, then, that seeing is to be valued more highly than looking.

E. It certainly must.

A. Knowledge, therefore, must be rated above reason.

E. I see that that follows logically.

A. Would you agree that brute beasts are more excellent or happier than men?

E. May God avert such monstrous madness.

A. You have good reason for shuddering at such a conclusion. But what you just said forces us to that conclusion, for you stated that they have knowledge, not reason. Man has reason by which he arrives at knowledge with great difficulty. But, granting that he reaches it with ease, how will reason help us to rank men ahead of brute animals, since they have knowledge, and knowledge, it has been found, must be rated higher than reason?

Chapter 28

(54) *E.*·I am forced either to grant that brute animals have no knowledge or to offer no objection when they are deservedly placed before me. But, please explain the story about Ulysses' dog; what is the point of it? For, mystified at the wonder of it, I have been barking up the wrong tree.

A. What do you think is the explanation, except a certain force of sense perception, not of knowing. Many animals surpass us in sense perception, and the reason for this is not to be gone into just now, but in mind and reason and knowledge God has placed us over them. The sense perception of animals, aided by the great force of habit, enables them to pick out the things that satisfy their souls, and this is done all the more easily because the brute soul is more closely bound to the body, and, of course, the senses belong to the body, the senses that the soul uses for food and for the pleasure that it derives from the body. But, because reason and knowledge, of which we are treating now, transcend the senses, the human soul, by means of reason and knowledge, withdraws itself as far as it can from the body and gladly enjoys the delights of the interior life. The more it stoops to the senses, the greater its similarity to the brute. Hence it is that nursing infants, the more they are devoid of reason, the sharper are they to recognize by sense the touch and proximity of their nurses and will not bear the odor of others to whom they are not accustomed.

(55) Therefore, although this is a digression, I am happy to emphasize the good advice that the soul should not pour itself out in the senses beyond the measure of necessity, but

rather should recall itself from the senses and become a child of God again, that is, be made a new man by putting off the old. There is surely need to begin at this reformation because of the neglect of God's law—and no other warning does Sacred Scripture utter more often in simple truth and in parable. I should like to develop this point and, of course, to bind myself by the same law, so to speak, that I lay down for you, namely, to render an account of myself to myself, to whom I ought before all others to render an account, and thus become to God, in the words of Horace,[1] 'a friend made a bond-servant to his lord.' This renovation cannot take place at all, unless we are remade in the image of Him who gave us that image to keep as a most precious treasure, when He gave us to ourselves with such a nature that only He Himself can rank before us.

But, to me no work is more laborious, no activity more like inactivity, than this renovation of spirit, for the soul has not the strength to begin or complete it, except with the help of Him to whom it turns itself. Hence it comes about that man's reformation must be sought from the mercy of Him whose Goodness and Power are the cause of man's formation.

(56) But we must get back to our subject. See now, therefore, whether it is proved to you that the brutes have no knowledge, and whether all that apparent knowledge which we admire is merely the result of sensation.

E. It is proved, indeed, and if any point of this question is to be investigated more thoroughly, I will find another time for that study. Now I would like to know what you are making of all this.

---

1 *Satires* II vii 2-3.

Chapter 29

A. What else, except to show you that our definition of sensation, which before somehow included more than sensation, now labors from the opposite vice, because it does not include every sensation. For, brutes have sensation, but not knowledge; and whatever is not hidden is known; and everything that is known surely comes under knowledge. On all these points we have already agreed. Therefore, either it is not true that sensation is a bodily experience of which the soul is not unaware, or else brutes have no sensation, because they are devoid of knowledge. But, we have made the admission that brutes have sensation. Therefore, that definition is defective.

E. I confess that I have no word to say against that.

(57) *A.* Here is another reason to make us still more ashamed of that definition. You remember, I believe, that the third defect of a definition, the worst blunder that could be made, is verified when the definition is false on both sides, as, for example, this definition of man: Man is a four-footed animal. Whoever says and affirms that every man is a four-footed animal, or that every four-footed animal is a man, is joking, or else is completely out of his mind.

E. You are right.

A. But, if our definition is found to have that very fault, do you think that we ought to explode it and eradicate it from our mind, and the sooner, the better?

E. Who would deny that? But, if possible, I would prefer not to be destined so long here again and to be plagued with little questions.

A. Have no fear, our task is done. Or, are you not convinced from our discussions of the difference between beasts and man that perceiving by sensation is entirely different from knowing?

E. To be sure, I am thoroughly convinced.

A. Therefore, there is a difference between sensation and knowledge.

E. There is.

A. We do not have sensation through reason, but by means of sight, or hearing, or smell, or taste, or touch.

E. I agree.

A. And everything we know, we know through reason. Therefore, no sensation is knowledge, but whatever one is aware of comes under knowledge. Therefore, 'to be not unaware of something' no more belongs to sensation than 'four-footed' to a man. Therefore, our definition, yours by adoption, is shown up as not only having trespassed beyond its own boundaries and quitted its own preserves, but as having had in fact no ground of its own whatsoever and as having been from the beginning an unabashed squatter.

E. What, then, shall we do? Will you allow this definition to make its way out of court in this condition? As for myself, I gave it as good a defense as I could, but you are the originator of the case that deceived us. Although I was unable to win the verdict, I was present in all good faith. That is enough for me. But you, if you are accused of lying, what will you do—you who are the author of the definition for this heated debate and the deviser of its shameful betrayal?

A. Is there any one here to act as a judge to whom I or this definition must show respect? My role here, you see, is like that of a private lawyer, namely, to attempt to prove you wrong for the sake of instructing you, so that you may stand prepared when you come into court.

(58) *E.* Can you say anything, then, in defense of this definition which you rashly committed to my unskilled hands to defend and protect?

A. Of course I can.

Chapter 30

E. What is it, I pray you?

A. Although sensation and knowledge are different, that 'not being unaware' is common to both, just as animal is common to man and the brute, although they differ very much. For, whatever is apparent to the soul, either through the condition of the body or through the purity of the intelligence, of that the soul is not unaware. Sensation claims for itself the first way; knowledge, the other.

E. Does that definition, then, remain safe and proved?

A. It certainly does.

E. Where, then, was I taken in?

A. When I asked you whether everything that one is aware of is known. You answered in the affirmative, without thinking.

E. What, then, would you have me say?

A. That knowledge is not had simply if one is aware of something, but only if that awareness results from an exercise of reason. For, if that awareness comes through the body, that is sensation; if the awareness is direct, that is said to be an experience of the body. Do you not know that some philosophers, and very good thinkers, too, thought that not even what is grasped by the mind is worthy of the name of knowledge, unless that comprehension is so firm that the mind cannot be moved from it by any argument?

(59) *E.* I accept your explanation very gratefully, but, now that sensation has been gone into most minutely, please

let us go back to the question which set us off on this explanation. For, I had presented an argument to prove that the soul is just as big as the body because it feels anyone touching it from the head to the little toe, whenever contact is made. We were then carried away to this definition of sensation, a definition perhaps necessary, but fraught with delay. And now, if you will, show me the result of all this labor.

A. There is fruit, indeed, and very rich fruit at that, for, all that we were looking for has been achieved. If sensation is a bodily experience of which the soul is not unaware directly—a definition which we have discussed at greater length than you wished, in order that we might hold on to it most firmly—you remember, then, that we found that the eyes perceive where they are not, or, rather, that they are acted upon where they are not.

E. I do remember.

A. You also granted this, unless I am mistaken, and now I believe you would make the same admission, that the soul is more excellent and more powerful than the whole body.

E. To hesitate on that point would be stupid.

A. Come now. If the body can experience something where the body is not, because of its union with the soul—we have found that this happens in the case of the eyes by seeing—shall we regard the soul, which furnishes the eyes with their marvelous power, as being so coarse and sluggish that an experience of the body would escape it, if it should not lie there at the place where the experience took place?

(60) *E*. That conclusion upsets me very much, so much, in fact, that I am completely stunned. I do not know what to answer and I do not know where I am. What shall I say? Shall I say that a bodily experience of which the soul is

aware directly is not sensation? What is it, then, if it is not that? Shall I say that the eyes experience nothing when we see? That is most absurd. Shall I say that the eyes experience where they are? But they do not see themselves and nothing is where they are, except themselves. Shall I say that the soul is not more powerful than the eyes, when the soul is the very power of the eyes? Nothing is more unreasonable. Or must this be said, that it is a sign of greater power to experience there where something is than to experience it where it is not? But, if that were true, sight would not be rated higher than the other senses.

A. But, when the eyes experience there where they are, a blow or something falling into them or a flow of moisture, the soul is aware of these things. That is not an experience of sight, but is classed as touch. Such experiences can befall the eyes of a corpse in which there is no soul that could be aware of them. But, the experience of the eye in a living body, namely, the experience of sight, is an experience of something that is there where the eye is not. From this argument it is clear to anyone that the soul is not contained in place, since the eye, which is a body, experiences something that is outside the eye and only things that are ouside, an experience it never has without the soul.

(61) *E*. What, then, shall I do, I ask you. By these reasons can it not be proved that our souls are not in our bodies? And, if that be true, I do not know where I am. For, who takes away from me the truth that I myself am my soul?

A. Do not be disturbed; rather, be of good heart. For, this thought and consideration recalls us to ourselves and, as far as may be, takes us away from the body. As for your suggestion that the soul is not in the body of a living person, although it may seem absurd to you, there were some very learned men who entertained that view and I believe there are some even now. As you see, the question is most difficult and one that requires a certain purification of the mind to solve it. But now, consider what other arguments you have to prove that the soul is long, or wide, or anything like that. For, that argument of yours from the sense of touch, you realize, does not come near the truth and has no force to prove that the soul is diffused throughout the whole body as is the blood. Or, if you have nothing to add, let us see what remains.

Chapter 31

(62) *E.* I would have nothing more to add, if I did not now remember how much we used to marvel, when we were boys, that the tails of lizards would quiver after we had cut them off from the rest of the body. That this movement can take place without a soul I am unable to convince myself. And it is also beyond me to understand how it can be that the soul has no material extension, when it can be cut off also with the body.

A. I might answer that air and fire, which are retained in a body of earth and moisture by the presence of the soul, so that a blending of all four elements is formed, in making their way to the upper region, when the soul departs, and in freeing themselves, start a vibration of those little bodies, more or less rapid in proportion to the freshness of the wound from which they make their hasty exodus; then the movement grows weak and finally ceases, while the escaping elements become less and less, and finally issue forth in their entirety. But, an incident recalls me from this explanation, an incident which I saw with my own eyes so recently that it deserves credence. A short while ago when we were in Liguria, these boys of ours[1] who were with me for the sake of studies, noticed lying on the ground in a shady spot a many-footed creeping animal, a long worm, I would say. The worm is well known but I had never experienced what I am telling. One of the boys cut the animal in half with the edge of the stylus that he carried, and both parts of the body then moved in opposite directions away from the cut with as much speed and energy as if they had been two living animals. Frightened at this novel sight, and eager to know the reason, they brought the living parts to me and to Alypius where we were sitting. We, too, were astonished to see the two parts running over the tablet wherever they could. One of them, touched by the stylus, would turn itself toward the place of the pain, while the other, feeling nothing, moved freely on its way. And, more surprising yet, when we tried to find how far this could go, and we cut the worm, or worms, in many sections, these would also move, so that if we had not cut them at all and if the fresh wounds were not visible, we would have believed that each section had been separately born and was living its own life.

(63) But, what I said to the boys when they looked at me, eager for an explanation, I am afraid to say to you now, for we have already gone so far that, unless I give you a different answer to support my case, our attention, after weathering the barrage of so many words, may appear to have succumbed to the bite of a single worm. I advised the boys to continue their studies, as they had begun, and thus they would come at the right time to search out and learn the answer to these problems, if they warranted an

1 Licentius and Trygetius, pupils whom Augustine took with him to the villa of Verecundus at Cassiciacum in October, 386. Cf. *De beata vita* 6.

answer. But what I said to Alypius, as the boys went away, and both of us, each in his own way, fell to sifting and spinning out hypotheses in our search for an answer, if I wished to explain all this, it would call for more words than we have used in this dialogue from its start, with all its meanderings and digressions. But, what I really think, I will not keep a secret from you. If I had not been well versed in questions about the nature of a body, the form that is in the body, about place, time and motion—questions that succeed in arousing sharp and learned clashes of wits because of their connection with our present topic—I should be inclined to bestow the palm of victory on the proponents of the doctrine that the soul is a body. Wherefore, as far as I can, I warn you not to allow yourself to be swept along in your reading or discussion by the torrent of words that pour out of men who rely too much on the senses of the body, until you make straight and steady the steps that lead the soul up to God. My counsel is given lest you be turned away from that unseen and silent haven to which the soul, while here on earth, is a stranger, lest you be turned away more readily by the turmoil of study than the repose of lethargy.

(64) Now as a reply to this difficulty, which, I see, terribly upsets you; here is one that is the quickest if not the best of many, and it is the best suited to you and not the easiest proof for myself that I can select.

E. Let me have it, I beg you, as quickly as you can.

A. First I say this: If the reason for this phenomenon that results from the cutting of certain bodies is especially elusive, we should not be so upset by this one fact, therefore, as to reverse our judgment on many things which before you saw to be true more clearly than light. For, it may be that the cause of this phenomenon is hidden from us because it is beyond the comprehension of human nature, or, if known to some one, it is not possible for us to question him, or, possibly, even if we could question him, our minds might be too dull to grasp his explanation. Does it become us, therefore, to slip and allow the truth to be wrenched from our hold, the truth of the opposite conclusion which we arrived at by most certain reasons and which we acknowledge to be indubitably correct? If the replies you made to my questions retain this full force of their truth and certainty, there is no reason for our childish fear of this little worm, even though we cannot establish the cause of its many lives.

For, if you had ascertained beyond the shadow of a doubt that a certain person is a man of honor, and if you had discovered him among a gang of thieves whom you had pursued, and if by some chance he were to drop dead before you could question him, you would think up any reason whatever to explain his association with criminals, even though it remained a perpetual enigma, rather than attribute it to a desire of crime and evil fellowship. Since, therefore, from the many arguments set forth earlier, which you accepted as most certain, it was made clear to you that the soul is not contained in place and for that reason lacks that quantity which we notice in bodies, why do you not take it for granted that there is some cause why a certain animal, when cut up, continues to live in each segment and that the cause is not that the soul can be divided with the body? If it is beyond our power to discover that cause, is it not better to continue our search for the true cause, rather than accept one that is false?

Chapter 32

(65) Finally, I ask you whether you think that the sound of words is different from their meaning.

E. I think they are both the same.

A. Tell me, whence does sound come when you speak?

E. Undoubtedly from me.

A. Does the sun, then, proceed from you when you name the sun?

E. You asked me about the sound, not about the reality itself.

A. Sound, then, is one thing and the reality that sound signifies is another thing. But, you said they were the same.

E. Go on. I admit now that mentioning the sun is one thing; the reality signified, another.

A. Tell me, therefore, whether, knowing the Latin tongue, you could name the sun in speaking, if the meaning of the sun did not precede the sound.

E. I could not, by any means.

A. What about this? If, aiming at proper enunciation, you paused in silence for a short interval before letting the word itself fall from your lips, does not that remain in your thought what the listener is about to hear when you open your mouth?

E. That is obvious.

A. Now then, while the sun has great magnitude, can that notion of it which you retain in your thought before pronouncing the word be possibly long, or wide or any such thing?

E. Not at all.

A. Come, now, tell me. When the word goes forth from your mouth and I hear it, and think of the sum which you were thinking of before you uttered and while you uttered the word, and now both of us are perhaps thinking of the same—does it not seem true to you that the word derived from you the meaning it was to carry to me when I heard it?

E. It does seem true.

A. Now, since a word is made up of sound and meaning, and the sound refers to the hearing, but the meaning to the understanding, does it not seem to you that, just as in some living body, the sound of the word is the body and the meaning is, as it were, the soul?

E. It does seem very likely.

A. Observe, now, whether the sound of a word can be split up into letters, while its soul, that is, its meaning, allows no division, since it is exactly the very thing which you said a little while ago appears to have neither width nor length in our thought.

E. I agree completely.

A. What of this? When the sound is split up into its single letters, does it seem to keep the same meaning?

E. How can the single letters mean the same as the word that is composed of them?

A. But, when the meaning is destroyed by splitting up the sound into its letters, does not that seem to you to be like the withdrawal of the soul from a mangled body? And has not a kind of death ensued?

E. Not only do I agree, but so heartily that nothing you have said affords me greater delight.

(67) *A.* If, therefore, this illustration makes it clear enough to you how it is possible to cut up the body without dividing the soul, understand now how the segments of a body can live, although the soul does not suffer any division. For, you have admitted, and correctly, I think, that the meaning—which is like the soul of the sound that is made in

uttering a word—cannot possibly be divided, while the sound itself—which is like the body—can be divided. Now, in the noun 'sun' any division of the sound leaves no meaning whatever in the parts. Therefore, after the body of the noun is rent, we would consider the letters simply as members bereft of all life, that is, without meaning. But, if we find some noun whose parts after division can have some meaning, you must allow that such division did not result in complete death, as it were, because the parts, considered separately, evidently retain some meaning and the breath of life, as it were.

E. I grant that entirely, and now I ask you to produce the sound.

A. Hear it, for when I turn my attention to the vicinity of the sun, which name we considered above, Lucifer comes to mind, and, when this word is split between the second and third syllable, the first part has a meaning when we say '*Luci.*' So, therefore, life exists in more than one half of its body. The part that is left also has a soul, for, when you are told to carry something, that is what you hear. How could you obey if some one were to say to you: 'Carry the book' [*fer librum*], if '*fer*' [carry] has no meaning? Then, when '*Luci*' is added, the sound is *Lucifer* and means a star. But, when that is taken away, it still signifies something and therefore retains life, in a certain sense.

(68) But, since everything that the senses perceive is contained in time and place, or rather, the senses perceive what time and space contain, then what we perceive by the eyes is divided by space; what we perceive by the ears is divided by time. For, just as that worm occupied more space as a whole than any part of it, so Lucifer takes a longer amount of time to pronounce than '*Luci.*' Wherefore, if this

part of the word has meaning and, therefore, life, in a shorter interval of time that was reduced by dividing the sound, not the meaning (for the sound and not the meaning is extended in time), so in the same way we ought to conclude about the worm. Namely, even though a part, just because it is a part, lives in a smaller space after the body has been cut, we should not conclude that the soul has been cut or that it is smaller in a smaller space, despite the fact that in the undivided living worm the soul was the equal possession of all the parts and the parts occupied a larger space. For, the soul did not occupy a place, but held the body which was moved by it. Just as the meaning of a word, without being extended in time, gave life, so to speak, and filled out all the letters that take up slight intervals of time [to pronounce]. With this illustration I ask you for the present to be content. And I see, indeed, that you are delighted with it. But for the present do not look for a learned disquisition on this subject. I do not mean one that goes in for deceiving appearances, but one that takes account of reality itself. This rambling discourse must be brought to a close and your mind must undergo training in many other subjects that you lack, for increasing your mental vision and discernment so that you may be able to understand most clearly whether what very learned men say is the objective truth or not, namely that the soul can in no way be divided in itself, but only by reason of the body.

(69) Now take my word for it or, if you will, with my help come to realize how great is the soul, not in extent of space or time, but in force and power; for, if you remember, long ago we so posed and divided the question. But, as to number referring to souls, since you thought that number refers to this problem, I know not what answer to give you: I would be more quick to answer that the question of number

should not be gone into or at least that you should postpone it, rather than say that number and multitude have no connection with quantity or that I could explain such an intricate question to you at this time. For, if I say the soul is one, you will be upset because in one it is happy, in another unhappy, and the same thing cannot be happy and unhappy at the same time. And if I say it is both one and many, you will laugh and I will not find it easy to restrain your mirth. But if I say the soul is many, I will laugh at myself, and I endure forefeiting my own esteem less gracefully than yours. Listen, now, to what I promise will be a profitable discourse, but heavy enough perhaps to overwhelm both of us, or at least one, and to make you decide to withdraw.

E. I accept the condition completely and now I wait for you to explain the problem which you feel you can handle conveniently with my help—such as it is.

Chapter 33

THE FIRST DEGREE OF THE SOUL

(70) *A.* I wish we both could question a man of learning about this problem, a man not only of learning, but one endowed also with eloquence and wisdom and every perfection. I can see him expounding the soul's power in the body, its power in itself, its power before God to whom it is nearest when undefiled and in whom it finds its supreme and every good. But now, since there is no one else, I dare not fail you. And this is my reward, that, while I explain to you the power of the soul out of my own poverty of learning, I am making an exhibition of my own power before a receptive audience.

First, then, let me deflate your soaring and boundless expectation. Do not think that I shall speak of every soul, but only of the human soul, which is our only care, if we care for ourselves. This, then, is my first observation,[1] one that is within easy reach of anyone: The soul by its presence gives life to this mortal and earthy body; it brings the body together into a unity and keeps it in unity; it prevents the body from breaking up and wasting away; it regulates the proper distribution of nourishment throughout the parts of the body, giving each its due share; it preserves the apt arrangement and proportion of the body, not only to delight the eye but to grow and generate. But, these powers are easily seen to be the common possession of men and plants. For, we say of them, too, that they live; we see and acknowledge that every one of them in its own way is preserved and nourished, grows and germinates.

THE SECOND DEGREE OF THE SOUL

(71) Rise, now, to the second degree and see the power of the soul in the senses where life is discerned with greater clarity. For, no attention should be paid to that foolish superstition which some illiterate people cherish, a super-

1 In this famous passage Augustine enumerates seven steps or levels of the soul's power. These steps fall into three groups: in the first three steps or stages the soul deals with the body or matter, 'acting' on it successively with greater power; in the next two stages or acts, the soul has to do with itself; finally, in the last two, the soul goes to God and dwells in Him. The last step is really not a step, but a 'mansion,' wherein the soul contemplates the Supreme and True Good, God Himself. V. Bourke, (*op. cit.* 102) renders the Latin as follows: Animation, sensation, ratiocination, evaluation, stabilization, fixation and contemplation. Rand (*Founders of the Middle Ages* 263) has this translation: Vitality, sensation, art, virtue, tranquillity, approach, contemplation. Augustine's words are: *animatio, sensus, ars, virtus, tranquillitas, ingressio, contemplatio* (35,79). In my translation I have tried to combine the best points of both translations. For the difference between Augustine's thought and that of Plotinus, cf. the study by Sister Mary Patricia Garvey, R.S.M. (*St. Augustine, Christian or Neo-Platonist?* 146-160). For an explanation of the mysticism of St. Augustine, cf. Dom Cuthbert Butler's *Western Mysticism,* 23-88.

stition that betrays closer affinity to a block of wood than do the very trees which it idolizes, namely, that the vine is pained when the grape is plucked, and that such things not only feel pain when they are cut, but even see and hear. Of this unholy error this is not the place to speak. Now, then, to follow my outline, notice in the higher living organism how great is the soul's power in the senses and in locomotion, which those things that are fixed to the earth by roots cannot possibly share with us.

The soul applies itself to the sense of touch; through it it feels and distinguishes hot and cold, rough and smooth, hard and soft, light and heavy. Then it distinguishes between unnumbered differences of taste and smell and sound and shapes, by tasting, smelling, hearing and seeing. And in all these it comes to know and seek what suits the nature of its body; it rejects and shuns what is unsuited. The soul withdraws itself at certain intervals of time from these senses and, by taking a vacation, you might say, restores their vigor and goes over the manifold and disconnected likenesses of realities which it took in through the senses, and all this is sleep and dreaming.

Often, too, the simplicity of moving makes it delight in making gestures and rambling about; without exertion it maintains order and harmony in its members, for the union of the sexes it does what it can, and from two natures through common life and love it aims at molding a new unity. It provides not only for the generation of offspring but also for their care, protection and nourishment. Through habit it becomes linked to the habitat and environment of the body, and from these it undergoes separation with reluctance as though they were parts of its body; this force of habit is called memory when the link with those places is not dissevered even by separation and the lapse of time.

But all this, no one denies, the soul can do even in brute beasts.

THE THIRD DEGREE OF THE SOUL

(72) Rise, now, to the third degree of the soul's power which is now proper to men, and consider memory not in its role as the link with familiar situations, but as the recorder and compiler of facts without number: so many arts of craftsmen, the tilling of the soil, the building of cities, the manifold marvels of various buildings and their construction, the invention of so many signs in letters, in words, in gesture, in the pronunciation of these, in paintings and carvings. Consider the languages of so many peoples, the varied teachings, some new, some renewed. Consider the great number of books and similar documents for preserving memory, and all this provision for posterity. Consider the grades of duties and powers and honors and dignities in families, in the state, in peace and war, in civil and ecclesiastical administration. Consider the power of reason and of thought, the flowing streams of eloquence, the varieties of poetry; the thousand forms of imitation for play and jest, the art of music, the accuracy of measurements, the study of numbers, the speculating on things past and future from the present. Great are these achievements, and distinctively human. Yet, this heritage, common to all rational souls, is shared in by the learned and the unlearned, by the good and the wicked.

THE FOURTH DEGREE OF THE SOUL

(73) Look up, now, and scale the fourth grade, where moral goodness begins and all true worth resides. From this point the soul dares to rank itself not only before its own body, if it is a part of the material world, but even before

the whole material world itself, and it dares to think that the good of the world is not its good and to distinguish and despise the counterfeits of its own power and beauty. Hence, the more it becomes the cause of its own delight, the more it dares to withdraw from baser things and wholly to cleanse itself and to make itself spotless and stainless; it dares to be strong against every enticement that tries to move it from its resolution and purpose, to esteem human society, to desire for another nothing that it would not wish for itself; to obey authority and the laws of wise men, and to believe that through these God speaks to it. In this noble task of the soul there is still toil, and against the vexations and allurements of the world a hard and bitter fight; in this work of purification there is underneath a fear of death, often not strong but sometimes overpowering—not strong, when its faith is most firm (to see whether this is true, indeed, is permitted only to the purified soul), that all things are so governed by the Providence and Justice of God that death cannot possibly come unjustly to anyone, even though the person who inflicts death be unjust. But, death is greatly feared on this plane now, when the Providence of God is so much the less firmly trusted as it is the more anxiously looked for, and it is the less seen as tranquillity grows less through fear—tranquillity so requisite for pursuing the study of these most puzzling matters. Finally, as the soul perceives more and more in proportion to its greater progress how great is the difference between itself purified and itself defiled, so much the more it fears, lest, when this body is put off, God may less endure it than it can endure itself defiled. But, there is nothing more difficult than to fear death and to refrain from the allurements of this world, as the risks involved demand. The soul, however, is so great that it can do even this with the help, of course, of the Justice of the supreme and true God—that

Justice which sustains and rules this universe; by which it is brought about that all things are, and not only are, but are in such order that they cannot be better. To this Justice, in the difficult task of purifying itself, the soul entrusts itself with complete filial devotion and trust to be helped and made perfect.

THE FIFTH DEGREE OF THE SOUL

(74) When this shall be accomplished, that is, when the soul shall have been freed from all disease and cleansed of all its stains, then finally it possesses itself in all joy and fears nothing whatever for itself and is not disturbed at all for any reason of its own. This, then, is the fifth degree. For, to make the soul pure is one thing; to keep it pure, another. And the action by which it restores itself from defilement is altogether different from the action by which it does not allow itself to be defiled again. On this plane it conceives in every way how great it is and, when it has grasped that truth, then, with certain unbounded and incredible confidence, it advances toward God that is, to the contemplation of Truth itself, that Truth, the highest and most hidden reward for all the labor it has exerted.

THE SIXTH DEGREE OF THE SOUL

(75) Now, this activity, namely, the yearning to understand what things are true and best, is the soul's highest vision. Beyond this it has nothing more perfect, more noble, and more true. This, therefore, will be the sixth degree of activity. For, it is one thing to have the eye of the soul so clear that it does not look about idly or incautiously and see what is unseemly, and another thing to protect and strengthen the health of the eye; and it is another thing, again, to direct

a calm and steady gaze upon that which is to be seen. Those who wish to do this before they are cleansed and healed are so driven back by the light of truth that they may think there is in it not only nothing good, but much of evil. They deny it the name of truth and, by reason of pitiable yielding to carnal indulgence, they draw back into the caverns of their own darkness, enduring it because they are ill and cursing the only remedy of their distemper. Whence, divinely inspired, the prophet most fittingly prays:[2] 'Create a clean heart in me, O Lord, and renew a right spirit in my breast.' The spirit is right, I believe, if it keeps the soul in its quest for truth from losing the way and going wrong. Such a spirit is not renewed in a man unless his heart first shall have been made clean, that is, unless he restrain his thoughts and draw them off from all mundane attachment and defilement.

THE SEVENTH DEGREE OF THE SOUL

(76) At length, in the vision and contemplation of truth, we come to the seventh and last step, not really a step, but a dwelling place to which the previous steps have brought us. What shall I say are the delights, what the enjoyment, of the supreme and true God; what breath of undisturbed peace and eternity? These are the wonders that great souls have declared, so far as they brought themselves to speak of these realities, great souls of incomparable greatness, who, we believe, beheld and now behold these things.

This I now dare say to you in all simplicity, that, if we hold with all perseverance to the course that God lays down for us and which we have undertaken to hold, we shall come by God's Power and Wisdom to that highest Cause, or Supreme Author, or Supreme Principle of all things, or

2 Ps. 50.12.

whatever other name you would deem worthy of so great a Reality. That being understood, we shall see truly how all things under the sun are no more than 'vanity of vanities.'[3] Vanity is pretense. Vain things are found out to be false, or deceiving, or both. One may recognize how great is the difference between vanity and truth. Even though all these visible things, considered in themselves, are marvelous and beautiful, having been created by God their Maker, still, in comparison with the unseen realities, they are as nothing. From this we shall realize how full of truth are the things we are commanded to believe, how excellently and healthfully we were nourished by Mother Church; else, what is the worth of that 'milk' which St. Paul[4] declared he gave as drink to little ones. It is very proper to take this nourishment when one is nourished by a mother, but shameful, when one is already grown; to reject it, when needed, is a pity; to find fault with it at any time or to despise it is a sign of impious wickedness, but to explain it and distribute it in a suitable manner is the clearest proof of goodness and of charity. We shall also see that this corporeal nature, in obedience to the divine law, undergoes so many changes and vicissitudes that we may hold even the resurrection of the body (which some believe too late; others, not at all) to be so certain that the rising of the sun, after it has gone down, is not more certain to us.

Then, indeed, we shall despise those who scoff at the fact that human nature was assumed by the Almighty, eternal, changeless Son of God, to be the exemplar and beginning of our salvation, and that He was born of a Virgin, and the other marvels of the Gospel narrative, and we shall esteem these scoffers to be like boys, who, since they see a painter

3 Eccle. 1.2.
4 I Cor. 3.2.

painting from other drawings which he places before him and carefully follows, think that a man cannot be painted unless the painter see another picture.

Moreover, in the contemplation of truth, no matter from what side we study it, so great is the joy, so great the purity, the sincerity, and the certainty of faith that one at length comes to think that the previous knowledge he thought he had is really nothing. Then death, which was an object of fear and an obstacle to the soul's fullest union with the full truth, death, namely, the sheer flight and escape from this body, is now yearned for as the greatest boon.

Chapter 34

(77) You have heard how great is the soul's force and power. Let me summarize what has been said. Just as we must acknowledge that the human soul is not what God is, so it must be set down that nothing is nearer to God among all the things He has created than the human soul. Therefore, it is handed down in the Catholic Church through special divine guidance that no creature is to be worshipped by the soul (gladly do I use the very words in which these truths were taught me), but that He alone is to be worshipped who is the Creator of all things that are, 'from Whom, by Whom, unto Whom'[1] are all things, that is, the unchanging Source, unchanging Wisdom, unchanging Love, One True and Perfect God, who never was not, never will not be; never was other, never will be other; than whom nothing is more hidden, nothing more present; with difficulty we find where He is, with greater difficulty, where He is not; with whom all cannot be, without whom no one can be And, if we human beings can with propriety predicate

1 Rom. 11.36.

anything more wonderful of Him, in keeping with His nature, that we attribute to Him. Hence, only God is to be adored by the soul, without discrimination or confusion. For, whatever the soul adores as God, it must deem more excellent than itself, and it is impossible to believe that the earth is superior to the nature of the soul, or the stars, or moon, or sun, or anything at all that is touched or seen by these eyes. Rather, reason proves with certainty that a single soul is of far greater value than all these material things, if only lovers of the truth will dare to pursue with unfaltering and respectful steps the path the soul points out, a path that is hard because it lies beyond the well-worn road of common experience.

(78) If there is in nature any other reality than those which the senses know, and which without exception occupy some dimension of space—and we have said that the human soul is more excellent than all such things—if, I say there is any other reality that God has created, it is less excellent or equal to the soul: less excellent, as the soul of the brute; equal, as the soul of an angel. But, better than the soul, there is nothing. And if, sometimes, any of these is more excellent, that is the result of sin, not of nature. And yet, even by sin the soul does not become so inferior as not to be preferred or even compared with the soul of the brute.

God, therefore, who alone is the Maker of the soul, is alone to be adored by the soul. But man, no matter who he is, though possessed of wisdom and every perfection, or any soul whatever, gifted with reason and blessed with all virtue, is to be loved only and imitated. To it, respect is due in keeping with its merit and station. For, 'Thou shalt adore the Lord, Thy God, and Him only shalt thou serve.'[2]

2 Deut. 6.13; Matt. 4.10.

We know that, as far as is lawful and commanded, we should assist souls of our own kind who have gone astray and struggle in error, and this task is to be undertaken with the conviction that its successful issue is to be attributed to God acting through us. Let us not appropriate anything to ourselves, deceived by the desire for vain glory, for, by this one vice we are brought down from the heights and sunk in the lowest depths. We ought to hate, therefore, not the victims of vice, but vice; not sinners, but sin. Toward all men we ought to have the will to help, even those who have injured us, or wish to harm us, or wish that we be harmed. This is the true, perfect, and only religion by which it belongs to the magnitude of the soul, which we are studying now, to be reconciled to God and by which it makes itself worthy of freedom. For He whom it is most useful for all to serve, and to delight in whose service is the only perfect freedom, frees from all things.

I see that I have almost exceeded the limits of my plan and, without stopping for any question, I have talked at great length; yet I do not regret it. For, while these principles are scattered throughout many writings of the Church, and though we may seem to have made a convenient digest of them, yet they cannot be clearly understood, unless one exerts manly efforts in the fourth of those seven degrees to preserve piety and to acquire health and strength for grasping them, and unless one makes each of these degrees the object of a searching and careful investigation. For, in each one of those grades, which we might better call acts, there is a distinct and proper beauty.

Chapter 35

(79) We are inquiring, of course, about the power of the soul, and the soul has the power to perform all these acts

simultaneously, although it may think that it is really doing only that act which implies some effort, or, at least, some fear. For, it performs that act with greater attention than the rest. To teach these grades to anyone, let the acts of the soul, from the lowest to the highest, be called, first, Animation; the second, Sensation; the third, Art; the fourth, Virtue; the fifth, Tranquillity; the sixth, Approach; the seventh, Contemplation. They can be named also in this way: 'of the body'; 'through the body'; 'about the body'; 'toward itself'; 'in itself'; 'toward God'; 'in God'. Or again, in this way: 'beautifully of another, beautifully through another, beautifully about another, beautifully toward a beautiful, beautifully in a beautiful, beautifully toward Beauty, beautifully in Beauty.'[1]

You may ask about any of these later on, if further clarification is needed. For the present I have decided to label these operations of the soul by these names so that you may not be troubled when other teachers use a different terminology or a different classification, and their diversity prevent you from accepting one or the other.

For, the same realities can be named in ways without number and be classified minutely according to different norms; in such a variety of means, each one uses the way he considers more suitable.

Chapter 36

(80) God, therefore, supreme and true, by an inviolable and unchanging law by which He rules all creation, subjects the body to the soul, the soul to Himself, and so everything to Himself. In no act does God abandon the soul either for

1 I have adopted Rand's translation (*op. cit.* 263-64), but I have written his 'beauty' with a capital.

punishment or reward. For, He has judged it to be the most beautiful, so that it is the exemplar of all reality, and all reality is so arranged in a hierarchy that anyone who considers the totality of things may not be offended by the lack of conformity in any part, and that every punishment and every reward of the soul should contribute something corresponding to the measured beauty and arrangement of all things.

To the soul, indeed, is given free choice, and they who endeavor to undermine it with futile reasonings are so blind that they do not understand that of their own will they are voicing these absurd and impious statements. And the gift of free choice is such that, making use of it in any way whatever, the soul does not disturb any portion of the divine order and law. It is conferred by the all wise and all prevailing Lord of all creation. But, to see these things as they should be seen is the gift of a few, and one becomes fit for the gift only by true religion. For, true religion is that by which the soul is united to God so that it binds itself again by reconciliation to Him from whom it had broken off, as it were, by sin.

Religion, then, in the third act forms a link with the soul and begins to lead it; in the fourth, it purifies; in the fifth, reforms; in the sixth, it leads into; in the seventh, it feeds. And this is done rather quickly, in some cases; in others, slowly—depending upon the worth of each one's love and merits. Yet God does all things justly, wisely and beautifully, no matter what attitude of will His creatures may assume. In this connection, again, a very difficult question is: What advantage is there in consecrating infants? We must believe that it accomplishes some good. Reason will discover this when the right time comes for investigating that question. Although I have presented this and many other problems for you to seek out the solution by personal study rather than to furnish you with the answer, my purpose will be accomplished if only you study with a sense of reverence.

(81) In view of our discussion, who can reasonably offer any complaint because the soul was given to move and manage the body, since an order of things so great and so divine could not be better linked together? Or who will think that we ought to inquire how the soul is affected in this mortal and frail body, since it is thrust together into death deservedly because of sin, but by virtue it has the power to rise above the body? Or what will be its state after death, since the pain of death must necessarily continue if sin remains, while for virtue and goodness God Himself, that is, Truth itself, is the reward?

Wherefore, if you will, let us finally conclude this long discourse, and let us make it our care to be most vigilant and exact in fulfilling the commandments of God. There is no other escape from such evils. But, if any statement of mine is not so clear as you would wish, make a mental note of it and ask about it at some other more opportune time.

And the Master of all, who is over us, will not fail us if we seek Him.

E. I was so thrilled by your discourse that I thought it would be wrong to interrupt it. If you wish to stop here and let this summary treatment suffice for the three last questions, I shall yield to your decision. For a further investigation of these important problems, I shall try to make both the occasion and my wits more responsive to the exigencies of your occupations.

ON MUSIC

(*De musica*)

Translated

by

ROBERT CATESBY TALIAFERRO, Ph.D.
Portsmouth Priory School
Rhode Island

INTRODUCTION

THESE SIX BOOKS *On Music* were begun, before Augustine's baptism, at Milan in 387 A.D., and finished later in Africa, after the *De magistro* in 391.[1] While they are, therefore, among the earliest work of his career, they are not the earliest, but follow the four philosophical dialogues of Cassiciacum. They also straddle the period of the *De immortaliate animae,* the *De quantitate animae* and the *De libero arbitrio.* They are, however, only one of a series of treatises on the liberal arts which Augustine started, but never finished. He speaks of finishing one on Grammar and of starting one each on Dialectic, Rhetoric, Geometry, Arithmetic, and Philosophy.[2] Treatises on Grammar, Rhetoric, and Dialectic which have come down to us under his name were not accepted as genuine by the Benedictines. Recent scholars accept the last one as being a draft of the original done probably by Augustine himself, and are doubtful about the first two.[3]

But if these six books *On Music* are only a fragment of a projected cycle on the liberal arts, they are, also, only a fragment of a larger treatise on music. They are, in the words of Augustine, 'only such as pertain to that part called Rhythm.'[4] Much later, in writing to Bishop Memorius, he speaks of having written six books on Rhythm and of having

1 See *Retractationes,* 1.6,11, Migne 33, and Portalié, 'Augustin,' in DTC.
2 *Retract.* 1.6.
3 See Marrou, *St. Augustin et la fin de la culture antique* 576-578, for a discussion of the authenticity of *De dialectica.*
4 *Retract.* 1.6.

intended to write six more on Melody (*de melo*).[5] As we shall see, this intended part would have been a treatise on Harmonics.

It is necessary, for the understanding of these books on Rhythm, to know what the ancients meant by music, by rhythm, and by melody. It is true St. Augustine tells us that, of these six books, the first five on rhythm and meter are trivial and childish,[6] but this is a rhetorical statement to introduce to us to the more serious business of the sixth book on the hierarchy of numbers as constitutive of the soul, the universe, and the angels. In the same letter to Memorius, written about 408 or 409 A.D., he also distinguishes the first five books from the sixth, considering them much inferior, and sends him only the sixth. This has given Westphal the opportunity to indulge in irony, to agree with Augustine, and so to dismiss his treatment of rhythm and meter as something strange and foreign to the correct ancient theories.[7] But Westphal, in his passion for everything Aristoxenian, did not always have good judgment; in another case, that of Aristides Quintilianus, he sacrificed a really excellent treatise on music, the only complete one to come down to us from the ancient world, as only a source of fragments of Aristoxenus. Schäfke, in a recent book,[8] has tried to bring Aristides' work back to its proper place.

It is usually dangerous procedure to ignore the technical details a thinker uses to test or suggest his general and more seductive theories. It is too easy to overlook the first five books and to concentrate on the sixth. It would seem neces-

5 *Epist.* 101 (Paris 1836).
6 *On Music,* 6.1.
7 R. Westphal, *Fragmente und Lehrsätze der Griechischen Rhythmiker* (Leipzig 1861) 19.
8 R. Schäfke, *Aristeides Quintilianus von der Musik* (Berlin-Schöneberg 1937).

sary, rather, to place these five technical books in the general picture of the theory of ancient music, and to try and read from the Augustinian variations on the ancient themes the intentions of his mind and doctrine.

As we have said, the only complete treatise on music to come down to us from the Greeks or Romans is that of Aristides Quintilianus, a Greek of probably the first part of the second century A.D.[9] There are a good many treatises on harmonics, those written from the Pythagorean point of view such as the Harmonics of Nicomachus, of Ptolemy, and of Theo of Smyrna, and the Harmonics of Aristoxenus from a less directly mathematical viewpoint. The treatise of Aristides combines the two approaches.

The Pythagorean harmonics starts from the fact that two strings of the same material and thickness, stretched by the same weight, form the two fundamental consonances (for the Greeks the only two) when they are in length in the ratio of 2 to 3 (the perfect fifth) and 3 to 4 (the perfect fourth). Thus, in moving from the lower to the higher pitch of the perfect fourth, the ear rests and is satisfied, and in passing from the higher to the lower pitch of the perfect fifth it also rests. For ancient music, no other ratios or intervals provided such a rest. Further, if from the first pitch to the second is a perfect fourth, and from the second to the third is a perfect fifth, then from the first pitch to the third is an interval called the octave, the ratio of the string lengths being $4/3 \cdot 3/2 = 2/1$. The characteristic of this interval is that the higher pitch seems to repeat the lower pitch and vice-versa: the higher pitch can replace the lower one (and vice-versa) in its relations with other pitches without changing the essential character of the relation. The octave, therefore, furnishes a cyclic

9 See Schäfke, *op. cit.*, for full discussion of possible dates.

pattern for the musical relations.[10] From the Pythagorean point of view the problem of musical intervals is the problem of whole-number ratios, the smallest possible numbers furnishing the octave and the next smallest the consonances.

The further musical problem was to fill in this octave, made up of the fourth and fifth, with other pitches to make a *systema* or scale. The interval between the fourth and fifth, called the tone, was taken as fundamental here, that is, in ratios of string-lengths 3/2 divided by 2/3 = 9/8. The diatonic scale is built by taking two pitches at intervals of a tone from the lower pitch of the fourth. What is left over of the fourth is called a leimma: $4/3$ divided by $(9/8 \cdot 9/8) = 256/243$, which is approximately a semitone. That is, two such leimmas add up nearly to a tone $(256/243)^2$ nearly equals 9/8. This is the diatonic scheme of the fundamental tetrachord. The scale can be completed by adding a tone and then another such tetrachord to fill out the octave: $(9/8)^2 \cdot 256/243 \cdot (9/8)^3 \cdot 256/243 = 4/3 \cdot 3/2 = 2/1$. This is one mathematical and one musical solution of the problem of the octave.[11] There were other solutions. It is also possible to combine tetrachords in other ways: either by taking the upper pitch of the fourth as the beginning of a new tetrachord and so continuing, or by constantly jumping a tone before beginning the new tetrachord.[12] But neither of these last two ways solves the problem of the octave as the first one which alternates the two.

10 For the reader interested in a more extended account of such relations there is the introduction to Lord Rayleigh's *The Theory of Sound*.

11 See Plato, *Timaeus* 35-36, for a particularly fine derivation of this solution. See also Theo of Smyrna, for a second-hand account.

12 Aristoxenus, *Harmonica* I 17, III 59. See also introduction by Macran to his edition, pp. 10-17.

Such principles could not be confined by Greek consonances. They could extend themselves to all kinds of relations, indeed to any relation. And although the purely Greek restrictions could be given a mathematical rationale in contradiction to what Aristoxenus and his modern supporters have had to say, since the supply of mathematical relations is seemingly inexhaustible and all plastic, yet Aristoxenus, a pupil of Aristotle, preferred to build a system which, if not totally unmathematical, preserving as it does a necessarily ordinal character, is certainly non-arithmetical. 'The science [of harmonics]' says Aristoxenus, 'is reduced to two things: hearing and reason. For by hearing we distinguish the magnitudes of the intervals, and by reason we consider the potentialities of the notes.'[13] By potentialities of the notes, he means their functions within a system of notes, a system which in turn obeys the fundamental restriction that the only consonances are the fourth, fifth, and octave, perceived as such by the ear. The tone is the interval which is the difference between the fourth and fifth as perceived by the ear. The fourth is the invariant interval to be filled in by two movable notes and only two. The movable notes can take their places continuously within certain limits, and these limits are further subdivided so that the positions of these movable notes fall into three classes which define the three kinds of scales: the diatonic, chromatic, and enharmonic. It is not necessary for our purpose to discuss these in detail. The tetrachords so formed can be added to each other (but only those of the same kind) by disjunction, by conjunction, or by a combination of both, as we have already explained above, that is, with a tone between, no tone between, or first one way, then the other.

13 *Ibid.* II 33.4-9.

The upper note of the lower tetrachord, that is, the upper limit of the lower fourth, properly filled in with the two movable notes, is called the mese and is the functional center of the system of two tetrachords; the potentiality of every note in the scale is with reference to this mese.[14] True, one or more of the lower notes of the lower tetrachord might be moved up an octave, or down an octave, and the pitch of the mese relative to the other notes would be different. With the survival of only the one method of combining teterachords, by alternate conjunction and disjunction, the different relations of pitch of the mese gave rise to the *tropoi* or modes of the one series of notes.[15] In these different modes the mese is no longer the center by position, but it remains the musical center.

Such, then, is the non-arithmetical Greek theory of harmonics which confines itself to principles laid down within a certain idiom of notes, abstractions from a certain ordered experience, but not constitutive of that experience as in the Pythagorean theory.

No strictly Pythagorean treatise on rhythm exists, and of the Rhythmics of Aristoxenus we have only the fragments piously and passionately collected by Westphal, first in *Fragmente und Lehrsätze der griechischen Rhythmiker* and last in *Aristoxenos von Tarent, Melik und Rhythmik des Classischen Hellenenthums.* A fragment of the Oxyrhynchus Papyri is also attributed to him. But the essential theses are repeated in Aristides Quintilianus. In both of these writers a clear distinc-

---

14 *Ibid.* II 33.32-34.10; Aristotle, *Problems* XIX 20; also Ptolemy, *Harmonica* II 7, quoted by Macran in his Introduction.

15 This, at least, is the interpretation of Macran, which certainly fits the facts and the texts better than the opposing theories of Westphal and Monro; see Introd. to *Harmonica* 21-40. See the same work also for an account of the extension of the octave and the consequent emergence of the modes as *tónoi* or keys.

tion is made between rhythmics and metrics, a distinction not so clear in Augustine and other Latin writers.

For Aristides, music is divided into theoretical and practical. The theoretical, in turn, is divided into the technical and natural, that which has to do with the art and that which has to do with the nature. The technical is divided into three parts: harmonics, rhythmics, and metrics. The natural is divided into two parts: the arithmetical and the physical. On the other hand, the practical is divided into the applied and the expressive. The first of these is divided into melopoeia, rhythmopoeia, and poetry, and the second into instrumental, vocal, and declamatory.[16]

And so the first book of Aristides' treatise is devoted to the discussion of the technical part of theoretic music: harmony, rhythm, and meter; the second book to ends served by the practical part of music: education and the State; the third book to the discussion of the natural part of theoretic music: whole-number ratios and cosmology. Thus, Aristides quite rightly assigns the Aristoxenian theory its place within the science of music as a technique, an art depending for its real validity on the Pythagorean theory. And he might well have added that it is only one of a possible many, a restricted set of rules, a particular idiom compared to the *mathesis universalis* of the Pythagorean theory.

Let us, then, focus our attention on rhythm. 'Rhythm,' say Aristides, 'is a scale of times collated in a certain order, and their affects we call arsis and thesis, strong and weak.'[17] 'Rhythm is determined in speech by syllables, in melody by the ratios of arsis and thesis, in movements by the figures and their limits . . . . And there are five parts of the art of rhythm.

16 Aristides, *op. cit.*, ed. Meibom, I 7,8.

17 *Ibid.* I, p. 49. We give only an outline here. Detailed discussion will be found in our notes to the treatise.

For we divide it thus: (1) in primary times, (2) on kinds of feet, (3) on rhythmical tempo, (4) on modulations, (5) on rhythmopoeia.'[18] A rhythmical foot is a part of the whole rhythm by means of which we comprehend the whole. And it has two parts, arsis and thesis.[19] And there are three kinds of rhythmical foot according to the ratio of arsis and thesis: the one-one ratio, the one-two, the two-three, and sometimes a fourth, the three-four. But the inner structure of these ratios is conditioned by the order of long and short syllables and, therefore, by the thing rhythmed.

'Metres,' says Aristides, 'are constructed of feet. Then meter is a scale of feet collated of unlike syllables, commensurable in length.'[20] Some say meter is to rhythm as part to whole; some, as matter to form; some say that the essence of rhythm is in arsis and thesis, and the essence of meter is in syllables and their unlikeness. And for this reason rhythm is constructed of like syllables and antithetical feet, but meter never of syllables all alike and rarely of antithetical feet.[21] Therefore, rhythm is the repeated sameness of ratio of arsis and thesis, which informs the syllables of speech, giving a variety of meters according to the variety of syllable structures and the variety of strong and weak.

If we compare Augustine's treatise with the traditional ones and, in particular, with that of Aristides, it does not appear as strange as some would make it out. The first five books deal with rhythm and meter. The last book deals with music in its cosmological and theological aspects, correspond-

18 *Ibid.* I, p. 32.
19 *Ibid.* I, p. 34.
20 *Ibid.* I, p. 49.
21 *Ibid.* I, pp. 49-50. See note to Book 2 p. 226, for discussion of meaning of 'antithetical.' In any case, Aristides seems here to consider rhythmn as only concerned with the ratio of arsis and thesis. Strong and weak as affects of the collated time of rhythm apparently belong to meter rather than to rhythm.

ing to the last book of Aristides and to the well known tradition of the *Timaeus*. The six books which were never completed would have dealt with harmony. All this is perfectly obvious and perfectly usual. It is, therefore, a grave mistake to accuse Augustine, along with Plato, of being unfortunately ignorant of musical sensibility and of the theory of it so highly developed in the nineteenth century. It is obvious that, in the case of both, the emphasis on music as a liberal art and science is the result of their being so well aware of the dangers of musical sensibility and of the consequent disorders arising from the irresponsible independence of music as a fine art. The mathematical theory of music has had a long and fruitful career, taking in such names as Ptolemy and Kepler; it has no apologies to make. The remarks of Laloy and Marrou and others like them on this subject, therefore, are quite beside the point.

If Augustine's treatise as a whole is well within the tradition, so also are the details of his treatment of rhythm and meter. The emphasis is decidedly on rhythm in the meaning of Aristides, and meter in any important sense is almost wholly ignored. For Augustine, there are two principles of rhythm which cannot be violated: the rhythmical feet must be equal with respect to the number of primary times, and the ratio of arsis and thesis within the rhythmical foot must be kept constant. The metrical foot, then, is entirely subservient to these two rhythmical principles and no deviation seems to be allowed; this subservience goes so far as to allow the complete dissolution of the molossus into its primary times for the sake of rhythm. There is no mention in Augustine of the rhythmical modulation found in Aristides, and, indeed, to some commentators trained in the tradition of certain Latin grammarians, it has seemed that Augustine tortures one line of poetry after another to fit them into the mold of his rhythmical principles. Every pleasing appearance must be explained by them. And Augustine pushes his investigations much like a physicist who must explain every phenomenon in the light of his fundamental premises. The use of the musical rest is one of his favorite devices in accomplishing this. But the theory of the musical rest, without any application, appears in Aristides' treatise, and there is evidence that the use was quite in tradition, although in a tradition different from that of the Latin grammarians such as Diomedes and Victorinus.[22] Yet the severity of Augustine's doctrine is remarkable, and, as we suggest later in our notes, seems to be the result of a deliberate attempt to restore a purely musical science of rhythmics against the usages of a whole tribe of grammarians and rhetoricians.

Given the Pythagorean themes of Augustine's dialectic in Book VI, this is not a surprising attempt. If it is also remembered that Augustine stands at the end of the classical quantitative metric and at the beginning of the stress or accentual metric, there may even be more point to it. In the quantitative metric, the thing rhythmed is informed by the rhythm through the pattern of primary times given by the syllables; in the stress metric it is the stress that determines the pattern primarily and the syllables only determine it secondarily. Since the stress is associated with each word as a whole, the stress metric gives more prominence to the word as a unit than does the quantitative metric. In the confused situation of metrics, the Augustinian theory, although it takes as its base the quantitative syllable with many protests at its mere conventionality, arrives at a pure musical rhythmics of whole-number ratios which can well apply to any system

22 The justification for these general remarks will be found in the notes to the treatise itself.

of metrics whatever. It stands above the metrical conflict of the period, therefore, and is, as Augustine continually points out, a purely musical discipline and not a grammatical one. Questions of stress, of the relative position of arsis and thesis, and even of syllabic quantity, are simply modes by which rhythm is incarnated in the rhythmed; they are not of its essence. And so Augustine gives the very innocuous definition of meter as the measuring off of rhythms, but a definition wholly traditional and mentioned by Aristides Quintilianus.

At first glance, we are tempted to consider the great concern of Augustine with these details of rhythm and meter as something of a tragedy. If we think of the comparable mathematical concerns of Plato, those of Augustine seem trivial, unworthy vehicles of the weighty dialectical truths they are supposed to carry. We think of Augustine as the victim of a period which had lost the profound mathematical insight of the great Greek age and could offer little for those living in it to reason on. There was not much a deep and sensitive soul could avail itself of, to escape the all-pervading rhetoric. But such a view is, perhaps, too simple, true in part though it may be.

For anyone reading the treatise *On Music* and then Books X and XI of the *Confessions,* the dovetailing of the themes is striking. Augustine remains a rhetorician. But, from the frivolous rhetorician that he was before his conversion, he becomes the real rhetorician, he who wins the outer to the inner man, the world to number, and the soul to its Redemption. Again and again he returns to the example of the syllable as a strange arbitrary quantum of time and of motion. And, properly, the locus of this rhetorical problem is the problem of motion and time. For, if time is an irreversible succession of before and after, then there is no Redemption possible; what has been, has been. And if mind and sense are to have a common point, it must be in memory and time, where motion as pure passage is caught in its numerableness and unchangingness, and number in its immobility is incarnate in change.

The problem of motion and time is also the focus for the problem of creation. Each moment of time, appearing ever as something new from a relative non-being, is symbolic of creation *ex nihilo.* If one is hypnotized as Aristotle by the successiveness of time, then no creation *ex nihilo* seems possible. But Plato sees not only this aspect, but the aspect of 'jump,' of the discontinuous and abrupt instant, indicative of the radical contingency of all temporal appearance. So, too, Augustine is fascinated by these instants which are and are not, and which are really understood only in so far as they are held distinct and together in the memory, just as the creation is only a whole and its parts as seen in Christ.

Memory, in the *Confessions,* is a principle of intellectual mediation like Christ. Through it the past is and the future is, and, therefore, through it repentance and salvation are possible. It is a cry of intellectual triumph, the cry of Augustine, *'In te, anime meus, tempora metior.'* For now necessity is overruled and the struggle with the implacable is won, not by denying nor escaping it, but by mediation and comprehension.

This is the train of thought begun in the treatise *On Music,* where Augustine finds his attention strained to number at the point where body meets soul and action meets passion, in the rhythmical song and speech of man.

SELECT BIBLIOGRAPHY

Texts of the treatise:

S. Augustinus, *De musica*, ed. J. P. Migne, *Patrologiae cursus completus: Series Latina* 32 (Paris 1877).

———, editio Parisina altera (Paris 1836).

Translations:

C. J. Perl, *Augustins Musik. Erste deutsche Übertragung* (Strassburg 1937).

R. Cardamone, *S. Agostino Della musica libri sei traduti ed annotati* (Firenze 1878).

Secondary works:

F. Amerio, 'Il "De musica" di S. Agostino,' *Didaskaleion*, Nuova serie 8 (1929) 1-196.

Aristides Quintilianus, *De musica libiri III* (in Meibom, *Antiquae musicae auctores septem*, Amsterdam 1652); also ed. A. Jahn (Berlin 1882).

Aristoxenus, *Harmonica*, ed. H. Macran (Oxford 1902).

J. Bartels, *Aristoxeni Elementorum Rhythmicorum Fragmentum* (Bonn 1854).

H. Edelstein, *Die Musikanschauung Augustins* (Ohlau in Schesien 1929).

E. Graf, *Rhythmus und Metrum* (Marburg 1891).

N. Hoffman, *Philosophische Interpretationen de Arte Musica* (Marlburg 1931).

J. Huré, *St. Augustin, musicien* (Paris 1924).

L. Laloy, *Aristoxène de Tarente et la musique de l'antiquité* (Paris 1904).

Martianus Capella, *De nuptiis Philologiae, ed. Meibom* (Amsterdam 1652, as above for Aristides Quintilianus).

H. I. Marrou, *St. Augustin et la fin de la culture antique* (Bibliothéque des Ecoles d'Athénes et de Rome 145, Paris 1938).

M. G. Nicolau, *L'origine du 'cursus' rhythmique et les débuts de l'accent d'intensité en latin* (Paris 1930).

R. Schäflke, *Aristeides Quintilianus von der Musik* (Berlin-Schöneberg 1937).

W. Scherer, 'Des hl. Augustins 6 Bücher *De musica,*' *Kirchenmusikalisches Jahrbuch* 22 (1909) 63-69. Not consulted.

K. Svoboda, *L'Esthétique de St. Augustin et ses sources* (Brno 1933).

Victorinus,*Ars grammatica, ed. H. Keil, grammatici Latini* 6 (Leipzig 1874).

H. Vincente, *Analyse du traité de métrique et de rhythmique de St. Augustin intitulé: De musica* (Paris 1849). Not consulted.

H. B. Vroom, *Le psaume abécédaire de St. Augustin et la poésie latine rhythmique* (J. Schrijnen [ed.], Latinitas Christianorum primaeva 4, Nijmegen 1933).

H. Weil, *Etudes de littérature et de rhythmique grecques* (Paris 1902).

K. Wenig, 'Über die Quellen der Schrift Augustins *de Musica,' Listy Philologicke* 33 (1906). Not consulted.

R. Westphal. *Aristoxenus von Tarent. Melik und Rhythmik des classischen Hellinenthums* (Leipzig 1883, 1893).

———, *Fragmente und Letrsätze der griechischen Rhythmniker* (Leipzig 1861).

A. Wikman, *Beiträge zur Ästhetik Augustins.* Not consulted.

C. F. A. Williams, *The Aristoxenian Theory of Musical Rhythm* (Cambridge 1911).

CONTENTS

ON MUSIC

BOOK ONE

The definition of music is given; and the species and proportion of number-laden movements, things which belong to the consideration of this discipline, are explained.

Chapter 1

(1) *MASTER*. What foot is *'modus'*?

DISCIPLE. A pyrrhic.

M. And it contains how many times?[1]

D. Two.

M. What foot is *'bonus'*?

D. The same as *'modus.'*

M. So, what is *'bonus'* is also *'modus.'*

D. No.

M. Why are they, then, the same?

D. Because they are the same in sound, but other in signification.

M. You say, then, the sound is the same when we say *'modus,'* and when we say *'bonus'*.

D. I see of course they differ in the sound of the letters, but are otherwise alike.

M. Now when we pronouce the verb *'pone'* and the adverb *'pone,'* except for the difference in meaning, do you perceive no difference in sound?

D. There is quite a difference.

1 The doctrine of the *tempus,* or *prótos chrónos,* is more thoroughly examined in 2.2.

M. Where is the difference, since both consist of the same times and the same letters?

D. The difference is they have the acute accent[2] in different places.

M. Now to what art does it belong to distinguish these things?

D. I have always heard them from grammarians, and that is where I learnt them. But whether they are proper to this art or taken from somewhere else, I don't know.

M. We shall see later. But for the present I shall ask you this. If I should strike a drum or a string at the same intensity and speed we pronounce '*modus*' or *bonus*,' would you recognize the times to be the same or not?[3]

D. I should.

M. Then you would call it a pyrrhic foot.

D. I should.

M. Where did you learn the name of this foot; wasn't it from the grammarian?

D. Yes.

2 The problem of the accent is never mentioned again in this treatise. This is probably because it is considered by Augustine as belonging to the purely grammatical side of metrics and not properly to rhythmics and music. As we shall see later, Augustine's definition and treatment of meter is a purely rhythmical and musical one.

If Nicolau is right, the accent, however, played a conspicuous role in the development of the vocal ictus as distinguished from the purely mechanical ictus. See his *L'Origine du 'cursus' rythmique et les débuts de l'accent d'intensité en latin* (Paris 1930). The fusion or confusion of the vocal ictus and the accent will in turn radically change the material to be rhythmed and finally establish accentual meters in the place of quantitative meters.

3 The primacy of rhythm and beat and the complete subordination of syllable and metrics are here suggested. Quite a part of this is Augustine's war on grammar. If we remember that rhythm was treated in the discipline of grammar by Marius Victorinus, Diomedes, and other Latin writers, and that the culture Augustine lived in was declining under the weight of grammar and grammarians, this flight of a rhetorician to rhythm, and to rhythm we shall see as pure number, is not without deep significance.

M. Then the grammarian will judge concerning all such sounds. Or rather, didn't you learn those beats through yourself, but the name you imposed you had heard from a grammarian?

D. That's it.

M. And you have ventured to transfer the name which grammar taught you to that thing you admit does not belong to grammar?

D. I see the measure of the times is the only reason for imposing the name of the foot. And so, wherever I recognize the proper measure, why shouldn't I just give it its name? But even if other names can be imposed when sounds have the same measure, yet they do not concern grammarians. So, why should I bother about names when the thing itself is clear?

M. I don't wish to, either. And yet when you see a great many kinds of sound in which distinct measures can be observed, and we admit these kinds are not to be attributed to the art of grammar, don't you think there is some other discipline which contains whatever is numerable or artful in utterances of this sort?

D. It would seem probable.

M. What do you think its name is? For I don't believe it is news to you that a certain omnipotence in singing is usually granted the Muses. If I am not mistaken, this is what is called Music.

D. And I also say it's that.

Chapter 2

(2) *M.* But we want to bother as little as possible about the name. Only let us inquire, if you will, into all the power and reason of whatever art this is.

D. Let's do so by all means. For I should like very much to know the whole of this affair.

M. Now define music.

D. I shouldn't dare to.

M. Well, you can at least test my definition?

D. I'll try, if you will give it.

M. Music is the science of mensurating well [*modulandi*].[4] Doesn't it seem so to you?

D. It might seem so, if it were clear to me what mensuration [*modulatio*] is.

M. This word 'to mensurate' [*modulari*]—you have at no time heard it used anywhere, except in what has to do with singing or dancing?

D. Just so. But because I know 'to mensurate' [*modulari*] is taken from 'measure' [*modus*], since in all things well made measure must be observed, and because I also know many things in singing and dancing, however much they charm, are very reprehensible, I want to understand fully what this mensuration is. For almost in this one word is contained the definition of a very great art. And certainly we are not to study here what any singer or actor knows.

---

4 It is impossible to render *modulari* by 'to modulate,' because 'modulate' in English has a technical musical meaning: it means a change from one mode or key to another mode or key according to certain reasonable rules. It is even used in rhythmics by Aristides to denote the art of changing from one rhythm to another. The Greek word for this is *metabolé*, which is also used in Latin. We have, therefore, used the rather harsh and strange 'mensurate.' Aside from the fact that it fits well with 'measure,' its adjective 'mensurable' has a musical connotation. See the *Oxford English Dictionary*. This definition appears in Cassiodorus, *Institutiones*, II,5,2 (ed. Mynors, Oxford 1937, p. 143). In the previous chapter, Censorinus to Quintus Carellius, *de Natali eius die* is mentioned as a source for musical doctrine. The same definition is found indeed in Censorinus, *de die Natali liber*, 10,3 (ed. Hultsch, Leipzig 1867, p. 16). Holzer therefore concludes it must be from the lost works of Varro on the liberal arts. See Holzer, *Varroniana* (Ulm 1890), 6, 14, 15.

M. Don't let this disturb you, that, as you just said, in all things made, music included, measure must be observed, and yet that this is called mensuration in music. For you are aware 'diction' is properly restricted to the orator.

D. I am. But what has that to do with this?

M. Because when your servant, no matter how uncultured and peasant-like he may be, replies with as much as one word to your question, don't you admit he is saying [*dicere*] something?

D. I do.

M. And therefore he is an orator?

D. No.

M. Then he hasn't used diction when he has said something, although we admit diction is derived from saying.

D. I agree. But I want to know what all this is about.

M. For you to understand that mensuration can regard music alone, while measure, from which the word is derived, can also be in other things. In the same way diction is properly attributed to orators, although anyone who speaks says something, and diction gets its name from saying.

D. Now I understand.

(3) *M*. Now what you said a while ago, that many things in singing and dancing are reprehensible, and that, if we take the word mensuration from them, the almost divine art becomes degraded—and that you have very prudently observed. So, let us first discuss what it is to mensurate; then what it is to mensurate well; for that is not added to the definition without reason. Finally, too, it shouldn't be forgotten the word science has been put there. For with these three, I believe, the definition is complete.

D. All right.

M. Now, since we admit mensuration is named from

measure, you never think, do you, you have to fear the measure's being exceeded or not fulfilled, except in things moving in some way or other? Or rather, if nothing move, we can't fear anything's being out of measure, can we?

D. No, not at all.

M. Then, mensuration is not improperly called a certain skill in moving, or at any rate that by which something is made to move well. For we can't say anything moves well unless it keeps its measure.

D. No, we can't, but, on the contrary, we have to understand this mensuration in all things well done. For I see nothing to be done, if not in moving well.

M. What if, perhaps, all these things are done by music, although the name mensuration is more used in connection with instruments of a certain kind, and not incorrectly? I am sure you think the thing fashioned, whether it be of wood or silver or some other material, is one thing, and the artist's movement by which these things are fashioned is another.

D. Yes, they differ a great deal.

M. Now you can't say, can you, the movement is desired for itself, and not for the sake of that which the artist wants to be fashioned?

D. That's evident.

M. But if he should move his limbs for no other reason than that they should be moved gracefully and harmoniously, we should say he was dancing and nothing more, shouldn't we?

D. It seems so.

M. When do you think a thing is superior, and you might say to rule, when it is desired for its own sake or for the sake of another?

D. For its own sake, of course.

M. Begin again with what we have just said about mensuration (for we had assumed it to be a certain skill in moving) and see where this name ought rather to be applied: to that movement which is free, that is, is desired for itself and charms through itself alone, or to that which serves in some way. For all those things are somehow servile which are not for themselves but are referred to something else.

D. To that which is desired for itself.

M. Then it is now to be assumed the science of mensurating is the science of moving well, in such a way that the movement is desired for itself, and for this reason charms through itself alone.

D. That is very likely the case.

Chapter 3

(4) *M*. Why, then, is 'well' added, since there cannot even be mensuration, unless the thing move well?

D. I don't know, and I don't know how it escaped me. For it had been in my mind to ask this.

M. There could be no dispute at all over this expression, so long as we dropped 'well' and defined music only as the science of mensurating.

D. And there would be none now, if you would clear it all up.

M. Music is the science of moving well. But that is because whatever moves and keeps harmoniously the measuring of times and intervals can already be said to move well. For it is already pleasing, and for this reason is already properly called mensuration. Yet it is possible for this harmony and measuring to please when they shouldn't. For example, if one should sing sweetly and dance gracefully, wishing thereby to be gay when the ocasion demanded gravity, such a person would in no way be using harmonious mensuration well. In other words, that person uses ill or improperly the motion at one time called good because of its harmony. And so it is one thing to mensurate, and another to mensurate well. For mensuration is thought to be proper to any singer whatever if only he does not err in those measurings of voice and sounds, but good mensuration to be proper to the liberal discipline, that is, to music. Now, even if the motion itself, because it is misplaced, does not seem to you good, even though you admit it is harmonious in construction, yet let us hold to our definition and keep it the same everywhere, not to have a merely verbal battle upset us where the thing itself is clear enough. And let us not bother whether music be described as the science of mensurating or as the science of mensurating well.

D. I prefer to get beyond a mere scuffle of words and to make light of such things. After all, I don't object to this distinction.

Chapter 4

(5) *M.* Finally, we must consider why the word 'science' is in the definition.

D. All right, for I remember the order of our discourse demands it.

M. Tell me, then, whether the nightingale seems to mensurate its voice well in the spring of the year. For its song is both harmonious, and sweet and, unless I'm mistaken, it fits the season.

D. It seems quite so.

M. But it isn't trained in the liberal discipline, is it?

D. No.

M. You see, then, the noun 'science' is indispensable to the definition.

D. I see it clearly.

M. Now tell me, then, don't they all seem to be a kind with the nightingale, all those which sing well under the guidance of a certain sense, that is, do it harmoniously and sweetly, although if they were questioned about these numbers or intervals of high and low notes[5] they could not reply?

D. I think they are very much alike.

M. And what's more, aren't those who like to listen to them without this science to be compared to beasts? For we see elephants, bears, and many other kinds of beasts are moved by singing, and birds themselves are charmed by their own voices. For, with no further proper purpose, they would not do this with such effort without some pleasure.

D. I judge so, but this reproach extends to nearly the whole of human kind.

M. Not as much as you think. For great men, even if they know nothing about music, either wish to be one with the common people who are not very different from beasts and whose number is great; and they do this very properly and prudently. But this is not the place to discuss that. Or after great cares in order to relax and restore the mind they very moderately partake of some pleasure. And it is very proper

5 We have here translated *intervallis acutarum gravumque vocum by* 'intervals of high and low notes.' These are more or less technical words in harmonics. 'Interval' is equivalent to the Greek word *diástema,* meaning difference of pitch; and *vox,*. in the usage of Martianus Capella, is equivalent to the *phoné* of Aristoxenus and Aristides and includes voice and the sound of instruments, covering both the speaking voice and the singing voice, that is, the *phoné synechés* and the *phoné diastematiké* of Aristides. See Aristoxenus, *Harmonica,* I, 3, 4-5; Aristides, *De Musica,* I, 7; Martianus Capella, *De Nuptiis Mercurii et philologae* IX, 182. Therefore, *vox* strictly should not be translated by 'note,' which is equivalent to *phthóngos,* and translated by Martianus as *sonus.* There are later passages where Augustine evidently uses *sonus* for sound in general. A discussion of these terms would have belonged to the *De melo* which Augustine never wrote.

to take it in from time to time. But to be taken in by it, even at times, is improper and disgraceful.

(6) But how about this? Those who play on flutes or lyres or any other instrument of this kind, they can't be compared to the nightingale, can they?

D. No.

M. How, then, do they differ?

D. In that I find a certain art in these instrument players, but only nature in the nightingale.

M. That's true. But do you think it ought to be called an art even if they do it by a sort of imitation?

D. Why not? For imitation seems to me to be so much a part of the arts that, if it is removed, nearly all of them are destroyed. For masters exhibit themselves to be imitated, and this is what they call teaching.

M. But don't you think art is a sort of reason, and those who use art use reason? Or do you think otherwise?

D. It seems so.

M. Therefore, whoever cannot use reason does not use art.

D. I grant that, too.

M. Do you think dumb animals, which are also called irrational, can use reason?

D. Not at all.

M. Then, either you would be forced to say magpies, parrots, and crows are rational, or you have been pretty rash in calling imitation by the name of art. For we find that these birds sing and make many sounds because of their intercourse with human beings, and that they utter them only by imitation. Or do you object to this?

D. I don't yet fully understand how you have reached this conclusion and how far it invalidates my reply.

M. I have asked you whether you would say lyre-players

and flute-players or any other men of this sort had an art, even if what they do in singing they do by imitation. You have said it is an art, and you have affirmed this so true it seems to you that, if imitation were done away with, nearly all the arts would be destroyed. And from this it can be concluded that anyone who does something by imitating uses an art, although, perhaps not everyone who uses an art acquired it by imitating. But if all imitation is art, and all art reason, all imitation is reason. But an irrational animal does not use reason; therefore, it does not possess an art. But it is capable of imitation; therefore, art is not imitation.

D. I said that many arts consist in imitation. I did not call imitation itself art.

M. And so you don't think those arts consisting in imitation consist in reason?

D. Certainly, I think they consist in both.

M. I have no objection. But where do you place science, in reason or in imitation?

D. Also in both.

M. Then you suppose those birds endowed with reason which you have supposed capable of imitation.

D. I do not. For I have supposed science to be in both, in such a way that it cannot be in imitation alone.

M. Well, do you think it can be in reason alone?

D. It can.

M. Then you think art is one thing, science another. If, then, science can be in reason alone, then art joins imitation with reason.

D. I don't see that follows. For I did not say all arts, but many arts, consisted in both reason and imitation together.

M. Well, will you also call that science which consists in these two together, or will you attribute only the reasonable part to it?

D. What is to prevent me from calling it science when imitation is joined with reason?

(7) *M.* Since now we are concerned with the cither-player and the flute-player, that is to say with musical things, I want you to tell me whether, when such people do something by imitation, that is to be attributed to the body, that is, to a kind of bodily obedience.

D. I think it ought to be attributed to both the mind and the body, although the word which you used, 'bodily obedience,' was properly enough introduced by you. For it can only obey the mind.

M. I see you are very careful about not wishing to attribute imitation to the body alone. But you won't deny science belongs to the mind alone, will you?

D. Who would deny that.

M. Then you certainly would not allow anyone to attribute the science of the sounds of strings and pipes to both reason and imitation together. For, as you admitted, there is no imitation without a body; but you have also said science is of the mind only.

D. I admit this conclusion follows from the premises I granted you. But what of it? For the piper will have science in his mind. And when he happens to be imitating, which I admitted impossible without a body, this act of his does not destroy what is embraced by the mind.

M. No, it doesn't. Nor do I affirm that all those who handle such instruments lack science, but I say they do not all have science. For we are considering this question for the following purpose: to understand, if we can, how correct it is to include science in the definition of music. And if all pipers, flute-players, and others of this kind have science, then I think there is no more degraded and abject discipline than this one.

(8) *M.* But be as attentive as possible, so that what we have been strenuously looking for may appear. For you have already granted me that science lives only in the mind.

D. And why shouldn't I?

M. Further, do you attribute the sense of hearing to the mind, to the body, or to both?

D. To both.

M. And memory?

D. To the mind, I think. For if we perceive by the senses something we commit to memory, that is no reason to think we must consider memory to be in the body.

M. This happens to be a great question, and one not proper to this discussion. But I believe you can't deny—and that is enough for the subject in hand—that beasts have memory. For swallows come back to their nests the next year, and it is very truly said of goats: 'And even goats remembering return to their sheds.'[6] And a dog is said to have recognized the hero, his master, already forgotten by his men. And we can bring up many cases, if we wished to prove our claim.

D. I don't deny it, and I am anxiously awaiting what help this will give you.

M. Why this, of course, that whoever attributes science to the mind alone refuses it to all irrational living things, and places it neither in sense nor memory, but in the intellect alone. For sense is not without body, and both sense and memory exist in beasts.

D. And I am still waiting to see how this will help you.

M. In this way. That all who follow sense and what is

6 Vergil, *Georgics* 3.316.

pleasing in it commit to memory, and in this way, by moving their body, acquire a certain power of imitation; and that they do not have science even if they seem to do many things cleverly and skillfully unless they possess in the purity and truth of the intellect the very thing they profess or exhibit. And if reason demonstrate these comedians to be just people, there is no reason, I believe, why you should hesitate to deny them science, and, therefore, music which is the science of mensurating.

D. Explain this. Let's see about it.

(9) *M.* I believe you attribute the greater or less mobility of the fingers not to science but to practice, don't you?

D. Why do you believe so?

M. Because just now you attributed science to the mind alone. But, although in this case the mind commands, you see the act belongs to the body.

D. But, since the knowing mind commands this of the body, I think the act ought to be attributed to the mind rather than the servile members.

M. But, don't you think it is possible for one person to surpass another in science, even though the other person move his fingers much more easily and readily?

D. I do.

M. But, if the rapid and readier motion of the fingers were to be attributed to science, the more science anyone had the more he would excel in the rapidity of the motion.

D. I concede that.

M. Consider this, too. For I suppose you have sometimes noticed how artisans or craftsmen of this sort keep striking the same place with an axe or hatchet and how the blow is only carried where the mind intends it, and how, when we try and can't do likewise, they often ridicule us.

D. It's as you say.

M. Then, since we can't do it, do you think we do not know what ought to be struck or how much ought to be cut?

D. Often, we don't know, often we do.

M. Suppose, then, someone who knows everything artisans ought to do and knows it perfectly, and yet is less able than they in practice; who nevertheless prescribes for these same people who work with such ease, more wisely than they could for themselves. Would you deny that came from practice?

D. I shouldn't.

M. Then, not only the speed and facility of moving but also the manner itself of the motion is to be attributed to practice rather than science. For, if it were otherwise, the cleverer one were the better he would use his hands. Now, we can translate this in terms of pipes or citherns, in order not to think that what fingers and joints do in such cases, because it is difficult for us, is done by science and meditation rather than by practice and diligent imitation.

D. I have to give in. For I am always hearing how even doctors, very learned men, in the matter of amputating or binding limbs, are often surpassed by less clever men in their use of the hand or knife. And this kind of curing they call surgery. The word itself signifies a certain operative habit of curing, developed in the hands. But pass on to other things, and let's finish up this question of ours.

Chapter 5

(10) *M.* I believe it remains for us to find, if we can, the arts which please us in the practical mastery they give our hands, and which do not derive immediately from science, but from sense and memory. For of course you can tell me

that it is possible for there to be science without practice, and very frequently greater science than in those who excel in practice; but that on the other hand they can't even acquire practice without science.

D. Go on, for it is clear that ought to be the case.

M. Have you never listened carefully to actors of this sort?

D. More perhaps than I should wish.

M. How do you explain the fact that an ignorant crowd hisses off a flute-player letting out futile sounds, and on the other hand applauds one who sings well, and finally that the more agreeably one sings the more fully and intensely it is moved? For it isn't possible to believe the crowd does all this by the art of music, is it?

D. No.

M. How then?

D. I think it is done by nature giving everyone a sense of hearing by which such things are judged.

M. You are right. But now consider this, too, whether the flute-player himself is also endowed with this sense. And if it is so, he can, by following his own judgment, move his fingers when he blows on the flute, and can note and commit to memory what he decides sounds well enough; and by repeating it he can accustom his fingers to being carried about without hesitation or error, whether he gets from another what he plays or whether he finds it himself, led on and abetted as he is by the nature we spoke of. And so, when memory follows sense, and the joints, already subdued and prepared by practice, follow memory, the player sings as he wishes, the better and more easily the more he excels in all those things which reason just now taught us we have in common with the beasts: that is, the desire of imitating, sense, and memory. Have you any objections to that?

D. No, I haven't. Now I want to know what kind of discipline this is I see so nicely appropriated by knowledge belonging to the lowest animals.

Chapter 6

(11) *M*. We haven't yet done enough. And I shall not allow us to pass to its explanation unless we have already agreed how actors without this science can satisfy the popular ear. And it also will have been established that actors can in no way be students of, and learned in, music.

D. It will be marvelous if you do this.

M. That is easy, but you must be more attentive.

D. Never that I know have I been even a little careless in listening from the very beginning of this dialogue. But now, I admit, you have made me more intent.

M. I am grateful, although you more or less suit yourself. But, tell me whether you think a man who wishes to sell a gold piece for a fair price, and judge it to be worth ten cents knows what it is.

D. Well, who would think so?

M. Then tell me, which is to be considered dearer, what is contained in our intellect or what is accidentally attributed to us by the judgment of an ignorant people?

D. No one doubts the first is far above all others, even those things which are not to be thought ours.

M. And so you don't deny, do you, all science is contained in the intellect?

D. Who does?

M. And, therefore, music is in the intellect.

D. That seems to follow from its definition.

M. Well then, don't the people's applause and all those theatrical rewards seem to you to be of the kind which is attributed to the power of chance and the judgment of the ignorant?

D. I don't suppose anything is more fortuitous and liable to chance, or subject to the domination and pleasure of the many, than these things are.

M. Would actors, then, sell their songs for this price, if they knew music?

D. I am not a little shaken by this conclusion, but I can't gainsay it. For it doesn't seem that the seller of the gold piece ought to be compared with the actor. For when he accepts applause or when money is given him, he doesn't give up his science, if he chanced to have any, to please the people with. But, heavier with pennies and happier with the praise of men, he returns home with the same discipline entire and intact. But he would be a fool if he despised these advantages. For, if he hadn't gotten them, he would be much poorer and more obscure; having gotten them, he is no less skilled.

(12) *M.* Let's see if we can get what we want in this way. For I suppose you think that for the sake of which we do a thing is much more important than the thing we do.

D. That's evident.

M. Then he who sings or who is learning to sing for no other reason than to be praised by many or some other man, doesn't he judge the praise to be better than the song?

D. It does seem so.

M. And he who judges wrongly about a thing, does he seem to you to know it?

D. Certainly not, unless he has somehow been bribed.

M. And so he who really thinks something inferior to be superior is, no doubt, lacking in the science of it.

D. That's so.

M. Therefore, when you have persuaded me or proved to me that any actor, if he has any talent, neither has developed it nor does he exhibit it to please the people for gain or fame, then I shall concede it is possible both to possess the science of music and to be an actor. But if it is very likely all actors conceive the end of their profession in terms of money and glory, then we must admit either that actors do not know music or one is right in seeking other people's praise or some chance gain rather than his own understanding.

D. I see that in conceding the other things, I must also accept these. For I don't believe there is any way of finding a man on the stage who loves his art for itself, and not for outside advantages. For it is hard to find one even from a school of higher learning. Yet if one exists or should exist, liberal artists are not for that reason to be despised; so why isn't it possible that actors ought sometimes to be honored. And then explain, if you will, this great discipline which now can't seem to me so degraded as you make out.

Chapter 7

(13) *M.* I shall do so; or rather you will do so. For all I shall do is question you. And by your answers you will explain all of what you now seem to be after, without knowing it. And now tell me whether anyone can run both fast and for a long time.

D. It is possible.

M. How about both slow and fast?

D. By no means.

M. Then 'for a long time' signifies something different from 'slow.'

D. Quite different.

M. Again, tell me what you think is the contrary of 'longness of time,' just as 'speed' is the contrary of 'slowness.'

D. No usual word occurs to me. And I find nothing I may oppose to 'of a long duration' except 'not of long duration,' so that the usual contrary of 'for a long time' is 'not for a long time.' Because if I didn't wish to say 'fast' and said 'not slow' instead, there would be no difference in meaning.

M. That's so. For it doesn't affect the truth any when we speak this way. And as for me, if this word exists you say hasn't occured to you, then either I don't know it or at present it doesn't come to my mind. And so let's go on, calling contraries each of the pairs, 'for a long time' and 'not for a long time,' 'slow' and 'fast.' And first, if you will, let's discuss 'of long duration' and 'not of long duration.'

D. Very well.

Chapter 8

(14) *M.* Now it is clear what is said to be done for a long time [*diu*] is done over a long period of time [*per longum tempus*], but what is said to be done not for a long time [*non diu*] is done over a short period of time [*per breve tempus*].

D. That's clear.

M. For example, doesn't a movement accomplished in two hours have twice the time of that accomplished in one hour?

D. Who would doubt it?

M. Therefore, what we call 'of long duration' or 'not of long duration' is capable of such measurements and numbers that one motion is to another as two to one; that is, that one has twice as much as the other. And again that one movement is to another as two to three; that is, that one has three parts of time to the other's two. And so it is possible to run through the rest of the numbers in a way that avoids indefinite and indeterminate spaces, and relates any two movements by some number. Either by the same number, as one to one, two to two, three to three, four to four; or not by same, as one to two, two to three, three to four, or one to three, two to six, and whatever measurements anything is capable of.

D. I want to get this point of yours more clearly.

M. Return, then, to the hours, and apply to each case what I thought sufficiently explained, since I explained it for one hour and for two. For certainly you don't deny the possibility of a movement of one hour, or another of two.

D. That's true.

M. Well, don't you admit the possibility of two-hour movement, and another of three?

D. I do.

M. And one of three hours, and another of four, again one of one hour and another of three, or one of two hours and another of six; isn't that clear?

D. It is.

M. Then why isn't the rest clear? For I said this same thing when I said two movements could be related by some number as one to two, two to three, three to four, one to three, two to six, and any others you wish to enumerate. For when you know these, you can follow through with the others, either seven to ten or five to eight and anything else consisting of two movements having parts so measured with respect to one another they can be described as so much to so much, either with equal numbers or with one larger and one smaller.

D. Now I understand, and I admit its possibility.

Chapter 9

(15) *M.* You understand this, too, I believe, that all measure and limit is preferred to infinity and immeasurableness.

D. That is very evident.

M. Then two movements which, as I said, are related by some numerical measurement are to be preferred to those which are not.

D. And this is evident and logical. For there is a certain limit and measure in numbers which connect them one with another. And those numbers lacking this measure are not joined together by any ratio.

M. Then, if you will, let us call those which are commensurable with one another rational, and those which are not commensurable, irrational.[7]

D. I am willing.

M. Now, tell me whether the agreement doesn't seem to you greater in the case of the rational movements of those things equal to each other than of those which are unequal?

D. Who wouldn't think so?

M. Again, of those which are unequal, aren't there some of which we can say by what *aliquot* part of the greater the greater is equal to, or exceeds, the less, as two and four or six and eight? But others of which that cannot be said, as in the numbers three and ten or four and eleven? You see immediately for the first two numbers that the greater is made equal to the less by its half. For those I mentioned next that the greater is in excess of the less by a fourth part of the greater. But for the others, such as three and ten

7 These are not the irrational feet defined by Aristoxenus and Aristides Quintilianus, but irrational movements incommensurable in the sense of magnitude without common measure.

or four and eleven, we find some agreement, because at least the parts are so related it can be said of them so many to so many. And yet we don't see such a relation as we saw in the earlier ones. For it can in no way be said by what *aliquot* part the greater is equal to the less or by what *aliquot* part it exceeds the less. For no one would say what *aliquot* part of ten three is, or what *aliquot* part of eleven four is. And when I tell you to consider what part it is, I mean the exact part, without any addition, like a half, a third, a quarter, a fifth, a sixth, and so on; so that thirds and twenty-fourths and such divisions are in no way added on.

D. I understand.

(16) *M.* Then, of these unequal rational movements, since I have also proposed two kinds of numbers in the examples adduced, which do you think are to be preferred, those in which the *aliquot* part can be given or those in which it cannot?

D. Reason seems to force my saying those in which it is possible to say by what *aliquot* part of itself the greater is either equal to the loss or exceeds it, ought to be preferred to those in which this is not the case.

M. But don't you think we ought to give them names, so that, when we have to recall them later on, we may speak of them more easily?

D. I do.

M. Then let us call those we prefer connumerate, and the others dinumerate, because the former not only have a common measure one, but also have as a common measure that part by which the greater is equal to or exceeds the less. But the latter only have a common measure one and do not have as a common measure the part by which the greater equals or exceeds the less. For in the case of these it is impossible to say either how many times the greater contains the less, or how many times both the greater and the less contain that by which the greater exceeds the less.

D. I accept these names, and I shall try as well as I can to remember them.

Chapter 10

(17) *M.* Come now, let's see what division there can be of the connumerate numbers. For I think it is pretty clear. For one class of the connumerate numbers is that in which the smaller number measures the greater, that is, the greater contains it a certain number of times, just as we said the numbers two and four do. For we see that two is contained twice in four, and it would be contained three times if we compared not four, but six to two, four times if it were eight, and five times if it were ten. The other class is that in which the part by which the greater exceeds the less measures both, that is, the greater and less contain it a certain number of times, and we have already noted this in the numbers six and eight. For the part by which the less is exceeded is two and that, you see, is contained four times in eight, three times in six. And so let us also mark out and designate with names the movements we are now talking about, and the numbers which reveal what we want to know about these movements. For I believe the distinction is already apparent. And so, if you will, those in which the greater is a multiple of the less are called complicate; the others sesquate, a name already long in use. For that is called '*sesque*' in which two numbers have such a ratio to each other that by whatever *aliquot* part of itself the greater exceeds the less, so many parts does it contain with respect to the less. For if it is three to two, the greater exceeds the less by a third part of itself; if four to three, by a fourth; if five to four, by a fifth, and so on. And

we have the same kind of ratio also in the case of six to four, eight to six, ten to eight; from these we can find this ratio in the larger numbers which follow. But I should find it hard to tell you the origin of this name, unless perhaps '*sesque*' is said for '*se absque*' or '*absque se*' [from itself], because in the case of five to four the greater minus [*absque*] a fifth of itself is the same as the less. And what is your opinion of all this?

D. Why, the ratio of measurements and numbers seems very correct to me. And the names you have given seem to be suitable for remembering the things we have understood. And the origin of the name you just explained to me is not absurd, although it may not be the one followed by the person starting the name.

Chapter 11

(18) *M*. I approve and accept your judgment. But do you see that all such rational motions, that is, those in some relation of numerical measure to each other can go on through numbers to infinity, unless some ratio should again delimit them and keep forcing them over and over again into a measure and form? For to speak of the equal pairs first: one to one, two to two, three to three, four to four, and if I follow through, what will be the end, since number has no end? For such is the power of number that every number named is finite, and not named is infinite. And what happens in the case of equal pairs also happens, as you see, in the case of unequal pairs, either complicate or sesquate or connumerate or dinumerate. For if you take one to two, and wish to continue with multiples by saying one to three, one to four, one to five, and so on, there will be no end. Or if only the double, as one to two, two to four,

four to eight, eight to sixteen, and so forth, here also there will be no end. And so, if you want to continue with only the triple, or whatever else you wish, they will go on to infinity. And this is true also of the sesquate. For when we say two to three, three to four, four to five, you see nothing keeps us from going on, for there is no limit. Or if you wish to proceed in the same class in this way, two to three, four to six, six to nine, eight to twelve, ten to fifteen, and so on. And so, either in this class of numbers or in all the others, no limit appears. And there is no need now to speak of the dinumerate numbers, since anyone can understand from what has been said that their continual recurrence allows no limit. Doesn't this seem true to you?

(19) *D.* What could be truer? But I am now waiting anxiously to learn about the ratio which forces such an infinity back into some measure, and prescribes a form it may not exceed.

M. You will find you already know this, too, as well as the other things, when you answer my questions right. For, since we are discussing numerically ordered movements, I wonder whether we first should not consider numbers themselves, and decide that whatever sure and fixed laws numbers make manifest are to be looked for and apprehended in the movements.

D. I certainly agree. I think nothing could be more orderly than that.

M. Then, if you will, let us start considering numbers from the very beginning and see, as far as we can grasp such things with the mind's strength we have, what the reason[8]

8 There is a continuous play on the Latin word *ratio,* which means both ratio and reason. This intentional ambiguity runs through the whole treatise. *Lógos* in Greek gives same ambiguity. Since ratio or *lógos is* defined by Euclid as 'a certain relation according to multiplicability

is that, although as we have said numbers progress to infinity, men have made certain articulations in counting by which they return again and again to one, the beginning or principle of numbers. For, in counting, we progress from one to ten, and from there we return to one. And if you wish to follow through with the intervals of ten, so that you go on with ten, twenty, thirty, forty, then the progression is to a hundred. If with intervals of a hundred, one hundred, two hundred, three hundred, four hundred, the articulation by which you return is at a thousand. Now why go farther? You certainly see the articulation I mean, whose first rule is given by the number ten. For, as ten contains one ten times, so a hundred contains the same ten ten times, and thousand contains a hundred ten times. And so you can go as far as you wish in these articulations, in a way predetermined by the number ten. Is there any thing in these matters you don't understand?

D. It is all very clear and true.

Chapter 12

(20) *M*. Then let us examine as diligently as we can what the reason is for there being a progression from one to ten and thence a return to one again. And next I ask you if what we call the beginning or principle can be a beginning at all unless it is the beginning of something.

D. Not at all.

M. Likewise, what we call the end, can it be an end, unless it is the end of something?

D. It can't either.

M. Well, you don't think you can go from the beginning to the end without going through the middle?

between magnitudes of the same kind,' it is obvious in what dialectical direction and toward what doctrine this intentional ambiguity directs us.

D. I don't think you can.

M. Then, for something to be a whole, it must consist of a beginning, middle, and end.

D. It seems so.

M. Now tell me, then, in what number do you think a beginning, middle, and end are contained.

D. I think you want me to say the number three, for three is one of those you are looking for.

M. You think right. And so you see there is a certain perfection in three because it is a whole: it has a beginning, middle, and end.

D. I see it clearly.

M. And don't we learn from boyhood every number is either even or odd?

D. You are right.

M. Recollect, then, and tell me which we usually call even and which odd.

D. That which can be divided into two equal parts is called even; but which cannot, odd.

(21) *M.* You have it. Now, since three is the first whole odd number, and consist of a beginning, middle, and end, then doesn't an even number have to be whole and perfect,[9] too, so that it also has a beginning, middle, and end?

D. It certainly must.

M. But this number, whichever it is, cannot have an indivisible middle like the odd one. For if it did, it could not be divided into two equal parts, for that, we said, was the property of an even number. Now, one is an indivisible middle; two is a divisible middle. But the middle in numbers is that from which both sides are equal to each other. Has

9 Not perfect in the technical sense of a number which is the sum of its different factors.

anything been put obscurely, and do you find it hard to follow?

D. On the contrary, this, too, is all very clear to me, and when I look for a whole even number, I first strike the number four. For how can the three things by which a number is whole, that is, beginning, middle, and end, be found in the number two?

M. You have answered the very thing I wished you to, and reason has forced you to. And now repeat the discussion beginning with the number one itself, and think. Then you will see immediately one has no middle and end, because there is only a beginning, or rather it is a beginning because it lacks a middle and end.

D. That's clear.

M. What, then, shall we say of two? We can't find a beginning and middle both in it, can we, since there can be no middle where there's no end? Nor a beginning and end both, since nothing can attain its end except through a middle?

D. Reason forces my admission, and I am very uncertain what to reply.

M. Be careful this number isn't also a beginning of numbers. For if it lacks a middle and end, as you have said reason forces us to admit, then there is nothing else for it to be but a beginning, is there? Or do you hesitate to set up two beginnings?

D. I hesitate very decidedly.

M. You would be right, if the two beginnings were made opposed to each other. But in this case the second beginning is from the first, so that the first is from none, but the second is from the first. For one and one are two, and so they are both beginnings in such a way that all numbers are really from one. But because they are made by combination and addition, and the origin of combination and addition is rightly attributed to two, therefore it is this first beginning from which [*a quo*], but the second through which [*per quod*], all numbers are found to be. Or have you objections to the things you are discussing.

D. I have none. And I ponder them with admiration, even though I am answering them myself under your questioning.

(22) *M.* Such things are more subtly and abstrusely examined in the discipline which concerns numbers. But here let us return as quickly as we can to the task in hand. And so, I ask, what does two added to one make?

D. Three.

M. So the two beginnings of numbers added together make the whole and perfect number.

D. So it is.

M. And in counting, what number do we place after two?

D. The same three.

M. And so the same number made out of one and two is placed after both of them as regards order, in such a way no other can be interposed.

D. So I see.

M. But now you must also see this can happen to none of the other numbers, the fact that, when you have singled out any two next to each other in the order of counting, the one immediately following them should be made up of these two.

D. I see that, too. For two and three, which are adjoining numbers, added together make five. And not five, but four, immediately follows them. Again, three and four make seven, but five and six have a place between four and seven. And the farther I should want to go, the more there are in between.

M. Therefore, this great harmony is in the first three

numbers. For we say one and two, and three, and nothing can be put between. But one and two themselves are three.

D. It is a great one certainly.

M. And have you no consideration for the fact that this harmony tends to a greater unity the more compressed and the more closely connected it is, and the more it makes a one from many.

D. On the contrary, the greatest consideration. And I don't know why, but I admire and love this unity you commend.

M. I very much approve. But certainly any conjunction and connection of things most definitely make something one when the means agree with the extremes, and the extremes with the means.

D. That certainly must be so.

(23) *M.* And so we must be careful to find it in this relation. For when we say one, two, three, isn't two exceeded by three as one is exceeded by two?

D. That's very true.

M. Well now, tell me, in this ordered set[10] how many times have I named one?

D. Once.

M. How many times three?

D. Once.

M. How many times two?

D. Twice.

M. Then once, and twice, and once, how many is that altogether?

D. Four times.

M. Then the number four rightly follows these three; to

10 We use 'ordered set' advisedly as a term from modern point-set theory, although there the term is used with a view to infinite sets.

it in fact is attributed this ordering by proportion. And it is now time you learn to know how important this thing is, because the unity you love can be effected in ordered things by that alone whose name in Greek is *analogía* and which some of our writers have called proportion. And we'll use this name, if you will, for, unless necessary, I should not like to bring a Greek word over into Latin speech.

D. I am quite willing. But go on with your story.

M. I shall. For we shall try and know more thoroughly by its place in this discipline what proportion is and how great is its authority in things. And the more advanced you are in learning, the better you will know its nature and power. But you see certainly, and that is enough for the present, that those three numbers whose harmony you were wondering at could only have been brought together in the same relation by the number four. And therefore, to the extent you understand, it has by rule obtained its own immediate succession to the other three to be joined with them in that closer harmony. So that now, not one, two, three only, but one, two, three, four is the most closely connected progression of numbers.

D. I entirely agree.

(24) *M.* But consider these further characteristics, lest you think the number four has nothing proper all other numbers lack, and nothing adequate to this relation I speak of, for making the interval from one to four itself a determinate number and the most beautiful art of progression. We agreed a while back something became most one when the means agreed with the extremes and the extremes with the means.

D. That's so.

M. Now, when we order one, two, three, tell me which are the extremes, and which the mean.

D. One and three seem to be the extremes, and two the mean.

M. Tell me now, one and three make what?

D. Four.

M. Well, two, the lone middle number, can't be joined with anything but itself, can it? And so tell me now what twice two makes.

D. Four.

M. So then, the mean agrees with the extremes and the extremes with the mean. And, therefore, just as there is a certain virtue in three in that it is placed in order after one and two, while consisting of one and two, so there is a certain virtue in four in that it falls in counting after one, two, and three, while consisting of one and three, or twice two. And this agreement of the extremes with the mean and of the mean with the extremes is by proportion which in Greek is called *analogía.* Now say, have you understood this?

D. I have.

(25) *M.* Try and see whether the property we attributed to the number four can be found in other numbers or not.

D. I shall. For if we fix upon two, three, four, the extremes added together make six, and the mean added to itself also makes six; yet not six, but five, is the number immediately following. Again I take three, four, and five. The extremes make eight, as also twice the mean. But between five and eight I find no longer one number but two, namely six and seven. And in the case of this ratio the farther I progress the greater these intervals become.

M. I see you have understood and know thoroughly what has been said. But now, not to delay, you certainly see that from one to four is the most complete progression, either from the point of view of odd and even numbers, since three is the first whole odd number and four the first whole even (this subject was treated a while ago). Or because one and two are the beginnings and seeds, as it were, of numbers, three is made from; and this accounts for three numbers. And when they are brought together by proportion, the number four appears and comes to be, and is joined to them by rule, to become the final number of the measured progression we seek.

D. I understand.

(26) *M.* Very well. But do you remember now what we had begun to look for? I believe it had been proposed we should find out, if we could, why, when definite articulations for counting had been established in the infinity of numbers, the first articulation should be at ten as the greatest. In other words, why those we count, having gone from one to ten, should return to one again.

D. I remember clearly it was for this we made our long digression, but I don't see what we have accomplished in the way of solving the problem. Unless all our reasoning has led to the conclusion the progression to ten is not a fixed and measured one, but the progression to four is.

M. But don't you see? What is the sum of one, two, three, and four?

D. I see now. I see and marvel at it all, and I admit the question which arose has now been solved. For one, two, three, and four together are ten.

M. And so it is fitting these first four numbers and the series of them and their relations be given more honor than any other numbers.

Chapter 13

(27) *M.* But it is time to return to the treatment and discussion of the movements properly attributed to this discipline, for whose sake we have considered with regard to numbers, plainly from another discipline, such things as seemed sufficient for the business in hand. Now, as aids to understanding, we took such movements in hour-intervals as reason showed to be related by some numerical measure. And so I ask you, supposing some one should run for an hour, then another for two hours, could you tell, without looking at a sun-dial or water-clock, or any time-piece of this sort, that one of these movements was single, the other double? And not being able to tell, would you nevertheless be delighted by the harmony and pleasurably affected?

D. I certainly could not.

M. And suppose an instrument struck in rhythm, with one sound a time's length and the next double repeatedly and connectedly, to make what are called iambic feet,[11] and suppose someone dancing to it moving his limbs in time. Then could you not give the time's measure, explain the movement's intervals alternating as one to two, either in the beats heard or the dancing seen? Or if you could not tell the numbers in its measure, wouldn't you at least delight in the rhythm you sense?

D. It is as you say. For those who know these numbers and discern them in the beats and dancing easily identify them. And those who don't know them and can't identify them admit, nevertheless, they get a certain pleasure from them.

---

11 This is the rhythmical foot, and the times here spoken of could well be, in the language of the school of Aristoxenus, *chrónoi podikoí.* This will be explained in greater detail in the next Book, which formally deals with the metrical foot.

(28) *M.* Now, although all well measured movements admittedly belong to the rationale of this discipline, if indeed it is the science of mensurating well, and especially those not referred to any thing else but keeping within themselves their end of ornament and delight, yet even in proper ratios these movements, as you just rightly said under my questioning, cannot be suited to our senses when accomplished in a long space of time, an hour or more. And since music somehow issuing forth from the most secret sanctuaries leaves traces in our very senses or in things sensed by us, mustn't we follow through those traces to reach without fail, if we can, those very places I have called sanctuaries?

D. We certainly must, and I earnestly pray we do so now.

M. Then let us not speak of those bounds of time extending beyond the capacity of our senses, and discuss, as far as reason goes, the short interval lengths which delight us in singing and dancing. Or do you, perhaps, think of some other possible way of following these traces which have penetrated, as we said, our senses and the things we sense with this discipline?

D. I think it can be done no other way.

BOOK TWO

Syllables and metrical feet[1] *are discussed.*

Chapter 1

(1) *M.* Then pay good attention and let's make something like a second beginning to our argument. But first, say whether you have learned well one of the things grammarians teach, that is, the difference between long and short syllables, or whether you prefer, knowing them or not, that we explore these matters as if we were altogether ignorant of them, in order to have reason bring us to all these conclu-

1 Augustine discusses now the metrical foot as distinguished from the rhythmical foot. In Book One the appeal has been to the rhythmical foot without any explicit mention of it and without any technical examination of it. It is not until the last half of this present Book (2.18) that mention is made of arsis and thesis, which are the distinctive parts of the rhythmical foot. Aristides is more explicit in distinguishing the two kinds of foot: 'Rhythm is a system [scale] of times collated in a certain order, and their affects we call arsis and thesis, and strong and weak' (*op. cit.* 1.20.) . . . 'Now foot is a part of the whole rhythm by means of which we comprehend the whole. And its parts are two: arsis and thesis' (*op. cit.* 1.34). So much for the rhythmical foot. As for the metrical foot, it depends fundamentally on the rhythmical foot, but emphasizes the *rhythmizómenon* or thing rhythmed as it appears within the rhythm or conditions it. 'Meters consist of feet. For meter is a system [scale] composed of feet of unlike syllables commensurable in length . . . . [Some say] the essence of rhythm is in arsis and thesis, but the essence of meter is in syllables and their unlikeness' (*op.cit.* 1.49). Thus, the rhythmical foot with one time to the upward beat and two to the downward beat could furnish two different metrical feet: a short syllable followed by two shorts or a short followed by a long. The problem of the difference which might arise from changing the upward and downward beat and whether it is rhythmical or metrical will come up later.

sions rather than having inveterate habit or the authority of another's judgment force us.

D. Not only reason, but also an inexperience—I might as well admit it—in matters of syllables certainly leads me to prefer a radical beginning.[2]

M. Well, then, tell me whether you yourself, by your own observation, have ever noticed that some syllables are enunciated very rapidly and briefly, but others more slowly and in a longer time.

D. It is certainly true I have not been insensible of such things.

M. But first I want you to know that the whole of that science called *grammatica* Greek-wise, but Latin-wise *litteratura,* professes the conservation of historical precedent—either that alone, as reason in its subtler moments teaches, or for the most part, as even stupid minds concede. And so, for example, when you say *cano,* or put it in verse, in such a way as to prolong its first syllable when you pronounce it or in such a place as to make it necessarily long, the grammarian will censure you; he, of course, the guardian of history, giving no other reason why this syllable should be contracted than that those who lived before us and whose books survive

2 This passage is not just an attack on grammar and grammarians in favor of the science of music, but it is also a recognition of a definite state of affairs. At this time and before this, the distinction of long and short syllables is no longer natural to the average person. Augustine (in his *Retractationes* 1.20), describes his *Psalm against the Donatist Faction* as written for the common people, *non aliquo carminis genere,* that is, not in quantitative meter. Vroom, in his analysis of the *Psalm,* describes it as rhythmical acatalectic trochaic tetrameter where the word-accent fails to coincide with the ictus only at the begining of the two hemistiches, but where quantity is not observed. Vroom supposes this to be the first case of such verses in trochaic meter in Latin literature, since those of Commodianus which are otherwise much like them are hexameters. See Vroom, *Le psaume abécédaire de St. Augustin et la poésie latine rythmique* (Nijmegen 1933).

and are discussed by grammarians used it as a short syllable, not as a long one. And so, whatever prevails here, prevails as authority. On the contrary, the reason of music, whose province is the rational and numerical measure of sounds, takes care only the syllable in this or that place be contracted or prolonged according to the rationale of its measures. For, if you should put this word where two long syllables ought to be, and should make the first syllable, which is short, long by pronunciation, the science of music will not for that be outraged in the least. For those sound-rhythms have been heard which were necessary to that number. But the grammarian orders its emendation and bids you put in a word whose first syllable must be long according to the authority, he says, of our ancestors of whose writings he is the watchdog.

Chapter 2

(2) *M.* Therefore, since we have undertaken to follow the theory of music, even if you do not know which syllables are to be shortened and which lengthened, we can nevertheless overlook this ignorance of yours and consider sufficient your saying you had noticed some syllables were shorter and some longer. And so I now ask you whether the sound of verses has ever moved you with pleasure.

D. In fact, so often I have almost never heard a verse without pleasure.

M. If, then, someone, in a verse which delighted you in hearing it, should lengthen or shorten the syllables contrary to the rationale of the verse, you can't enjoy it in the same way, can you?

D. On the contrary, hearing it is offensive.

M. So there is no doubt about it, you enjoy a certain

measuring out of numbers in the sound you say pleases you and which when disturbed cannot give you that pleasure.

D. That's evident.

M. Then tell me, in so far as it concerns the verse's sound, what differences does it make whether I say *Arma virumque cano, Troiae qui primus ab oris* or *qui primis ab oris*.

D. Both sound the same to me as far as measure is concerned.

M. And that's because of my pronunciation, with a fault, of course, grammarians call a barbarism. For '*primus*' is made up of a long and a short syllable. And in '*primis*' both ought to be long, but I shortened the last one. So your ears were right. Therefore, we must repeatedly test to see whether, on my pronouncing, you sense what is long and not long in syllables, in order to have the discussion continue, with me questioning and you replying as we began it. So I shall repeat the same verse I committed the barbarism in, and the syllable I shortened, not to offend your ears, I shall lengthen, as the grammarians order. You will tell me whether the rhythm of the verse gives your senses the same pleasure. So let me recite this way, *Arma virumque cano, Troiae qui primis ab oris*.

D. No, I can't deny I am disturbed by a sort of deformity of sound.

M. You are quite right. For, although there was no barbarism, yet there was a fault both grammar and music condemn: grammar, because a word whose syllable is to be pronounced long has been put where a syllable to be pronounced short should be, but music only because some sound has been lengthened where it ought to have been shortened, and the proper time demanded by the numerical measure has not been rendered. And so, if you now discriminated between what the sense of hearing demands and what authority demands, it follows we should see why that sense sometimes enjoys either long or short sounds and sometimes does not. For that is what concerns 'for a long time' and 'not for a long time.' And I am sure you remember we undertook to explain just that.

D. I made the discrimination, I remember, and I am waiting very eagerly for what follows.

Chapter 3

(3) *M.* Don't you think we should begin by comparing syllables with each other and seeing by what numbers they are related to each other, just as we have already done with movements in a very long discussion? For all that sounds is in movement, and syllables are certainly sound. Do you deny any of these premises?

D. Not at all.

M. Therefore, when syllables are compared with each other, movements containing numbers found by measure of the length of time are compared with each other.

D. That's so.

M. Then, one syllable cannot be compared with itself, can it? For singleness escapes all comparison. Or have you something else to say about this?

D. I haven't.

M. But that one syllable to one syllable, or one to two, or two to three and so on, you don't deny they can be compared with each other, do you?

D. Who would?

M. And then, consider this, any short syllable you will, pronounced in the shortest time, dying as soon as it begins, yet occupies some interval of time and has some brief stay of its own.

D. What you say seems necessary.

M. Tell me, now, what number we begin with.

D. One, of course.

M. Then the ancients were not absurd in calling one time a sort of minimum interval,[3] proper to the short syllable. For we go from the short to the long.

D. That's true.

M. It follows, then, you also perceive that, since as in numbers the first progression is from one to two, so in syllables where we clearly go from short to long, the long ought to be double time. And therefore, if the interval the short syllable occupies is rightly called one time, likewise the interval the long one occupies is rightly called two times.[4]

D. Very rightly, for I agree reason demands it.

Chapter 4

(4) *M.* Now, let us consider the ordered sets themselves. For I want to know what ratio you think one short syllable has to one short syllable or what these movements

---

3 This refers to the doctrine of the *prótos chrónos,* or primary time, of Aristoxenus. The *prótos chrónos* is that time which can never be divided by the *rhythmizómenon,* the thing rhythmed, either *léxis, mélos,* or *kínesis somatiké,* that is, speech, melody, or bodily movement. See fragments in Westphal, *Aristoxenos von Tarent,* II 79, 18-20.

Aristides gives the same doctrine: 'Primary time is then an indivisible and least time which is called a point. And I call that least with respect to us which is the first [time] capable of being grasped by sense' (*op.cit.* II.32). It is not only relative to the thing rhythmed and to us in general, but also from occasion to occasion, since it can be varied by change or tempo or *agogé.* This quasi arbitrary and creative act by which we make a divisible sensible thing stand for an indivisible one has a deep significance for the theory of time. Thus the syllable is no longer the measure of time but the thing measured, and Aristoxenus (*op. cit.* II. 76) expressly respects the theory of Aristotle in *Meta.* 13.1,7. The *diesis* plays the same role as the least interval in harmonics.

4 This is the doctrine of Aristoxenus (*op.cit.* II.76), although in the fragment in the Oxyrhynchus Papyri attributed to him the long is considered as capable also of representing three times. See H. Weil,

are called in relation to each other. For you remember, if I am not mistaken, in the discussion a while back we imposed names on all movements having certain numerical relations to each other.

D. I remember they were named equal, for they were so related with respect to time.

M. Now, you don't think this ordered set of syllables, furnishing its constituents with numbers with respect to one another, ought to be left without a name, do you?

D. I do not.

M. Well, the ancients called such an ordered set of sounds a foot.[5] But we must be careful to notice just how far reason allows a syllable to go. And so next tell me in what ratio a short and a long syllable are with respect to each other.

D. I believe this ordering comes from that genus of numbers we called complicate. At least that is so if I am right in thinking a unit is here ordered with a double, that is, the short syllable's one time with the long syllable's two.

Etudes de littérature et de rythmique grecques (Paris 1902), 200-201; Laloy, *Aristoxène de Tarente, et la musique de l'antiquité* (Paris 1904), 329. Aristides also allows a long of three times. This is, of course, a metrical question and not a rhythmical one.

---

5 Augustine here approaches the foot more from its metrical side than its rhythmical. We have already shown how Aristides Quintilianus defines the foot rhythmically, and makes the metrical foot depend on it. Likewise, Aristoxenus, having defined rhythm as a certain order of primary times, adds: 'That by which we signify the rhythm and make it known to sense, is one foot or more than one' (*op.cit.* II.81). The foot, then, he proceeds to show, is the ratio of arsis and thesis which orders the primary times. An ordered set of syllables, as Augustine says, rather than of primary times within the arsis and thesis, introduces into the notion of foot the metrical considerations of the order of longs and shorts. Marius Victorinus defines a mixture. *Pes est certus modus syllabarum, quo cognoscimus totius metri speciem, compositas ex sublatione et positione.*—'The foot is a certain measure of syllable collated from arsis and thesis, by means of which we know the species of meter' *Ars Gramm., Keil,* VI.43). But both he and Diomedes tend to confuse what the Greeks had stated clearly and with the conviction of a coherent system.

M. And what if the order should be first the long syllable and then the short syllable? But the change in order doesn't change the ratio of complicate numbers, does it? For just as in the first foot it was one to two, so in this one it is two to one.

D. That is so.

M. And in a foot of two long syllables, aren't two times compared with two times?

D. Evidently.

M. Then from what ratio is such a set taken?

D. Why from those called equals.

(5) *M.* Now tell me, how many ordered sets of feet we have treated starting from two short syllables and reaching two long syllables.

D. Four. For, first there were two shorts; second, a short and a long; third, a long and a short; and fourth, two longs.

M. There can't be more than four when the comparison is of two syllables, can there?

D. Certainly not. For, with syllables measured to give a short syllable one time and a long one two, and every syllable either short or long, how can two syllables be compared with each other or combined to make a foot otherwise than as short and short, short and long, long and short, or long and long?

M. Tell me, now, the number of times in the shortest two-syllable foot, and the number in the longest.

D. The first has two; the other, four.

M. Do you see there could be no other progression than from one to four either in feet or times?

D. I see it plainly, and I remember the ratio of progression in numbers. And with great intellectual pleasure I find that power residing here also.

M. Then, since feet consist of syllables, that is, of distinct and articulate movements of sound, and syllables are extensions of times, don't you think the progression within the foot should go to four syllables, just as the progression of feet and times goes as we have seen to four?

D. I feel about it as you say and I know it is perfectly reasonable. And what should be I want very much to see done.

Chapter 5

(6) *M.* Proceed then. First, in good order, let's see how many three-syllable feet there can be, just as we found out there were four two-syllable feet.

D. All right.

M. You remember we laid the beginning of the ratio in one short syllable, that is, in one time, and you understood well enough why it should be so.

D. I remember we resolved one must not depart from that law of counting which enjoins a start from one, the beginning of numbers.

M. Since, then, in two-syllable feet the first consists of two short syllables (for reason first demanded one time be added to one time before two times), what do you think ought to be first among three-syllable feet?

D. It could only be that composed of three short syllables.

M. And how many times is it?

D. Three, certainly.

M. Then, how are its parts compared to one another? For, according to number sets, every foot must have two parts to be compared with each other by means of some ratio. And I seem to remember we discussed this before. But can we divide this foot of three short syllables into two equal parts?

D. Not at all.

M. How is it divided, then?

D. The only way seems to be for the first part to contain one syllable and the second two, or for the first part to contain two syllables and the second one.

M. Then tell me what number pattern this is from.

D. It seems to be from the genus of complicate numbers.

(7) *M*. Well now, consider this: How many permutations are there of three syllables with one long, that is, how many different feet can be gotten from them? Answer, if you find out.

D. I find a foot consisting of one long and two shorts. I don't find any other.

M. And so you think only the foot having the long syllable in first place is a foot having one long in three?

D. No, I don't, since the two shorts can be first and the long last.

M. Think whether there is a third.

D. There clearly is, for the long can be placed between the two shorts.

M. See if there is any fourth possibility.

D. There certainly can't be.

M. Can you tell me now how many permutation there are of three syllables with one long and two shorts, that is, how many different feet they can produce?

D. I certainly can, for there were three permutations and three different feet.

M. Now, can you see at one glance how these three feet are to be ordered, or do you have to go through them one by one?

D. Because you don't like the order I found them in? For first I noticed a long and two shorts, then two shorts and a long, and finally a short and a long and a short.

M. And so you wouldn't be disturbed at an order going

from the first to the third, and from the third to the second, rather than from the first to the second and then to the third?

D. I don't like it at all. But where, I ask, have you seen that in this case?

M. Because in this tripartite differentiation you have placed that foot first containing the long syllable in first place, feeling, no doubt, the long syllable's unity gives it preeminence (if it really is a unit) and on that account ought to bring forth order by making that the first foot where it itself is first. And so you should also have seen at the same time the second foot is where it is second, and third where it is third. Or do you still think it ought to be in the order you first named them?

D. I certainly do not. For who wouldn't agree this is the better order, or rather, this is order?

M. Now, then, in what number pattern are these feet divided and their parts related?

D. The first and last I see are divided according to the equal pattern, because the first can be divided into a long and two shorts, and the last into two shorts and a long, each part, therefore, having two times and so being equal. But in the case of the second, since it has a long syllable in the middle, whether it be attributed to the first or to the second part, there is a division either into three times and one time, or into one and three. And so the ratio of complicate numbers presides at its partition.

(8) *M.* Now I want you to tell me, unaided if you can, what feet you think ought to be ordered next after those we have just been discussing. For first we discussed the two-syllable feet with an order fashioned after the order of numbers so as to begin from the short syllables. Then we undertook the longer three-syllable feet, and with an easy deduction

from former reasoning we began with three shorts. And then it was natural we should see how many forms a long syllable and two shorts would produce. And we have seen. And accordingly three feet found a necessary place after that first one. And it's up to you to see what follows next if we are not to get everything out of you by these short tedious arguments.

D. You are right. For any one would see the next feet are those with one short and the rest long. And since by former reasoning preeminence is given the shorter syllable because there is only one, that will be the first foot where it is first, second where it is second, and third where it is third, which is also the last.

M. I suppose you also see into what ratios they are divided for the comparison of their parts.

D. I certainly do. For the foot consisting of one short and two longs can only be divided to give a first part containing a short and a long and so three times, and a second part containing the one long syllable's two times. And the third foot is like the first in allowing only one division, but unlike it in the one's being divided into two and three times while the other is divided into three and two. For the long syllable occupying the first part embraces two times, and there remain a long and short, a three-time interval. But the middle foot with a middle short syllable allows a double division, because the same short syllable can be attributed to either the first or second part, and, therefore, it is divided into either two and three times or three and two. Hence the ratio of sesquate numbers dominates these three feet.

M. Have we now considered all the three-syllable feet, or does any remain?

D. I find one left consisting of three longs.

M. Then discuss its division, too.

D. Its divisions are one syllable and two or two syllables and one, that is, two times and four times or four and two. And so this foot's parts are related in the ratio of complicate numbers.

Chapter 6

(9) *M.* Now, let's consider the four-syllable feet properly and in order, and tell me yourself which of these is to be first, and give, too, the ratio of division.

D. Very evidently, there's the foot of four shorts divided into two parts of two syllables, having each two times in the ratio of equal numbers.

M. I see you understand. And so, now go on by yourself, following through with the others. For I don't think you need to be questioned through each one. For there is the method [*ratio*] of removing short syllables one by one and substituting long syllables for them until you come to all long syllables, and so of considering what varieties result and how many feet are produced as the shorts are removed and the longs substituted. And clearly, the syllable, either long or short, which is alone of its kind, holds precedence of order. And you have already had practice in these things. But when there are two shorts and two longs, a case we have not yet faced, what syllables do you think are to have precedence?

D. Now this, too, is clear from what has been done before. The short syllable with one time certainly has more unity than the long with two. And it was for that we put the foot consisting of shorts at the head and beginning of them all.

(10) *M.* There is nothing, then, to keep you from going through with all these feet while I listen and judge without questioning.

D. I shall, if I can. To begin with, one short must be subtracted from the four shorts of the first foot and one long substituted in the first place because of unity's precedence. But this foot is divided in two ways: either into one long and three shorts or into a long and short and two shorts, that is, either into two times and three times or into three and two. But when the long syllable is put second, it makes another foot with one way division, that is, into three times and two, with the first part containing a short and long and the second part two shorts. Next, when the long is put third, it makes a foot again divided one way, but in such a way the first part has two times with two short syllables, the second part three with a long and a short. A final long syllable produces the fourth foot, divided in two ways as when the long was first. For it can be split either into two shorts and into a short and long, or into three shorts and into a long, that is, into two and three times or into three and two times. And all these four feet, where the long syllable is variously placed among the three shorts, have their parts interrelated in the ratio of sesquate numbers.

(11) Next, from the four shorts we take away two and substitute two longs, and consider how many forms and feet can be produced with two longs and two shorts. Then I find two shorts and two longs are to be considered first, because the beginning is more correctly made with the shorts. But this foot has a twofold division. For it is split either into two times and four or into four times and two, so that either two shorts comprise the first part and two longs the second; or two shorts and a long comprise the first part while the remaining long comprises the second. Another foot is produced when the two shorts we placed at the beginning, according to order's demands, have been put in the middle. And the division of this foot is into three times and three. For a long

and a short syllable take up the first part, and a short and a long the second. But when they are placed last, for this is the next case, they produce a foot of two divisions, either with the first part containing two times in one long syllable and the second four times in one long syllable and two shorts, or with the first part containing four in two longs and the second two in two shorts. And the parts of these three feet are interrelated, in the case of the first and third, by a ratio of complicate numbers, and in the case of the middle, by equality.

(12) Next, these two shorts which were placed together must be split apart. It is the least separation of the two shorts we must begin with, and it is such the two shorts have a long syllable between them. And the greatest separation, such they have two between. But when one long syllable separates them, this is possible in two ways and two feet are produced. And the first of these ways is with a short syllable at the beginning followed by a long; then again a short and the remaining long. The other way is with the short syllables second and last, and the long syllables first and third; so it will be a long and a short, and a long and short. But the greatest separation occurs when the two longs are between, and the shorts are first and last. And those three feet with the short syllables separated are divided into three times and three, that is, the first into a short and long, and a short and long; the second into a long and short, and a long and short; and the third into a short and long, and a long and short. And so, six feet are produced from two short and two long syllables placed in relation to each other in as many different ways as possible.

(13) There remains the subtraction of three shorts from the four and the substitution of three longs. So there will be

one short. And a short syllable at the beginning followed by three longs makes one foot; placed second, a second foot; third, a third foot; and fourth, a fourth. And the first two of these four feet are divided into three and four times, but the last two into four and three. And they all have parts ordered in the ratio of sesquate numbers. For the first part of the first foot is a short and a long with three times, the second part is two long with four times. The first part of the second foot is a long and a short, and, therefore, three times; the second part two longs or four times. The third foot has a first part of two longs or four times; a short and long make up the second part, that is three times. Likewise, two long or four times make up the first part of the fourth foot; and a long and short or three times, the second part. The remaining foot is four syllables with all shorts removed, so that the foot consists of four longs. And it is divided into two longs and two longs according to equal numbers or into four times and four. —There you have what you wished me to explain by myself and unaided. Now you go on questioning with the rest.

Chapter 7

(14) *M.* I shall. But have you sufficiently considered to what extent that progression to four, demonstrated for numbers, is also true for feet?

D. I certainly judge this ratio of progression to exist in the ones as in the others.

M. Well, just as feet are made by joining syllables, doesn't it seem something can be made by joining feet, something called neither a foot nor a syllable?

D. It seems so.

M. And what do you think it is?

D. Verse, I suppose.

M. What if one should wish to keep adding feet together so as to impose no measure on them or no end to them except from a failing in voice, chance interruption, or the necessity of doing something else? Would you also call it a verse when it has twenty, thirty, a hundred feet or more, in any length of uninterrupted succession the person putting them together could or would wish?

D. No. For when I see feet of all sorts thrown together, many and without end, I shall not call them a verse. But I can learn from some discipline the genus and number of feet, that is, what feet and how many go to make up a verse, and judge accordingly whether I have heard verses or not.

M. Certainly, this discipline, whatever it be, has not established a rule and measure for verses in any way at all, but rather by some ratio.

D. For it should not and could not do otherwise, if it is a discipline.

M. Then, if you will, let us look for and follow out this ratio. For if we regard only authority, a verse will be whatever an Asclepiades or Archilochus, the ancient poets, or Sappho, a poetess, and others wished to be so. And the kinds of verses they first invented and sang are called by their names. For there are verses called Asclepiadean, and Archilochian, and Sapphic, and a thousand other names belonging to Greek authors have been given to verses of various kinds. And in view of this it would not be absurd to think that, if someone, to suit himself, has ordered in a certain way feet of whatever number and kind he wishes, then, just because no one before him has established this order and measure in feet, rightly and lawfully he will be called the creator and propagator of this new kind of verse. But if this sort of license is not given man, then one must ask complainingly what merit has been theirs if, following no ratio, they had the sequence of feet it pleased them to throw together considered and called a verse. Doesn't it seem so to you?

D. It is just as you say, and I certainly agree a verse is generated by ratio rather than authority. And I pray we see it right away.

Chapter 8

(15) *M.* Let us see first which feet are to be joined together; next, what is done with what has been joined, for a verse doesn't stand all by itself; finally we shall discuss the whole rationale of verse. But you don't imagine we can easily get through all this without names for the feet, do you? It is true we have arranged them so they can be called by their ordinal number; for we can say first, second, third, and so on in this way. Yet, because the old names are not to be despised and custom should not be lightly violated unless it is opposed to reason, we should use the names of feet the Greeks instituted, now in use among the Latins. And we take them over without inquiring into the origins of the names, for this matter has much talk about it and little usefulness. For in speaking you don't name bread, wood, and stone the less usefully because you don't know why they are called so.

D. I think it is certainly as you say.

M. The first foot is called a pyrrhic, constructed of two shorts, consisting of two times, as *fuga.*

The second an iamb, of a short and long, as *parens,* three times.

The third a trochee, or choree of a long and a short, as *meta,* three times.

The fourth a spondee, of two longs, as *aestas,* four times.

The fifth a tribrach, of three shorts, as *macula,* three times.

The sixth a dactyl, of a long and two shorts, as *Maenalus,* four times.

The seventh an amphibrach, of a short and a long and a short, as *carina,* four times.

The eight an anapest, of two shorts and a long, as *Erato,* four times.

The ninth a bacchius, of a short and two longs, as *Achetes,* five times.

The tenth a cretic or amphimacer, of a long and a short and a long, as *insulae,* five times.

The eleventh an antibacchius, of two longs and a short, as *natura,* five times.

The twelfth a molossus, of three longs, as *Aeneas,* six times.

The thirteenth a proceleusmatic, of four shorts, as *avicula,* four times.

The fourteenth a first paeon, of a first long and three shorts, as *legitimus,* five times.

The fifteenth, a second paeon, of a second long and three shorts, as *colonia,* five times.

The sixteenth a third paeon, of a third long and three shorts as *Menedemus,* five times.

The seventeenth a fourth paeon, of a fourth long and three shorts, as *celeritas,* five times.

The eighteenth a lesser ionic, of two shorts and two longs, as *Diomedes,* six times.

The nineteenth a choriamb, of a long and two shorts and a long, as *armipotens,* six times.

The twentieth a greater ionic, of two longs and two shorts, as *Junonius,* six times.

The twenty-first a diiamb, of a short and long and a short and long, as *propinquitas,* six times.

The twenty-second a dichoree or ditrochee, of a long and short and a long and short, as *cantilena,* six times.

The twenty-third an antispast, of a short and two longs and a short, as *Saloninus,* six times.

The twenty-fourth a first epitrite, of a first short and three longs, as *sacerdotis,* seven times.

The twenty-fifth a second epitrite, of a second short and three longs, as *conditores,* seven times.

The twenty-sixth a third epitrite, of a third short and three longs, as *Demosthenes,* seven times.

The twenty-seventh a fourth epitrite, of a fourth short and three longs, as *Fescenninus,* seven times.

The twenty-eight a dispondee, of four longs, as *oratores,* eight times.

Chapter 9

(16) *D.* I have them. Now discuss the question of which feet are joined with which.

M. You will easily decide this for yourself, if only you judge equality and similitude superior to inequality and dissimilitude.

D. I believe everyone does.

M. Then this is the principal rule to be followed in combining feet, and there should be no deviation from it without very just cause.

D. I agree.

M. You will not hesitate, then, to combine pyrrhic feet with each other, nor iambic, nor trochaic also called choric, nor spondaic. And so you will have no doubts about combining any foot with others of the same kind. For you have the greatest equality when feet are in sequence with those of their own kind and name. Wouldn't you say so?

D. I don't see any other way of looking at it.

M. So, then, you accept the principle any foot is to be combined with any other provided an equality is preserved. For what can give the ear more pleasure than being both delighted by variety and uncheated of equality?

D. I accept.

M. And only those feet having the same measure are to be considered equal, aren't they?

D. I should say so.

M. And only those with the same stretch of time are to be considered of the same measure?

D. That's true.

M. Then any feet found having the same number of times, those you will put together without offending the ear.

D. I see that follows.

Chapter 10

(17) *M.* Quite rightly. But the subject has still matter for debate. For although the amphibrach[6] is a foot of four times, certain people deny it can be mixed either with dactyls or anapests or spondees, or proceleusmatics. Yet these are all four-time feet. And they not only deny it can be joined with these feet,[7] but they think also the number does not proceed correctly and legitimately, even when amphibrach is combined with amphibrach in a repetition of itself alone.

6 This doctrine of Augustine on the amphibrach is that of Censorinus also. See. F. Amerio, Il "De Musica" di S. Agostino, *Didaskaleion,* Nuova serie 8 (Turin 1939) 173.

7 Both Aristoxenus and Aristides disallow the 1:3 ratio. Aristoxenus indeed only allows the 1:1, 1:2, and 2:3 ratios, that is, what he calls the dactylic, iambic, and paeonic. He refuses the epitritic or 3:4 ratio. Aristides accepts all four but no others. There is a good Pythagorean reason for this doctrine of Aristides and Augustine. These four ratios are exactly the ratios of the string-lengths of the intervals of coincidence, of the octave, of the perfect fifth, and of the perfect fourth, the only consonances admitted in Greek music. This establishes another correspondence between Rhythmics and Harmonics. Schäfke is also of this same opinion. See Westphal, *Aristox.* II 83-85. These ratios,

And we must consider their opinion, not to overlook a reason deserving our compliance and approval.

D. I want very much to hear what they say. For it seems to me this is very interesting, that, of the thirty-two feet given us by reason, this one alone should be excluded from the succession of numbers, occupying as it does the same time-stretch as dactyls and others equal to them just enumerated, combinations of which are not forbidden.

M. To understand this you must consider the interrelation of the parts within the other feet. For this way you will find a strange and peculiar accident in the amphibrach, well justifying the judgment it is little fit to be much applied in numbers.

(18) But in considering this we must first learn two names, the arsis [upward beat] and thesis [downward beat]. In making a beat, since the hand is raised and lowered, the arsis claims one part of the foot, the thesis the other. And I call these the parts of a foot which we discussed thoroughly a while ago in treating them in order.[8] If, then, you accept this, begin briefly recounting the measures belonging to every foot's parts, in order to find the peculiar accident of the one we are discussing.

---

for Aristoxenus and Aristides, distinguish rhythmical feet according to genus. This is the second differentia of feet for Aristoxenus of which the first is according to magnitude. There are five others of which the last is according to antithesis, mentioned in another note.

---

8 In this treatment of arsis and thesis, Augustine seems to recognize only the mechanical ictus, that is, upward and downward strokes whose only purpose is to break the rhythmical foot into parts in certain ratios. There is not a trace here of *psóphos kai eremía* of Aristides' definition quoted in our first note in this Book which, according to Nicolau's interpretation, marks the recognition of a vocal ictus accompanying the arsis. Consequently, there is no recognition by Augustine of Aristides' differentiations of feet *katá antíthesin*, a distinction which appears also in the fragments of Aristoxenus. Accord-

D. I see the first foot or pyrrhic has as much in the arsis as in the thesis. The spondee, the dactyl, the anapest, proceleusmatic, choriamb, diiamb, dichoree, antispast, and dispondee are also divided in the same ratio. For the best takes as much time going down as coming up. I see the second foot or iamb has the ratio of one to two. And I find this ratio also in the choree, tribrach, molossus, and in both ionics. Now the arsis and thesis of the amphibrach (for it comes in turn, and I look for others like it) are in the ratio of one to three. But I certainly find no other in the sequel with parts in the same relation. For when I look at those consisting of a short and two longs, that is the bacchius, cretic, and antibacchius, I find their arsis and thesis in the ratio of sesquialter numbers. There is, again, the same ratio in those four consisting of a long and three shorts, called the four paeons in order. There remain the four epitrites, similarly named in order, where the sesquitertian number dominates the arsis and thesis.

(19) *M.* You don't think it's too little reason for excluding this foot from the numerical series of sounds simply be-

---

ing to Aristoxenus: 'Feet differ from each other by antithesis in having the up-time and the down-time reversed in position. And this difference will be in feet which are equal but have an unequal order of up-times and down-times' (*op.cit.* II.84). According to Aristides: 'Difference according to antithesis occurs whenever of two feet considered, the one has the greater time first and the less time second, and the other vice-versa' (*op. cit.* I.34). Again Aristides says: '. . . rhythm is constructed from like syllables and antithetical feet. But meter is never constructed from feet having all syllables like, and rarely from antithetical feet' (*op.cit.* I.49-50).

In line with the definition of arsis and thesis of Aristides, it is interesting to consider the text of a later writer, contemporary of Augustine, Marius Victorinus: *Arsis igitur ac thesis quae Graeci dicunt, id est sublatio et positio, significant pedis motum. Est enim arsis sublatio pedis sine sono, thesis posito cum sono: item arsis elatio temporis, soni, vocis, thesis depositio et quaedam contractio syllabarum.*—'Therefore the arsis and thesis the Greeks speak of, that is rise and fall, cause its parts differ to the extent of one to three, do you? For the nearer the similarity of parts is to equality, the more worthy of consideration it is. And so, in the rule of numbers going from one to four, there is nothing nearer each one than itself. And, therefore, those feet take precedence whose parts are in relation of equality to each other. Then the union of single and double emerges in one and two; the sesquialter union in two and three; and the sesquitertian in three and four. But the single and triple, although dominated by the law of complicate numbers, are not brought together by this ordering. For we do not count three after one, but from one three is reached by way of two. And this is the reason in virtue of which the amphibrach is judged to be fittingly excluded from the combinations of feet we are now discussing. And if you agree to this, let us go on to the rest.

D. I do agree, for it is all very clear and certain.

---

signifies the motion of the foot. For arsis is the raising of the foot without sound, thesis the putting down of the foot with sound: likewise arsis is a lengthening out of the time and sound and a raising of the voice, thesis the lowering and a contraction of the syllables' (Marius Victorinus, *Ars Grammatica,* Keil, VI.40).

Nicolau finds the same combination of mechanical and vocal ictus in the text of Victorinus, and furthermore in the *'elatio vocis'* and *'contractio syllabarum'* he finds the confusion of vocal ictus and accent, an accent which is no longer musical and which becomes more and more the pivotal point of rhythm, meter, and word in accordance with the natural laws of accent of Latin. The accent becomes the 'soul of the word' and the totality of the word must be preserved in scansion. See texts of Pompeius, Capella, and Sacerdos quoted by Nicolau, *op.cit.* 65-66. It is for this reason, according to Nicolau, that the Latin metricists at times invert the use of arsis and thesis, the arsis for the strong time and the thesis for the weak. The exact meaning of the antithetical difference in Aristoxenus and Aristides and whether it is exactly the same thing in both is hard to determine. Bartels, in his *Aristoxeni Elementorum Rhythmicorum Fragmentum* (Bonn 1854) 51-52, considers it simply a difference in up-time and down-time and chides Aristides for his clumsy rendition of these terms by 'greater time' and 'less time.' Nicolau follows Desrousseaux in considering the difference to be one of strong time, the simple fact of the occurrence of a constantly repeated pattern of long times.

Chapter 11

(20) *M.* Since, then, you are willing all feet save only the amphibrach can be combined one with another regularly and without violation of the principle of equality, no matter what their mutual relations in syllables if only they are the same quantity in time, it is perhaps well to inquire whether those also are regularly combined which, although equal in time, yet do not agree in the beat where arsis and thesis throw the foot's one part against the other. For the dactyl, anapest, and spondee are not only similarly timed, but they are also beat to the same stroke. For in all of them the arsis carries equal weight with the thesis.[9] And so these are more properly put together than any of the ionics with the other feet of six times. For each of the ionics is beat to one-two time, that is, two times against four. The molossus, too, is like them in this. But the other six-time feet have equal divisions, for here three times go to the arsis and thesis each. And so, although all of them have an acceptable beat—for the first three are beat in a one-two ratio and the other four in equal parts—yet, because such a combination gives unequal strokes, I don't at all know if reason's judgment would countenance it. Or have you something to the point?

Thus a spondee in a series of dactyls would be antithetical to a spondee in a series of anapests. See Nicolau, *op.cit.* 47, n.2. Nicolau, of course, denies the existence of a vocal ictus in Aristoxenus and at any time much previous to Aristides. In any case, Augustine must have been aware of these evolutions in doctrine and practice. His *Psalm against the Donatist Faction* would seem to guarantee that. This flight of his, therefore, into a purely musical rhythmics, into a sort of metarhythmics, has more significance than has been supposed. Amerio, in his study of Augustine's sources, considers it a return to an older tradition of pure rhythmical doctrine. See F. Amerio, *op.cit.* 167-193.

---

9 Obviously arsis and thesis are not essentially different, except for the numerical division of the foot.

D. I am readier to pass judgment here. For I do not see how an unequal beat could avoid offending the sense of hearing. And if it offends, it cannot occur without a flaw in the combination.

(21) *M.* But you know the ancients judged such feet to be properly combined and they constructed verses composed this way. But, not to oppress you with authority, take a verse of that sort and see if it offends your ear. For if it should not, but rather delight you, there will be no reason for rejecting this combination. And here are the verses I wish you to listen to:

At consona quae sunt, nisi vocalibus aptes,
Pars dimidium vocis opus proferet ex se:
Pars muta soni comprimet ora molientum:
Illis sonus obscurior impeditiorque,
Utrumque tamen promitur ore semicluso.[10]

I believe that's enough for judging what I want. And so tell me now if this number hasn't been pleasing to hear.

D. True, nothing seems to me to flow and sound more agreeably.

M. Now look to the feet. You will quickly find that, of the five verses, the first two run in ionics only, and the last three have a dichoree mixed in, although all of them are equally pleasing.

D. I have already noticed this, and more readily while you recited.

M. Why, then, do we hesitate to agree with the ancients, conquered not by their authority but by the very reason of those who think feet of the same time-measure can with reason be combined if only their beat is proper although diverse?

10 Terentianus Maurus, *De Litteris*, 11. 89-93 (Keil VI,328).

D. I am ready now to give way. For their sound gives me no ground for contradiction.

Chapter 12

(22) *M.* In the same way listen to these verses:

> *Volo tandem tibi parcas, labor est in chartis,*
> *Et apertum ire per auras animum permittas.*
> *Placet hoc nam sapienter, remittere interdum*
> *Aciem rebus agendis decenter intentam.*

D. That is enough.

M. Too true, for these verses I was forced to compose on the spur of the moment are pretty rude. And yet I want to know the judgment your sense passes in the case of these four, too.

D. And here again what else is there to say except they sounded correct and smooth?

M. Do you see here, also, the first two verses are composed of second ionics, called lesser, but the last two have a diiamb thrown in?

D. I was very conscious of your putting it in when you recited.

M. Well, aren't you interested in the fact that in the verses of Terentianus a dichoree was thrown in with the ionic called greater, but in these verses of ours a diiamb has been cast in with the other ionic called lesser? Or do you think this is trivial?

D. It is quite important and I seem to see the reason. For, since the greater ionic begins with two longs, it ought rather to be joined with the dichoree where there is a first long. But the diiamb because it begins with a short is more suitably combined with the other ionic beginning with the two shorts.

(23) *M.* Your understanding is good. And so it must be held, given the equality of times, a symmetry of this kind must have some weight in combining feet. For, though it is not of the greatest importance, yet it is not negligible. For your own sense of hearing can judge any six-time foot capable of substitution for any other six-time foot. First let us have an example of a molossus, *virtutes*; then a lesser ionic, *moderatas;* then of a choriamb, *percipies;* a greater ionic, *concedere;* a diiamb, *benignitas;* a dichoree, *civitasque;* an antispast, *volet justa.*

D. I have them.

M. Then put them together and recite them, or better, listen to me recite them so your sense of hearing may be freer of its time for judging. For to introduce the equality of a continued number without offending your ears, I shall give the whole combination three times. And I am sure that will be enough. *Virtutes moderatas percipies, concedere benignitas civitasque volet justa. Virtutes moderatas percipies, concedere benignitas civitasque volet justa. Virtutes moderatas percipies, concedere benignitas civitasque volet justa.* You don't find anything in this flow of feet, do you, to rob your ears of equality and smoothness?

D. Not at all.

M. Were they pleased, then? Although, in this kind of thing, it logically follows what does not offend delights.

D. I can't say I have been affected otherwise than you expect.

M. Then your decision is, all these six-time feet can with propriety be combined and mixed.

D. It is.

Chapter 13

(24) *M.* Aren't you afraid some one may think these

feet were capable of this equal balance in sound because of this particular order, and another order would destroy it?

D. That is certainly an objection, but it is not hard to find out.

M. You will do that when there's time, and you'll only find your hearing is delighted by a single equality and a multiform difference.

D. I shall go through with it, although everyone foresees what will happen here.

M. You are right. But what is more to the point I shall run through them with the accompanying beats to enable you to decide whether there is a flaw or not. But as soon as you have made some trial of the possible permutations we have already declared harmless, make the change and, as you will, give me for recitation and rhythmical delivery these same feet placed otherwise than I had them.

D. First I want the lesser ionic, next the greater ionic, third the choriamb, fourth the diiamb, fifth the antispast, sixth the dichoree, seventh the molossus.

M. Now, fix your ears on the sound and your eyes on the beats. For the hand beating time is not to be heard but seen, and note must be taken of the amount of time given to the arsis and to the thesis.

D. I shall follow as well as I can.

M. All right, then, for the order of feet you have given me and their beats: *Moderatas, concedere, percipies, benignitas, volet justa, civitasque, virtutes.*

D. I see no flaw in the beat, and as much time is given to the arsis as to the thesis. But I certainly wonder how those feet with a division in a one-two ratio could have been beat to this time, such, for example, as the ionics and the molossus.

M. Well, what do you think is done here with three measures in each the arsis and thesis?

D. Only this, that the long syllable, second in the greater ionic and molossus, but third in the lesser ionic, is divided by the beat itself so that, of its two times, one is attributed to the first part and one to the second, and so the arsis and thesis are each allotted three times.[11]

(25) *M.* There is nothing more to be said or understood on this score. But why couldn't the amphibrach we so utterly struck from the list also be combined with the spondee, dactyl, and anapest, or itself produce a numerical or harmonious line with a succession of amphibrachs? For the middle syllable of this foot, being long, can also be divided by the beat into a like ratio, so that, when each side has in this way been given a time, the arsis and thesis no longer claim one and three times respectively, but each two. Have you anything to say to that?

D. Nothing except to say the amphibrach must also be allowed.

M. Then let us beat the time to an ordered composition of four-time feet with an amphibrach included, and find out if there is any inequality to offend this sense of hearing. And now listen to this number, given three times to facilitate a judgment. *Sumas optima, facias honesta. Sumas optima, facias honesta. Sumas optima, facias honesta.*

D. Please spare me. For, even without the accompaniment of the beat, the very flow of the feet runs away in that amphibrach.

11 This dissolution of the syllabic structure of the molossus to allow it to be beat with any other six-time foot is another sign of the character of this treatise. Everywhere we find the dissolution of the inner structure or purely metrical structure of the foot in favor of an all embracing and entirely rational arithmetic rhythmics. E. Graf has already remarked on this in his *Rhythmus und Metrum* (Marburg 1891) 66 and n.1. He points out this might well lead to the breaking up of an overlapping ionic and gives an example from Marius Victorinus.

M. What, then, is the cause what could be done in the case of the molossus and ionics cannot be done here? Is it because in the first case the sides are equal to the middle? For, six is the first even number where the sides are equal to the middle. Then, since the six-time feet have two times in the middle and two each on the sides, the middle falls in happily with the sides fitting with complete equality. But it is not the same in the amphibrach, where the sides are not equal to the middle, for there is one time in each of the sides and two in the middle. And so in the ionics and the molossus, when the middle has been dissolved into the sides, the times are three each. And in each of these sides again are found equal sides with an equal middle. And this doesn't occur in the amphibrach either.

D. It's as you say. And it's not without cause the amphibrach, put in that sequence, offends my hearing, while the others please it.

Chapter 14

(26) *M*. Come now, explain briefly on your own, as far as you can, which feet are to be mixed with which, beginning with the pyrrhic and in accordance with the ratios just given.

D. None with the pyrrhic, for no other foot with the same number of times is to be found. The choree can be combined with the iamb. But this combination is to be avoided on account of the unequal beat, for one begins with a single beat, the other with a double. And so the tribrach can be fitted in with either one. I find the spondee, dactyl, anapest, and proceleusmatic are compatible and permit of combination. For they agree not only in the number of times, but also in the beat. But the amphibrach we excluded could not be reduced by any ratio; equality of times was of no avail, for its division and beat are discordant. It is clear the cretic and first, second, and fourth paeons agree in times and beat with the bacchius. And this same cretic, and the first, third, and fourth paeons with the antibacchius. Therefore, all the other five-time feet can be combined, without any hitch, with the cretic and the first and fourth paeons, since a division can be made of them, beginning either with two or three times. It has already been sufficiently argued there is a strange agreement of all the six-time feet among themselves. For even those where the status of the syllables results in a different division do not clash in beat with the others, so great is the force of the equality of the sides with the middle. To go on, of the four seven-time feet called epitrites, I find the first and second can be combined, for the division of both begins with three times and, therefore, they disagree neither in time-interval nor in beat. Again the third and fourth are readily combined, because both have a first division of four times, and so have an equal time and beat. There remains the eight-time called dispondee, and just as with the pyrrhic there is no foot equal to it. Now you have what you asked of me and as much as I have been able to do. You go on with the rest.

M. I shall. But let's breathe a little after such a long discussion, and let's recall those verses fatigue prompted me with on the spur of the moment, a little while back.

> *Volo tandem tibi parcas, labor est in chartis,*
> *Et apertum ire per auras animum permittas.*
> *Placet hoc nam sapienter, remittere interdum*
> *Aciem rebus agendis decenter intentam.*[12]

D. I am very willing, and gladly obey.

12 'And now I want you to spare yourself (there is drudgery in letters), and to let your mind run free to the winds. For this is a judicious pleasure, to relax at times your attention when it has been properly strained to business.'

BOOK THREE

The difference between rhythm, meter, and verse; then rhythm is discussed separately; and next the treatise on meter begins.

Chapter 1

(1) *M.* Now, since enough has been said about the harmony and agreement of feet among themselves, this third discussion warrants our seeing what arises from their composition and from the sequences of them. And so first I ask you whether those feet which can properly be put together can be combined to create a sort of continuing number without definite end, as when chorus-boys beat castanets and cymbals with their feet according to numbers whose combinations are pleasing to the ear, but yet in an unending flow so that, unless you should hear the flutes, you could in no way mark how far the combination of feet runs forward and from where it returns to begin again. It's as if you should want a hundred pyrrhics or more, as many as you please, or any other feet belonging together, to run on in continuous combination.

D. I now understand, and I agree a certain combination of feet can be made in which it is fixed just how many feet the progression is to be, before it starts over again.

M. Then you are not doubting the existence of this sort of thing, since you don't deny there's a certain discipline for making verses, you who have always confessed to hearing them with pleasure?

D. It's evident there's such a thing, and that it's distinct from the other kind we talked about before.

(2) *M.* Then, since it's proper for things distinct from each other to be distinguished by names, it's well to learn the first kind of combination is called rhythm by the Greeks; the second, meter. In Latin they could be called, the first, number [*numerus*]; the second, measure [*mensio or mensura*].[1] But, since these names are very current with us, and since we must be careful not to speak ambiguously, we find the use of the Greek names more convenient. Yet you see, I believe, how correctly each of these names is imposed. For, since there is a rolling forward in fixed feet, and a hitch if dissonant feet are mixed together, this sort of thing is rightly called rhythm or number. But, because the rolling forward has no measure, and there has been no decision as to what foot is to be used as a definite end, this ought not to be called meter because there is an absence of measure in the succession. But meter has both: it runs in fixed feet and in fixed measure. And so it is not only meter because of a distinct end, but it is also rhythm be-

1 The result of Augustine's theories is seen clearly in this definition of meter, as Graf has pointed out. It is not a new definition, but other writers usually give it, along with the other definitions stressing the strictly metrical qualities of the foot.

To say meter is simply the measuring off of rhythm is to deny anything specifically metrical. Quite different is the approach of Aristides Quintilianus; for him, meter is the differentiation within the rhythmical foot, its inner structure. But for Augustine, only two things are demanded: that the feet be equal in length and that the ratio of their parts be the same. There is no mention of rhythmical modulation as in Aristides. The real differentiation between arsis and thesis is ignored as something outside of the rhythm.

Many scholars consider this definition to be from Varro, but Aristides also gives it among others and Diomedes reports Varro as giving quite another '*inter rythmum, qui latine numerus vocatur, et metrum hoc inherere, quod inter materiam et regulam.*' See Graf, *op.cit.* 64.

Amerio points out that Censorinus, one of the oldest of the metricists, gives also the same notion of homogeneity of meter: '*Numerus est aequalium pedum legitima ordinatio.*' See Amerio, *op. cit.* 168-172.

cause of the rational composition of feet. And so all meter is rhythm, but not all rhythm is meter. For the name rhythm makes such an extensive appearance in music that the whole part of it having to do with longs and shorts has been called rhythm. But it has seemed good to both the learned and the wise that there need be little trouble about the name since the thing itself is clear. Or do you perhaps have something to oppose, or think there ought to be some doubt about what I have said?

D. On the contrary, I agree with you.

Chapter 2

(3) *M.* Now then, consider this question with me: Whether just as all verse is meter, so all meter is verse.

D. I am considering the question, but I find nothing to reply.

M. Why do you think you have gotten into this difficulty? Isn't it because it's a question of names? For we can't reply to a question about names as to one about things belonging to a discipline, because things are implanted in the minds of all in common, but names are imposed arbitrarily, and their force depends for the most part on authority and usage. And so there can be a diversity in tongues, but in the very truth of constituted things there certainly cannot be. Take from me, then, what you could nowise get for yourself: the ancients spoke of meter, not verse only. And so, what you are to do is to say and see (for it is not a matter of names) whether there is a difference between the following two things: the one case where a certain number of feet are so defined by a fixed end there is nothing in the way of an articulation before this end is reached; the other case where there is not only a closure by a fixed end, but also before the end a division appears in a definite place to produce two members as it were.

D. I don't understand.

M. Listen to these examples:

Ite igitur, Camoenae
Fonticolae puellae,
Quae canitis sub antris
Mellifluos sonores;
Quae lavitis capillum
Purpureum Hippocrene
Fonte, ubi fusus olim
Spumea lavit almus
Ora jubis aquosis
Pegasus, in nitentem
Pervolaturus aethram.

You certainly see the first five of these so-called versicles have the break in discourse in the same place, that is, at the choriambic foot, to which is added a bacchius to complete the versicle (for these eleven versicles consist of choriambic and bacchic feet, but the others, except one, namely, *Ora jubis aquosis,* do not have the break in discourse in that same place.

D. I see that, but I don't see what it's about.

M. Why so you may understand, this meter doesn't have a place somehow laid down by law for a break in discourse before the end of the verse. For if it did, all would have this articulation in the same place or at least one which didn't would be rarely found among them. But, here of these eleven, six do, and five do not.

D. I see that and I am still waiting to see where reason is going.

M. Well, listen then to the well-worn words, *Arma virum-*

que cano, Troiae qui primis ab oris.[2] And not to take up time, since the poem is very well known, exploring each verse as far as you wish, you will always find a part of the discourse completed in the fifth half-foot, that is, two and a half feet from the beginning. For these verses consist of feet of four times, and so this completion of a part of the discourse in the tenth time is laid down by law, you might say.

D. That's evident.

(4) *M.* Then you see there is a difference in the two kinds I have just given examples of. For one meter before its close has clearly no fixed and determined division, as we saw in those eleven little verses, but the other has, as the fifth half-foot in the heiroic meter sufficiently indicates.

D. What you say is now clear.

M. Now the first kind, you should know, is not called verse by the learned men among the ancients in whom there is great authority, but that is defined as verse and so called which consists, you might say, of two members joined in a fixed measure and ratio. But don't trouble yourself too much about a name you couldn't possibly come out with on any amount of questioning without its being thrown at you by me or someone else. But what reason teaches, keep your mind first and foremost on that, as we are now doing. For reason teaches there is a difference between these two kinds, no matter what names they are called by. And so, if questioned correctly, you could put your finger on the difference, confident in the truth itself, but the names you couldn't without following authority.

D. I was already very clear about that. And what you so constantly harp on I now consider as important as you do.

M. Then I want you to learn by heart these names we are

---

2 Vergil, *Aeneid* 1.1.

forced to use from the necessities of discourse itself: rhythm, meter, and verse. And these are distinct in such a way that all meter is also rhythm, but not all rhythm meter. And likewise that all verse is also meter, but not all meter verse. Therefore, all verse is rhythm and meter. For you see, I am sure, this follows.

D. I certainly do, for it's clearer than light.

Chapter 3

(5) *M.* First, then, if you will, let's discuss as far as we can the rhythm that's without meter, then the meter without verse, and finally verse itself.

D. Very willingly.

M. Now, take from your own head pyrrhic feet, and compose a rhythm of them.

D. And now if I should be able to do this, what will be its length?

M. It will be enough to extend it (for we are doing it as an example) up to ten feet. For verse, which will be thoroughly discussed in its proper place, does not go as far as this number of feet.

D. You do well not to ask me to put many feet together. But just the same you don't seem to me to remember you have already sufficiently distinguished the difference between the grammarian and the musician when I told you I didn't possess the knowledge of long and short syllables, a knowledge passed down by grammarians. Unless, perhaps you let me show the rhythm in beats and not in words. For I don't deny I am capable of ear-judgments for regulating the values of times. But as to what syllables are to be pronounced long or short, since it's a matter of authority, I am altogther ignorant.

M. I admit we distinguished a grammarian from a musician in the way you say, and you confessed your ignorance of this sort of thing. And so take this by way of example from me: *Ago celeriter agile quod ago tibi quod anima velit.*

D. I have it.

(6) *M.* Now, by repeating this as many times as you will, you could make the length of this rhythm as great as you wished, although these ten feet are enough for an example. But I want to know this. If anyone should tell you this rhythm is composed not of pyrrhic feet but of proceleusmatics, what will you say?

D. I certainly don't know. For where there are ten pyrrhics I can measure five proceleusmatics, and therefore there is a greater doubt about the decision to be made in the case of a rhythm flowing on without stop. For eleven or thirteen or any odd number of pyrrhics cannot contain a whole number of proceleusmatics. And so, if there were a fixed end to the rhythm in question, we could at least say it ran rather in pyrrhics than in proceleusmatics in the case where all the feet would not be whole proceleusmatics. But this infinity confounds our judgment even when the feet are counted out for us, but in an even number, as these ten are.

M. But the question isn't even clear as it seemed to you in the case of the uneven number of pyrrhics. For what if, given eleven pyrrhic feet, one should say they are five and a half proceleusmatics? What's wrong with that since we find many verses closing with a half-foot?

D. I have already said I don't see what to do about this matter.

M. But you aren't at a loss about this, are you, that, if the proceleusmatic is made of two pyrrhics, then the pyrrhic is prior to the proceleusmatic? For, just as one is prior to two, and two to four, so the pyrrhic is prior to the proceleusmatic.

D. That's very true.

M. Then, since we fall into this ambiguity of both the pyrrhic's and the proceleusmatic's being measured in the one rhythm, to which are we to give preference? To the prior one the other is composed of, or to the secondary one the other is not composed of?

D. To the prior one certainly.

M. Why, then, on being consulted about this do you hesitate to reply this rhythm is to be called pyrrhic rather than proceleusmatic?

D. I don't hesitate at all now. I am ashamed at not having immediately noticed such an evident reason.

Chapter 4

(7) *M.* Do you now see by this reasoning you are forced to the conclusion there are certain feet not able to continue the rhythm uninterruptedly? For, what was found to be true of the proceleusmatic with its priority usurped by the pyrrhic can also be proved, I think, for the dichoree and the diiamb. Or does it appear otherwise to you?

D. How can it, for, after the reason has been established, I cannot disprove what follows from it.

M. Then consider all this too, and compare and judge. For it seems when such an uncertainty occurs the distinction ought to be made by the beat rather than by the foot it runs in. And so if you wish to run in pyrrhics, you'll have one time for the arsis, one for the thesis; if in proceleusmatics, two and two. And in this way the foot will be unambiguous, and no foot will be excluded from a purely rhythmical succession.

D. I am more inclined toward the opinion leaving no foot free of this kind of succession.

(8) *M.* You are right, and for your greater approval think what we could reply in the case of the tribrach, if someone should further contend this rhythm runs not in pyrrhics or proceleusmatics, but in tribrachs.

D. I see judgment must be referred to the beat, so that, if there is one time in the arsis and two in the thesis, that is one and two syllables, or if two in the arsis and one in the thesis, the rhythm is said to be tribrach.

M. That's right. Therefore, tell me now whether the spondaic foot can be joined with the pyrrhic rhythm.

D. Not at all. For the same beat will not continue, since the arsis and thesis in the pyrrhic have each one time, but in the spondee each two times.

M. Then it can be joined with the proceleusmatic.

D. It can.

M. Then suppose it is, what will we say when we are asked whether the rhythm is proceleusmatic or spondaic?

D. How can you decide, unless preference is to be given the spondee? For since the beat does not here decide the case—in both rhythms the arsis and thesis take two times—what else is there to do except to prefer that which is prior in the order of feet?

M. I quite approve the reasoning you have followed. And you see, I am sure, what that entails.

D. Well, what?

M. Why that no other foot can be mixed with the proceleusmatic rhythm. For whatever foot consisting of the same times is mixed in—and otherwise the mixing is not possible—the name of the rhythm would necessarily be transferred to it. For all those feet consisting of the same number of times are prior to the proceleusmatic. And since reason forces us, as we have seen, to prefer the prior, that is, to name the rhythm by them, there will no longer be any proceleusmatic rhythm with some other four-time rhythm mixed in, but a spondaic or dactylic or anapestic rhythm. For it is agreed the amphibrach is rightly excluded from the composition of such numbers.

D. I admit it's so.

(9) *M*. Now, next in order let's consider the iambic rhythm, since we have now sufficiently discussed the pyrrhic and proceleusmatic born of the double pyrrhic. And so tell me what foot is to be mixed in, with the iambic rhythm's still keeping its name.

D. Why, the tribach, of course, agreeing as it does in beat and times. And yet, being posterior, it cannot prevail over the iambic. The choree is also posterior and of the same number of times, but it hasn't the same beat.

M. Now examine the trochaic rhythm, and here again give me a reply to the same purpose.

D. My reply is the same, for the tribach can fit in with it not only in extent of time but also in beat. But it's clear the iambic must under these conditions be avoided. For even if it were of equal beat, yet in the mixing it would carry off the palm.

M. And further, what foot shall we compound with the spondaic rhythm?

D. In this case there is evidently a very great number of choices. For I see the dactyl, the anapest, and the proceleusmatic can be mixed in with it without inequality of times, without any hitch in the beat, and without claims of priority.

(10) *M*. I see now you can easily explain the others in order. And so without my questioning, or rather as if questioned about them all, tell as briefly and clearly as you can how each of the remaining feet, with others lawfully mixed in, gets its name in the rhythm.

D. I shall. For it's no trouble with such a light of reasons cast before. And none will be mixed with the tribach, for all equal to it in time are prior to it. The anapest can be mixed with the dactyl, for it is posterior and runs in equal time and beat. But the proceleusmatic is compounded with both for the same reason. Now the cretic, and the first, second, and fourth paeons can be mixed with the bacchius. Further, all the five-time feet after the cretic are by right mixed with the cretic itself, but they are not all of the same division. For, some are divided in the ratio of two to three, and others of three to two. But the cretic can be divided both ways, because the middle short is attributed to either part. But the antibacchius, because its division begins with two times and ends with three, is suited to, and composable with, all the paeons except the second. Of the trisyllabic feet there remains only the molossus, the beginning of the six-time feet, all of which can be joined with it: partly on account of the one-two ratio, and partly on account of that partition of the long syllable giving up to each part one time, because in the num-six the middle is equal to the sides. And therefore the mollossus and both ionics can be given not only a one-two beat, but also a three-three beat in equal parts. And so all posterior six-time feet can be compounded with any six-time foot. And so there is only the antispast allowing no mixture. The four epitrites follow: the first accepting the second; the second, none; the third, the fourth; and the fourth none. And finally there is the dispondee, it, too, beating out its rhythm only alone, because it finds no foot posterior to it or equal to it. And so of all the feet there are eight giving rhythm of their own only if no other foot is mixed in: the pyrrhic, tribrach, proceleusmatic, fourth paeon, antispast, second and fourth epitrites, and dispondee. The others allow those posterior to them to be compounded with them without dropping their name from the rhythm even if they are fewer. And this, I believe, is what you wanted of me, sufficiently digested and explained. It is up to you now to explain what is left.

Chapter 5

(11) *M*. And up to you, too, along with me, for we are both in the search. But what do you think there is left to say about rhythm? Isn't it pertinent to find out if there isn't a foot more than four syllables in length although it doesn't exceed the eight times of the dispondee?

D. Why, I ask?

M. And you, why do you ask me rather than yourself? Or don't you think two short syllables can be substituted for one long without deceiving or offending the ear either with respect to the beat and division of feet or to the matters concerning time?

D. Who would deny they could?

M. And so in this way we substitute a tribrach for an iamb or choree, and a dactyl or anapest or proceleusmatic for a spondee, when we substitute two shorts for the second long or for the first, or four shorts for both longs.

D. I agree.

M. Do this same thing in any ionic, or in any other four-syllable foot of six times, and substitute two shorts for any one long. There is no loss in the time or hitch in the beat, is there?

D. Not at all.

M. Let's see, then, how many syllables there are.

D. I see there are five.

M. You see, then, the four syllables can certainly be exceeded.

D. I certainly do.

M. And what if you should substitute four shorts for the two longs there? Wouldn't six syllables have to be measured in one foot?

D. So they would.

M. What if you dissolve all the longs of any epitrite into shorts? It would certainly make seven syllables, wouldn't it?

D. Certainly.

M. And what about the dispondee? Doesn't it make eight syllables when we substitute two shorts each for all the longs?

D. That's very true.

(12) *M.* What, then, is this ratio we are forced to measure feet of so many syllables by, and do we admit in accordance with ratios already discussed a foot used for numbers does not exceed four syllables? Don't these seem to you contradictory?

D. Very much so, and I don't see how it can be patched up.

M. This is easy enough, if you again ask yourself whether a while back we rationally established the pyrrhic and proceleusmatic ought to be determined and distinguished by beat so there might be no foot lawfully divided not producing a rhythm, that is, not having a rhythm named after it.

D. I certainly remember this, and I don't see why I should have misgivings about its having seemed right to me. But where is this leading?

M. Well, clearly all the four-syllable feet, except the amphibrach, produce a rhythm, that is, they hold priority in rhythm, and bring it about in use and name. But many having more than four syllables can be substituted for these, yet they cannot themselves produce the rhythm nor impose their name upon it. And so I shouldn't have thought they ought to be called feet. And therefore those contradictions troubling us are now, I believe, arranged and laid at rest when it is possible to substitute more syllables than four for any foot and yet not to call foot anything not producing a rhythm. For it was proper to establish for the foot some measure of syllable-progression. But that measure could best be established, transferred from the ratio of numbers and consisting in fours. And so there could be a foot of four long syllables. And when, instead, we construct one of eight shorts, occupying the same interval of time, it can be substituted for the other. But because the eight shorts exceed the lawful progression, that is, the number four, not the sense of hearing but the law of the discipline forbids their being substituted for it and producing a rhythm.—Perhaps you wish to oppose?

(13) *D.* I very much intend to, and I shall do so right now. For what kept the foot from going on up to eight syllables, since we see that number can be allowed as far as rhythm is concerned? And your saying it can be substituted for another doesn't move me, but on the contrary it puts me in mind to ask about or, rather, to complain about a thing's being substituted for another without also taking over its own name.

M. It's not surprising you are deceived, but there's an easy explanation of the truth. For, omitting the many things already disputed in favor of the number four, and why the syllable-progression should only go so far, suppose I have given in to you and have agreed the length of a foot ought to be extended to eight syllables. You can't object, then, to the possibility of a foot of eight long syllables? For, certainly, the maximum length of a foot in terms of syllables applies alike to both longs and shorts. And so, when the law permitting the substitution of two shorts for a long is again applied—and it can't be cut short—we get to sixteen syllables. And at that point if you should want again to decree the foot's increase, we arrive at thirty-two shorts. Your reason compels you to bring the foot that far, too, and the law again compels you to substitute a double number of shorts for the longs. And in this way no limit will be established.

D. Well I give in to your reason of taking the foot only as far as four syllables. But I don't reject the fact it's proper for feet of more syllables to be substituted for these legitimate feet, with two shorts in the place of one long.

Chapter 6

(14) *M*. Then it is easy for you also to see and agree there are certain feet put in place of those having priority in rhythm, others which are placed with them. For, where two shorts are substituted for each long, we put another foot in place of the one holding the rhythm: for example, a tribrach in place of an iamb or trochee, or a dactyl or anapest or proceleusmatic in place of a spondee. But where that is not the case, whatever lower foot is mixed in is placed with, not in place of: for example, an anapest with a dactyl, and a diiamb or a dichoree with either ionic, and similarly for the others according to their peculiar laws. Or does this seem false to you, or too obscure?

D. No, I understand now.

M. Then tell me whether the feet put in place of others can also produce rhythms on their own.

D. They can.

M. All?

D. All.

M. Then even a five-syllable foot can produce a rhythm in its own name, because it can be put in place of a bacchius or cretic or any of the paeons.

D. But it cannot. For we no longer call this a foot, if I

remember well enough the progression to four. But when I replied all could, I replied only feet could.

M. And I praise your diligence and vigilance in retaining a name. But it is true, you know, many have thought it proper for even six-syllable groups to be called feet. Yet, as far as I know, for more than that no one has thought it proper. And even those favoring the six-syllable foot have denied its applicability in producing a rhythm or meter of its own. And so it wasn't even given a name. And so the four-syllable measure of progression is the truest, since all those feet, at whose division two cannot be made, have been able, joined together, to make a foot. And so, those who have gone as far as the sixth syllable have dared give only the name of foot to those exceeding the fourth syllable; but they have not allowed them to aspire to the domination of rhythms and meters. But when the shorts are substituted by twos for the longs, even the seventh and eight syllables are reached, as reason has already shown. But no one has extended the foot this far. But since I see we have agreed any foot of more than four syllables, when we have substituted two shorts for each long, can be put in place of, but not with, the legitimate feet and cannot create a rhythm of its own, lest in this way things determined by reason go on to infinity, let us pass on to meter, if you will, having, I belived, talked enough about rhythm.

D. I am willing, certainly.

Chapter 7

(15) *M.* Tell me, then, would you say meter is made of feet or feet of meter?

D. I don't understand.

M. Do feet joined together produce meter, or meters joined together produce feet?

D. I know now what you are saying, and I think meter is produced by the joining together of feet.

M. But why do you think that?

D. Because you said there was this difference between rhythm and meter: in rhythm the conjunction of feet has no determinate end, but in meter it has. So this joining together of feet is understood to belong to both rhythm and meter, but in one case it is infinite, in the other finite.

M. Then one foot is not a meter.

D. Not at all.

M. What about a foot and a half?

D. That isn't, either.

M. Why? Is it because meter is made of feet, and that can't be called feet where there is less than two?

D. That's it.

M. Then let's look at those meters I recited a while back and see what feet they consist of, for it's no longer right you should be untrained in discerning this sort of thing. They were:

Ite igitur Camoenae
Fonticolae puellae,
Quae canitis sub antris
Mellifluos sonores.

I think these are enough for what I intend. Measure them, now, and tell me what feet they consist of.

D. I am altogether unable to do it. I believe those feet are to be measured that can be legitimately put together, and I can't see my way out of this. For if I should make the first a choree, an iamb follows, equal in times, but not the same in beat. And if I should make the first a dactyl, nothing follows even equal in time. If a choriamb, there's the same difficulty, for what's left over doesn't agree with it either in time or beat. Then, either this is not meter or what we said about the joining together of feet is false. For I don't see what else I can say.

(16) *M.* And by the ear's judgment it is certainly proved to be meter, both because it is more than one foot and because it has a determinate ending. For it would not sound with such sweet equality or be beaten with such a skillfully adjusted motion, if there were not some numerical quality in it proper only to this part of music. But I am surprised you think false those things we decided on, for nothing is surer than numbers, or more orderly than the recitation and placing of feet. For we have seen whatever is expressed in the nowise deceptive ratio of numbers is capable of delighting the ear and dominating rhythm. But rather listen as I keep repeating *Quae canitis sub antris*, and charm your senses with its numerical quality. What difference is there between this and what results from the adding of a short syllable also repeated in this same way, *Quae canitis sub antrisve*?

D. To my ears both seem to flow agreeably. Yet I am forced to admit the second you added a short syllable to occupies more space and time, if it has been made longer.

M. And when I repeat the first, *Quae canitis sub antris,* in such a way I don't stop at all after the ending? Do you experience the same pleasure?

D. I don't know what sort of hitch it is here offending me unless perhaps you drew out that last syllable more than other long ones.

M. Then do you think either what is more extended or what is given as a rest [*siletur*][3] have both a time-value?

D. How can it be otherwise?

3 The doctrine of rests and their wide use are not just Augustinian novelties as many have thought, but they are traditional rhythmical

Chapter 8

(17) *M.* You are right. But tell me what interval you think there is.

D. It's very hard to measure.

M. That's true. But doesn't that extra short syllable seem to measure it? And when we added it on, doesn't it seem your senses didn't demand any unusual lengthening of the last long or any rest [*silentium*] as the meter was repeated?

D. I entirely agree. For while you were just reciting and repeating the first, I was repeating the second after you to myself in the same way. And so, since my last short exactly fitted your rest, I sensed the same time-interval occurs in both.

M. Then you must hold there are fixed rest-intervals in meters. And so when you have found some defect in a regular foot, you ought to consider whether there will be compensation when the rest has been measured and accounted for.

D. I now understand that. Go on.

(18) *M.* It seems to me we ought now to examine the measurement of rest itself. For in this meter where we found the bacchius after the choriamb, the ear very easily sensed the one time's lack to make it six like the choriamb, and forced us, in repetition, to interpose a rest length of a short syllable. But if a spondee should be placed after the choriamb, on repeating it we have to cross a two-time rest, as in this case,

---

and musical elements. Thus in Aristides: 'An empty time is one without sound for the filling out of the rhythm. A leimma in rhythm is the least empty time; a prothesis is a long empty time, double the least' (*op.cit.* 40-41).

Amerio reports two other places. One is the Paris Fragment where the word for rest is *siópesis*. The other is in the scholiast of Hephaestion and worth quoting: 'Heliodorus says that a foot-division in paeons is perfectly regular practice, so that the rest gives a time, makes the rhythmical unit six-timed and in a 1 to 1 ratio like the others.' See Amerio, *op. cit.* 177 n.1.

Quae canitis fontem. For I believe you now feel there ought to be a rest, for the beat not to hit amiss when we return to the beginning. But in order for you to experience the time of this rest, add a long syllable to have, for example, *Quae canitis fontem vos*, and repeat this with the beat. You will see the beat occupies as much time as it did before, although in the first case two longs are placed after the choriamb, in the other three. And so it appears a two-time rest is put in there. But if an iamb is placed after the choriamb, as, for example, *Quae canitis locos,* we are forced to a three-time rest. To experience it, the times are added either by means of another iamb or by a choree or by a tribrach, to have, for example, either *Quae canitis locos bonos* or *Quae canitis locos monte* or *Quae canitis locos nemore*. For since with these added an harmonious and equable repetition moves on without a rest, and since with the beat applied each of these three is found to occupy just such a time-interval as with a rest, evidently there is a three-time rest there. Again, one long syllable can be put after the choriamb to give a four-time rest. For the choriamb can also be divided so as to have an arsis and thesis in a one-two ratio. An example of this meter is *Quae canitis res*. And if you add to this either two longs, or a long and two shorts, or a short and a long, and a short, or two shorts and a long, or four shorts, you will fill out a six-time foot bearing repetition without need of a rest. Such are *Quae canitis res pulchras, Quae canitis res in bona, Quae canitis res bonumve, Quae canitis res teneras,* and *Quae canitis res modo bene*. With these things known and agreed to, I believe it is already evident enough to you there cannot be a rest less than one time or more than four. For this is that very same measured progression so much has already been said about. And in any foot no arsis or thesis takes more than four times.

(19) And so when something is sung or recited having a determinate ending, more than one foot, and a natural motion pleasing the senses by a certain equableness even before consideration of the numbers involved, then it is already meter. For though it should have less than two feet, yet because it exceeds one foot and forces a rest, it is not without measure, but what is needed for filling out the times is owing the second foot. Instead of two feet, the ear accepts what occupies the times of two feet up to the return to the beginning of the foot, with the fixed and measured silence of the interval also counted out by sound. But I want you to tell me now whether you understand and agree with what has been said.

D. I understand and agree.

M. Do you simply believe, or do you see for yourself they are true?

D. For myself certainly, although it's from your talk I know they are true.

Chapter 9

(20) *M.* Come, then, since we have now found out where meter starts, let's also find out where it ends. For meter begins with two feet, either filled by sound, or to be filled with whatever the numericaly determined silence lacks. And therefore you must now consider that fourfold progression, and tell me to what number of feet we ought to extend meter.

D. That is certainly easy. For reason teaches eight feet are enough.

M. Well, do you remember we said that is called a verse by the learned consisting of two members joined and measured in fixed ratio?

D. I remember it well.

M. Then, since it was not said a verse consists of two feet, out of two members, and since it is clear a verse hasn't one foot but several, doesn't this very fact indicate a member is longer than a foot?

D. So it does.

M. But if the members of a verse are equal, can't the order be inverted so, without distinction, the first part becomes the last, and the last first?

D. I see.

M. Then to keep this from happening and to have one thing in the verse sufficiently apparent and discernible as the member it begins with, and another as the member it ends with, we must admit the members have to be unequal.

D. That's so.

M. Let's consider this first then in the case of the pyrrhic, if you will, where I believe you have already seen there can't be a number of less than three times, since that's the first greater than a foot.

D. I agree.

M. Then how many times will the least verse possess?

D. I would say six, if the inversion you spoke of didn't belie me. It will have seven then, because a member cannot have less than three, but to have more is not yet gainsaid it.

M. Your understanding is right. But tell me how many feet seven times contain.

D. Three and a half.

M. Then a one-time rest is due before the return to the beginning, to fill out the foot's interval.

D. It is certainly due.

M. How many times will there be when this is counted in?

D. Eight.

M. Then as the least which is the first foot cannot have less than two times, so the least which is the first verse cannot have less than eight times.

D. So it is.

M. What is the largest verse than which there is no greater and how many times must there be? Won't you see immediately if we refer back to that progression so much has been said about?

D. Now I see a verse can't be greater than thirty-two times.

(21) *M.* What about the length of meter? Do you think it ought to be greater than verse, since the least meter is much less than the least verse?

D. I do not.

M. Since, then, meter begins with two feet, verse with four, or the first with a two-foot interval, the second with four if the rest is counted in, but since meter does not exceed eight feet, doesn't verse, being also meter, necessarily not exceed too that same number of feet?

D. That is so.

M. Again, since verse can't be longer than thirty-two times, and since meter is a length of verse if it does not have a conjunction of two members such as is the rule in verse, but is only closed with a determinate ending, and since it must not be longer than verse, isn't it evident just as verse should not exceed eight feet so meter should not exceed thirty-two times?

D. I agree.

M. There will be, then, a same time-interval and a same number of feet both in verse and meter, and a certain common limit beyond which neither should progress, although meter is bounded by a fourfold number of times for its beginning, and verse by a fourfold number of feet[4] for its beginning. And so this quaternary ratio is kept, and meter evidently shares with verse its manner of expansion in feet, verse with meter in times.

D. I understand and am satisfied, and I am delighted they agree and are in harmony this way.

4 I have interchanged the terms 'times' and 'feet.'

BOOK FOUR

The treatise on meter is continued.

Chapter 1

(1) *M.* Let's return to the consideration of meter. It was in connection with its length and expansion I was forced to talk with you a little on verse which we decided was to be treated afterwards. But first, tell me if you don't reject the opinion of poets and their critics, the grammarians, thinking it of no importance whether the last syllable ending the meter be short or long.

D. I certainly do. For this doesn't seem rational.

M. Then tell me, please, what pyrrhic meter is shortest.

D. Three shorts.

M. What quantity must the rest be when it is repeated?

D. One time, the length of one short syllable.

M. Come now, carry this meter through, not by voice but by beat.

D. I have.

M. Then beat out the anapest this way, too.

D. I have also done that.

M. What's the difference?

D. None at all.

M. Well, can you give the cause?

D. It seems clear enough. For what is ascribed to the rest in one is ascribed to the lengthening of the last syllable in the other. For the short syllable in the one case is given the same beat as the long in the other, and after an equal interval there is a return to the beginning. But, in the first case there is a stop to fill the space of a pyrrhic foot; in the second, to fill that of a long syllable. So in each there is an equal delay before we return.

M. Then they haven't been so absurd in saying it makes no difference whether the last syllable of the meter is long or short. For the ending is followed by as great a rest as necessary to finish out the meter. Or do you think in this matter of the cause they ought to have considered some repetition or return to the beginning, and not only the fact it ends as if nothing were to be said after it?

D. I now agree the last syllable must be considered indifferently.

M. Right. But if this is due to the rest, it being in this way considered the end as if no sound were to follow it to give it an ending, and if because of the very large time-span in the rest it makes no difference what syllable is pronounced there, doesn't it follow the very indifference of the last syllable, conceded on account of the large interval, comes to this that whether there be a long or short syllable there, the ear always takes it as long?

D. I see that certainly follows.

Chapter 2

(2) *M*. And when we say the last pyrrhic meter is three short syllables with a rest for the space of one short before the return to the beginning, do you see, too, there is no difference between repeating this meter and repeating anapests?

D. I already saw this a while ago in the beat.

M. Don't you think the confusion here ought to be separated out by some ratio?

D. I certainly do.

M. Tell me, do you find any ratio to distinguish them except the pyrrhic meter in three shorts is not a minimum as it seemed, but in five? For the similarity of the anapest doesn't allow us, after a foot and a half, to rest for the space of the half necessary to fill out the foot and so to return to the beginning, and to establish this as the minimum pyrrhic meter. Therefore, if we wish to avoid confusion, that one time is to be taken as a rest at the end of two and a half feet.

D. But why aren't two pyrrhics the minimum meter in pyrrhics, and rather four short syllables without a rest than five with a rest?

M. Quite on the lookout, but you aren't noticing the proceleusmatic forbids this just as the anapest did the other.

D. You are right.

M. Do you agree, then, to this measure in five shorts and a one-time rest?

D. I certainly do.

M. Well, it seems to me you have quite forgotten the method we set up for discerning whether a rhythm was running in pyrrhics or proceleumatics.

D. You are right in warning me, for we found these numbers were to be distinguished from each other by beat. And so in this case I am no longer afraid of the proceleusmatic, for I can distinguish it from the pyrrhic when the beat is applied.

M. Why didn't you see this same beat is to be applied to distinguish the anapest from those three shorts or pyrrhic and a half, followed by a one-time rest?

D. Now I understand, and I go back and confirm the least pyrrhic meter as three syllables occupying with an added rest the time of two pyrrhics.

M. Then your ears approve this sort of number: *Si aliqua, Bene vis, Bene dic, Bene fac, Animus, Si aliquid, Male vis, Male dic, Male fac, Animus, Medium est.*

D. They do, especially when I now remember how they are to be beaten out so anapests aren't confused with pyrrhic meter.

(3) *M*. Consider these, too: *Si aliquid es, Age bene, Male qui agit, Nihil agit, Et ideo, Miser erit.*

D. These too run harmoniously, except in one place, where the end of the third is joined with the beginning of the fourth.

M. That's just what I wanted of your ears. It's not for nothing they are offended, since they expect one time each for all syllables and no rests between. But the concourse of two consonants, '*t*' and '*n*,' immediately cheat this expectation, forcing the preceding vowel to be long and extending it to two times. And the grammarians call this kind a syllable long by position. But because of that famous indifference of the last syllable no one incriminates this meter, even though unspoiled and exacting ears condemn it without benefit of an accuser. For see, if you will, the difference there is, if for *Male qui agit, Nihil agit* you should say *Male qui agit, Homo perit.*

D. This is quite clear and right.

M. Then, for the sake of musical purity let us observe what the poets do not observe for the facility of composing. So, for example, as often as we must put in meters where nothing is owing the foot to be compensated by a rest, so often do we put those syllables last the law of that number absolutely demands, so as not to return from the end to the beginning with offense to the ear and falsity of measure. But we concede, of course, there are meters ending as if nothing were to be said following them, and in that case they may treat the last syllable as either long or short with impunity. For in a succession of meters they are clearly convicted of error by the ear's judgment that no syllable is to be placed last except by the law and ratio of the meter itself. But this succession exists when nothing is owing the foot to force a rest.

D. I understand, and am thankful you promise examples of the kind giving the senses no offense.

Chapter 3

(4) *M.* Come, now report on the pyrrhics too, in order:

Quid erit homo
Qui amat hominem,
Si amat in eo
Fragile quod est?
Amet igitur
Animum hominis,
Et erit homo
Aliquid amans.

How do these seem to you?

D. Why, to flow very smoothly and vigorously.

M. What about these:

Bonus erit amor,
Anima bona sit:
Amor inhabitat,
Et anima domus.
Ita bene habitat,
Ubi bona domus;
Ubi mala, male.

D. I also find these follow along smoothly.

M. Now three and a half feet, see:

Animus hominis est
Mala bonave agitans.
Bona voluit, habet;
Mala voluit, habet.

D. These, too, are enjoyable with a one-time rest put in.
M. Four full pyrrhics follow; listen to them and judge:

Animus hominis agit
Ut habeat ea bona,
Quibus inhabitet homo,
Nihil ibi metuitur.

D. In these, too, there is a fixed and agreeable measure.
M. Listen now to nine short syllables, listen and judge:

Homo malus amat et eget;
Malus etenim ea bona amat,
Nihil ubi satiat eum.

D. Now try five pyrrhics.
M. *Levicula fragilia bona,*
Qui amat homo, similiter habet.

D. That's enough; they pass. Now add a half-foot.
M. I shall.

Vaga levia fragilia bona
Qui amat homo, similis erit eis.

D. Very well: now I am waiting for six pyrrhics.
M. Then listen to these:

Vaga levicula fragilia bona,
Qui adamat homo, similis erit eis.

D. That's enough; add another half-foot.

Fluida levicula fragilia bona
Quae adamat anima, similis erit eis.

D. That's enough, and very good; now give seven pyrrhics.
M. *Levicula fragilia gracilia bona*
Quae adamat animula, similis erit eis.

D. Add a half-foot to these, for this is all very fine.

M. *Vaga fluida levicula fragilia bona,*
Quae adamat animula, fit ea similis eis.

D. Now I see the eight-foot lines remain before we can get beyond these trifles. For, although the ear approves, by a natural measuring, what you give out in sound, yet I shouldn't wish you to look for so many short syllables. And, if I am not mistaken, they are more difficult to find woven in a succession of words than if some longs could be mixed in.

M. You are quite right, and to show my gratitude at our being allowed to get this far I shall compose the one remaining meter of this kind with a more joyful sentence:

Solida bona bonus amat, et ea qui amat, habet.
Itaque nec eget amor, et ea bona Deus est.

D. I now have with abundance a complete set of pyrrhic meters. The iambics come next; two examples of each meter are enough. And it is pleasant to hear them without interruption.

Chapter 4

(5) *M.* I'll obey you. But how many kinds have we already gone through?

D. Fourteen.

M. How many iambic meters do you think there are too?

D. Also fourteen.

M. What if I should wish in these meters to substitute a tribrach for an iamb, wouldn't the variety of forms be greater?

D. That's very evident. But, not to be too long, I want to hear these examples only in iambics. For it's easy art to substitute two shorts for any long.

M. I shall do as you wish, and I'm thankful your keen intelligence lessens my labor. But listen now to the iambics.

D. I am listening; begin.

M. Bonus vir
Beatus.

Malus miser,
Sibi est malum.

Bonus beatus,
Deus bonum eius.

Bonus beatus est,
Deus bonum eius est.[1]

Bonus vir est beatus,
Videt Deum beate.

Bonus vir, et sapit bonum,
Videns Deum beatus est.

Deum videre qui cupiscit
Bonusque vivit, hic videbit.

Bonum videre, qui cupit diem,
Bonus sit hic, videbit et Deum.

Bonum videre qui cupit diem illum,
Bonus sit hic, videbit et Deum illic.

Beatus est bonus fruens enim est Deo,
Malus miser, sed ipse poena fit sua.

Beatus est videns Deum, nihil cupit plus,
Malus bonum foris requirit, hinc egestas.

Beatus est videns Deum, nihil boni amplius,
Malus bonum foris requirit, hinc eget miser.

Beatus est videns Deum, nihil boni amplius vult,
Malus foris bonum requirit, hinc egenus errat.

1 There is a misprint in the Migne Edition which has been corrected according to the Benedictine Edition.

Beatus est videns Deum, nihil boni amplius volet,
Malus foris bonum requirit, hinc eget miser bono.

Chapter 5

(6) *D.* The trochee is next; give the trochaic meters, for these are the best.

M. I shall, and in the same way as the iambic:

Optimi
Non egent.

Veritate,
Non egetur.

Veritas sat est,
Semper haec manet.

Veritas vocatur
Ars Dei supremi.

Veritate factus est
Mundus iste quem vides.

Veritate facta cuncta
Quaeque gignier videmus.

Veritate facta cuncta sunt,
Omniumque forma veritas.

Veritate cuncta facta cerno,
Veritas manet, moventur ista.

Veritate facta cernis omnia,
Veritas manet, moventur omnia.

Veritate facta cernis ista cuncta,
Veritas tamen manet, moventur ista.

Veritate facta cuncta cernis optime,
Veritas manet, moventur haec, sed ordine.

Veritate facta cuncta cernis ordinata,
Veritas manet, novans movet quod innovatur.

Veritate facta cuncta sunt, et ordinata sunt,
Veritas novat manens, moventur ut noventur haec.

Veritate facta cuncta sunt, et ordinata cuncta,
Veritas manens novat, moventur ut noventur ista.

Chapter 6

(7) *D.* The spondee clearly follows; I have had enough of trochees.

M. Here are the spondaic meters:

Magnorum est,
Libertas.

Magnum est munus
Libertatis.

Solus liber fit,
Qui errorem vincit.

Solus liber vivit,
Qui errorem iam vicit.

Solus liber vere fit,
Qui erroris vinclum vicit.

Solus liber vere vivit,
Qui erroris vinclum iam vicit.

Solus liber non falso vivit,
Qui erroris vinclum iam devicit.

Solus liber iure ac vere vivit,
Qui erroris vinclum magnus devicit.

Solus liber iure ac non falso vivit,
Qui erroris vinclum funestum devicit.

Solus liber iure ac vere magnus vivit,
Qui erroris vinclum funestum iam devicit.

Solus liber iure ac non falso magnus vivit,
Qui erroris vinclum funestum prudens devicit.

Solus liber iure ac non falso securus vivit,
Qui erroris vinclum funestum prudens iam devicit.

Solus liber iure ac non falso securus iam vivit,
Qui erroris vinclum tetrum ac funestum prudens devicit.

Solus liber iure ac non falso securam vitam vivit,
Qui erroris vinclum tetrum ac funestum prudens iam devicit.

Chapter 7

(8) *D.* I have all the spondees I need; let's go to the tribrach.

M. All right. But since all four of the preceding feet have each given birth to fourteen meters, making fifty-six all told, more are to be expected from the tribrach. For when there is a half-foot rest in those fifty-six, the rest is never more than a syllable. But in the case of the tribrach you certainly don't think the rests are only for the space of a short syllable, or do you think there are also rests for the space of two short syllables? For there is a double division here, you know, since the tribrach either begins with one short and ends with two, or begins with two and ends with one. And so it must generate twenty-one meters.

D. That's very true. For they begin with four times and, therefore, a two-time rest; then five times with a one-time rest; third, six times with no rest; fourth, seven with a two-time rest; then eight with a one-time rest; sixth, nine with no rest. And so, when they are added on one by one until you come to twenty-four syllables or eight tribrachs, there are twenty-one meters all told.

M. You have certainly very readily followed reason here. But do you think we ought to give examples of all of them, or ought we to think those we have given for the first four feet will furnish light enough for the rest?

D. In my opinion, they are sufficient.

M. I only need yours, now. But, since you already know very well how with a change of beat tribrachs can be forged out of pyrrhic meters, tell me whether the first pyrrhic meter can also have a tribrach meter.

D. It cannot, for the meter must be greater than the foot.

M. How about the second?

D. It can, for four shorts are two pyrrhics and a tribrach and a half, so in the one case there is no rest and in the other a two-time rest.

M. Then with a change of beat the pyrrhics give you examples of tribrachs up to sixteen syllables or five and a half tribrachs. And you will have to be content with that, for you can compose the others yourself either by voice or beat, if you still think these numbers ought to be explored by the sensible ear.

D. In any case I shall do as seems best. Let's see about the others.

Chapter 8

(9) *M.* The dactyl is next, and divisible only one way, isn't it?

D. Certainly.

M. What part of it, then, can be given as a rest?

D. Why, the half.

M. Well, if someone should put a trochee after a dactyl and want to have a one-time rest in the form of a short syllable to fill out the dacytl, what shall we say? For we can't say it's impossible to have a rest of less than a half-foot. For that reason we've discussed convinced us there could be no rest, not of less, but more than a half-foot. For there is certainly a rest of less than a half-foot in the choriamb, when a bacchius follows it, and an example of this is *Fonticolae puellae*. For, you know, we have here a short-syllable rest, needed to fill out the six times.

D. That's true.

M. Then, when a trochee follows a dactyl, isn't it also permissible to have a one-time rest?

D. I am forced to admit it.

M. Yet who could have forced you, if you had only remembered what has been said? You are in this plight because you forgot the demonstration about the indifference of the last syllable, and how the ear takes upon itself a final long syllable even if it's short, when there's an interval to prolong it in.

D. Now I understand. For, if the ear takes the final short syllable as long when there's a rest as we found out by that reason discussed with examples, then it will make no difference whether a trochee or spondee is pronounced after the dactyl. And so, when the repetition is to be punctuated by a rest, it is proper to place a long syllable, to have a two-time rest.

M. What if a pyrrhic should be put after a dactyl? Do you think it would be right to do so?

D. It would not. Whether a pyrrhic or an iamb, there is no difference; although it must be taken for an iamb because with the rest the ear makes the last syllable long. But every one knows it's not proper for an iamb to be put after a dactyl because of the difference in the arsis and thesis, neither of these in the dactyl having three times.

Chapter 9

(10) *M*. Very good and to the point. But what do you think about the anapest? Or does the same reason hold?

D. Exactly the same.

M. Then, let's consider the bacchius, if you will, and tell me what its first meter is.

D. I think it is four syllables, one short and three longs: two longs belonging to the bacchius, but the last one to begin the foot properly placed with the bacchius, with a rest to make up for what is lacking. Yet I should like to explore this with my ear in some example or other.

M. It is easy to give examples, and yet I don't think you could be so delighted with these as with those just given. For these five-time feet, and the seven-time ones, too, do not flow so smoothly as those divided either into equal parts, or into one and two or two and one, so great is the difference between the sesquate movements and the equal or complicate movements we talked about so much in our first discussion. And so, just as the poets treat these five- and seven-time feet contemptuously, so prose adopts them more happily than others. And this can be easily seen in the examples you asked for. Such is *Laborat magister docens tardos*. Repeat this with a three-time rest in between. And for you to feel it more easily, I have put a long syllable after the three feet because it is the beginning of the cretic, which can be put with the bacchius. And I haven't given you an example of the first meter, of four syllables, lest one foot wouldn't be enough to impress on your senses how much of a rest should follow the one foot and a long. Listen now, I shall give it and repeat it myself so you may feel the three times in the rest: *Labor nullus, Amor magnus*.

D. It is evident enough these feet are more suitable to prose, and there is no need to go through the others with examples.

M. You are right. But when there's to be a rest, you don't think only a long syllable can be put after the bacchius?

D. Certainly not. Also a short and a long, the first half-foot of the bacchius itself. For, if we were allowed to begin a cretic on the grounds it can be put with a bacchius, how much more will we be allowed to do it with the bacchius itself, and especially since we did not even put all that part of the cretic equal in times to the first part of the bacchius.

Chapter 10

(11) *M.* Now, then, if you will, go through the rest yourself, while I listen and judge, and in all those feet, where the left-over is filled in by a rest, describe what is placed after the full foot.

D. What you ask is very short and easy now, I believe. For what has been said of the bacchius can also be said of the second paeon. But after the cretic it is permissible to put one long syllable, and an iamb, and a spondee, so there is a rest either of three times, or two, or one. And this applies also to the first and last paeon. After the antibacchius may be placed either one long syllable or a spondee, and so in this meter there will be a three-time or a one-time rest. The same thing is true of the third paeon. Certainly, wherever a spondee can properly be put, there also an anapest. But after the molossus, because of its division, we put one long syllable with a four-time rest, or two longs with a two-time rest. But since, both by experience and reason it has been ascertained all six-time feet can be ordered with the molossus, there will be a place after it both for the iamb with a three-time rest, for the cretic with a one-time rest, and in the same way for the bacchius. But if we resolve the cretic's first long and the bacchius' second long into two shorts, there will be a place for the fourth paeon too. And what I have said of the molossus, I could also say of the other six-time feet. Now I think the proceleusmatic is to be referred back to the other four-time feet, except when we place three shorts after it. And this is the same as putting an anapest after it, because of the final syllable habitually taken as long when followed by a rest. And the iamb is rightly subordinated to the first epitrite and so also the bacchius, cretic, and fourth paeon. And let the same be said of the second epitrite so there is either a four-time or two-time rest. But the spondee and molossus can properly follow the other two epitrites, on the condition it is possible to resolve the spondee's first long and the molossus' first or second into two shorts. Therefore, in these meters there will be either a three-time or one-time rest. The dispondee is left. If we should put a spondee after it, there will be four times to rest; if a molossus, two, and there remains the possibility of dissolving a long into two shorts either in the spondee or molossus, with the exception of the final long syllable. You have what you wanted me to run through. Perhaps you have corrections.

Chapter 11

(12) *M.* Not I certainly, but you, when you put your ear to judging the matter. Tell me, when I say or beat this meter, *Verus optimus,* and this one, *Verus optimorum,* and this one, *Veritatis inops,* whether your senses receive the third as happily as the other two. And they will judge this easily by your repeating them and beating them with the necessary rests.

D. They clearly receive the first two with pleasure, but not the last.

M. Then it's not right to put an iamb after a dichoree.

D. So it isn't.

M. But when he has repeated the following meters with a proper regard for the interposing of rests, everyone agrees it can be put after the other six-time feet:

Fallacem cave,
Male castum cave,
Multiloquum cave,
Fallaciam cave,
Et invidum cave,
Et infirmum cave.

D. I understand what you say, and I agree.

M. See, too, if there isn't a hitch when this last meter, repeated with a two-time rest interposed, continues on, unequal. For it wouldn't sound like the following, would it?

Veraces regnant.
Sapientes regnant.
Veriloqui regnant.
Prudentia regnant.
Boni in bonis regnant.
Pura cuncta regnant.

D. These last have an even and agreeable sound, but that other was quite awkward.

M. Then we shall hold, in meters of six-time feet the dichoree is dissonant with the iamb, and the antispast with the spondee.

D. We certainly shall.

(13) *M.* Well, can't you put your finger on the cause if you notice a foot is so divided into two parts by the arsis and thesis that, if it has any middle syllable, either one or two, they are either attributed to the first part or second part or divided between them both?

D. I certainly know this, and it's true. But what's the point?

M. Listen, then, to what I am going to say; then you will see more easily what you are looking for. For I suppose it is clear to you there are some feet without middle syllables, like the pyrrhic and other two-syllable feet; others, where the middle agrees in length with the first part or last part, or both, or neither. With the first part as in the case of the anapest or antibacchius or first paeon; with the last part as in the case of the dactyl or bacchius or fourth paeon; with both as in the case of the tribrach or molossus or choriamb or any ionic; with neither as in the case of the cretic or second and third paeons, or diiamb or dichoree or antispast. For in those feet capable of division into three equal parts, the middle is in accord with the first and last parts. But in those not capable of such division the middle is in accord with the first part only, or with the last, or with neither.

D. And I know this, too, and I am waiting to see where it all leads.

M. Why to this point, of course: the iamb with a rest is improperly placed after the dichoree because its middle part is equal neither to the first part nor to the last, and so is not in accord with the arsis and thesis. The same thing is true in the case of the spondee, similarly ill at ease when placed with a rest after the antispast. Have you anything to say to the contrary?

D. Nothing, except the shock the ear feels when these feet are so placed is in comparison with the sweetness diverting it when these feet along with a rest are placed after the other six-time feet. For if without the others you were to give examples and ask me how the iamb sounded after the dichoree or the spondee after the antispast, accompanied by a rest in each case—to say what I feel, I should perhaps approve and praise them.

M. And I don't contradict you. It's enough for me, however, these arrangements offend in comparison with numbers of the same kind, but more consonant as you say. For they are to be rejected from the fact that, since these feet we admit run on more happily end in the same half-feet, and are of the same kind, there should have been no discrepancy between them. But don't you think in line with this reasoning an iamb with a rest shouldn't be put after the second epitrite? For in the case of this foot, too, the iamb occupies the middle in such a way it is equal neither to the times of the first part nor of the second.

D. This reasoning compels my agreeing to that.

Chapter 12

(14) *M*. Come now, give me, if you will, an account of all the meters we have discussed, that is, of those beginning with full feet of their own with no rests interposed in the cyclic return, or with feet not full, followed by a rest, but such as reason has shown to be in harmony. And the number of them begins with two incomplete feet and goes as far as eight complete ones in such a way however, as not to exceed, thirty-two times.

D. What you impose is laborious, yet it is worth the work. But I remember a little while ago we had already gotten to seventy-seven meters in going from the pyrrhic to the tribrach. For the two-syllable feet each produced fourteen, making all together fifty-six. But the tribrach, because of its two-way division, produced twenty-one. Then to these seventy-seven we add fourteen from the dactyl and as many from the anapest. For the full feet, when arranged without rests, go from two to eight feet and produce seven meters, but when the half-feet are added with rests and the meters begin with one foot and a half and go to seven and a half, there are seven more. And now there are all together one hundred and five. But the bacchius cannot stretch its meter to eight feet, lest it exceeed the thirty-two times, nor can any of the five-time feet, but they can go to six. The bacchius, then, and the second paeon, equal to it not only in times but also in division, produce each five meters going from two to six feet when the full feet are ordered without rests; but with rests, beginning with a foot and a half and going to five and a half feet, they produce five meters each when followed by a long, and likewise five each when followed by a short and a long. And so they produce each fifteen meters, or thirty all told. And now all together there are a hundred and thirty-five meters. But the cretic and the first and fourth paeons, being divided in the same way, can be followed by a long and an iamb and a spondee and an anapest, and therefore come to seventy-five meters. For, since there are three of them, they each produce five without rests, but twenty with rests, making a total, as we said, of seventy-five. And this, added to the former sum, makes two hundred and ten. The antibacchius and the third paeon, alike in division, each produce five meters in the case of full feet without rests, but with rests they produce five meters each when followed by a long, five each by a spondee, five each by an anapest. We add these to the last sum, and we have in all two hundred and fifty meters.

(15) The molossus and the other six-time feet, seven in all, each produce four meters with full feet, but with rests, since they can be followed each one by a long or an iamb or spondee or anapest or bacchius or cretic or fourth paeon, they each produce twenty-eight, or a total of a hundred and ninety-six meters. And these, added to the four each, make two hundred and twenty-four. But eight must be subtracted from this sum, because the iamb doesn't properly follow the dichoree

nor the spondee the antispast. That leaves two hundred and sixteen, and this added to the whole sum makes all together four hundred and sixty-six meters. The ratio of the proceleusmatic cannot be considered along with those it agrees with, on account of the greater number of half-feet placed after it. For one long syllable with a rest can be put after it just as after the dactyl and the feet like it to give a two-time rest, and three shorts to give a one-time rest. And the final short can in this way be taken for a final long. The epitrites each produce three meters with full feet, beginning with a two-foot meter and going as far as a four-foot meter. For if you should add a fifth foot, you would exceed the allotted thirty-two times. But with rests the first and second epitrites produce three meters each when followed by an iamb, three each when followed by a bacchius, three each by a cretic, and three each by a fourth paeon. And with the full meters this makes all told thirty. But the third and fourth epitrites each produce three meters before the introduction of rests. With the spondee they each produce three, with the anapest three, with the molossus three, with the lesser ionic three, and with the choriamb three. And together with the full meters this makes a total of thirty-six. Therefore, all the epitrites together produce sixty-six meters, and these, with the proceleusmatic's twenty-one, added to the former sum makes five hundred and fifty-three. There remains only the dispondee, producing three meters with full feet; but when rests are used, with the spondee it produces three, three with the anapest, three with the molossus, three with the lesser ionic, and three with the choriamb. And this makes a total of eighteen. So there will be five hundred and seventy-one meters all told.

Chapter 13

(16) *M.* There certainly would be if three were not

to be substracted because of the iamb's difficulties with being placed after the second epitrite. But this is all fine. And so tell me, now, how this meter affects your ear, *Triplici vides ut ortu Triviae rotetur ignis.*

D. Very agreeably.

M. Can you tell me the feet it consists of?

D. I can't; I can't find out how any I measure off go together. For, if I should start with a pyrrhic or an anapest or a third paeon, those following don't fit in. And I can find a cretic after a third paeon, leaving a long syllable allowable after a cretic. But this meter couldn't properly consist of these with a three-time rest interposed. For there is no rest when its repetition is pleasing to the ear.

M. See if it shouldn't begin with a pyrrhic followed by a dichoree, and then a spondee filling out the times owing the foot you started with. Likewise, you can begin with an anapest followed by a diiamb, so the final long when placed with the anapest's four times makes six times, to harmonize with the diiamb. And so from that you understand it is permissible for parts of a foot to be placed, not only at the end, but also at the beginning of meters.

D. I now understand.

(17) *M.* What if I should take away the final long to have a meter like this, *Segetes meus labor;* you notice it's repeated with a two-time rest? And so it is clear some part of the foot can be put at the beginning of the meter, some at the end, and some in a rest.

D. That's clear.

M. But this is clearly true if you measure off a full dichoree in this meter. On the other hand, if you should measure off a diiamb with an anapest at the start, you find a four-time part of the foot at the beginning, and the two times left due in a rest at the end. And thus we learn a meter can begin with a part of a foot ending with a full foot, but never without a rest.

D. This is very clear.

(18) *M.* Further, can you measure off this meter, and tell the feet it consists of?

Iam satis terris nivis, atque dirae
Grandinis misit Pater, et rubente
Dextera sacras iaculatus arces.[2]

D. I can establish a cretic at the beginning and measure off the two remaining six-time feet, one a greater ionic, the other a dichoree, and add a one-time rest to fill out six times with the cretic.

M. Something is amiss in your consideration. For when the dichoree is at the end with a rest left over, its last syllable, a short, is taken for a long. Or do you deny this?

D. I certainly admit it.

M. Then a dichoree must not be put at the end if it is to be followed by a rest in repetition, lest it be perceived no longer as a dichoree but as a second epitrite.

D. That's evident.

M. How, then, shall we measure off this meter?

D. I don't know.

Chapter 14

M. Then see if it sounds well when I recite it with a one-time rest after the first three syllables. For there will be nothing due at the end to keep a dichoree from properly being there.

2 Horace, *Odes* I.2.1-3. The 'traditional' method of scanning this, that of Marius Victorinus, is quite different. But Masqueray, *Traité de métrique grecque* (Paris 1899) scans as Augustine does.

D. It sounds very pleasing.

(19) *M.* Then let's add this rule also to the art, that not only at the end, but also before the end, there may be rests. And it must be applied either when what is necessary for filling out the times of a foot cannot properly be given as a final rest because of a final short, or when two incomplete feet are established, one at the beginning and the other at the end, such as here, *Gentiles nostros inter oberrat equos.* For you saw, I believe, I introduced a two-time rest after the five long syllables, and one of the same length must be introduced at the end, when a cyclic return is made to the beginning. For, if you should measure off this meter by the six-time law, you will have first a spondee, second a molossus, third a choriamb, fourth an anapest. Therefore, two times are due the spondee in order to complete a six-time foot. And so there is a two-time rest after the molossus and before the end, and again after the anapest, and at the end. But, if you measure it off by the four-time law, there will be a long syllable at the beginning, then we measure off two spondees, then two dactyls, and it will finish with a long. And so we have a two-time rest after the two spondees and before the end, and again at the end in order to fill out both of those feet whose halves have been placed at the beginning and the end.

(20) Yet sometimes, what is due two incomplete feet, placed one at the beginning the other at the end, is rendered by the final rest alone, if it be of such a quantity as not to exceed the half-foot, as in the case of these two,

Silvae laborantes, geluque
Flumina constiterint acuto.[3]

For the first of these begins with an antibacchius, from there

3 Horace, *Odes* I.9.3-4.

runs into a molossus, and ends in a bacchius. And so there is a two-time rest, and when you have given one of these to the bacchius and the other to the antibacchius, the six-time intervals will everywhere be filled. But the second begins with a dactyl, from there goes into a choriamb, and closes with a bacchius. It will then be necessary to have a three-time rest. Out of that we shall give one time to the bacchius and two to the dactyl, so there will be six times in every foot.

(21) But what is due for filling out the last foot is given before that due for the first foot. Our ears don't allow it to be otherwise. And no wonder. For when we repeat, what comes last is certainly joined with what comes first. And so in the meter we gave, *Flumina constiterint acuto,* since three times are due to fill out the six-time intervals, if you should wish to give them, not with a rest but with words, they could be rendered by an iamb, choree, or tribrach because each of these contains three times. But the senses themselves would not allow them to be rendered by the choree where the first syllable is long; the second, short. For that first ought to sound, due the last bacchius, that is, the short syllable; not the long belonging to the first dactyl. This can be seen in these examples:

Flumina constiterint acuto gelu.
Flumina constiterint acute gelida.
Flumina constiterint in alta nocte.

And it is evident to anyone the first two are proper when repeated, but the last one not at all.

(22) Likewise, when a single time is due each incomplete foot, if you want to render them by word, the senses don't allow them to be compressed into one syllable. Quite justly, of course. For it is not proper for what is to be rendered sep-

arately not to be constructed separately. And, therefore, in the meter *Silvae laborantes geluque,* if you should add a long syllable to the end in place of the rest, as in *Silvae laborantes gelu duro,* your ears do not approve as when we say *Silvae laborantes gelu et frigore.* And you perceive this well enough, when you repeat each one.

(23) Likewise, when there are two incomplete feet, it is not proper a greater be put at the beginning than at the end. For the hearing condemns this, too, for example, if you should say *Optimum tempus adest tandem* with the first foot a cretic, the second a choriamb, and the third a spondee, with the result that we have a three-time rest, two times being due the last spondee for filling out the six, and one to the first cretic. And so, if it should be said in this way, *Tandem tempus adest optimum,* with the same three-time rest, who would not find its repetition most enjoyable? And, therefore, it is proper either the final incomplete foot be of the same quantity as the first one, as in *Silvae laborantes geluque;* or the first one be the smaller and the last one the larger, as in *Flumina constiterint acuto.* And this is not arbitrary, because on the one hand there is no discord where there is equality. But where the number is unequal, if we should come from the less to the greater, as is usual in counting, this very order again effects an accord.

(24) And so it also follows, when these incomplete feet just mentioned are put in, if a rest is interposed in two places, that is, before the end and at the end, then there is a rest before the end of a quantity owing the last foot, but a rest at the end of a quantity owing the first foot. For, the middle tends toward the end, but a return is to be made from the end to the beginning. But, if to each the same amount is owing, there is no dispute, and in this case there must be a rest before the

end of the same quantity as at the end. Moreover, there must be no rest except where there is an end to a part of the discourse. In the case of those numbers not made by words, but by some beat or breath or even by the tongue, there is no way to make the distinction after what sound or beat a rest should come, so a legitimate rest may intervene according to the preceding ratios. And, therefore, a meter also can begin with two incomplete feet, on condition the combined quantities of both should not be less than one foot and a half. For we have already affirmed two incomplete feet are properly inserted when what is due both does not exceed the length of a half foot. An example is *Montes acuti,* so either we have a three-time rest, or a one-time rest after the spondee with a two-time rest at the end. For this meter cannot be properly measured otherwise.

Chapter 15

(25) Let this [prescription], too, be part of the discipline: when we have a rest before the end, that part of the discourse may not end in a short syllable, to keep the senses from taking it because of the rest following it, for a long syllable in accordance with the continually repeated rule to that effect. And so in the meter *Montibus acutis* we cannot make a one-time pause after the dactyl as we could after the spondee in the example before, for then no longer a dactyl but a cretic would be perceived, with the result the meter would not seemingly consist of two incomplete feet, the object of our present explanation, but a full dichoree and a final spondee with a two-time rest owing at the end.

(26) And it must be noted, too, when an incomplete foot is placed at the beginning, what is owing is repaid either in rest right on the spot, as in *Iam satis terris nivis atque dirae;* or at

the end, as in *Segetes meus labor*. But to an incomplete foot at the end, what is due is repaid in rest either right on the spot, as in *Ite igitur Camoenae;* or somewhere in the middle, as in *Ver blandum viget arvis, adest hospes hirundo*. For the one time owing the last bacchius can be a rest either after the whole number, or after the number's first foot, the molossus, or after its second, the lesser ionic. But what is owing incomplete feet in the middle can only be repaid on the spot, as in *Tuba terribilem sonitum dedit aere curvo*. For, if we should so measure out this meter as to make the first an anapest, the second either of the ionics expressed as five syllables with either the first or final long resolved into two shorts, the third a choriamb, the last a bacchius, then there will be three times owing, one to the final bacchius and two to the first anapest to fill out the times each ought to have. But this whole three-time interval can be rendered as a final rest. But, if you should begin with a complete foot, meting out the first five syllables for either ionic, then a choriamb follows. From there on you will not find a complete foot, and so there will have to be rest for the space of one long syllable; when this is added, the choriamb will be completed. A bacchius whose last time will be repaid by a final rest is left to close the meter.

(27) And so I now think it's clear, when there is a rest in the middle places, it redeems either those times owing at the end, or those owing where the pause is made. But sometimes it is not necessary for the pause to be in the middle places, since the meter can be measured off another way as in the example we just gave. But sometimes it is necessary, as in *Vernat temperies, aurae tepent, sunt deliciae*. For it is clear this number runs in either four-time or six-time feet. If in four, there must be a one time rest after the eighth syllable, and two-time rest at the end. First, measure off a spondee; second, a

dactyl; third, a spondee; fourth, a dactyl, adding a rest after the long syllable because it is not proper to do so after the short syllable; fifth, a spondee; sixth, a dactyl, with a final long closing the line and its two missing times redeemed by a rest at the end. But, if we measure off six-time feet, the first will be a molossus, the second a lesser ionic, the third a cretic becoming a dichoree when a one-time rest is added, the fourth a greater ionic, and a final long followed by a four-time rest. It could be otherwise with one long placed at the beginning, followed by a lesser ionic, then a molossus, then a bacchius becoming an antispast when a one-time rest has been added. A final choriamb would close the meter, with a four-time rest being given the first long. But the ear rejects such a measuring, because, unless the part of the foot placed at the beginning is greater than a half foot, the lack cannot be properly restored where it is owing by the final rest after the complete foot. But with other feet inserted, we know how much is wanting. But the sense does not take in there is such a long rest, unless there is less owing in the rest than is put in sound, because, when the voice has traversed the greater part of the foot, the remaining lesser part easily presents itself anywhere.

(28) And so, although in the case of the meter we have just given as an example, *Vernat temperies, aurae tepent, sunt deliciae,* there is one necessary measuring if there is a one-time rest after the tenth syllable and a four-time rest at the end, yet there is a voluntary measuring if one should wish to have a two-time rest after the sixth syllable, a one-time rest after the eleventh, and a two-time rest at the end, resulting in a spondee at the beginning, a choriamb next, third a spondee with a two-time rest added on to make a molossus or lesser ionic, fourth a bacchius likewise becoming an antis-

past by the addition of a one-time rest, fifth a choriamb to close the number as far as sound is concerned, with a two-time rest at the end redeeming the first spondee. And likewise there is another way. For if you wish, you can have a one-time rest after the sixth syllable, and again after the tenth and eleventh, nd a two-time rest at the end. With the result the first foot is a spondee, the second a choriamb, the third an antibacchius becoming an antispast by the addition of the one-time rest, the fourth a spondee becoming a dichoree by the insertion and addition of one-time rests, finally a choriamb closing the number to give at the end a two-time rest owing the first spondee. And there is a third way of measuring it, if there should be a one-time rest after the first spondee with the other rests just as before except for there being a final one-time rest because of the usually beginning spondee's becoming an antibacchius with the addition of the one-time rest following it, with the result only a one-time measure is owing it to appear as a final rest. And so now you see how rests are inserted in meters, some necessary, some voluntary: necessary when something is owing for completing the feet, but voluntary when the feet are whole and complete.

(29) But what has just been said about the rule of avoiding rests of more than four times was said of necessary rests where times due are filled out. For in those we have called voluntary rests, it is also proper to sound a foot and rest a foot. But, if we should do this at equal intervals, there will not be a meter, but a rhythm with no fixed end appearing as a means to a return to the beginning. And so, if you should wish, for example, to punctuate a line with rests so as to pause after the first foot for the length of a foot, this must not be continued. But it is proper to prolong a meter up to the legitimate number of times with rests inserted in

any sort of arrangement, as in *Nobis verum in promptu est, tu si verum dicis.* It is proper here to have a four-time rest after the first spondee, and another after the following two, but no rest after the last three, because the thirty-two times have already been completed. But it is much more apt, and somehow more just, there be a rest either only at the end, or at the end and in the middle, too, and this can be done with one foot subtracted, to give *Nobis verum in promptu est, tu dic verum.* And this rule is to be maintained for meters of other feet that, in the case of necessary rests the times due to fill out the feet ought to be redeemed either by final or middle rests. But the rest must not be greater than that part of the foot occupied by either the arsis or thesis. But in the case of rests by choice it is possible to rest either for the space of a whole foot or of part of a foot, as we have shown in the examples just given. But let this finish the treatment of the ratio of rest-insertion.

Chapter 16

(30) Now let us say a few things about the mixing of feet and the conjunction of their respective meters, since many things were said when we were investigating what feet ought to be mixed together, and since some things must be said about the composition of meters when we begin to talk about verse. For, feet are conjoined and mixed according to the rules we disclosed in our second discourse. But here it is in order to remember all the meters already celebrated by poets have had each one its author and inventor to keep us from transgressing certain fixed laws they laid down. For it is not proper, when they have fixed them by reasoning, to make any change in them, even if we could make the change according to reasoning and without any offense to the ear.

And the knowledge of this sort of thing is handed down not by art, but by history. And, therefore, it is believed rather than known. For, if some Falerian or other has composed meters to sound like these

Quando flagella ligas, ita liga,
Vitis et ulmus uti simul eant;[4]

we can't know it, but only believe it by hearing and reading. It belongs to the discipline we are treating, to see whether it consists of three dactyls and a final pyrrhic, as most of those unskilled in music affirm (for they do not see a pyrrhic cannot follow a dactyl), or, as reason shows, the first foot in this meter is a choriamb, the second an ionic with a long syllable resolved into two shorts, the last an iamb followed by a three-time rest. And half-taught men could see this, if it were recited and beaten out by a learned man according to both laws. For they would judge from natural and common sense what the discipline's norm would prescribe.

(31) Yet the poet's wishing these numbers to be unchangeable when we use this meter has to be respected. For it satisfies the ear, although it would be equally well satisfied if we should put a diiamb for the choriamb or the ionic, without resolving the long syllable into shorts, and whatever else might fit in. In this meter, then, nothing will be changed, not for the reason by which we avoid inequality, but for that by which we observe authority. For reason certainly teaches some meters are established as immobile, that is, where nothing should be changed, as in this one we have just talked about; others as mobile, where one may substitute certain feet

4 'When you bind switches, bind so the elm and vine go together.' Amerio points out this is the way Marius Victorinus and Terentianus treat this meter, *op. cit.* 184.

for others, as in *Trioae qui primus ab oris, arma virumque cano.* For here an anapest may be substituted for a spondee in any place. Others are neither completely immobile nor completely mobile, as

Pendeat ex humeris dulcis chelys
Et numeros edat varios, quibus
Assonet omne virens late nemus,
Et tortis errans qui flexibus.[5]

For you see here both spondees and dactyls can be placed everywhere, except in the last foot which the author of the meter always wished to be a dactyl. And you see, even in these three kinds, authority has some weight.

(32) But as regards what in the composition of feet belongs to reason alone to judge concerning these things perceived, you know those parts of feet harmoniously placed with a rest after certain feet, as the iamb after the dichoree or second epitrite, and the spondee after the antispast, are still badly placed after other feet these have been mixed with. For it is evident the iamb is well placed after the molossus, as we see in this example with the final three-time rest we are so often repeating. *Ver blandum viret floribus.* But, if you should put a dichoree first in place of the molossus, as in *Vere terra viret floribus,* the ear rejects and condemns it. It is easy, too, to discover this in the other cases, if the ear only search it out. For it is a most sure reasoning, when feet are combined capable of such combination, only those parts of a foot agreeing with all the feet in that sequence be added

5 Terentianus Maurus quotes this from Pomponius. See his *de Metris* 11.2135 ff. (Keil VI 389).
'Let the sweet harp hang from the shoulders and bring forth varied numbers every far-green wood resounds with, and wandering with curious turns . . .

on at the end, to avoid any discord arising one way or another among friends.

(33) This is more wonderful that, although a spondee completes both the diiamb and the dichoree without dissonance, yet when these two feet, either alone or in one way or another mixed with others agreeable to them, have been put in one sequence together, it is the sense's judgment a spondee cannot be put at the end. For no one would doubt, would he, the ear accepts willingly each of these repeated separately; *Timenda res non est* and *Iam timere noli.* But, if you should join them so, *Timenda res, iam timere noli,* I should not want to hear it outside of prose. Nor is it less awkward if you put another foot in anywhere, for instance, a molossus in this way, *Vir fortis, timenda res, iam timere noli,* or in this way, *Timenda res, vir fortis, iam timere noli,* or again in this way, *Timenda res, iam timere noli,* or again in this way, *Timenda res, iam timere vir fortis noli.* And the cause of the awkwardness is this: the diiambic foot can also be beaten in the proportion of two to one, just as the dichoree in the proportion of one to two. But the spondee is equal to their two-part. But, since one pulls it to the first part, the other to the last part, a certain disagreement arises. And so in this way reason relieves us of our wonder.

(34) And the antispast produces something just as marvelous. For if no other foot, or the diiamb alone of all of them, should be mixed with it, it allows the meter to be closed by an iamb, but not so when placed with others. In the case of the dichoree, it is because of the dichoree itself; and I wonder very little at that. But why with the other six-time feet it refuses to allow that particular three-time foot at the end, I do not know. The cause is perhaps too secret for us to be able to find

it out and show it. But I judge it is so by these examples. For there is no doubt each of these two meters, *Potestate placet* and *Potestate potentium placet,* is repeated harmoniously with a three-time rest at the end; but each of these with the same rest, inharmoniously: *Potestate praeclara placet, Potestate tibi multum placet, Potestate iam tibi sic placet, Potestate multum tibi placet, Potestatis magnitudo placet.* Now, in so far as the senses are concerned, they have done their duty in this question, and have indicated what they would approve and what they would not. But reason must be consulted as to why it is so. And mine in all this obscurity only sees this: the antispast has its first half in common with the diiamb, for each begins with a short and a long, but its last half in common with the dichoree, for both end with a long and short. And so the antispast either when it is alone allows the iamb to close the meter as its own first half, or again when it is with the diiamb it has this half in common. And it would allow it with the dichoree, if such an ending were harmonious with the dichoree, but not in the case of others, and it is not joined with them in such company.

Chapter 17

(35) But, with regard to the composition of meters, it is enough at present to see diverse meters can be joined together so long as they agree with respect to beat, that is, to their arsis and thesis. But they differ either in quantity, as when greater are joined with less, for example,

Iam satis terris nivis atque dirae
Grandinis misit Pater, et rubente
Dextera sacras iaculatus arces,
Terruit urbem.

For this fourth line made up of a choriamb and final long, you see how small it is compared to the first three, all equal to each other. Or in feet, as these,

Grato Pyrrha sub antro,
Cui flavam religas comam.[6]

You see, certainly, the first of the two consists of a spondee and choriamb, and a final long due the spondee for completing the six times; the second, of a spondee and choriamb, and two final shorts likewise filling out the spondee to six times. They are equal, then, in times, but somewhat different in feet.

(36) And there is another difference in combinations of this kind: some are so combined they have no rests placed between them as these last two; others require a rest of some kind in between them, like these,

Vides ut alta stet nive candidum
Soracte, nec iam sustineant onus
Silvae laborantes, geluque
Flumina constiterint acuto.[7]

For, if each of these is repeated, the first two acquire a one-time rest, the third a two-time, the fourth, a three-time. Considered together, in going from the first to the second there is necessarily a one-time pause, from the second to the third a two-time, from the third to the fourth a three-time one. But, if you should return from the fourth to the first, you will pause for one time. And whatever ratio is used for the return to the beginning is also used for passing to another such combination. We rightly call this kind of combination a cycle [*circuitum*], in Greek called *períodos*. So the cycle cannot be less than two numbers, nor have they wished it to be more than four. It is

6 Horace, *Odes* 1.5.3-4.
7 Horace, *Odes* 1.9.1-4.

proper, then, to call the least bi-membered, the middle one tri-membered, the last quadri-membered; for the Greeks call them *díkolon, tríkolon, tetrákolon.* And, since we shall treat of this whole class more thoroughly, as I have said, in our discussion of verses, let this be enough for the moment.

(37) I think you now certainly understand there are a great many kinds of meter. In fact, we found there were five hundred and sixty-eight, when no examples were given of rests except final ones, and no mixture of feet made, and no resolution of long syllables into two shorts stretching the foot to more than four syllables. But, if you wish to get the number of meters with every possible insertion of rests applied, and every combination of feet, and every resolution of long syllables, the number is so great its name perhaps is not at hand. But, although these examples we have given and those we can give, poets judged proper in making them, and common nature in hearing them, yet, unless a learned and practised man's recitation should commend them to our ears and the sense of hearing should not be slower than humanity requires, the ones we have treated cannot be judged true. But let's rest a little, and then let's discuss verse.

D. Good.

BOOK FIVE

Verse is discussed.

Chapter 1

(1) *M.* The controversy among ancient learned men in their attempt to find out what verse is, has been great and not without fruit. For the subject has been discovered and written down for the knowledge of posterity, and has been confirmed, not only by serious and certain authority, but also by reason. Now, they noticed there is a difference between rhythm and meter, so all meter is rhythm, but not all rhythm meter. For every legitimate composition of feet is numerable, since the composition containing meter cannot not be number, that is, not be rhythm. But, since it is not the same thing to roll forward, although in legitimate feet, yet without any definite end, and to progress likewise in legitimate feet, but to be bounded by a fixed end, these kinds, therefore, had to be distinguished by names. So the first was called only by the name proper to it, rhythm, but the other by meter as well as rhythm. Again, since of those numbers bounded by a definite end, that is of meters, there are some where there is no ratio of division within them and others where there certainly is, this difference also had to be noted in names. And so the kind of rhythm where this ratio is not has been properly called meter; where it is, they have named it verse. And reason will perhaps show us the origin of this name as we go on. And do not think this so prescribed it is not permissible also to call verses meters. But it's one thing to abuse a name with the license of a resemblance; another to call a thing by its name. Anyhow, let's be

done now with telling over names. For in their case, as we have already learned, the willingness of those speaking and the authority of age count for everything. Let's investigate these other things, if you will, as we are wont, with sense announcing and reason discovering, so you may know the ancient authors did not institute these things as if not already existing whole and finished in the nature of things, but found them by reasoning and designated them by naming them.

Chapter 2

(2) And so I first ask you whether a foot only pleases the ear if the two parts in it, one the arsis, the other the thesis, answer to each other in a numerical and skillful joining?

D. I have already been persuaded and apprised of this.

M. Now, meter, resulting as it does from the conjunction of feet, isn't to be thought to belong to the class of things incapable of division, is it? For no indivisible thing can extend through time, and it would be absurd, wouldn't it, to think what consists of divisible feet is indivisible?

D. I certainly say it isn't indivisible.

M. But aren't all things capable of division more beautiful if their parts agree in some equality than if they should be discordant and dissonant?

D. There's no doubt about it.

M. Well, what number, then, is the author of equal division? The number two?

D. It is.

M. Then, just as we found the foot is divided into two harmonious parts and in this way delights the ear, if we also find a meter of this kind, won't it be rightly preferred to such as are not?

D. I agree.

Chapter 3

(3) *M.* Very well. Now, tell me this. Since in all things we measure by a part of time, one thing precedes and another follows, one begins and another ends, would you think there ought to be no difference between the part preceding or beginning and the part which follows or ends?

D. I think there must be.

M. Tell me, then, what the difference is between the two parts of a verse where one is *cornua velatarum,* and the other *vertimus antennarum.*[1] For, if it should be recited, not as the poet wrote it, with *obvertimus,* but in this way, *Cornua velatarum vertimus antennarum,* doesn't it become uncertain by more or less frequent repetition which part is first, which last? For it is no less the same verse said this way: *Vertimus antennarum cornua velatarum.*

D. I see it becomes very uncertain.

M. Do you think that ought to be avoided?

D. I do.

M. See, then, whether it has been properly avoided in this case. One part of the verse, the first, is, *Arma virumque cano,* and the other following it, *Troiae qui primus ab oris.* And they differ from each other to the extent, if you change the order and recite them this way, *Troiae qui primus ab oris, arma virumque cano,* you would have to measure off other feet.

D. I understand.

M. But see whether this ratio is kept in the other lines. Now whatever measure *Arma virumque cano* begins, you know these do likewise: *Italiam fato, Littora multum ille et, Vi superum saevae, Multa quoque et bello, Inferretque deos, Albanique patres.* In short, you can go through as many of the

---

1 Vergil, *Aeneid* III.549.

other lines as you wish, you will find these first verse-parts to be of the same measure, that is, five distinct half-feet. Very rarely, indeed, if not in this way; so the end-parts are no less equal to each other: *Troiae qui primus ab oris, Profugus Lacinaque venit, Memorem Iunonis ob iram, Passus dum conderet urbem, Latio genus unde Latinum, Atque altae moenia Romae.*

D. That's very evident.

(4) *M.* And so, five and seven half-feet divide into two parts, the heroic verse consisting, as everyone knows, of six four-time feet. And without the harmonious conjunction of two members, either this one, or some other, there is no verse. And in all these examples reason has shown this much must be observed: the first part cannot be second, nor the second first. And if it is otherwise, they will no longer be called verses except through misuse of the name. But they will have rhythm and meter, and it is not improper to stick in such things at long intervals in long poems composed of verses. And just of such a kind is the one I recited a while back: *Cornua velatarum vertimus antennarum.* And so I don't believe a verse is so called, as some think, because it returns from a fixed ending to the beginning of the same member, so the name is taken from those who turn around [*se vertunt*] when retracing their steps. For verse seems to have this in common with those meters which are not verses. But, on the contrary, perhaps the name came about rather in the way the grammarians have called a deponent verb one not deposing the letter '*r*,' for example '*lucror*' and '*conqueror*'; just so whatever is made up of two members, neither able to be put in the place of the other without violating the law of the numbers, is called verse because it cannot be reversed. But you can accept either of these derivations or reject them both, and look for another, or with me

disapprove of any question of this kind. It has nothing to do with the present affair. For, since the thing itself signified by this name is sufficiently apparent, there's no need to labor the word's derivation. Perhaps you have some objections?

D. I have none, certainly, but go on with the rest.

Chapter 4

(5) *M.* Next we must look to the ending of the verse. For they wanted this also to be marked and distinguished by some difference, or rather reason itself wanted it so. Don't you think it better the ending confining the number's forward roll, with the equality of times undisturbed, should stand out, rather than be confused with the other parts not effecting an ending?

D. Who doubts it? It's too evident.

M. See, then, whether those people were right in wanting the spondaic foot to be the distinctive ending of the heroic verse. For in the other five places it is permissible to put either a spondee or a dactyl, but at the end only a spondee. For what they reckon a trochee becomes a spondee on account of the last syllable's indifference we spoke enough about in the treatment of meter. But according to them the six-foot iambic either will not be a verse or will be one without this distinction of ending. But either is absurd. For no one, either among very learned men or moderately or even slightly learned, has ever doubted this was a verse: *Phaselus ille quem videtis, hospites,*[2] and whatever is formed of words in this number-form. And yet the more serious authors, and so the most skillful, have judged nothing to be a verse without a distinctive ending.

(6) *D.* You are right. And, therefore, I believe some other

2 Catullus, 4.1.

mark of its ending must be looked for, and the spondee story is not acceptable.

M. What is it? You don't doubt, do you, whatever it is, it is either a difference in foot, time, or both?

D. What else can it be?

M. But which of these three do you think it is? For I, since ending a verse to keep it within its proper bounds is proper only to the time-measure, I don't think this mark can be taken elsewhere than from time. Or do you find something else better?

D. I certainly agree.

M. Do you see this, too. Since time in this case can only be different in the one's being longer, the other shorter, the end-mark must consist in a shorter time, because, when the verse is ended, it is done to prevent it's proceeding farther?

D. I see that. But to what does the added 'in this case' refer?

M. To the fact we do not everywhere get the time-difference only in brevity and length. You don't say, do you, the difference of summer and winter is one of time or rather of a shorter and longer interval, and don't you place it in the power of cold and hot, or of dry and wet, and any other thing like that?

D. I now understand, and I agree this mark we are looking for must be taken from shortness of time.

(7) *M*. Listen then to this verse, *Roma, Roma, cerne quanta sit deum benignitas,* called trochaic, and measure it and say what you find out about its members and the number of its feet.

D. I should easily reply about the feet, for it is evident there are seven and a half, but as to the members the matter is not clear enough. For I see the ends of parts of discourse in many places, yet I believe the partition is in the eighth half-foot with the first member *Roma, Roma, cerne quanta,* and the second *sit deum benignitas.*

M. And how many half-feet does it have?

D. Seven.

M. Reason has most certainly led you to this. For since nothing is better than equality, it would be proper to approach it in any division. If only less can be gotten, an approximation to it must be sought, not to stray too far from it. And so, since here the verse has in all fifteen half-feet, it could not be divided more equally than into eight and seven. But there is the same approximation in seven and eight. Yet in this way the distinctive ending would not be preserved, as reason itself has taught us it must be. For if there were such a verse as *Roma, cerne quanta sit tibi deum benignitas,* beginning with a member of seven half-feet, *Roma, cerne quanta sit,* and ending with one consisting of these eight, *tibi deum benignitas,* then the verse could not close with a half-foot, for eight half-feet make four whole feet. At the same time there would result another deformity in our not measuring the same feet in the last member as in the first, and rather would the first member finish with the mark of shorter time, that is, with a half-foot, than the second this ending by rights belongs to. For in the one there are three and a half trochees, *Roma, cerne quanta sit;* in the other four iambs would be scanned *tibi deum benignitas.* But in the case we have before us, we scan trochees in both members, and the verse closes with a half-foot so the ending has the mark of a short syllable. For there are four in the first, *Roma, Roma, cerne quanta,* but three and a half in the second, *sit deum benignitas.* Or are you prepared to say something to the contrary?

D. Nothing at all; I willingly agree.

(8) *M*. Let us keep these laws unchanged, then, if you

will, that a verse should not be without a partition into two members approaching equality, as this one is, *Cornua velatarum obvertimus antennarum.* That this equality should not make the members convertible, so to speak, as it does in *Cornua velatarum vertimus antennarum.* And when this convertibility is avoided, that the members should not have too great a discrepancy between them, but nearly equal each other, as much as possible by proximate numbers, not to say they can be divided such a way, eight half-feet are in the first member, *Cornua velatarum vertimus,* and four in the last, that is, *antennarum.* That the second member should not have an even number of half-feet, as *tibi deum benignitas,* lest the verse, finishing with a full foot, should not have an ending distinguished by a shorter time.

D. I now have them, and I shall commit them to memory as far as I can.

Chapter 5

(9) *M.* Since, then, we now hold a verse ought not to end with a full foot, how do you think we ought to measure the heroic verse so as to preserve the law of members and the end-marks?

D. Well, I see there are twelve half-feet, and the members cannot each have six half-feet, because convertibility must be avoided. Nor is it proper for there to be a great discrepancy between them as in three and nine or nine and three. Nor should an even number of half-feet be given the second member, resulting in a division of eight and four or four and eight, and a verse ending with a full foot. The division must be made into five and seven or seven and five. For these numbers are both odd and proximate, and the members certainly approach each other more nearly than they would in the numbers four and eight. To be very certain about it, I see the end-parts of discourse always or nearly always in the fifth half-foot, as in Vergil's first verse, *Arma virumque cano*; and in the second, *Italiam fato*; and in the third, *Littora multum ille et*; likewise in the fourth, *Vi superum saevae*; and so on, for nearly the whole poem.

M. That's true. But you must look to what feet you are measuring; to dare no violation of these laws just so firmly established.

D. Although the reason is sufficiently clear to me, yet I am disturbed by the novelty. For, usually, in this kind of line we scan nothing but spondees and dactyls, and almost no one is so uneducated as not to have heard of that, even if he is less able to do it. And so, if we should in this case wish to follow that very common custom, the law of ending has to be abrogated, for the first member would close with a half-foot, but the second with a full foot, and it ought to have been just the contrary. But, since it seems very unsuitable to abolish this law and I have now learned to know it is permissible, in numbers, for us to begin with an incomplete foot, we are left to judge it is not a dactyl with a spondee here, but an anapest. So the verse begins with one long syllable; then two feet, either spondees or anapests or both, end the first member; then again three feet for the other member, either anapests or spondees in any place or in all; and finally one syllable to rightly end the verse. Do you accept this?

(10) *M.* I, too, judge it quite correct, but the public is not easily persuaded of such things. For the force of custom, if it is old and born of false opinion, is so great nothing is more hostile to the truth. For you understand, as far as making the verse goes, there is no difference whether in this kind of line the anapest or the dactyl is placed with the spondee. Yet, for measuring it rationally, something not proper to the ear but

to the mind, this fact is discerned by a true and fixed reason, not by irrational opinion. And we are not the first to have found it out, but it was noticed long before this custom grew up. And so, if people should read those who have been most learned in this discipline either in the Greek or Latin tongue, they, chancing to hear this, will not be too surprised, although one is ashamed of the stupidity of seeking an authority for strengthening men's reason, since nothing is to be preferred to the authority of truth and reason itself, certainly better than any man. For we do not in this case look only to the authority of the ancients as in the lengthening or shortening of a syllable, to use our words as they also used them. Yet, because in a matter of this kind it is the part of slothfulness to follow no rule, and of license to establish a new one, so in the measuring of verse the inveterate will of man and not the eternal ratio of things is to be considered, since we first perceive its measured length naturally by the ear, and then establish it by the rational consideration of numbers, and since anyone judging this meter to be properly completed more surely than other meters judges it must close with a distinctive ending, and since it is clear such an ending must be marked by a shorter time. For this confines the length of the time and somehow checks it.

Chapter 6

(11) And since all this is so, how can the second member end if not with an incomplete foot? But the beginning of the first member is either a complete foot, as in the trochaic verse, *Roma, Roma, cerne quanta sit deum benignitas,* or part of a foot, as in the heroic verse, *Arma virumque cano, Troiae qui primus ab oris.* And so, with all hesitation now removed, measure if you will the verse, *Phaselus ille quem videtis, hospites,* and tell me about its members and feet.

D. I see its members are certainly distributed into five and seven half-feet, so the first is *Phaselus ille* and the second *quem videtis hospites.* The feet, I see, are iambic.

M. But I ask, aren't you to take care at all the verse doesn't end with a full foot?

D. You are right; I was off the track. For who wouldn't be bright enough to see it must end in a half-foot like the heroic verse. And considered in this genus, we measured the verse, not with iambs, but with trochees, to have a half-foot close it.

(12) *M.* It's just as you say. But look, what do you think is to be said about this one they call Asclepiadean, *Maecenas atavis edite regibus.*[3] For a part of the discourse ends in the sixth syllable, and not inconsistently, but in nearly all verses of this kind. Its first member is *Maecenas atavis;* the second, *edite regibus.* And one can well hesitate as to what ratio it's in. For if you should measure it off in four-time feet, there will be five half-feet in the first member and four in the second. But the law forbids the last member's consisting of an even number of half-feet so ending the verse in a full foot. It remains for us to consider six-time feet, with each member consisting of three half-feet. And in order for the first member to end with a full foot, we must begin with two longs; then a whole choriamb divides the verse so the second member begins with another choriamb following it, and the verse closes with a half-foot of two short syllables. For this number of times together with the spondee placed at the beginning fill out a six-time foot. Do you have anything perhaps to add to this?

D. Nothing, certainly.

M. You are willing for both members to consist of the same number of half-feet.

D. Why not? For conversion here is not to be feared, because

3 Horace, *Odes* 1.1.1.

if the first member were put in place of the second with the first becoming second, the same law of feet will no longer hold. And so there is no cause why the same number of half-feet should not be allowed the members in this case, since this equality can be maintained without any fault of convertibility, and since also the law of a distinctive ending is preserved when the foot doesn't end in a full foot—and this ought to be most consistently preserved.

Chapter 7

(13) M. You have quite seen through the matter. And so, since now reason has found there are two kinds of verses, one where the number of half-feet in the members is the same, another where it is not, let us diligently consider, if you will, how this inequality of half-feet may be referred to some equality by a somewhat more obscure but certainly very subtle ratio of numbers. For look, when I say two and three, how many numbers do I say?

D. Two, of course.

M. So two is one number, and three one, and any other you might have said.

D. That's so.

M. Doesn't it seem to you from this, one can be joined not absurdly with any number? For one can't say one is two, but in a certain way two is one; likewise it can be truly said three and four are one.

D. I agree.

M. Listen to this. Tell me what does three times two make all together?

D. Six.

M. Six and three aren't the same number, are they?

D. Not at all.

M. Now, I want you to take four times three and tell me the product.

D. Twelve.

M. You see, also, twelve is more than four.

D. And a great deal more certainly.

M. To dilly-dally no longer, this rule must be fixed: whatever two numbers you choose from two on, the less multiplied by the greater must exceed the greater.

D. Who could have any doubt about this? For, what is so small in the plural number as two? And yet, if multiplied by a thousand, it will so exceed a thousand as to be its double.

M. You are right. But take the number one and then any other greater number and, just as we did with the others, multiply the lesser by the greater. The greater will not be exceeded in the same way, will it?

D. Clearly not, but the lesser will be equal to the greater. For two times one is two, ten times one is ten, and a thousand times one is a thousand, and by whatever number I multiply one, the result must be equal.

M. So one has a certain right of equality with other numbers, not only in any number's being one, but also in one's giving, multiplied by any number, that same number as a product.

D. That's very evident.

(14) *M.* Come now, look to the numbers of half-feet the unequal memebrs in the verse are made of, and you will find a wonderful equality by means of the ratio we have discussed. For, I believe, that is the least verse in two members of an unequal number of half-feet which has four half-feet and three, as for instance *Hospes ille quem vides.* For the first member, *Hospes ille,* can be cut equally into two parts of two half-feet each, but the second, *quem vides,* is so divided one

part has two half-feet, the other one half-foot. And so this last member is as if it were two and two by that law, just discussed, of the equality one has with all numbers. And so by this division the first member is in some way the same length as the second. And where there would be four and five half-feet, as in the case of *Roma, Roma, cerne quanta sit,* it doesn't work out this way, and so that will be a meter rather than a verse, because the members are unequal in such a way they can be referred to no law of equality by any division whatsoever. You certainly see, I believe, the four half-feet, *Roma, Roma,* of the first member can be separated into two each; and the five last ones, *cerne quanta sit,* can be divided into two and three, where, by no law whatsoever, does equality appear. For in no way can the five half-feet, because of the two and three, be accounted the same as the four, the way we found in the shorter verse just given, the three half-feet because of the one and two have the same value as four. Is there anything you haven't followed or anything displeasing you?

D. Why, on the contrary, everything is evident and thought out.

(15) *M.* Well, now, let's consider five and three half-feet, like this little verse, *Phaselus ille quem vides,* and let's see how such an inequality may fall under a law of equality. For all agree this kind of line is not only a meter, but also a verse. And so, when you have cut the first member into two and three half-feet, and the second into two and one, join together the subordinate parts you find alike in both, since in the first section we have two's, and in the second there are two parts left, one of three half-feet from the first member, the other in one half-foot from the last member. And so we also join the last two together because it is in community with all members, and, added together, one and three make

four, the same as two and two. By this division, therefore, five and three half-feet are brought into agreement, too. But tell me if you have understood.

D. I certainly have, and very much approve.

Chapter 8

(16) *M.* We should next discuss five and seven half-feet. Of this kind are those two noblest verses, the heroic and what is popularly called the iambic, a six-foot verse, too. For *Arma virumque cano, Troiae qui primus ab oris* is so divided its first member is *Arma virumque cano,* or five half-feet, and its second *Troiae qui primus ab oris,* or seven. And *Phaselus ille quem videtis, hospites* has for its first member *Phaselus ille,* in five half-feet, and for its second, in seven half-feet, *quem videtis, hospites.* But this great nobleness labors within this law of equality. For when we have divided the first five half-feet into two and three, and the last seven into three and four, the parts of three half-feet each will certainly go together. And if the other two should combine so one of them consisted in one half-foot and the other in five, they would be joined together by the law permitting the union of one with any number, and added together they would make six, the sum also of three and three. But now, because two and four are found in this case, together they will give six, but by no law of equality is two as much as four, to produce, you might say, a necessary joining. Unless you could say, perhaps, it is sufficiently subsumed under a rule of equality by having two and four make six just as three and three. And I don't think this ratio is to be attacked, for this is an equality, too. But I should not be willing for five and three half-feet to enjoy a greater harmony than five and seven. For the name of one is not so famous as that of the other, and in

the case of the first you see not only the same sum is found when one and three are added together as when two and two, but also the parts are much more concordant when one and three are joined together because of the harmony of one with all numbers, than when two and four are joined as in the second case. Do you find anything not clear?

D. Nothing at all. But somehow it offends me these six-foot verses, although more celebrated than other kinds and said to have the first place among verses, should have less harmony in their members than those of obscurer fame.

M. Don't be discouraged. For I shall show you so great a harmony in the six-foot verses as they alone among all others have merited, so you may see they have been justly preferred. But, since its treatment is a little longer, although more interesting, we ought to leave it to the end when we have sufficiently discussed the others and are free of all care for a closer scrutiny of the secrets of these verses.

D. Willingly. But I should wish to have explained what we first started out to do so as to understand it now more easily.

M. In comparison with those already discussed, those you are waiting for become more agreeable.

Chapter 9

(17) And so now consider whether in two members, one six half-feet and the other seven, is found the equality necessary to a real verse. For you see this must be discussed after five and seven half-feet. And an example of this is *Roma, cerne quanta sit deum benignitas.*

D. I see the first member can be distributed into parts having three half-feet each; the second into three and four. And so when the equals are added they make six half-feet, but three and four are seven and are not equal in number to the first lot. But if we should consider two and two in the part with four, and two and one in the part with three, then, when the parts with two have been added, the sum is four, but when those with two and one are added, if we take these also as four because of one's agreeing with all other numbers, then they become all together eight, and they exceed the sum of six by more than when they were seven.

(18) *M*. It's as you say. Now, seeing this kind ot combination doesn't fall under the law of verses, let's consider now next in order those members with the first having eight half-feet, the second seven. Well. this combination has what we want. For, joining the half part of the first member with the part of the second member nearest that half, since they are each four half-feet, I make a sum of eight. And so there are left four half-feet from the first member and three from the second. Two from the one and two from the other together become four. Again two from the one and one from the other, combined according to that law of agreement constituting one equal to all the other numbers, are in a way taken for four. So now this eight agrees with the other eight.

D. But why don't I get an example of this?

M. Because it's been so often repeated. Yet, so you may not think it's been left out at its proper place, here it is, *Roma, Roma, cerne quanta sit deum benignitas,* or this, too, *Optimus beatus ille qui procul negotio.*[4]

(19) And so now examine the combination of nine and seven half-feet. An example of this is *Vir optimus beatus ille qui procul negotio.*

D. It is easy to recognize these harmonies. For the first

4 A variation on Horace, *Epodes* 1.2.

member is divided into four and five half-feet and the second into three and four. The lesser part of the first member, then, joined with the greater part of the second, makes eight, and the greater part of the first member with the lesser part of the second likewise makes eight. For the first combination is four and four half-feet, and the second five and three. Further, if you should divide five into two and three half-feet, and three into two and one, there appears another harmony of two with two and of one with three, because one is joined with all other numbers by that law of ours. But, unless reason fails me, there remains nothing more for us to seek on the combination of members. For we have already come to eight feet, and we recognized some time ago a verse can't lawfully exceed eight feet. And so, come now, open up these secrets of the six-foot verses, the heroic and iambic or trochaic, you have excited and disturbed my attention for.

Chapter 10

(20) *M.* I shall; at least, that reason common to us both will. But say, don't you remember when we were talking about meters, we said and wholly exhibited by our very senses, those feet whose parts are in the superparticular ratio, either in two and three, as the cretic or paeons, or in three and four, as the epitrites, are thrown out by the poets because of their less pleasing sound and harmoniously embellish the severity of prose when a period's close is bound by them?

D. I remember. But where does this get us?

M. It's because I want us first to understand, once feet of this kind have been denied use in poetry, there only remain those whose parts are in a one-to-one ratio as the spondee, or two-to-one as the iamb, or in both as the choriamb.

D. That's so.

M. But if this is the matter of the poets and prose is at variance with verse, no verse can be made except of this kind of feet.

D. I agree, for I see poems in verse are on a grander scale than those other meters proper to lyric poems. But so far, where this reasoning leads us I can't see.

(21) *M.* Be patient. Now let's talk about the excellence of six-foot verse. And first I want to show you, if I can, the most proper six-foot verses can only be of two kinds, also the most famous of all: one the heroic like *Arma virumque cano, Troiae qui primus ab oris,* measured according to custom with the spondee and dactyl, but according to a more subtle reasoning with spondee and anapest; the other called iambic, and by the same reasoning found to be trochaic. Now, I believe you see clearly somehow the sound-intervals are dull, unless the long syllables are interspersed with short ones; likewise they become too cut up and too tremulous, you might say, unless the shorts are interspersed with longs; and in neither case is there a proper compounding even though they burden the ear with an equality of times. And so, neither those verses with six pyrrhics nor those with six proceleusmatics aspire to the dignity of heroic verse, nor those with six tribrachs to the dignity of trochaic verse. Further, in those verses reason itself prefers to all others, if you should convert the members, the whole will be so changed we will be forced to measure off other feet. And so you might say these are more inconvertible than those consisting either all of shorts or all of longs. And, therefore, it makes no difference whether the members in these more properly organized verses are ordered with five and seven half-feet or with seven and five. For in neither of these orders can the verse be converted without so much change it turns out to run in other feet. Yet, in the

case of these verses, if the poem is begun with verses having the first members of five half-feet, those with first members of seven half-feet should not be mixed in, lest it then be possible to convert them all. For no substitution of feet cancels conversion. Yet the rare interspersion in heroic verses of an all spondaic verse is allowed, although this latter age of ours has very little approved it. But in the case of trochaic or iambic verses, although it is permissible to put in a tribrach anywhere, yet it has been judged very bad in poems of this sort to resolve a verse entirely into shorts.

(22) And so when the epitrites have been excluded from the six-foot mode of verse, not only because they are more fitted to prose, but also because with six of them, like the dispondee, they would exceed thirty-two times, and when the five-time feet have also been excluded because prose claims them more eagerly for closing periods, and when likewise the molossi and all other six-time feet, although they do well in poems, have been excluded from this present affair because of the number of times, there remain the verses composed all of short syllables having either pyrrhics or proceleusmatics or tribrachs, and all of longs having spondees. And though they are admitted to the six-foot mode, yet they must give way to the dignity and harmony of those varied with shorts and longs and on this account much less convertible.

Chapter 11

(23) But it can be asked why the six-foot verses are judged better measured by that subtle ratio in terms of anapests or trochees, than when they are measured in terms of dactyls or iambs. For without reference to meaning, since we are now discussing numbers, if the verse were in the one case *Troiae qui primus ab oris arma virumque cano,* or in the

other *Qui procul malo pius beatus ille,* each of these would certainly be a six-foot verse, and not less tempered with a good disposition of longs and shorts, nor any more convertible. And the members in each case are so ordered a part of discourse ends in the fifth and seventh half-feet. Why, then, should they be thought better if they are rather so: *Arma virumque cano, Troiae qui primus ab oris* and *Beatus ille qui procul pius malo?* And to this question I could too easily and rapidly reply, it happened by chance these were first noticed and repeated. Or if not fortuitous, I believe it seemed better the heroic verse should close with two longs rather than with two shorts and a long, because the ear finds its rest more easily in the longs. And the other verse would better have a long syllable than a short in the final half-foot. Or perhaps it's this way. Whichever of the two pairs are chosen first necessarily rob of their supremacy those they could become by a conversion of members. And so that kind is judged best *Arma virumque cano, Troiae qui primus ab oris* is an example of, and immediately the other, its converse, would be improper, for instance, *Troiae qui primus ab oris, arma virumque cano.* And this must also hold for the trochaic kind. For if *Beatus ille qui procul negotio* is better, then the kind it would become on conversion, *Qui procul negotio beatus ille,* certainly should not be. Yet, if anyone should dare make such verses, it is evident he will make other kinds of six-foot verse not so good as these.

(24) And so these, the most beautiful of all six-foot verses, have not been able, the two of them, to maintain their integrity against the license of men. For in the case of the trochaic kind, the poets think all four-time feet applying to numbers should be mixed in, not only with the six-foot verse, but with the least up to the greatest magnitude of eight feet.

And the Greeks, in fact, put them alternately, beginning with the first and third places, if the verse began with a half-foot; if with a full trochee, these longer feet are put alternately beginning with the second and fourth places. And in order for this corruption to be tolerable, they haven't divided each foot into two parts by beat, one to the arsis, the other to the thesis, but, putting the arsis on one foot and the thesis on the next (and so they call the six-foot verse trimeter), they bring the beat back to the division of the epitrites. At all events, if this should be constantly held to, although the epitrites are feet belonging to prose rather than to poetry and it would turn out to be, no longer six-foot, but three-foot verse, yet in any case that equality of numbers would not be wholly destroyed. But now it is allowed, provided only they are also put in the places already mentioned, to put the four-time feet not only in every place, but wherever one pleases and as many times as one pleases. And even the ancients of our race could not keep these places at intervals free of feet of this kind. And so with respect to this kind of verse the poets have gone all the way in this corruption and license, because, we are to think, they wished dramatic poetry to be very much like prose. But now that enough has been said as to why these among six-foot verses are of greater nobleness, let's see why the six-foot verses themselves are better than any others constructed of any number of feet whatsoever. Perhaps you have something to say against this?

D. No, I agree. And now I am eagerly waiting to know about that equality of members you so much interested me in a while ago—if it is now proper to turn to it.[5]

5 The curious argument on the six-foot verse which follows is referred to very definitely by Aulus Gellius, XVIII.15.2, who refers it back to Varro. See Weil, *op.cit.* 142.

Chapter 12

(25) *M.* Then let me have your entire attention and tell me if you think any length can be cut into any number of parts.

D. I have been sufficiently persuaded of that, and I don't think I can doubt every length called a line has its half and in this way can be cut into two lines. And, since the lines made by this cut are certainly lines, it is clear the same thing can be done with them. And so, any length can be cut into any number of parts.

M. Very readily and truly explained. And can't it be rightly affirmed every length, on being extended its length in width, is equal to the square of its width? For, if the line move sideways any more or less than the length of the line itself, it isn't the square; if just that, it is the square.

D. I understand and agree. Nothing could be truer.

M. I am sure you see this follows: if counters, laid out one after another at equal distances, are substituted for the line, their length will only take on the form of a square when the stones have been multiplied by an equal number. For example, if you put down two stones, you will not get a square unless two others are added in width. And if three, six must be added, apportioned in width in two rows of three each. For, if they should be added in length, no figure results. For length without width is not a figure. And it is possible to consider the other numbers in proportion. For, as two times two and three times three make square figures in numbers, so also do four times four, five times five, six times six, and so on for the rest.

D. This, too, is reasoned and evident.

M. See, now, if time has length.

D. Who would doubt there's no time without length?

M. And further, can a verse be without time-length?

D. It certainly cannot.

M. What in this length is to be substituted for the counters: the feet necessarily divided into two parts, that is, into an arsis and thesis, or the half-feet, each containing only an arsis or thesis?

D. I judge it more proper to substitute the half-feet for the counters.

(26) *M*. Come, then, repeat how many half-feet the heroic verse's shorter member contains.

D. Five.

M. Give an example.

D. *Arma virumque cano.*

M. You only wanted the other seven feet to be in harmony by an equality with these five didn't you?

D. That's all, certainly.

M. Further, is there any verse seven half-feet can complete by themselves?

D. There certainly is. For the first and smallest verse has just this number of half-feet with a rest added at the end.

M. You are right. But for it to be a verse, into what two members is it divided?

D. Into four and three half-feet.

M. Then bring each part under the law of squares, and see what four times four makes.

D. Sixteen.

M. What three times three?

D. Nine.

M. What's the whole?

D. Twenty-five.

M. Since, then, seven half-feet can have two members,

when each of its members has been referred to the ratio of squares they add up to the number twenty-five. And this is one part of the heroic verse.

D. So it is.

M. Then the other part of five half-feet, since it cannot be divided into two members and must harmonize by means of some equality, isn't the whole of it to be squared?

D. I judge so. And yet I already see a marvelous equality. For five times five gives twenty-five. And so, not without cause have the six-foot verses become more famous and more noble than the others. For it is hard to say how great the difference is between the equality of these unequal members and that of all others.

Chapter 13

(27) *M.* Then my promise didn't fail you, or, rather, reason itself both of us follow. And so, to finish this talk soon enough, you see certainly, although the meters are almost innumerable, yet a meter can only be a verse if it has two members harmoniously joined together, either with an equal number of half-feet with their endings inconvertible, as in *Maecenas atavis edite regibus,* or again with an unequal number of half-feet yet combined according to some equality as four and three, or five and three, or five and seven, or six and seven, or eight and seven, or seven and nine. For the trochaic can begin with a full foot, as in *Optimus beatus ille qui procul negotio,* and with an incomplete foot, as in *Vir optimus beatus ille qui procul negotio,* but it can certainly only end with an incomplete foot. Whether these incomplete feet contain whole half-feet, as in the case of the example just cited, or less than a half-foot, as the two last shorts in this choriamb, *Maecenas atavis edite regibus,* or more than

a half, as the first two longs at the beginning or the bacchius at another choriambic verse's end, as for example, *Te domus Evandri, te sedes celsa Latini*,[6] still all these incomplete feet are called half-feet.

(28) Now, not only are there such poems as those of the epic or even of the comic poets, made in verses so as to be of one kind, but also the lyric poets composed the circular kind called by the Greek *períodoi*, not only on those meters not governed by the law of verse, but also in verses. For that famous one of Flaccus,

Nox erat, caelo fulgebat luna sereno
Inter minora sidera.[7]

is a circular two-membered poem consisting of verses. And the two verses cannot harmonize unless they are both reckoned in six-time feet. For the heroic mode does not harmonize with the iambic or trochaic mode, because one set of feet is divided in a one-one ratio, the other in a double ratio. And so, the circular poems are made either of any meter without verse, like those in the discussion before this one when we were talking just about meters, or are made only of verses like those we have just been talking about, or are measured both in verses and other meters, as in this case:

Diffugere nives, redeunt iam gramina campis,
Arboribusque comae.[8]

But in what order you place either the verses with the other meters, or the greater members with the lesser, makes no difference in the ear's pleasure, provided the circular meter

6 Terentianus quotes this, according to Maurist ed.
7 Horace, *Epodes* 13.1-2.
8 Horace, *Odes* IV.7.1-2.

is not shorter than a two-membered verse nor longer than a four-membered one. But, if you have nothing to the contrary, let this be the end of the discussion, so we may next come with as much wisdom as we can from these sensible traces of music, all dealing with that part of it in the numbers of the times to the real places where it is free of all body.

BOOK SIX

The mind is raised from the consideration of changeable numbers in inferior things to unchangeable numbers in unchangeable truth itself.

Chapter 1

(1) *M.* We have delayed long enough and very childishly, too, through five books, in those number-traces belonging to time-intervals. And let's hope a dutiful labor will readily excuse our triviality in the eyes of benevolent men. For we only thought it ought to be undertaken so adolescents, or men of any age God has endowed with a good natural capacity, might with reason guiding be torn away, not quickly but gradually, from the fleshly senses and letters it is difficult for them not to stick to, and adhere with the love of unchangeable truth to one God and Master of all things who with no mean term whatsoever directs human minds. And so, whoever reads those first books will find us dwelling with grammatical and poetical minds, not through choice of permanent company, but through necessity of wayfaring. But when he comes to this book, if, as I hope and pray, one God and Lord has governed my purpose and will and led it to what it was intent upon, he will understand this trifling way is not of trifling value, this way we, too, not very strong ourselves, have preferred to walk, in company with lighter persons, rather than to rush with weaker wings through the freer air. So, as far as I can see, he will judge either we haven't sinned at all or very little, if only he is of the number of spiritual men. For if by chance the other crowd from the schools, with tumultous tongues taking vulgar delight in the noise

of rhythm-dancers, should chance upon these writings, they will either despise all or consider those first five books sufficient. But this one the very fruit of those is found in, they will either throw aside as not necessary, or put off as over and above the necessary. But, brother-fashion, I warn those others not educated to understand these things, if, steeped in the sacraments of Christian purity and glowing with the highest charity for the one and true God, they have passed over all these childish things, for fear they descend to them and, having begun to labor here, bewail their backwardness, not knowing they can pass over difficult roads and obstacles in their path, even if unknown, by flying. But, if those read who because of infirm or untrained steps cannot walk here, having no wings of piety to disregard and fly by these things with, let them not mix themselves up with an improper business, but nourish their wings with the precepts of the most salutary religion and in the nest of the Christian faith, and carried over by these let them leave behind the labor and dust of this road, more intent on the fatherland itself than on these tortuous paths. For these books are written for those who, given up to secular letters, are involved in great errors and waste their natural good qualities in vanities, not knowing what their charm is. And if they would notice it, they would see how to escape those snares, and what is the place of happiest freedom.[1]

Chapter 2

(2) And so you, my friend, sharing reason with me,

1 Because of the passages of Letters 101 to Memorius, Marrou conjectures that this first chapter of Book 6 is really an introduction tacked on in order to make Book 6 a self-sufficient unit. For this was the only Book he sent to Memorius. *Sextum sane librum quem emendatum reperi, ubi est omnis fructus caeterorum, non distuli mittere Charitati tuae* (*Epist.* 101.4). See Marrou, *St. Augustin et la fin de la culture antique* (*Bibl. des Ecoles d'Athènes et de Rome*, cvix, 1939) 580-83.

that we may pass from corporeal to incorporeal things, tell me if you will, when we recite this verse, *Deus creator omnium,* where you think the four iambs and twelve times are it consists of. Is it to be said these numbers are only in the sound heard or also in the hearer's sense belonging to the ears, or also in the act of the reciter, or, because the verse is known, in our memory too?

D. In all of them, I think.

M. Nowhere else?

D. I don't see what else there is, unless, perhaps, there is some interior and superior power these proceed from.

M. I am not asking for what is to be merely suspected. And so if these four kinds are so apparent to you, you see no others equally evident, then let us look at them, if you will, separately one by one and see whether any one of them can be without any other. For I am sure you won't deny the possibility of a sound's beating the air by the drop of liquid or the shock of bodies, with pauses and limits of this sort, and existing where no hearer is present. And when this takes place, of the four there is only this first kind where the sound has the numbers.

D. I don't see any other.

(3) *M.* What about this other kind in the sense of the hearer? Can it be if nothing sounds? For I am not asking whether the ears have, if something sounds, a power [*vis*] of perceiving they don't lack even if the sound is wanting. For, even when there is a silence, they differ somewhat from deaf ears. But I am asking whether they have the numbers themselves, even if nothing is sounding. For it is one thing to have the number, another to be able to sense the harmonious sound. For if you should touch with your fingers a sentient place in the body, the number of times it's touched is sensed by the sense of touch. And when it is sensed, the sensor pos-

sesses it. But it is likewise a question whether, not the sensing, but the number is in the sensor, when nothing is touching.

D. I couldn't easily say the sense is lacking in such numbers determined in themselves, even before anything sounds; otherwise it would neither be charmed by their harmony nor offended by their absurdity. And so, whatever it is we either approve or disapprove by when something sounds, when we do so not by reason but by nature, that I call the number of the sense. For this power of approval and disapproval is not created in my ears, when I hear the sound. The ears are certainly not otherwise accessible to good sounds than to bad ones.

M. Watch out you don't confuse the following two things. For, if any verse is sometimes pronounced shorter, sometimes longer, it cannot occupy the same interval of time, although the same ratio of feet may be preserved. And so, pleasing the ears by its peculiar kind of harmony is the doing of that power we accept harmonious things and reject disagreeable ones by. But its being perceived in a shorter time when it is spoken more quickly than when it is spoken more slowly makes no difference except how long the ears are touched by sound. So this affection of the ears when they are touched with sound is in no way such as if they should not be so touched. For as hearing differs from not hearing, so hearing this tone differs from hearing another. Therefore, this affection is neither prolonged beyond nor restrained to less, since it is the measure of the sound producing it. So it is one thing in the iamb, another in the tribrach, longer in the longer iamb, shorter in the shorter, nothing in a rest. And if it is produced by an harmonious sound, it must be harmonious. Nor can it be except when its author, the sound, is present; for it is like a trace imprinted in water, not found before your pressing a body into it, and not remaining when you have taken it away. But that natural power, belonging to the judiciary, you might say, present in the ears, is still there during the rest, and the sound does not bring it into us, but is rather received by it to be approved of or disapproved of. And so, if I am not mistaken, these two must be distinguished, and it must be admitted the numbers in the passion of the ears when something is heard are brought in by the sound and taken away by the rest. And it is inferred the numbers in the sound itself can be without those in the hearing, although these last cannot be without the first.

Chapter 3

(4) *D.* I agree.

M. Notice, then, this third kind, being in the practice and operation of the person pronouncing, and see whether these numbers can be without those in the memory. For silent within ourselves we can also by thinking go through certain numbers in the amount of time they would be gone through by the voice. It is evident these are in a certain operation of the mind which, since it produces no sound and visits no passion on the ear, shows this kind of number can be without the other two, namely, the one in the sound, the other in the hearer when he hears. But we ask if it would be without memory's accompanying it. Yet, if the soul produces the numbers we find in the beat of the veins, the question is solved. For it is clear they are in the operation and we are no whit helped with them by the memory. And if it is not sure in the case of these whether they belong to the soul operating, certainly about those we produce in recurrent breathing, there is no doubt there are numbers in its time-intervals, and the soul so operates them they can also be changed in many ways when the will is applied. Nor is there need of any memory for their production.

D. It seems to me this kind of number can be without the

other three. For, although I don't doubt the various vein-beats and respiration-intervals are created for the equilibrium [*temperatio*] of bodies, yet who would so much as deny they are created by the soul in operation? And if the flow, according to the diversity of bodies, is faster for some, slower for others, yet, unless there is a soul to produce it, there is none.

M. Consider, too, the fourth class, that is, the class of those numbers in the memory. For, if we draw them out by recollection, and, when we are carried away to other thoughts, we again leave them as if hidden in their own hiding places, I don't think it is difficult to see they can be without the others.

D. I don't doubt they can be without the others. But just the same, unless they were heard or thought, they could not be sent on to the memory. And so, although they remain at the death of those that are heard or thought, yet they are imprinted by them.

Chapter 4

(5) *M*. I don't contradict you, and I should like now to ask which of these four kinds you judge the principal one. Except, I believe, while we were discussing these things, a fifth kind appeared from somewhere, a kind in the natural judgment of perceiving when we are delighted by the equality of numbers or offended at a flaw in them. For I am mindful of your opinion our sense could have in no way done this without certain numbers latent in it. Or do you, perhaps, think a great power like this belongs to some one of those four?

D. On the contrary. I think this kind is to be distinguished from all of them. For it is one thing to sound and this is attributed to a body; another to hear, and in the body the soul is passive to this from sounds; another to produce numbers either more slow or less so; another to remember them; and another, by accepting or rejecting, to give sentence on them all as if by some natural right.

(6) *M.* Come, now, tell me which of these five is the most excellent.

D. The fifth, I think.

M. You are right, for, unless it excelled, it could not bring judgment on them. But again, I want to know of the other four which you judge the greatest.

D. The kind in the memory, certainly. For I see those numbers are of greater duration than when they sound or are heard or are produced.

M. Then you prefer things made to things making. For you said a while ago those in the memory are imprinted by the others.

D. I should rather not prefer them. But still, how can I not prefer those of greater duration to those of less, I don't see.

M. Don't let this disturb you. For not as eternal things to temporal are those decaying through a longer time to be preferred to those passing away in a shorter time. Because one day's sanity is to be preferred to many days' folly. And if we compare desirable things, one day's reading is better than many days' writing, if the same thing is read in one day, written in many. So numbers in the memory, although they remain longer than those they are imprinted by, yet it is not proper to prefer them to those we cause, not in the body, but in the soul. For they both pass away, one by cessation, others by forgetting. But those we operate seem to be snatched from us, even though we have not yet stopped, by the succession of those immediately following, when the first by disappearing give place to the second, the second to the third, and continuously those before to those after, until a complete stop destroys the last. But in the case of forgetting, several numbers are wiped away together, even though by degrees. For they do not remain entire for any time. For what is not found in the memory after a year, for instance, is also already less after a day's time. But this decrease is not sensed, yet it is not therefore falsely conjectured. Because the whole does not disappear suddenly the day before the year is finished, and so the understanding grants it begins to lapse from the time it comes into the memory. That is why we often say, 'I vaguely remember,' whenever we repeat something, recalling it after a time before its complete destruction. And, therefore, both these kinds of numbers are mortal. But things making are by right preferred to those made.

D. I accept and approve.

(7) *M.* Now, then, consider the other three, and explain which of them is the best, and so to be preferred to the others.

D. That's not easy. For, according to the rule things making are to be preferred to those made, I am forced to give the prize to the sounding numbers. For, when we hear we sense them, and when we sense them we are passive to them. And so, these last make those others existing in the ear's affection when we hear, but, again, these we have by sensing produce in the memory others they are rightly preferred to, since they are produced by them. But here, because sensing and remembering both belong to the soul, I am not disturbed if I should prefer something produced in the soul to something else likewise produced in it. But I am disturbed how the sounding numbers, certainly corporeal or somehow in a body, are to be considered of more worth than those found in the soul when we sense. And yet, again, it is disturbing how these last are not rather to be more highly considered since they make, and the others are made by them.

M. Be rather amazed at the body's being able to make anything in the soul. For it could not, perhaps, if the body the soul used to animate and govern without trouble and with the greatest ease, changed for the worse by the first sin, were not subject to death and corruption. And yet, it has a beauty of its own, and in this way it sets its dignity off to fair advantage in the eyes of the soul. And neither its wound nor its disease has deserved to be without the honor of some ornament. And the highest Wisdom of God designed to assume this wound, by means of a wonderful and ineffable sacrament, when He took upon Himself man without sin, but not without the condition of sin. For He was willing to be humanly born, to suffer, and to die. None of these things was accomplished by our merit, but by this most excellent goodness, in order we might rather look to the pride we most deservingly fell into those things by, than to the humiliations He undeservingly suffered, and so with calm mind we might pay the death owed, if He, too, was able to bear it unowed on our account, and anything else more secret and more atoned for in such a sacrament to be understood by saintly and more holy people. And so it is not surprising a soul operating in mortal flesh feels the passion of bodies. And not because it is better than the body ought all taking place in it be considered better than all taking place in the body. I suppose you think the true is to be preferred to the false.

D. Who wouldn't.

M. But what we see in our sleep isn't a tree?

D. Not at all.

M. But its form is in the soul. And the form of what we now see has been made in the body. And so, since the true is better than the false, and although the soul is better than the body, the true in the body is better than the false in the soul. But as the latter is better in so far as it is true, not in so far as it is made in the body, so the former is worse in so far as it is false, not in so far as it is made in the soul. Have you anything to say about this?

D. Nothing, certainly.

M. Listen, then, to this other thing, nearer to the mark, I believe, than 'better.' For you won't deny what is proper is better than what is not proper.

D. I certainly admit that.

M. But no one doubts a man would be improper in the same clothers a woman would be proper in.

D. That's evident.

M. Well, then, it isn't to be greatly wondered at, is it, if this form of numbers is proper in the sounds falling on the ears, and improper in the soul when it has them by sensing and being passive?

D. I don't think so.

M. Why, then, do we hesitate to prefer sounding and corporeal numbers to those made by them, even though they are made in the soul which is better than the body? Because we are preferring numbers to numbers, producers to produced, not the body to the soul. For bodies are the better the more harmonious [*numerosiora*] they are by means of these numbers. But the soul is made better through lack of those numbers it receives through the body, when it turns away from the carnal senses and is reformed by the divine numbers of wisdom. So it is truly said in the Holy Scriptures, 'I have gone the rounds, to know and consider and seek wisdom and number.'[2] And you are in no way to think this was said about those numbers shameful theaters resound with, but about those, I believe, the soul does not receive from the body, but receiving from God on high it rather impresses on the body. And what kind of thing this is, is not to be considered in this place.

2 Eccle. 7.26.

Chapter 5

(8) But, lest it turn out the life of a tree is better than our own, because it doesn't receive numbers from the body by sensing (for it has no sense), it must be carefully considered if there is really nothing called hearing unless something is produced in the soul by the body. But it is very absurd to subordinate the soul like a matter to the body as an artisan. For the soul is never inferior to the body, and all matter is inferior to the artisan. The soul, then, is in no way a matter subordinated to the body as an artisan. But it would be, if the body worked numbers in it. Therefore, when we hear, numbers are not made in the soul by those we know in sounds. Or do you think otherwise?

D. What happens, then, when a person hears?

M. Whatever it is—and perhaps we cannot find or explain it—it won't result, will it, in our denying the soul's being better than the body? And when we admit this, can we subordinate it to the body working and imposing numbers, so the body is an artisan but the soul a matter something harmonious is made from and in? And, if we believe this, we must believe the soul is inferior to the body. And what more miserable and detestable thing than this can be believed? And since things are thus, I shall try as much as God will help me to conjecture at and discuss whatever lies there. But if, because of the infirmity of either or both of us, the result should be less that we wish, either we ourselves shall investigate it at another time when we are less agitated, or we shall leave it to more intelligent people to examine, or, unworried, we shall leave it unsolved. But we must not for that reason let these other more certain things slip from our hands.

D. I shall hold that as unshaken if I can, and yet I shouldn't wish that secret place to remain impenetrable to us.

(9) *M.* I shall say right away what I think. But you must either follow or go ahead of me, if you can, when you see me stop and hesitate. For I think the body is animated by the soul only to the purpose of the doer. Nor do I think it is affected in any way by the body, but it acts *through* it and *in* it as something divinely subjected to its dominion. But at times it acts with ease, at times with difficulty, according as, proportionately to its merits, the corporeal nature yields more or less to it. And so, whatever corporeal things are taken into this body or come into contact with it from without, have in the body itself, not in the soul, some effect either opposed to its operation or agreeing with it. And so, when it fights the body's opposition and with difficulty throws the matter subjected to it into the ways of its operation, it becomes more attentive to the actions because of the difficulty. And this difficulty on account of the attention, when not unobserved, is called feeling, and this is named pain or trouble. But when what is taken in or touches it easily agrees, all that or as much as is necessary is projected into the course of its operation. And this action of the soul by which it joins its body to an outside body harmonizing with it, since it is accomplished more attentively because of an unusualness, is not unobserved, but because of the harmony is felt with pleasure. But when those things the soul uses to mend the wear and tear in the body are lacking, need follows. And when the soul becomes more attentive on account of the difficulty of the action and this operation does not pass unobserved, then this is called hunger or thirst or some such thing. But when there is a superfluity of things taken in, from the burden of these is born a difficulty of operation and an awareness accompanies the issue. And since this action does not pass unobserved, indigestion is felt. It also operates with attention when it gets rid of the superfluity: if smoothly, with pleasure; if roughly, with pain. The soul also occupies

itself attentively with any sickly disturbance of the body, desiring to succor it as it declines and disintegrates. And when this action does not pass unobserved, it is said to feel sickness and illness.

(10) In short, it seems to me the soul, when it has sensations in the body, is not affected in any way by it, but it pays more attention to the passions of the body. But this sense, even while we do not sense, being nevertheless in the body, is an instrument of the body directed by the soul for its ordering so the soul may be more prepared to act on the passions of the body with attention to the end of joining like things to like and of repelling what is harmful. Further, I think, it operates something luminous in the eyes, a most clear and mobile air in ears, something misty in the nose, something damp in the mouth, something earthy and muddy you might say in the touch. But whether these are put together in this way or by some other distribution, the soul acts quietly if the things within are in unity of health as if they agreed to some domestic pact. But when things affecting the body, you might say with otherness, are applied, it exerts more attentive actions accomodated to certain places and instruments. Then it is said to see or hear or smell or taste or touch. And by such actions it willingly associates proper things and resists improper ones. I think the soul, then, when it senses, produces these actions on the passions of the body, but does not receive these passions.

(11) And so, when we now examine the numbers of sounds and the sense of hearing is called into doubt, it isn't necessary to digress any longer. Let's return, then, to the question, and see if sound causes anything in the ear. Or do you deny that it does?

D. Not at all.

M. Well, you agree ears are an animated member?

D. I do.

M. Since, then, what in this member is like air is moved when the air is moved, we don't believe, do we, the soul, with a vital motion quickening in silence the body of the ears before this sound, can either stop from the work of moving what it animates, or can move the air of the ear now moved extrinsically in the same way it moved before the sound slipped in?

D. It seems it must be in another way.

M. Then, to move it in another way, mustn't it be said to act, not to be acted on?

D. That's true.

M. So we are not absurd in believing the movements of the soul, or its actions or operations—find any easier name you can—do not escape the soul's notice when it senses.

(12) But these operations are applied to these passions of the body either as when figures interrupt the light of our eyes, or sound enters the ears, or odors move into the nostrils, or savors to the palate, and to the rest of the body solid and bodily things; or as when something runs and crosses from place to place in the body itself; or as when the whole body is moved by its own weight or that of another. These are operations the soul applies to these passions of the body, delighting the soul when it agrees with them, offending it when it opposes them. But when it is affected by its own operations, it is affected by itself, not by the body. But clearly when it adapts itself to the body, it is less with itself, because the body is always less than it is.

(13) And so, when the soul is turned from its God to its servant, it is necessarily deficient; but, when it is turned from its servant to its God, it necessarily progresses and furnishes its servant a very easy life, and, therefore, the least laborious and

full of business, no attention being given it in its surpassing peace. Just so is the bodily affection called health. Indeed, it needs none of our attention, not because the soul then does nothing in the body, but because it does nothing more easily. For in all our operations the greater the difficulty we operate with, the more attentively we do it. But this health will be the most firm and certain when this body will have been restored to its former stability, in its own time and order. And this its resurrection is properly believed before it is fully understood. For the soul must be ruled by the superior, and rule the inferior. But God alone is superior to it, and only body is inferior to it, if you mean the soul whole and entire. And so as it cannot be entire without the Lord, so it cannot excel without a servant. But as its Lord is greater than it, so its servant is less. And so, intent on its Lord, it understands His eternal things and is greater, and its servant, too, is greater in its kind through the soul itself. But when the Lord is neglected, intent on its servant with the carnal concupiscence it is seduced by, the soul feels the movements it gives its servant, and is less; yet not so inferior as its servant, even when it is at the lowest in its own nature. But the body by this offense of its mistress is much less than it was, since she was much greater before it.

(14) And so, for one now mortal and fragile, it is dominated with great difficulty and attention. And from there does this error fall upon the soul that it esteems the body's pleasure because the matter yields to its attention, more than it esteems its health needing no attention. No wonder it is involved in troubles, preferring unquiet to security. But a greater unquiet arises for one turning back to God for fear he be turned away. And it is so until the push of carnal business, excited by daily habit and inserting itself into the heart of the conversion by disorderly memories, comes to rest. When a man's movements

that carry him away into outside things have been in this way quieted, then he enjoys an interior freedom of peace signified by the sabbath. So he knows God alone is his Lord, and He is served with the greatest freedom. But, although he starts those carnal movements as he wishes, he does not stop them as he wishes. For, again, the reward of sin is not in his power as sin itself is. For, indeed, this soul is a thing of great worth, and yet it doesn't remain apt for suppressing its own lascivious movements. For it sins in its strength, and by divine law made weaker after sin it is less able to undo what it has done. 'Unhappy man I am, who will deliver me from the body of this death? The grace of God through Jesus Christ our Lord.'[3] Then a movement of the soul, conserving its force and not yet extinct, is said to be in the memory. And, when the mind is intent on something else, it is as if that previous movement were not in the mind and were lost, except, before it dies away, it be renewed by some affinity of similar things.

(15) But have you anything to say to the contrary?

D. You seem to me to say what is probable, and I shouldn't dare oppose.

M. Since, then, feeling itself is a moving the body against the movement made in it, don't you think then we do not feel when bones and nails and hair are cut, not because these are not at all alive in us, for otherwise they would neither be held together nor be fed nor grow, nor show their strength in begetting their kind. But because they are penetrated with an air less free or mobile than is necessary for the soul's causing a movement there so rapid as that movement it is against when it's said to feel. Although some such life is understood in trees and other vegetation, it is nowise proper to prefer it, not only to our own life exceeding it in reason, but also to that of brutes.

3 Rom. 7.24-25.

For it is one thing not to sense because of very great solidity, and another not to sense because of very great health of body. For in the one case the instruments moving relatively to the passions of the body are lacking, and in the other these passions themselves are lacking.

D. I approve and agree.

Chapter 6

(16) *M.* Let's get back to the problem proposed, and tell me, of the three kinds of numbers, one in the memory, the other in sensing, and another in sound, which of these seems to you the most excellent.

D. I put sound after these other two, both in the soul and in some sense living. But of these last two I am uncertain which I consider superior. But, perhaps, since we said those in action are to be preferred to those in the memory only because the ones are active and the others are caused by them, so for the same reason it is proper to prefer also those in the soul while we are listening to those in the memory caused by them. That's the way it seemed to me before.

M. I don't think your reply absurd. But since it has been argued those numbers in sensing are also operations of the soul, how do you distinguish them from those we see to be in act even when the soul in silence and not remembering performs something harmonious through intervals of time? Or do the ones belong to the soul moving itself with respect to its body, while those others inhering belong to the soul moving itself with respect to the body's passions?

D. I accept this distinction

M .Well, do you think it acceptable those relative to the body be judged superior to those relative to the body's passions?

D. Those existing in silence seem to me to be freer than those exerted not only on the body but also on the body's passions.

M. It seems we have distinguished five kinds of numbers and ordered them in some sort of scale of merits. And if you will, we shall impose names proper to them, to avoid in the rest of our discourse using more words than things.

D. Very willingly.

M. Then let the first be named judicial, the second advancing [*progressores*], the third reacting [*occursores*],[4] the fourth memorial, the fifth sounding.

D. I understand and I am glad to use these names.

Chapter 7

(17) *M.* Come now, tell me, which of these seems to you undying, or do you think they all fall in their time and die?

D. I think the judicial alone are undying. For the others, I see, either pass away when they are made or are striken out of the memory by forgetfulness.

M. You are just as certain, then, of the immortality of the first as you are of the destruction of the others? Or is it proper to inquire more diligently whether they are undying?

D. Let's look into the matter thoroughly.

M. Say, then, when I pronounce a verse sometimes longer, sometimes shorter, provided I comply with the law of times putting feet in a one-two ratio, I don't offend the judgment of your senses with any kind of hitch or fraud, do I?

D. Not at all.

M. Well, but that sound, given out in shorter and, you

---

4 *Occursores* is here translated as 'reacting,' but with the understanding, of course, that the sounding numbers cause the reacting numbers only as something like occasional causes.

might say, faster syllables, it can't occupy more time than it sounds, can it?

D. How can it?

M. Then, if those judicial numbers are time-bound in just the interval the sounding numbers were disposed in, can they hope to judge those other sounds based on the same iambic law, but slower?

D. In no way.

M. Then it appears those judicial numbers are not confined to a span of time.

D. It certainly appears so.

(18) *M.* You are right in agreeing. But if they are confined to no interval, then no matter how slowly I should emit iambic sounds in regular intervals, they could still be used for judging. But now, if I should say a syllable of such a stretch as three steps in walking (to make it small), and another syllable double that, and if I should order the succeeding iambs at such a pace, then the law of one to two would nevertheless be preserved. And yet we couldn't apply that natural judgment to confirming these measurements, could we?

D. I can't deny you seem right, for my opinion of the matter is very simple.

M. Then the judicial numbers are also confined to certain limits of time-spans they cannot exceed in their judgments. And whatever exceeds these intervals, they find no way to judge. And if they should be confined in this way, I do not see how they are immortal.

D. And I don't see what I can say to that. Although now I shall be less forward in presuming on their immortality, yet I do not understand how they are in this way proved mortal. For it is possible whatever intervals they can judge they can always judge, since I cannot say they are destroyed as the others by forgetfulness, or their length of time is so long as a sound's movement, or of such a stretch as reacting numbers, or as the numbers we have called advancing, impelled in time and prolonged in length. For each of these passes away with the time of its operation. But the judicial remain certainly in the nature of man, whether also in the soul I do not know, to pass judgment on things given even if varied within certain lengths, by approving harmonies in them and rejecting discords.

(19) *M.* At least you concede some men are more quickly offended by discordant numbers, some more slowly, and most judge them defective only by the comparison with sound ones on hearing them agree and disagree.

D. I agree to that.

M. Well, what do you think this difference arises from, if not from nature or practice or both?

D. That's true.

M. Then, I want to know if someone at sometime could pass judgment on and approve longer intervals than another could.

D. I believe that's possible.

M. Well, anyone who can't, if he should practice properly and should not be really dull, could, couldn't he?

D. Certainly he could.

M. But he couldn't go so far as to judge even longer intervals, comprehending in that judicial sense intervals in the ratio of one to two hours or days or months or years (for they'd at least be hindered by sleep) and approving them as iambs of motion.

D. They can't.

M. Why can't they do so? Unless it's because to each living thing in its proper kind and in its proportion with the universe is given a sense of places and times, so that even as its body is so much in proportion to the body of the universe whose part it is, and its age so much in proportion to the age of the universe whose part it is, so its sensing complies with the action it pursues in proportion to the movement of the universe whose part it is? So this world, often called in Sacred Scriptures by the name of heaven and earth, is great by containing all things whose parts being all diminished in proportion it remains just as large, or increased in proportion it still remains just as large. For nothing is large of itself in space and time-stretches, but with respect to something shorter; and again nothing is small of itself, but with respect to something larger.[5] And so, if there is attributed to human nature for the actions of carnal life a sense such that it cannot pass judgment on greater stretches of times than the intervals pertaining to the use of such a life demand, then, since this nature of man is mortal, so I think also this sense is mortal. For it is not for nothing custom is called a sort of second and fitted-on nature. But we see new senses in the judging of this kind of corporeal things, built up by custom, by another custom disappear.

Chapter 8

(20) But whatever kind of thing these judicial numbers may be, they are certainly superior to any other in this, that we doubt and with difficulty find out if they are mortal. But of the other four kinds there is no question they are mortal. And although they do not embrace some members

---

5 Just as the thing rhythmed was considered only as a matrix for ratios, so here the extended world is such a matrix, and so is the sensible life of man. Being then belongs more to the relations that to the relata and this doctrine will find its keystone in the Trinity where the distinction of Persons involves a certain primacy of relations. It is interesting to note in this connection that Boethius, who mentions Augustine, carefully pointed this out in his discussion of the categories of Aristotle in his *De Trinitate.*

of these four classes because they have been extended beyond their laws, yet they appropriate the kinds themselves for their very consideration. For even the advancing numbers, when they seek a certain harmonious operation in the body, are modified by the secret will of the judicial numbers. For whatever restrains and keeps us from walking with unequal steps, or from beating out in unequal intervals, or from eating or drinking with uneven motions of the jaw, and from scratching with unequal motions of the nails, or to be brief, from unequal movements in any application of ourselves to doing something with our bodily members, and tacitly demands a certain equality, that very thing is something judicial, I don't know what, introducing God the builder of the animal, properly believed to be the author of all fittingness and agreement.

(21) And these reacting numbers, brought forth certainly not according to their own will, but in virtue of the body's passions, in so far as the memory can keep their intervals, just so far they given over to the judgment of the judicial are numbers and are judged. For the number consisting in time-intervals can in no way be judged by us unless we are aided in the judging by memory. For any syllable, no matter how short, since it begins and stops, has its beginning at one time and its ending at another. Then it is stretched over some little interval of time and stretches from its beginning through its middle to an end. So reason finds spatial as well as temporal intervals have an infinite division and so no syllable's end is heard with its beginning. And so, even in hearing the shortest syllable, unless memory help us have in the soul that motion made when the beginning sounded, at the very moment when no longer the beginning but the end of the syllable is sounding, then we cannot say we have heard anything. And from this it often comes about, being occupied with another thought, we do not

in conversation seem to have heard even ourselves. This is not because the soul does not at that time put in motion those reacting numbers, since certainly the sound reaches the ears, and the soul cannot be idle at its body's passion and since it cannot move differently than if that passion of the body should occur, but because the impetus of the motion is immediately blotted out by the attention [*intentio*] on something else, an impetus which, if it remained, would remain in the memory so we would also know and feel we had heard. But if a rather slow mind follows not too easily what reason discovers in the case of a short syllable, in the case of two syllables there's certainly no doubt no soul can hear both at the same time. For the second does not sound unless the first stops. For how can what cannot sound together be heard together? Then, as the diffusion of rays shining out into the open from tiny pupils of the eye, and belonging therefore to our body, in such a way that, although the things we see are placed at a distance, they are yet quickened by the soul, so, just as we are helped by their effusion in comprehending place-spans, the memory too, because it is somehow the light of time-spans, so far comprehends these time-spans as in its own way it too can be projected. But when a sound beats a longer time on the ears, in no way articulated and again another, double it, or equal it, is added on from some stopping place or another, then that motion of the mind, created by its attention on the past and finished sound in its transition, is repressed by its attention on the continuously succeeding sound, and so it does not remain in the memory. And so mustn't these judicial numbers be thought of as extended in a certain interval of time? For they can't judge the numbers situated in the time-spans unless the memory should come to their assistance, with the exception of the advancing numbers whose very advance they regulate. But there intervene the time-spans where we forget or remember what they judge. And so we cannot judge round or square or any other solid definite things in those bodily forms which are properly objects of the eyes, unless we turn them around to the eyes. But when one part is seen, if for that reason it should blot out what is seen in another, then the attention of the person judging would be in vain, because it, too, is accomplished in a certain time-span. And it is up to memory to see to this diversity.

(22) But it is much more evident we judge memorial numbers by judicial when the memory itself presents them. For, if reacting numbers are judged in so far as they are presented by it, much more are those found to live in the memory itself which are brought back by memory itself as if they had been stored up by other applications of our attention. For what else do we do when we recall to memory except examine somehow what we've stored up? But a motion of the mind, not destroyed, runs back into our cogitation on the occasion of similar ones, and it's this that's called remembering. And so, either in thought alone or also in the movement of our members, we enact numbers we have already enacted sometime or other. But for that reason we know they haven't just come, but come back into our cogitation, because whenever they were being committed to memory, they were repeated with difficulty, and we needed prior practice in order to follow through. And with this difficulty overcome, when the numbers offer themselves without trouble and at will, comformably to the times and in their proper order, so easily, indeed, those inhering more forcibly come forth as if of their own will even while we are thinking of something else, we then feel they are not new. There is also another thing, I think, giving us to feel the present motion of the mind has already existed at some time: that is, to recognize when we compare by an interior light of some

sort the recent, and certainly more lively, movements of the action we are in the midst of when we remember, with the now more composed memorial numbers. And such knowledge is recognition and remembering. Then the memorial numbers are also judged by these judicial numbers, never alone, but along with active or reacting numbers or with both, bringing them from their hiding-places to the light, and recalling these numbers, lost before and now brought to life again. So, since the reacting numbers are judged in so far as the memory presents them to those judging, in turn the memorial numbers can be judged as the reacting numbers exhibit them. So this is the difference: for the reacting numbers to be judged, the memory presents what might be called recent traces of their flight, but when we hear and judge the memorial numbers, the same traces relive with the passage of the reacting numbers. Now, why do we need to say anything further about the sounding numbers, since, if they are heard, they are judged in the reacting numbers? But if they sound where they can't be heard, who doubts they can't be judged by us? And just as in sounds with the ears as instruments, so in dancing and other visible motions, we judge, by means of these same judicial numbers with the help of the memory, whatever pertains to temporal numbers.

Chapter 9

(23) Since things are so, let us try if we can and transcend those judicial numbers and see if there are any superior to them. Although in the case of these judicial numbers we now see a minimum of time-spans, yet they are only applied for judging those things in a time-span, and not even all such, but only those articulated memory-wise. Do you object to this?

D. The force and power of these judicial numbers moves me to the utmost. For it seems to me it's to them the functions of all the senses are referred. And so, I don't know whether among numbers any thing more excellent than these can be found.

M. There is nothing lost in our looking more carefully. For, either we shall find in the human soul superior ones, or, if it should be clear there are none in it higher, we shall confirm these to be the highest in it. For it is one thing not to be, and another not to be capable of being found either by us or any man. But I think when that verse *Deus creator omnium* we quoted is sung, we hear it through reacting numbers, recognize it through memorial numbers, pronounce it through advancing numbers, are delighted through judicial numbers, and appraise it by still others, and in accordance with these more hidden numbers we bring another judgment on this delight, a kind of judgment on the judicial numbers. Do you think it's the same thing to be delighted by sense and to appraise by reason?

D. I admit they are different. But I am disturbed first by the name. Why aren't those called judicial numbers where reason rather than where delight resides? Second, I fear this appraisal of reason is only a more diligent judgment of judicial numbers concerning themselves. Not one kind of number in delight and another in reason, but one and the same kind of number judges at one time those produced in the body when memory presents them as we just proved, and at the other times of themselves, in a purer manner and more remote from the body.

(24) *M.* Don't worry about names; the thing is in the meaning [*potestas*]. Names are imposed by convention, not by nature. But your thinking them the same and not wishing to accept them as two kinds of number—the same soul's doing both, I guess, wrings that out of you. But you must notice in

advancing numbers the same soul[6] moves the body or moves to the body, and in reacting numbers the same soul goes to meet its passions, and in memorial numbers it fluctuates in motions, you might say, until they somehow subside. And so we see the motions and affections of one nature, that is, the soul, in these kinds which are necessarily enumerated and distinguished. And, therefore, if, as it is one thing to be moved to those things the body is passive to, and this is done in sensing; another, to move oneself to the body, and this is done in operating; another, to hold in the soul what is gotten from these motions, and that is to remember; so it is one thing to accept or reject these motions either when they are first produced or when revived by the memory, and this is done in the delight at the fitness or in the distaste at the absurdity of such movements or affections; and another thing to appraise whether they delight rightly or not, and this is done by reasoning—if all this is true, then we must admit these last are of two kinds just as the first are of three kinds. And, if we have been right in our judgment, the very sense of delight could not have been favorable to equal intervals and rejected perturbed ones, unless it itself were imbued with numbers; then, too, the reason laid upon this delight cannot at all judge of the numbers it has under it, without more powerful numbers. And, if these things are true, it appears five kinds of numbers have been found in the soul, and, when you add to these those corporeal numbers we have called sounding, you will see six kinds of numbers in rank and order. And now, if you will, let those that tried to take first place be called sensuous, and those found to be more excellent receive the name of judicial numbers, since that is more honorable. And again I think the name of sounding numbers ought to be

6 I read *eamdem animam* for *eadem animam* in Migne, an obvious misprint not in Benedictine Edition.

changed, since, if they should be called corporeal, they will also evidently signify those involved in dancing and in any other visible motion. Do you approve, then, of what's been said?

D. I do. For it seems to me both true and evident. And I am willing to accept your corrections in vocabulary.

Chapter 10

(25) *M.* Well, now examine the force and power of reason in so far as we can examine it in its works. For reason itself, to mention the most extraordinary thing it attains in its operation, first has considered what is good mensuration, and seen it to be in a free movement, and directed it to the end of its own beauty. Then it saw there was something in the movements of bodies varying in the brevity and length of time, in so far as it was greater or less in time, and something else varying in the beat of spatial intervals in certain degrees of swiftness and slowness. After this division, it articulated into different numbers whatever was in a time-stretch by means of moderate intervals convenient to the human senses, and followed through their kinds and order to the measurements of verses. Lastly, it turned its attention to what the soul it's the head of would do in the measuring, operating, sensing, and retaining of these things. And it separated all these numbers of the soul from bodies. And it saw itself could not notice, distinguish or rightly enumerate all these things without certain numbers of its own, and it set them above the others as of an inferior order, by means of a kind of judicial appraisal.

(26) And now of its own delight, that looks so closely into the balancings of times and shows its decisions in measuring these numbers, it asks this question: 'What is it we love in sensible harmony?' Nothing but a sort of equality and

equally measured intervals, isn't it so? Does the pyrrhic foot or spondaic or anapestic or dactylic or proceleusmatic or dispondaic delight us for any other reason than its comparing the one of its parts to the other by an equal division of itself? And what beauty does the iamb, trochee, or tribrach have if not the division of their greater part into two such as their lesser? And, too, do the six-time feet sound more smooth and gay except through their division according to either law: that is, either into two equal parts with three times each, or into one part single and the other double; that is, so the greater part is twice the less and is in this way divided equally by it, since the four times are measured off and cut in two by the two times? What about the five and seven-time feet? How is it they seem more adapted to prose than to verse, if not because their smaller part does not divide their larger in two? And yet, whence are they themselves admitted in the order of their own kind to the numberliness of times, if not because the smaller part also in the five-time foot has two such sub-parts as the greater has three, and in seven-time feet the smaller three such as the greater four? So in all feet, no measuring net marks off any least part others as many as possible are not equal to.

(27) Consider in the case of feet joined together, whether this conjoining be continued on as far as one wishes as in rhythms, or whether it be restrained by some definite end as in meters, or whether it be divided into two members symmetrical to one another by some law as in verses—by what now other than equality is one foot in accord with another? And how is it the molossus' and ionic's middle syllable, a long one, can be divided, not by division, but by the will of the person reciting and beating time, into two equal moments, so even the whole foot is in harmony with each three-time

part when it is added to others divided in the same way? Isn't it only because the law of equality dominates, that is, because it's equal to its sides, each of two times, and it itself is of two times? Why can't the same thing be done in the case of the amphibrach when it is added to other four-time feet, if it isn't because an equality of this sort isn't found there, the middle syllable being double and the sides single? Why in rests isn't our sense offended by a deficiency, if not because what is due that same law of equality, although not in sound, is yet made up in spread of time?[7] Why, too, is a short syllable taken for a long one when followed by a rest—and not by convention, but by natural consideration directing the ears—if not because by the same law of equality we are prevented, in a longer time-span, from forcing the sound into a shorter

7 There is more in this sentence than meets the eye. In the first place we have here the appearance in rhythm of the being of non-being. The rest, the absence of a sensible motion, is itself the object of the time-count and plays its role on the same level as a sensible sound. Its absence is counted by the 'spread of time' (*spatium temporis*). This is the forerunner of the *distentio animi* of the *Confessions,* all of which is certainly tied in with Plotinus' doctrine of *tó parakoloúthema* in his treatise *On Time and Eternity*: 'What it means then to say [time] is the accompaniment of movement . . . .' (III. 7.10.1-2), For the essential point of Plotinus' attack on Aristotle's 'Time-is-the-number-of-movement' theory is that there is something like the synthesis of the constantly recurring motions which necessitates an intellectual accompaniment of the motion. For, without this there would be no unity of the past and present, no one magnitude to be numbered. Nor can the movement itself establish its own homogeneity so that it can be said for instance that the daily motion of the heavens is always equal to itself. It is the intellectual accompaniment which in view of equality considers one or another cyclic movement in the sensible world as equal one cycle to another and so perceives an order there. 'For on the one hand one will refer a body moving for such and such a time to the [uniform] movement of such and such magnitude (for it is the principle) and to its time. But the time of this movement, on the other hand, one will refer to the movement of the soul which divides out the equal intervals' (*Enn.* III. 7.13.58-62). So in mechanical theories the choice of equal motions is made with a view to the convenient ordering of all the others. One should hasten to add this does not reduce time to a purely

time? And so the nature of hearing and passing over in silence allows the lengthening of a syllable beyond two times: so what is also filled with rest can be filled with sound. But for a syllable to occupy less than two times, with a span left and rests at will, is a sort of deception of equality, because there can be no equality in less than two. And finally in the case of that equality of members, the circuits the Greeks call *periodoi* are varied by and verses are formed by, how is a return made somehow to the same equality unless the members joined together as unequals be found to have a force of equality so that in the circuit the shorter member harmonize in beat with the greater by equal feet, and in the verse by a more subtle consideration of numbers?

(28) And so reason wonders and asks the sensuous delight of the soul which reserves to itself the judicial role whether, when an equality in the number of time-spans pleases it, any two short syllables one hears are really equal, or could it be one of them is pronounced longer, not to the long syllable's measure, but a little under, yet enough to exceed its like. You can't deny this is possible, can you, when the soul's delight does not sense these differences, but delights in unequals as equals?

psychological being. Any thing perceived by an act of the intellect is an object in its own right.

It is not too far-fetched, perhaps, to consider along with these texts of Plotinus and Augustine a text of Aristoxenus: 'It is clear that the comprehending of melody is the accompanying with hearing and understanding of the notes gone by in their every difference (For melody like the other parts of music is in becoming) . . . For the comprehension of music consists of these two, sensing and memory. For we must sense what is becoming and remember the become. There is no other way to follow the things of music' (*Harmonica* II 38, 29-39.3).

The doctrine of Augustine certainly starts with these same terms and insights. Obviously, the doctrine of creation *ex nihilo* and of the Incarnation will force him to more intellectualist conclusions. See Guitton, *Le temps et l'eternité chez Plotin et St. Augustin* (Paris 1933), which, however, does not treat the problem profoundly enough.

And what is worse than this error and inequality? And so we are advised to turn away from the enjoyment of things imitating equality. For we cannot perceive whether they perfectly fill out their time, although we can perhaps perceive they do not perfectly do so. And yet in so far as they imitate we cannot deny they are beautiful in their kind and order.

Chapter 11

(29) Let's not, then, be envious of things inferior to ourselves, and let us, our Lord and God helping, order ourselves between those below us and those above us, so we are not troubled by lower, and take delight only in higher things. For delight is a kind of weight in the soul. Therefore, delight orders the soul. 'For where your treasure is, there will your heart be also.'[8] Where delight, there the treasure; where the heart, there happiness or misery. But what are the higher things, if not those where the highest unchangeable undisturbed and eternal equality resides? Where there is no time, because there is no change, and from where times are made and ordered and changed, imitating eternity as they do when the turn of the heavens comes back to the same state, and the heavenly bodies to the same place, and in days and months and years and centuries and other revolutions of the stars obey the laws of equality, unity, and order. So terrestrial things are subject to celestial, and their time circuits join together in harmonious succession for a poem of the universe.

(30) And so many of these things seem to us disordered and perturbed, because we have been sewn into their order according to our merits, not knowing what beautiful thing Divine Providence purposes for us. For, if someone should be

8 Matt. 6.21.

put as a statue in an angle of the most spacious and beautiful building, he could not perceive the beauty of the building he himself is a part of. Nor can the soldier in the front line of battle get the order of the whole army. And in a poem, if syllables should live and perceive only so long as they sound, the harmony and beauty of the connected work would in no way please them. For they could not see or approve the whole, since it would be fashioned and perfected by the very passing away of these singulars. So God has ordered the man who sins as vicious, but not viciously. For he has been made vicious by will, thus losing the whole he who obeyed God's precepts possessed, and has been ordered in part so who did not will to fulfill the law has been fulfilled by the law. But whatever is fulfilled by the law is also fulfilled justly; and whatever justly is not fulfilled viciously, because God's precepts possessed, and has been ordered in part so he far as he is man is something good. But whatever is unchaste in so far as it is unchaste is a bad work. But man for the most part is born of unchastity, that is to say, from man's bad work, God's good work.

(31) And so, to return to the subject all this was said for, these numbers are pre-eminent by virtue of the beauty of ratio. And if we were absolutely separated from them, then whenever we should be disposed to the body, the advancing numbers would not alter the sensuous numbers. But by moving bodies they produce the sensible beauties of times. And so reacting numbers are also made opposed to sounding numbers. And the same soul receiving all its own motions multiplies, you might say, in itself, and makes them subject to recall. And this force it has is called memory, a great help in the everyday business of this life.

(32) Then whatever this memory contains from the

motions of the mind brought to bear on the passions of the body are called *phantasíai* in Greek. And I don't find in Latin anything I should rather call them. And the life of opinion consists in having them instead of things known and things perceived, and such a life is at the very entrance of error. But when these motions react with each other, and boil up, you might say, with various and conflicting winds of purpose, they generate one motion from another; not indeed those impressed from the senses and gotten from the reactions to the body's passions, but like images of images, to which we give the name phantasms. For my father I have often seen I know, in one way, and my grandfather I have never seen, another way. The first of these is a phantasia, the other phantasm. The first I find in my memory, the last in that motion of my mind born of those the memory has. But it is difficult both to find out and to explain how they are born. Yet, I think, if I had never seen human bodies, I could nowise imagine them by thinking with a visible form. But what I make from what I've seen, I make by memory. Yet it's one thing to find a phantasia in the memory and another to make a phantasm out of the memory. And a power of the soul can do all these things. But it is the greatest error to hold even true phantasms for things known, although in both kinds there is that we say, not absurdly, we know, that is, we have sensed such and such things, or imagined them. After all, I am not afraid to say I had a father and a grandfather. But I should be mad to say it is they themselves my mind holds in the phantasia or phantasm. But some follow their phantasms so headlong the only ground for all false opinions is to hold phantasias or phantasms for things known, known by the senses. And so let us resist them as much as we can, nor so fit our mind to them that, while our thinking is on them, we believe we see them with the understanding.

(33) And this is why, if numbers of this kind, coming to be in a soul given over to temporal things, have a beauty of their own, yet, even though they continually effect it by passing away, this beauty is grudged by a Divine Providence born of our punishable mortality merited by God's most just law, where yet He has not so forsaken us we may not turn back and be fetched again from the delight of the carnal senses, under the spread of His merciful hands. For such a delight strongly fixes in the memory what it brings from the slippery senses. And this habit of the soul made with flesh, through carnal affection, in the Holy Scriptures is called the flesh. And it is struggling with such a mind in that apostolic sentence: 'In mind I serve the law of God, but in flesh the law of sin.'[9] But when the mind is raised to spiritual things and remains fixed there, the push of this habit is broken, too, and, being little by little repressed, is destroyed. For it was greater when we followed along with it; not altogether nothing, but certainly less when we check it. And so with a determined retreat from every wanton movement where lies the fault of the soul's essence, and with a restored delight in reason's numbers, our whole life is turned to God, giving numbers of health to the body, not taking pleasure from it; which happens when the exterior man is corrupt, even when there is a change for the better.

Chapter 12

(34) But the memory not only takes in the carnal motions of the mind, and we have already spoken of these numbers, but also the spiritual motions I shall now speak of briefly. For in so far as they are simpler, they demand fewer words, and the greatest possible serenity of mind. That equal-

9 Rom. 7.25.

ity we could not find sure and fixed in sensible numbers, but yet we knew shadowed and fleeting, the mind could never indeed desire unless it were known somewhere. But this could be nowhere in the spans of places and times; for those swell up and these pass away. Where, then, do you think, tell me, if possible. For you don't think it's in the forms of bodies, and you'll never dare say they are equal by pure experiment; nor in intervals of times where we do not know whether they are insensibly longer or shorter than they should be. I want to know where you think that equality is on seeing which we desire certain bodies or motions of bodies to be equal, and on more careful consideration we dare not trust them.

D. There, I think, where it is more excellent than bodies, but whether it is in the soul itself or above the soul I do not know.

(35) *M*. If, then, we look for that rhythmical or metrical art we use for making verses, do you think it possesses the numbers verses are made by?

D. I can't suppose anything else.

M. Whatever these numbers are, do they seem to you to pass away with the verses or to remain?

D. To remain, certainly.

M. Therefore, it must be agreed some things that pass away are made from some numbers that remain?

D. Reason forces me to agree.

M. Well, you don't think this art is other than some affection of the artisan's minds, do you?

D. So I believe.

M. Do you believe this affection also to be in one unskilled in this art?

D. Nowise.

M. And in the one having forgotten it?

D. Not even in the one himself unskilled even though he has been skilled at some time or other.

M. Well, if anyone reminds him by questioning, do you think those numbers return to him from the persons questioning, or he moves himself to something within his own mind whence returns to him what he had lost?

D. I think he does it within himself.

M. You don't think, by questioning, he could also be forcibly reminded which syllable is short or which is long if he has forgotten completely, do you? Since by an old agreement and custom of man, to some syllables a lesser, to others a greater stretch is given. For indeed if it were by nature or by discipline fixed and stable, then the learned men of our time would not have lengthened some syllables the ancients shortened, nor shortened some they lengthened.

D. I believe this can be so, since however much is forgotten can again be brought to memory by a remindful questioning.

M. I can't believe you think anyone by questioning could get you to remember what you ate a year ago.

D. I confess I couldn't, and I don't think now I could be reminded about syllables whose spans were completely forgotten.

M. Why so, except because, in the noun *Italia,* the first syllable by the will of certain men is shortened, and now by the will of others lengthened? But that one and two should not be three and that two should not be the double of one, none of the dead or living or of those to be can bring it about.

D. Evidently not.

M. What, then, if we asked very clearly all the other things pertaining to numbers the way we have with one and two, and if one were questioned, unskilled, not by forgetting, but because he had never learned? Don't you think then he could likewise know this art except for the syllables?

D. How doubt it?

M. How, then, do you think he would move himself so these numbers may be impressed on his mind, and make that affection called art? Or will the questioner give them to him?

D. I think he does it within himself this way that he understands the things asked to be true and replies.

(36) *M.* Come, tell me now whether these numbers under discussion seem to you to be changeable?

D. Nowise.

M. Then you don't deny they're eternal.

D. I admit it.

M. Well, is there no lingering fear some inequality won't spoil them?

D. Nothing at all is surer for me than their equality.

M. From where, then, must we believe what is eternal and unchangeable to be given the soul if not from the eternal and unchangeable God?

D. I don't see what else to believe.

M. Well, then, isn't it evident he, who under another's questioning moves himself within to God to know the unchangeable truth, cannot be reminded by any outside warning to see that truth, unless his memory hold his own same movement?

D. It's evident.

Chapter 13

(37) *M.* I wonder, then, how he falls away from the contemplation of these things to need another's recalling it to his memory. Or must the mind even when intent on it be thought to require such a return?

D. I think so.

M. Let us see, if you will, what this could be could so incite to turn away from the contemplation of the highest and unchangeable equality. For I only see three kinds. For the mind is either intent upon something equal when it is turned away or something higher or lower.

D. There is need only to discuss two of them, for I see nothing superior to eternal equality.

M. Then, do you see anything could be equal to it and yet other?

D. I don't.

M. It only remains, then, to inquire what the lower is. But don't you think first of the soul avowing that equality to be certainly unchangeable, but knowing it itself changes from its intuiting at one time this equality and at another time something else and so following the variety of time, not found in eternal and unchangeable things, works this and that?

D. I agree.

M. Then this affection or motion of the soul by which it understands eternal things and counts temporal things below them even within itself and knows these higher things are rather to be desired than those lower, don't you think that's prudence?

D. I certainly do.

(38) *M*. Well, then, don't you think it worth pondering, at once there's not in the soul the inhering in eternal things, there's yet in it the knowing they should be inhered in?

D. I want us very much to ponder this, and I want to know how it comes about.

M. You will easily see, if you notice the things we direct the mind to most, and have the greatest care for. For I think they're those we very much love, isn't that so?

D. No others.

M. Say, then, we can only love beautiful things, can't we? For, although some people seem to love ugly things, those the Greeks commonly call *saprophíloi,* it is yet a matter of how much less beautiful they are than those things pleasing most people. For, clearly, no one loves those things whose foulness his sense is offended by.

D. It's as you say.

M. These beautiful things, then, please by number, where we have shown equality is sought. For this is found not only in that beauty belonging to the ears or in the motion of bodies, but also in the very visible forms where beauty is more usually said to be. Don't you think it's only equality when equal numbers reply to equal numbers in twos, but in ones, when they have a mean place so equal intervals are kept for them on each side?

D. I certainly do.

M. What is it in light itself holding the origin of all colors (for color also delights us in the forms of bodies), what is it in light and colors we seek if not what suits the eye? For we turn away from too great a flare, and we are unwilling to face things too dark, just as also in sounds we shrink from things too loud, and do not like whispering things. And this is not in the time-intervals, but in the sound itself, the light, you might say, of such numbers, whose contrary is silence, as darkness to colors. When, then, we seek things suitable for the way of our nature and reject things unsuitable we yet know are suitable to other living things, aren't we here, too, rejoicing in some law of equality when we recognize equals allotted in more subtle ways? This can be seen in smells and tastes and in the sense of touch—and for this a long time to follow out more clearly but very easy to explore. For there's not one of these sensibles doesn't please us from equality or likeness. But where equality and likeness, there numberliness [*numerositas*]. In fact, nothing is so equal or like as one and one, isn't that so?

D. I agree completely.

(39) *M*. Well, didn't we persuade ourselves a while ago the soul effects these things in bodies, and doesn't suffer from bodies?

D. We did.

M. Then the love of acting on the stream of its bodily passions turns the soul away from the contemplation of eternal things, diverting its attention with the care of sensible pleasure; it does this with reacting numbers. But the love of operating on bodies also turns it away, and makes it restless; this it does with advancing numbers. The phantasias and phantasms turn it away; these it does with memorial numbers. Finally, the love of the vainest knowledge of such things turns it away; this it does with sensible numbers where lie rules of an art, as if glad in their imitation. And from these is born curiosity by its very care an enemy of peace, and in its vanity impotent over truth.

(40) But the general love of action turning away from the true arises from pride by which vice the soul has preferred imitating God to serving God. And so it is rightly written in Holy Scripture: 'The beginning of man's pride is to fall from God,'[10] and 'The beginning of all sin is pride.' What pride is could not have been better shown than where it is said: 'What does earth and ashes take pride in, since in its own life it gives up its inmost things?' For since the soul is nothing through itself—for it would not otherwise be changeable and sufler a flight from essence—since then through itself it is nothing, but whatever it is is from God,

10 Eccli. 10. 14, 15, 9, 10.

staying in its order, it is quickened in mind and conscience by the presence of God Himself. And so it has this good inmost. And so to puff with pride is to go forth to the outermost and, we might say, to become empty, that is to be less and less. But to go forth into the outermost what is that but giving up the inmost things, that is, putting yourself away from God, not in the span of places, but in affect of mind?

(41) But that appetite of the soul is to have under it other souls; not of beasts as conceded by divine law, but rational ones, that is, your neighbors, fellows and companions under the same law. But the proud soul desires to operate on them, and as much as every soul is better than every body, just so much does the action on them seem more excellent than on bodies. But God alone can operate on rational souls, not through a body, but through Himself. But such is the state of sin that souls are allowed to act upon souls moving them by signifying by one or the other body, or by natural signs as look or nod, or by conventional signs as words. For they act with signs by commanding or persuading, and if there is any other way besides command and persuasion, souls act with or upon souls. But by rights it has come about those souls wishing to be over others command their own parts and bodies with difficulty and pain, in part being foolish in themselves, in part, oppressed by mortal members. And so with these numbers and motions souls set upon souls by, with the desire of honor and praise they are turned away from the sight of that pure and entire truth. For God alone honors the soul making it blessed in secret when it lives justly and piously before Him.

(42) The motions the soul thrusts upon those cleaving to it and servant to it, then, are like the advancing ones, for it acts as if on its own body. But those motions it thrusts

out, wishing to attach some to itself or to enslave, are counted as reacting motions. For it acts as if in the senses forcing a thing moving up outside to become one with it, and a thing not able to do so to be kept out. And the memory takes in both these motions, and makes them memorial, likewise boiling up in tumultuous fashion with the phantasias and phantasms of these acts. Nor are there lacking the corresponding judicial numbers seeing what moves suitably and unsuitably in these acts, not wrongly to be called sensible, for it is by sensible signs souls act toward souls. What wonder if the soul wound up in so many and great concerns is turned away from the contemplation of the truth? And it sees it in so far as it breathes free of them. But, because it has not yet turned them out, it cannot remain there. And so it is the soul has not at once the knowledge of where it ought to be and the power to be there. Do you agree?

D. Nothing, I daresay, to the contrary.

Chapter 14

(43) *M.* What's left, then? Since we have considered as far as possible the stain and oppression of the soul, isn't it to see what action is divinely commanded it for its return, after purgation and forgiveness, to peace, and for its entry into the joy of its Master?

D. Yes.

M. And what more do you think there's for me to say when Holy Scripture, in so many volumes endowed with such authority and holiness, exhorts us only to love our God and Lord with all our heart, with all our soul, and with all our mind, and to love our neighbor as ourself? If, then, we refer all those motions and numbers of human action to this end, we shall certainly be cleansed. Isn't it so?

D. It certainly is, but how short this is to hear, and how hard and arduous to do.

(44) *M.* What, then, is easy? To love colors and voices and sweets and roses and soft bodies? Is it then easy for the soul to love these things where it only desires equality and likeness, yet, considering a little more carefully, knows hardly the last shadow and trace of them? And is it difficult for the soul to love God thinking upon whom, as thoughts till then upon mean and sickly things allow, it finds these nothing unequal, nothing unlike, nothing divided in places, nothing changed in time? Or is there rather delight in throwing up a vast extent of building and passing the time in works of this kind where if the numbers please—there's nothing else—what can there be called equal and like, the discipline's reason would not laugh to scorn? And if this is so, why then does it sink from the truest height of equality to these things, and build up earthly machines in its own ruins? Was this not promised by Him who knows not to deceive? 'For my yoke,' He says, 'is light.'[11] The love of this world is more wearisome. For, what the soul seeks in it, constancy and eternity, it does not find, since the lowest beauty is finished out with the passage of things, and what there imitates constancy is thrown through the soul by the highest God. For the form [*species*] changeable only in time is prior to that changeable both in time and place. And just as souls have been told by the Lord what to love, so they are told through the Apostle John what not to love. 'Do not love this world,' he says; 'because all things in the world are concupiscence of the flesh, concupiscence of the eyes, and secular ambition.'[12]

(45) But what manner of man do you think this is, re-

11 Matt. 11.30.
12 1 John 2.15,16.

ferring all those numbers from the body and over against the body's passions and held from them by memory, not to carnal pleasure, but only to the body's health? A man referring all those numbers operating on souls bound to him or those numbers put out to bind them, and therefore sticking within the memory, not to his own proud excelling, but to the usefulness of those souls themselves? A man also using those numbers in either kind as directing, in the role of moderators and examiners of things passing in the senses, not for an idle or harmful curiosity but for a necessary approval or disapproval? Doesn't such a man work all these numbers and yet not get caught in them? For he only chooses the body's health not to be hindered, and refers all those actions to the good of that neighbor he has been bidden to love as himself in the natural tie of common right.

D. You talk of a great and very manlike man.

(46) *M*. It's not those numbers below reason and beautiful in their kind do soil the soul, then, but the love of lower beauty. And whenever the soul finds to love in it not only equality, concerning which we have said enough for this work, but also order, it has lost its own order. Nor yet does it depart from the order of things even at this point, and so it is whenever and however a thing is, it is highly ordered. For it is one thing to keep order and another to be kept by order. That soul keeps order that, with its whole self, loves Him above itself, that is, God and fellow souls as itself. In virtue of this love it orders lower things and suffers no disorder from them. And what degrades it is not evil, for the body also is a creature of God and is adorned in its own beauty, although of the lowest kind, but in view of the soul's dignity is lightly esteemed, just as the value of gold is degraded by a mixture with the finest silver. And so whatever numbers result from our

criminal mortality, we shall not except them from the making of Divine Providence, since they are beautiful in their own kind, but let us not love them to become happy in their enjoyment. For we shall keep free of them since they are temporal, by using them well, as with a board in a flood by not throwing them aside as burdensome and not grasping them as stable. But the love of our neighbor commanded us is our most certain ascent to inhere in God and not so much to be kept by His ordering as to keep our own order firm and sure.

(47) Or perhaps the soul does not love order as even those sensible numbers attest? But how, then, is the first foot a pyrrhic, the second an iamb, the third a trochee, and so on? But in this law you will have rather told the following of reason, not of sense. Well, isn't this so of sensible numbers that when say eight long syllables take up as much time as sixteen short ones, yet the shorts look rather to be mixed with the longs? And when reason judges of sense and for it proceleusmatic feet are declared equal to the spondaic, it finds here only the power of ordering, because long syllables are only long in comparison with short syllables, and again short syllables are only short in comparison with long. And so the iambic verse, no matter how long it's pronounced, if it does not lose the rule of one and two, does not lose its name. But that verse consisting of pyrrhic feet with the gradual lengthening of its enunciation becomes suddenly spondaic, if you consult not grammar with music. But if it is dactylic or anapestic, since longs are perceived by comparison with shorts mixed in, no matter how long its enunciation, it keeps its name. Why are additions of half feet not to be kept with the same law, in the beginning as at the end; nor all used, although fitting the same beat? Why the sometime placing of two shorts rather than one long at the end? Aren't they measured off by sense

itself? Nor in these is there found an equality-number, suffering no change, but only a bond of order. It would take too long to go over all the other things like this having to do with the numbers of times. But even the senses reject visible forms, either leaning the wrong way or upside down, and like things, where it's not the inequality—for the equality of the parts remains—but the perverseness that's condemned. And finally in all our senses and works when we familiarize many unusual and therefore unpleasing things by gradual steps to our taste, we first accept them with a kind of toleration and then gladly, haven't we kept our pleasure with order, and don't we turn from them unless the first are harmoniously bound with the middle, and the middle with the last?

(48) And so, let us put our joy neither in carnal pleasure, nor in the honors and praises of men, nor in the exploring of things touching the body from without, having God within where all we love is sure and unchangeable. And in this way it comes to be, when temporal things are present, yet are we not involved in them, and those things outside the body can be absent without sense of pain, and the body itself taken away with little or no sense of pain and brought back transformed by the death of its nature. For the soul's attention in the direction of the body contracts endless business, and the love of some special work to the neglect of universal law, a work yet inseparable from the universe of God's rule. And so who loves not the law is subject to the law.

Chapter 15

(49) For if, for the most part, thinking intently on things incorporeal and being always what they are, we meanwhile effect temporal numbers in some bodily movement, easy and useful, by walking or singing, then they pass straight

through us unnoticed, although they would not be were we not acting. And then, if, when we are occupied in our empty phantasms, likewise these, too, pass by as we act without feeling, how much more and more constantly 'when this corruptible has put on incorruption, and this mortal has put on immortality,'[13] that is, to speak plainly, when God has vivified our mortal bodies, as the Apostle says, 'for the spirit remaining in us.'[14] How much more, then, intent on one God and manifest truth, face to face, as it's said, shall we feel with no unquietness and rejoice in the numbers we move bodies by. Unless perhaps one is to believe the soul, although it can rejoice in things good through it, cannot rejoice in the things its good from.

(50) But this action the soul, its God and Master willing, extracts itself from the love of an inferior beauty by fighting and downing its own habit that wars against it; on that point of victory within itself over the powers of this alloy from whose envious desire to entangle it, it soars to God—its support and station—isn't such an action for you called the virtue temperance?

D. I see and understand.

M. Well, when it advances along this way, now divining eternal joys nor quite grasping them, no loss of temporal things nor any death can deter it from saying to weaker fellows, can it: 'It is good I be dissolved and be with Christ; but for your sakes it is necessary to remain in the flesh'?[15]

D. So I think.

M. And this disposition where it fears neither adversity nor death, that can only be called fortitude, can't it?

D. I see that.

---

13 I Cor. 15.53.
14 Rom. 8.11.
15 Phil. 1.23,24.

M. Now, this ordering itself, according to which it serves only one God, desires to be co-equal to only the purest souls and to have dominion only over animal and corporeal nature, what virtue do you think that is?

D. Who doesn't know that's justice?

M. Right.

Chapter 16

(51) But now I want to know, when we decided a while ago among ourselves prudence to be the virtue the soul knows its proper station by, its ascent to it being through temperance, that is, conversion of love to God called charity, and aversion from this world attended by fortitude and justice, I want to know whether you think when it will have come to the fruit of its delight and zeal by perfect sanctification, by that perfect vivification, too, of its body, and, the swarm of phantasms wiped from its memory, will have begun to live with God Himself for God alone, when will have been fulfilled that divinely promised us in these words: 'Beloved, now we are sons of God, and it has not yet appeared what we shall be. We know when He will have appeared we shall be like Him, since we shall see Him as He is,[16]—I want to know then whether you think these virtues we've recalled will then be there too.

D. I don't see, when those things the fight's about have passed by, how either prudence can be there, only choosing what to follow in opposition, or temperance, only turning love from things opposed, or fortitude, only bearing up under things opposed, or justice, only desiring to be equal to the most blessed souls and to master its lower nature in opposition, that is, not yet in possession of that it desires.

16 I John 3.2.

(52) *M*. Your reply is not absurd so far. And I don't deny it has seemed this way to certain learned men. But I, on consulting the books whose authority none surpasses, found this said, 'Taste and see, since the Lord is sweet.'[17] The Apostle Peter also puts it this way: 'If yet you have tasted, since the Lord is sweet.'[18] I think this is what is effected in those virtues purging the soul by conversion. For the love of temporal things could only be dislodged by some sweetness of eternal things. But when it has come to what is sung, 'But the sons of men will hope under the cover of your wings; they will be drunk of the abundance of your house, and you will give them to drink in a torrent of pleasure; for in you is the fountain of life,' it does not say the Lord will be sweet to taste, but you see what a flood and flow is said of the eternal fountain; even a drunkenness follows on it. And by this name is wonderfully signified, it seems to me, that forgetfulness of secular vanities and phantasms. Then the rest follows, and it says, 'In your light we shall see light. Stretch forth your mercy to those knowing you.' 'In light' is to be taken as in Christ, who is the Wisdom of God, and is often called light. When therefore it is said 'We see,' and 'knowing you,' it can't be denied there'll be prudence there. Or do you think the true good of the soul can be known where there's no prudence?

D. I now understand.

(53) *M*. Well, can there be those right in heart without justice?

D. I know justice is very often signified by this name.

M. Then isn't it that the same prophet later says when he sings, 'And your justice to those who are of right heart'?

D. Evidently.

---

17 Ps. 33.9.
18 I Peter 2.3.

M. Come, then, recall if you will we have already sufficiently expounded the soul lapses by pride into certain actions of its own power, and neglecting universal law has fallen into doing certain things private to itself, and this is called turning away from God.

D. I remember, certainly.

M. When, therefore, it acts, so this never again delights it, doesn't it seem to you to fix its love in God and to live most temperately and chastely and securely away from all filth?

D. It seems to be.

M. See, then, too, how the prophet goes on saying, 'Let not the foot of pride come upon me.' For, saying 'foot' he signifies the distraction or fall, and in freedom from this the soul inheres in God and lives eternally.

D. I agree and follow.

(54) *M*. Then fortitude remains. But as temperance against the lapse in the free will, so fortitude avails against the force anyone can be broken by if less strong in the face of attackers or if wretchedly lying down. And this force is usually well signified in the Scriptures by the name of hand. Then who besides sinners try to apply this force? Well, in so far as the soul is barricaded through this very thing and secured by God's support so nothing befalls it from anywhere, it sustains an enduring and you might say impassible power called fortitude; and I think this is said when it is added, 'Nor let the hand of sinners disturb me.'[19]

(55) But whether this or something else is to be understood by these words, will you deny the soul fixed in that perfection and blessedness sees the truth, remains unspotted, suffers no harm, is subject to the one God, and rises above other natures?

19 Ps. 35.8-12.

D. I don't see how it can otherwise be absolutely perfect and blessed.

M. Then, either this contemplation, sanctification, impassibleness, and ordering of it are those four virtues perfected and consummated, or, not to split hairs over names when the things fit, instead of these virtues the soul in labor uses, some such powers are to be hoped for it in eternal life.

Chapter 17

(56) We have only recalled what belongs most to this present discussion, that all this is done by God's Providence He has created and rules all things through, so even the sinful and miserable soul may be moved by numbers and set numbers moving even to the lowest corruption of the flesh. And these numbers can be less and less beautiful, but they can't lack beauty entirely. But God, most good and most just, grudges no beauty whether fashioned by the soul's damnation, retreat, or perseverance. But number also begins from one, and is beautiful in equality and likeness, and bound by order. And so, whoever confesses there's no nature of any kind, but desires unity, and tries as much as it can to be like itself, and holds its salvation as a proper order in place or time or weight of body, must confess all things whatever and of any size are made from one beginning through a form equal to it and like to the riches of His goodness, by which they are joined together in charity as one and one gift from one.[21]

(57) And so that verse proposed by us, '*Deus creator om-*

21 For Augustine the doctrine of creation from nothing is not only an article of faith, but a dialectical truth which follows from a sound doctrine of oneness. It rests on the recognition of beings, objects of the human intellect but independent of it. A scrutiny of these beings leads immediately to the further recognition that their very being as object supposes an absolute sufficiency in itself participated in

nium,' sounds with the harmony of number not only to the ears, but even more is most pleasing in truth and wholeness to the soul's sentiment. Unless, perhaps, you are moved by the stupidity, to speak mildly, of those denying anything can be made from nothing, even though God Almighty be said to have made it. Or is it rather the artisan can operate the sensible numbers of his habit by the reasonable numbers of his art, and by sensible numbers those advancing numbers, his numbers in their operation move by, and time-spans belong to; and from these again he can fashion visible forms in wood numbered with place-spans; and the nature of things serving God's will cannot make this wood from earth and other elements; and could not even make these final things from nothing? In fact the time-numbers of a tree must precede its place-numbers. For there's no stem does not in fixed time-measures spring up to replace its seed, germinate, break out into the air, unfold its leaves, become strong, and bring back either fruit or, by very subtle numbers of the wood itself, the force of the seed. And how much more the bodies of animals where the placing of the members presents a much more numbered equalness to

---

by all the others. This is oneness in itself, the ground of all recognition and knowledge. For Plato and Augustine, as soon as one understands what it means to know, one is forced to admit oneness in itself. Any proof which proceeds only from premises to conclusion by the methods of discursive knowledge is insufficient. For one can always deny premises. To find that without which one cannot even deny premises is the task of the upward dialectic.

Since for Augustine time is a kind of unity and order contemplated by the human intellect by which the sensible things existing seemingly only at this moment and hardly existing then take on significance and have a history, it therefore is more than the sensible things themselves, and the acuity of such a question as that of the eternity of motion is greatly diminished and perhaps has little meaning. The appearance here of the phrase 'Creator of all things' and its constant appearance throughout the book is indicative that the great problem of time is to give the sensible world meaning and being rather than to save us from the intellectual horror of self-perpetuating 'eternal' moving things of which time is only an abstraction.

sight. Can these be made of the elements and these elements not have been made of nothing? For which among them is more ordinary and lowly than earth. Yet first it has the general form of body where a unity and numbers and order are clearly shown to be. For any part of it, no matter how small, must be extended from an indivisible point in length, third takes on breadth, and fourth height, to fill the body. From where, then, is the measure of this progression of one to four? And from where, too, the equality of the parts found in length, breadth, and height? From where a corrationality (for so I have chosen to call proportion), so the ratio length has to the indivisible point, breadth has to length, and height to breadth? Where, I ask, do these things come from, if not from the highest and eternal rule of numbers, likeness, equality, and order? And if you abstract these things from earth, it will be nothing. And therefore God Almighty has made earth, and earth is made from nothing.

(58) Then, too, this form earth is differentiated from the other elements by, doesn't it present something one in so far as it has received it, and no part of it is unlike the whole? And doesn't it have the soundest final ground in its kind by the connection and agreement of the same parts? And the nature of water extends above it, itself abounding in unity, more beautiful and more pellucid because of the greater likeness of its parts, keeping the place of order and its own soundness. And what shall I say of the nature of air, sweeping to unity with a greater reach and as much more beautiful than water is than earth, and so much higher in worth. And what about the supreme circuit of the heavens where the whole universe of visible bodies ends, the highest beauty in its kind, and the soundest excellence of place? Now all these things we've enumerated with the help of the carnal senses, and all things in

them, can only receive and hold local numbers seemingly in a kind of rest, if temporal numbers, in motion, precede within and in silence. Likewise, a vital movement measures off and precedes these as they move in time-spans, a vital movement serving the Master of all things, having in its numbers no temporal spans divided out, but with a power providing times.[22] And above this power, the rational and intellectual numbers of the blessed and saintly souls[23] transmit the very law of God no leaf-fall breaks and our hairs are numbered by, to the judgments of earth and hell, without toll from any nature between.

(59) I in my littleness have gathered with you what I could and as I could on such great matters. But, if any read this talk of ours committed to writing, they must know these things have been written by persons much weaker than those who, having followed the authority of the two Testaments, by believing, hoping, and loving, venerate and worship the consubstantial and unchangeable Trinity of the one highest God from whom, through whom, and in whom are all things. For they are purified, not by flashing human reasoning, but by the effective and burning fire of charity. And while we do

---

22 Augustine seems to be saying that the root of all dispersion is the temporal and that the spatial dispersion depends upon it. He then proceeds to enumerate the hierarchy of numbers. As Svoboda has pointed out, we can consider this as a hierarchy of rhythms since *numerus* is an ambiguous word. Conceptually it makes litttle difference, but rhetorically this systematic ambiguity may have great effect. Time has much the same position in the system of Kant as in that of Augustine: it is the mediating principle between the intelligibles and the sensible world. So it is, too, for Plotinus.

23 'The rational and intellectual numbers of the blessed and saintly souls' refer, as Augustine points out in *Retractationes* 1.11.3, to the angels. He finds the word 'souls' inappropriately used.
This whole book is a bold development of the traditional Platonic phrase stemming from Xenocrates: *psyché arithmós autón kinon*. 'The soul is a self-moving number.'

not think those the heretics deceive with the promises of reason and false science ought to be neglected, yet, in the consideration of the ways themselves, we go more slowly than holy men who deign not to wait in their flying ascent. And yet we should dare not do this if we did not see that many pious sons of that best of mothers, the Catholic Church, who in their youthful studies have sufficiently developed the faculty of speaking and arguing, have, for the confuting of heretics, done this same thing.

THE ADVANTAGE OF BELIEVING

(*De utilitate credendi*)

Translated

by

LUANNE MEAGHER, O.S.B., Ph.D.
College of St. Benedict
St. Joseph, Minnesota

INTRODUCTION

In A.D. 373, the nineteen-year-old Augustine was lured into an attachment with the Manichaeans; in 382, when he came to know one of the most prominent among them, the highly reputed Faustus, the enchantment was dispelled and the attachment ended.[1] While in those nine years Augustine never passed from the lower Manichaean grade of 'Hearer' to that of one of the 'Elect,'[2] his eminence among them was such that his withdrawal occasioned them deep regret.[3] Whatever the extent to which he actually embraced the tenets of the heresy, he certainly acquired a detailed knowledge of Manichaean doctrine and usages, evidence of which is abundant in the long series of works he directed against the Manichaeans, especially in the years between his ordination to the priesthood (391) and his consecration as bishop (395). Among the earliest of these works and by no means the least important is the present treatise, *The Advantage of Believing* (*De utilitate credendi*).

While this work is not a text from which to learn in detail the full nature and content of the Manichaean heresy,[4] it is in order here to inquire how the Manichaeans could draw to

1 See *De utilitate credendi* 8.20. On Augustine and Manichaeism see also *Confessions*, Bks. 3-5.

2 See *De util. cred.* 1.2 and note thereon.

3 Cf. *Secundini Manichaei Epistola*, to which St. Augustine's *Contra Secundinum Manichaeum* is a reply (both works in Migne, PL 42).

4 The passages cited below on *De util. cred.* 1.2 are effective summaries by St. Augustine himself on the Manichaean position; (cf. also *Conf.* 3.6-7, 5.3-7). A convenient bibliography of St. Augustine's anti-Manichaean writings and of modern studies in Manichaeism appears in Hugh Pope, O.P., *Saint Augustine of Hippo* (London 1937) 83 nn. 6, 7.

themselves the passionately truth-hungry Augustine and to hold him for nearly a decade. The causes were manifold: 'The Manichaeans attracted him'—to quote Dr. Anton C. Pegis's recent summation of the matter[5]—'for various reasons. They appeared, by their promises at least, to be able to satisfy important intellectual and moral difficulties. Their materialism and dualism, eternal warring principles, eased his inability to avoid conceiving God in a material way, and, by absolving the individual from moral guilt, soothed his tortured conscience. Their pretension to scientific knowledge was a considerable attraction, and Augustine remained among them by expectation more than by conviction.' He was to find that the Manichaean claim to scientific knowledge—to truth and to reason which had no need of the prior action of faith—was indeed a pretension and nothing more. He was to find, too, that the Manichaeans' rejection of the Old Testament and their corollary that whatever in the New Testament confirmed and guaranteed the Old was interpolated[6] were insupportable positions, taken by men whose right to judge the Old Testament was initially violated by their having declared, in principle, a merciless hostility to them.[7] Here indeed are the two chief preoccupations of the book: (1) to vindicate the true position of authority in matters of religion and to justify the priority of belief over reason, and (2) to refute the negative position of the Manichaeans concerning the Old Testament. While the second task is more elaborately accomplished in other writings, the *The Advantage of Believing* penetrates the

5 'The Mind of St. Augustine,' *Mediaeval Studies* 6 (1944) 1-2. Dr. Pegis's treatment of 'Faith and Wisdom' in St. Augustine (pp. 12-19) draws frequently on the *De. util. cred.*

6 *De util. cred.* 2.4 ff.; *De haeresibus* 46; *Conf.* 5.11; *De moribus ecclesiae Catholicae* 1.2.

7 *De util. cred.* 6.13.

first problem in a manner that is deep and close to definitive.[8] The search for wisdom to which the book bears witness was one which, by way of the influence of St. Ambrose and certain books of the Platonists, was to lead to the fruitful retirement at Cassiciacum and to the author's last days at Milan, from which the deeply-searching work *The Immortality of the Soul* was to issue, as also the first part of *On Music,* both translated in the present volume.

As with St. Augustine's treatment of Manichaeism in the *Confessions,* so here his argument is set against a background of his personal history. The book may indeed be seen, as Batiffol observed,[9] as a first sketch of the relevant passages of the later work. We are given glimpses of the author's schoolboy days,[10] of his youthful quest for truth,[11] and finally of his tortuously reached conclusion that his search for truth among the Manichaeans had been in vain.[12]

The autobiographical turn of the work is derived in part from the circumstances of its composition. It was written, as its author tells us,[13] 'to a friend whom I knew to have been taken in by the Manichaeans and to be still held in that error, deriding in the discipline of the Catholic faith the fact that men

---

8 The judgment of J. Martin (quoted by Pegis, *op. cit.* 15 n. 63) on one passage (13.28) of this portion of the *De util. cred.* is striking: 'the most vigorous page, and, more than this, the only completely true page on this subject written by an eminent philosopher from Aristotle to Kant and after.'

9 P. Batiffol, 'Autour de *De utilitate credendi* de Saint Augustin,' *Revue Biblique,* Nouv. Serie 14 (1917) 11. Batiffol's article as a whole (pp. 9-53) is useful especially as culling from other writings of St. Augustine parallel statements of the principal themes of the *De util. cred.*

10 Cf. *De util. cred.* 6.13.

11 *Ibid.* 1.1-2 and *passim.*

12 *Ibid.* 8.20.

13 *Retractationes* 1.14. The detailed comments made in this work on particular passages of the *De util. cred.* are found below in the notes to the translation.

were bid to believe but were not taught, by reason most certain, what truth was.' More than one passage of the work indicates that Augustine and Honoratus were not only both Manichaeans but had become so in consequence of earlier common experiences and aspirations.[14] Nothing more than what the present book tells is surely known about the Honoratus in question.[15] If he is the Honoratus addressed in St. Augustine *Letter 140* (hardly written to a Manichaean),[16] we see that success waited upon St. Augustine's appeal here[17] that Honoratus should 'follow the path of Catholic teaching, which has come down to us from the Apostles through Christ Himself, and will continue hence to posterity.'

Since St. Augustine, in his *Retractations,*[18] lists the *De utilitate credendi* first among those of his writings which followed his ordination to the priesthood (391), the date of composition is reliably established.

The present translation is based on Zycha's text in the Vienna *Corpus*. The translator has occasionally profited from consulting the English rendering of C. L. Cornish[19] and the more recent Italian translation of the Barnabite Father, Domenico Bassi, whose introduction and notes have also been especially useful. An edition by C. Marriott (1869 and 1885)[20] has not been available to the translator, nor the

---

14 See especially *De util. cred.* 1.1, 4.10, 6.13.

15 There is no reason to connect him with the presbyter referred to in *Letter 83* or with the bishop addressed in *Letter 228*.

16 *Letter 140* (cf. *ca.* 412) is a not inconsiderable treatise *De gratia Novi Testamenti*. The Honoratus who had asked the five questions which the book answers (cf. *Retract.* 2.36) was not yet baptized (*Letter 140* 19.48).

17 *De util. cred.* 8.20.

18 *Retract.* 1.14.

19 See below, Select Bibliography. Earlier English renderings are those in *Seventeen Short Treatises by Saint Augustine* (Oxford 1836) and, according to Pope, *op. cit.* 369, one by H. de Romestin (1885).

20 Noted by Pope, *loc. cit.*

German renderings of K. Frh. v. Piesport (Fulda 1771) and F. M. Berghaus (Münster 1808) and the Italian of N. Casacca (Florence 1930). Except where St. Augustine's Biblical quotations showed significant departures from the Vulgate (when adaptation had to be made), quotations from the Holy Scriptures have been taken from the Reims-Douai version as revised by Bishop Challoner.

SELECT BIBLIOGRAPHY

Attention need here be drawn to the critical text used in the present translation, that of J. Zycha, in *Corpus Scriptorum Ecclesiasticorum Latinorum* XXV (Vienna 1891) 1-48; to the (sometimes more readable) Maurist text, now most conveniently found in J. P. Migne, *Patrologia Latina 42* (Paris 1841) 63-92; to the English rendering of the Rev. C. L. Cornish, in *A Select Library of the Nicene and Post-Nicene Fathers*, First Series, III (Buffalo 1887) 347-366; and to the Latin text (Maurist) with introduction, Italian translation and notes by P. Domenico Bassi (*Corona Patrum Salesiana*, Serie Latina, III), (Turin 1936); the same volume gives text and annotated translation of the *De moribus ecclesiae Catholicae* and the *De moribus Manichaeorum*. The most valuable monograph on the *De util. cred.* is that of Batiffol cited above. See also the final paragraph of the Introduction.

CONTENTS

THE ADVANTAGE OF BELIEVING

Chapter 1

If I were to believe, Honoratus,[1] that a heretic and a man who believes heretics were one and the same, I should think it well to rest both my tongue and my pen in this matter. Now, actually, there is a vast difference between these two. The heretic, in my opinion, is one who for some temporal advantage, especially for the sake of glory and preeminence, originates or follows false and new opinions. But he who believes men of this kind is deceived by a certain image of truth and piety. Under these circumstances, I did not think I should be silent before you as to my views of finding and retaining truth. And you know how ardently I have loved it from my youth. But truth is far removed from the minds of the vain men who, having gone too far in these corporeal things, mistakenly think nothing else exists except what they perceive with the five well-known messengers of the body. The impressions and images they receive from these they revolve within themselves even when they try to get away from the senses, and, according to the fatal and utterly false standard supplied by these impressions and images, they think that they can accurately measure the ineffable mysteries of truth. Nothing is easier, my dear friend, than not only to say but even to think that one has found truth; but, how difficult it is in reality you will realize, I trust, from this letter of mine. That it may be profitable to you, or at least in no way harm you and all those into whose hands it may accidentally come, has been and is the object of my prayers to God. And I am hopeful that this will be

1 On Honoratus see Introduction.

the outcome, in that I am fully conscious that I have taken up my pen devoutly and dutifully without any desire for empty fame or worthless ostentation.

(2) It is, accordingly, my purpose to prove to you, if I can, that the Manichaeans are sacrilegiously and rashly attacking those who, following the authority of the Catholic faith, before they can gaze upon that truth which pure minds behold, are, by believing, both fortified in advance and prepared for God who will enlighten them. And you know, Honoratus, that for no other reason did we fall in with such men than that they kept saying that by pure and simple reason, apart from all formidable authority, they would lead their willing listeners on to God and free them from all error. For, what else forced me for almost nine years, during which time I rejected the religion which my parents had implanted in me as a child,[2] to follow these men and diligently to listen to them, save that they said we were terrified by superstition, and that faith was demanded of us before reason, while they, on the other hand, were forcing faith on no one without first hunting for and disentangling the truth. Who would not be enticed by these promises? And would there not be special enticement for a youthful mind desirous of truth, and yet haughty and talkative in disputations in the school of certain learned men? Such a one they then found me, spurning, of course, what seemed to be old wives' tales and desiring to get hold of and drink in the sincere and open truth which they promised. But, again, what reason kept me from embracing them completely so that I remained in that rank which they call Hearers[3] (so as not

---

2 Cf. *Conf.* 1,11; 5.14.

3 The Manichaeans of the lower rank. Members of the upper rank were called the 'Elect' and employed rigid ascetic practices not required of the 'Hearers.' For St. Augustine's account of these two classes and a brief statement concerning Manichaean doctrine and discipline, see his *De haeresibus* 46.

to lose the hope of this world together with its affairs), except that I noticed that they themselves also were more fluent and eloquent in refuting others than they were strong and sure in proving their own beliefs? But what shall I say about myself, I who was already a Catholic Christian? Almost exhausted, and parched after this excessive period of thirst, with intense desire I again sought these breasts [of Holy Mother Church], and, weeping and groaning deeply, I beat them violently and wrung them out that there might trickle forth just enough nourishment to refresh me, affected as I was, and to restore the hope of life and safety. What, then, shall I say about myself? You, not yet a Christian, since you were vehemently denouncing them, could scarcely be persuaded by me that you had to hear and investigate them. By what else were you delighted—please try to recall, I pray—save by a certain inordinate presumption and promise of reasons? But because they disputed widely and vigorously for a long time and in much detail over the errors of the unlearned—something which I learned too late was very easy for anyone of average learning—we thought that we should necessarily retain whatever they implanted in us of their own doctrine, since we met no other with which we might be satisfied. And so they did to us what deceitful bird-catchers are wont to do, who fix lime-smeared branches near water to deceive thirsty birds. These men cover over and conceal in any way they can the other surrounding waters or even ward off the birds by formidable devices, so that they fall into snares, not through choice, but out of pure need.

(3) But, why do I not reply to myself that these elegant and charming comparisons and censures of this kind against all who teach anything can be poured out cleverly and smartly by any adversary? The purpose I had in mind in thinking some

such admonition should be put into my letter was to urge them to cease from such action, so that, as that famous man says,[4] when trifling commonplaces have been separated out, matter may clash with matter, cause with cause, and reason with reason. Therefore, let them cease to utter that saying, which they have on their lips as if of necessity, whenever they are deserted by anyone who has been a Hearer over a rather long period of time, 'The light hath made its way through him.' For you see—you, who are my greatest care (for about them I am not too concerned) how empty this can be and how very easy for anyone to censure. And so I leave this for your prudence to investigate. For I am not afraid that you may think that I was possessed by light at the time that I was entangled in the life of this world, having a darksome hope from the beauty of my wife, from the pomp of riches, from the emptiness of honors and other harmful and destructive pleasures.[5] And all these (and this was not unknown to you), I did not cease to desire and hope for, as long as I remained their attentive Hearer. Nor do I attribute this to their teaching, for I admit that they assiduously advise that such things be shunned. But to say that I have been deserted by light now that I have turned away from all these shadows of things and determined to be content with only the necessary sustenance for bodily health, but that I was enlightened and resplendent when I loved these things and was held enmeshed in them, is characteristic of a man who, to put it very gently, gives superficial consideration to matters on which he loves to talk much. But, please, let us come to the issue.

---

4 Cicero seems to be meant. See his Second Oration against Catiline 11.25 (. . . *si his rebus omissis causas ipsas, quae inter se confligunt, contendere velimus* . . .).

5 Cf. *Soliloquia* 1.10.17.

Chapter 2

(4) You well know that the Manichaeans, by finding fault with the Catholic faith and, in chief, by tearing apart and mangling the Old Testament, stir up the unlearned who surely do not know to what extent these criticisms are to be accepted, and how these, once swallowed, descend effectively into the veins and marrow of souls still, as it were, emitting infant wails; and because [in the Old Testament] there are certain things which give some offense to souls that are ignorant and neglectful of their own interest (and this is the largest group), these points can be attacked from a popular point of view, while, on the other hand, they cannot be popularly defended by very many on account of the mysteries which they contain. The very few who know how to do this have no liking for public and much advertised contests in disputation, and, for this reason, are little known except to those who seek them out most urgently. As to the rashness, then, with which the Manichaeans criticize the Old Testament and the Catholic faith, learn, I beg of you, what disturbs me. And I desire and I hope that you will receive these remarks in the same spirit in which they are uttered. For God knows (and to Him are known all the hidden thoughts of my conscience) that I engage in this discussion with no malice. But, as I think, it should be received for the sake of proving the truth (and for this one purpose we had long since decided to live); and with incredible solicitude, so that it may not have been very easy for me to err with you, but very difficult (not to put it too harshly) to hold with you the straight path. But in the expectation with which I anticipate your holding the way of wisdom with me, I trust that He will not desert me, He to whom I am consecrated. Night and day I try to keep my gaze upon Him, and, with the eye of my soul wounded, both because of my sins and my way of life, by

the blows of spiritless opinions, often with tears I recognize my own weakness. After long darkness and blindness, the eyes, scarcely opened, still throbbing and turning away, refuse the light—which they yet desire—especially if anyone tries to show them the sun itself. This is what is now happening to me, for I do not deny that there is a certain ineffable and singular good of the soul which is seen with the mind, but with sighs and tears I confess that I am not yet fit to contemplate it. He will not then desert me, if I am not deceitful, if I am influenced by duty, if I love truth, if I esteem friendship, if my great fear is that you may be deceived.

Chapter 3

(5) All of that Scripture called the Old Testament is handed down fourfold, therefore, to those eagerly bent on knowing it: according to history, according to aetiology, according to analogy, and according to allegory. Do not think me inept for using the Greek words. In the first place, I learned them in this form, and I do not dare to reveal them to you other than as I learned them. Then, you will also realize that we have in common use no names for these things. If I had made them up through translation, I should surely be all the more inept, but if I were to use circumlocution, I would be less unhampered in discussing them. I only ask that you believe that, howsoever I may err, I am not acting as one swollen with pride or vanity. Things are handed down according to history, when the teaching concerns what has been written or done and what has not been done, but only written as though it were done; according to aetiology, when the reason is given as to why anything has been done or said; according to analogy, when it is shown that the two Testaments, the Old and the New, are not opposed to each other;

according to allegory, when one is taught that certain writings are not to be taken according to the letter, but are to be understood figuratively.

(6) All these ways were used by our Lord Jesus Christ and the apostles. For that incident was taken from history in which He was reproached because His disciples had plucked ears of corn on the sabbath day: 'Have you not read,' He said,[1] 'what David did when he was hungry, and they that were with him: how he entered into the house of God and did eat the loaves of proposition, which it was not lawful for him to eat, nor for them that were with him, but for the priests only?" But to aetiology belongs the instance in which His questioners, when Christ had forbidden a wife to be put away except for fornication, protested that Moses had permitted this freedom by giving a bill of divorce: 'This,' He said,[2] Moses did 'by reason of the hardness of your heart.' For here the reason was given why Moses had wisely permitted it for a time. But this precept of Christ seemed to indicate that now the times were other [than those of Moses]. It would be tedious to explain the changes of these times and their order, arranged and settled by a certain wonderful disposal of Divine Providence.

(7) Now, furthermore, as to analogy, by which the harmony of the two Testaments is clearly seen, why should I say that all those have used it to whose authority the Manichaeans have yielded? They themselves can ponder over how much they usually say has been interpolated into Sacred Scripture by some, I know not what, corruptors of truth. This statement has always seemed to me to be very weak, even at the time that I was one of their Hearers; and not only to me,

---

1 Matt. 12.3-4.
2 Matt. 19.8.

but also (I well remember it) to you, and to all of us who were trying to exercise a more careful judgment than the general run of believers. But now, many things which disturbed me have been explained and unraveled, especially those matters about which in their discourses they generally boast, and wax all the more eloquent whenever, in the absence of an adversary, they do not have to be careful. And for all that, they seem to me to have said nothing more shamelessly, or to put it more gently, more carelessly or weakly, than that the divine Scriptures have been corrupted, for no copies are extant in so recent a matter whereby they can prove this. If they were to say that they did not think that they could accept the Scriptures completely, on the ground that they had been written by men who, they thought, did not write the truth, somehow or other their refusal would be more just or their mistake more human. For this is what they have done about that book which is entitled the Acts of the Apostles. And at this plan of theirs, when I myself consider it, I cannot sufficiently wonder. For it is not the wisdom of men that I miss here, but the absence of average understanding. For that book has so many things which are similar to those which they do accept that it seems to me to be utter stupidity not to accept it also and to consider false and interpolated whatever in it offends them. Or, if such language is impudent, as it is, why do they think these things are more valid in the epistles of St. Paul, or why in the four books of the Gospel? And, I am inclined to think that these books contain more things, proportionately, which they would like to consider corrupt interpolations than the books of the Acts could possibly contain. But, without doubt, this is what seems to me to be the situation, and I ask you to consider it with me with a calm and serene judgment. For you know that the Manichaeans, working to include the person of Manichaeus, their founder, among the number of the apostles, say that the Holy Spirit, whom the Lord promised He would send to His apostles, came to us through him. And so, if they were to accept the Acts of the Apostles in which the coming of the Holy Ghost is clearly asserted,[3] they could not find a way in which to say that this had been interpolated. As they would have it, there were some corruptors of the divine books before the time of Manichaeus himself, and the corruptors were those who were eager to combine the Jewish law with the Gospel. But this about the Holy Spirit they cannot say, unless, perhaps, they assert that the [authors] prophesied and put into their books the charge which would be brought against Manichaeus, who at some future time would be and would say that the Holy Spirit had been sent through him. But about the Holy Spirit we will speak more plainly elsewhere. Now, let us get back to my original intention.

(8) For I think I have sufficiently demonstrated that both the history of the Old Testament and aetiology and analogy can be found in the New Testament; it remains to point out allegory. Our Redeemer Himself uses in the Gospel an allegory from the Old Testament. 'This generation', He says,[4] 'seeketh a sign: and a sign shall not be given it but the sign of Jonas the prophet. For as Jonas was in the whale's belly three days and three nights: so shall the Son of man be in the heart of the earth three days and three nights.' And what shall I say about the apostle Paul, who also in his first Epistle to the Corinthians indicates that the story of the Exodus itself was an allegory of the future Christian people:[5] 'For I would not have you ignorant, brethren, that our fathers were all under the cloud and all passed through the sea. And all in Moses

3 Acts. 2.2-4.
4 Matt. 12.39-40.
5 1 Cor. 10.1-11.

were baptized, in the cloud, and in the sea: And did all eat the same spiritual food, and all drank the same spiritual drink: (And they drank of the spiritual rock that followed them: and the rock was Christ). But with most of them God was not well pleased; for they were overthrown in the desert. Now these things were figures of ourselves, that we should not covet evil things as they also coveted. Neither let us worship idols, as some of them, as it is written, "The people sat down to eat and drink and rose up to play."[6] Neither let us commit fornication, as some of them committed fornication, and there fell in one day three and twenty thousand men. Neither let us tempt Christ, as some of them tempted and perished by the serpents. Neither let us murmur, as some of them murmured and were destroyed by the destroyer. Now all these things happened to them in figure: and they are written for our correction, upon whom the end of the world is come.' There is likewise in the apostle a certain allegory which, in fact, pertains especially to our case for the very reason that the [Manichaeans] themselves are in the habit of presenting and using it in their disputations. For the same Paul says to the Galatians:[7] 'For it is written that Abraham had two sons: the one of a bondwoman, was born according to the flesh; but he of the free woman was by promise. Which things are said by an allegory. For these are the two testaments. The one from Mount Sina, engendering unto bondage, which is Agar. For Sina is a mountain in Arabia, which hath affinity to that Jerusalem which now is, and is in bondage with her children. But that Jerusalem which is above is free: which is our mother'.

(9) Here, then, those exceedingly wicked men, while they try to render void the Law, force us to accept those Scriptures.

6 Exod. 32.6.
7 Gal. 4.22-26.

For they note the saying that they are in servitude who are under the Law, and this last point they air widely in preference to the others:[8] 'You are made void of Christ, you who are justified in the law: you are fallen from grace.' We grant all this to be true, and we do not say that the Law is necessary except to those to whom its servitude is still profitable. For this reason was the Law well enacted, that men who could not be recalled by reason from sin had to be forced by such a law, that is, by the threats and terrors of those penalties which can be seen by fools. And when the grace of Christ frees us from these, it does not condemn the Law, but invites us at times to be obedient to its love, not to be a slave to fear of the Law. This itself is a grace, that is, a blessing, which they who still desire to be under the chains of the Law do not realize has providentially come to them. Paul rightly rebukes these as infidels because they do not believe that they have now been set free through Jesus Christ our Lord from the servitude to which for a fixed period they had been subjected according to the very just dispensation of God. Hence that statement of the same apostle:[9] 'For the Law was our pedagogue in Christ.' He accordingly gave men a pedagogue to fear, who later gave them a master to love. And yet, in these precepts and commandments of the Law[10] which it is not now lawful for Christians to use, such as the sabbath or circumcision or sacrifices or anything of this kind, such

---

8 Gal. 5.4.

9 Gal. 3.24. The duty of the ancient Greco-Roman pedagogue was primarily to conduct the child to school and back.

10 In his *Retract.* 1.14.1, St. Augustine quotes the sentence, 'And yet in these precepts . . . quickeneth,' and then comments: 'But I have otherwise explained those words of the apostle Paul, and as it seems to me or rather as it appears from the very nature of the case, much more appropriately, in that book which is entitled, *De spiritu et littera;* though this sense [that given in the present treatise] is not to be rejected.'

great mysteries are contained that every faithful soul realizes that nothing is more dangerous than to take whatever is there literally, that is, according to the word, while nothing is more healthful than a revelation according to the spirit. Hence the saying:[11] 'The letter killeth, but the spirit quickeneth'; and also:[12] 'The selfsame veil, in the reading of the Old Testament, remaineth not taken away (because in Christ it is made void).' What is made void in Christ is not the Old Testament, but its veil; that through Christ there may be understood and, as it were, laid bare, that which without Christ is obscure and covered over. And at once, to be sure, the same apostle adds:[13] 'But when you shall be converted to Christ, the veil will be taken away.' But he does not say, 'The Law will be taken away' or 'The Old Testament.' These, then, have not been taken away through the grace of the Lord as though they concealed useless things; rather, there was removed their covering by which useful things were hidden. This is the treatment followed in the case of those who studiously and faithfully, not turbidly and rashly, seek the sense of the Scriptures. A careful demonstration is made of the order of things, and of the causes of deeds and words, and of the harmony of the Old Testament with the New, so pervading that no tittle is left in disagreement. And among the figures, too, such hidden riches are found that the resulting allegories, when interpreted, force an admission of their own misery upon those who wish to condemn them in advance rather than to learn them.

Chapter 4

(10) But in the meantime, passing over the depths of

11 2 Cor. 3.6.
12 2 Cor. 3.14.
13 2 Cor. 3.16.

knowledge, let me deal with you as I think I should with my good friend, that is, as I can, not as I have marveled that learned men can. There are three kinds of mistakes according to which men err when they read anything. Let me speak about them one by one. The first kind is that in which what is false is thought to be true, though the writer has thought otherwise. The second kind, not so widespread but no less harmful, occurs when what is false is considered true and is so thought because the writer also thought so. The third is the perception of some kind of truth from the writing of another, though the writer himself did not understand it. In this kind there is no little profit; nay, if one considers carefully, therein lies the whole, entire fruit of reading. An instance of the first kind would be to have anyone say and believe, for example, that Rhadamanthus hears and judges the cases of the dead for the reason that he has read this in Maro's poetry.[1] Such a one errs in two ways: both because he believes an incredible statement, and also because it should not have been thought that the author believed it. The second one can be observed in this case: If, because Lucretius[2] writes that the soul is made up of atoms and is after death dissolved into the same atoms and perishes, anyone thinks that this is true and ought to be believed. For he is no less wretched who, about a matter of so great moment, persuades himself of the truth of what is false, even though Lucretius, by whose books he was deceived, had this opinion. For what value is it to this man to be sure about the opinion of an author when he has selected for himself not one through whom he would escape error, but one with whom he would go astray? The third class is exemplified by the following instance: If, having read some

1 Virgil, *Aeneid* 6.566-569.

2 Roman follower (1st cent. B. C.) of Epicurus. The third book of his poem *On the Nature of Things* is especially devoted to the thesis here mentioned.

passage in his books in which he praises continence,[3] anyone should insist that Epicurus has placed the highest good in virtue, and is, therefore, free from fault. What harm is the error of Epicurus to this man, even though the former believes that the highest good of man is bodily pleasure? For the man has not surrendered himself to so base and vile a sentiment, and it is for no other reason that Epicurus pleases him than that he thinks he was free from all improper opinions. This mistake is not only human, but is often even most worthy of a man. Suppose I were told about some man I loved that he, now when bearded, had said in the presence of many that boyhood and infancy were so pleasant that he even took an oath expressing his willingness to live in the same way; and suppose this were so clearly proved to me that it would be shameful to deny it. I should not seem worthy of censure, should I, if I thought that, by saying this, he wished to indicate that he was pleased with innocence and with that state of mind which was a stranger to those pleasures in which mankind is enmeshed, and if for this reason I should love him still more, and more than I loved him previously, even if what he had foolishly loved in the years of boyhood was a certain freedom in playing and eating and an idle leisure? Suppose that he had died after I had heard this, so that I could not by questioning find out his real sentiments. Would there be anyone so base as to be angry with me for praising the man's purpose and intention through those very words which I had heard? Even a just critic would doubtless not hesitate to praise my opinion and my intention in that I had been pleased with innocence, and, as one man about another, I had pre-

3 St. Augustine may have had in mind some such document as the 'Letter to Menoeceus' (handed down under the name of Epicurus, 4th-3rd cent. B. C.): W. J. Oates, *The Stoic and Epicurean Philosophers* (New York 1940) 30-33.

ferred to think well in a matter of doubt even when I could have thought ill.

Chapter 5

(11) Such being conditions and distinctions that affect reading, let me now speak of those that relate correspondingly to writing; these are necessarily of the same number. For, either the author writes with profit, and is not profitably understood by some reader; or both [the writing and the reading] are done without profit; or the reader understands with profit, while the author has written to the contrary. Of these three situations, I have no blame for the first, and about the last I am not concerned. For, neither can I blame the man who through no fault of his own has been misunderstood, nor can I be annoyed at anyone being read who has not seen the truth, as long as I see that there is no harm done to his readers. One kind, therefore, meets with complete approval, and is, as it were, entirely without fault, that in which good things have been written, and also received in good part by the readers. And yet this kind can still be subdivided into two parts, for it does not completely exclude error. For it frequently happens that, when the writer has clearly understood, the reader also clearly understands, but differently than he, sometimes in a better sense, sometimes in a poorer sense, and yet with profit. But when, in the matter of doctrine perfectly aimed at the good life, we hold the same sense as does he whom we read, we have truth in abundance, and there is no room anywhere for falsehood. This kind is for the most part exceedingly rare when the reading treats of matters that are very obscure; nor can it, in my opinion, be clearly known, but only believed. For, from what evidence am I to ascertain the intention of the man, absent or dead, so that I can swear to it? Even if he were questioned personally, there would be much that he,

if he were a good man, would conceal as a matter of courtesy. I think, too, that what sort of man the writer was would be of little help in understanding the matter itself; yet he is most creditably believed a good man whose writings have had at heart the good of the human race and of posterity.

(12) Therefore, I wish these men would tell me in what class they place the supposed error of the Catholic Church. If in the first, it is a very serious charge. But the required defense is not far to seek, for it is sufficient to say that our understanding is not what they think it is when they attack us. If in the second class, it is no less serious. But they will be refuted by the same statement. If in the third class, it is no charge at all. Come, then, and consider the Scriptures themselves. Why do they object to the books of the so-called Old Testament? Is it that they are good, but misunderstood by us? But they themselves do not accept them. Or is it that they are neither good nor well understood? Our defense above is sufficient refutation. Or, perhaps they will speak as follows: Even though you may understand them in a good sense, they are still bad. What else is this than to acquit living adversaries with whom there is a controversy, and to accuse the long ago dead with whom there is none? Indeed, I believe that the sacred writers both profitably handed down all things and were themselves great and divine, and I believe that it was the command and the will of God that proclaimed and established that Law. And (though I know very few of this kind of books) I can easily persuade to my belief anyone who comes to me with a mind open and free from stubbornness. This I will do when you give me the opportunity of influencing your benevolent ears and mind. But this when I can. Is it not sufficient for me now, in whatever way the matter stands, not to have been deceived?

Chapter 6

(13) I call to witness, Honoratus, my own conscience and the God who dwells in pure minds that I think nothing is more prudent, more chaste, more worthy of reverence, than are those writings, all of them, which the Catholic Church preserves under the name of the Old Testament. You wonder, I know. For I cannot conceal the fact that once I had been persuaded far differently. But, surely, there is nothing more full of rashness (and we boys had no lack of that) than, whatever books are in question, to desert those expositors who profess that they can preserve these books and hand them down to their disciples, and to seek out the opinion of those who, under I know not what compulsion, have declared a bitter war against the framers and authors of these books. For, who ever thought, to speak of teachings in which the reader may perhaps err without committing sacrilege, that the obscure and recondite works of Aristotle should be explained by one who was his enemy? And who has ever wished to read or learn the geometric writings of Archimedes, with Epicurus as his teacher? Against these the latter argued much and boldly, but, as I think, with no understanding of any of them. Or are those Scriptures of the Law of a manifest clarity, against which, as though publicly exposed, these men make their attack in vain and with no profit? And they seem to me to be very similar to that silly woman whom these same men usually deride: angry because the sun was praised to her and commended by a certain Manichaean woman as worthy of worship, and, being very simple-minded in her religious thinking, she leaped up excitedly and, repeatedly beating with her foot that spot on which the sun shone as it streamed through the window, began to cry out—quite foolishly (who will say otherwise?) and woman-like—'Lo, I

am trampling on the sun and your god.' But do not these men seem to you to be like her in respect to things which they do not understand—either why they exist or what indeed their nature is: things which, though apparently of no value, are still subtle and divine to those who understand them—they think they accomplish something by tearing them to pieces with the mighty force of their prayers and imprecations because they secure the applause of the ignorant? Believe me, whatever there is in the Scriptures is something lofty and divine. Truth is there absolutely, and a discipline well adapted to refresh and renew minds, which is so simply ordered that everyone can draw thence what is sufficient for his needs if only he approaches to partake devoutly and faithfully as true religion demands. To prove this to you, one needs many reasons and a longer treatise. But I must so deal with you that first you will not hate the authors; then, that you will love them. And this I must do in any other way, rather than by explaining their meanings and words. For, if we hated Virgil —rather, if we did not love him through the recommendations of our forebears before we had an understanding of him, never would we have been satisfied about those innumerable questions over which grammarians are generally agitated and disturbed;[1] nor would we listen willingly to one who resolved these questions to the poet's credit, but would favor him who tried to show, through them, that he had erred and was off the track. But now, since many are trying to explain these questions, and each according to his own bent, those men get the most applause through whose exposition the poet is found better, one who is believed (even by those who do not understand him) not only to have erred in no respect,

1 The student will find in the commentaries of Servius (4th-5th cent. A.D.) on Virgil abundant examples of the type of question here intended.

but to have written nothing save what was praiseworthy. And so we rather become annoyed at the teacher who fails in some little question and has no answer to give than think that he is silent through Maro's fault. Now if, toward his own defense, he should wish to assert a defect in so great an author, it is not likely that his students will stay with him, even though their fees have been paid. How great a thing it would be to show similar good will to those through whom so old a tradition confirms that the Holy Spirit has spoken. But, of course, we brilliant young men and wondrous searchers-out of reason, not even having opened those books, without having looked for teachers, without directing the least accusation at our own dullness, and, finally, not even conceding an average understanding to those men who for so long a time had wished books of this kind to be read and guarded and expounded throughout the entire world, we thought that no confidence should be placed in these men; and we were moved to this opinion by the words of those who were their enemies and foes and among whom we would be forced to cherish and believe under the false pretence of reason, untold thousands of fables.

Chapter 7

(14) But now I will continue what I have begun, if I can, and thus treat with you, not so as to open up the Catholic faith in the meantime, but, with a view to scrutinizing its great mysteries, that, for those who have a care for their souls, I may show forth the hope both of divine fruit and of finding the truth. No one doubts that he who seeks true religion either already believes the soul to be immortal if that religion is to be of any profit to him, or that it is just that very truth he wishes to discover in this same religion. It is for the sake of the soul that all religion exists; for, how it may be with

the nature of the body causes no worry or solicitude, especially after death, to one whose soul possesses that by which it may be happy. It is for the sake of the soul, then, either entirely or most of all, that true religion, if there is any, has been established. But this soul—I will see for what reason, and I confess that this matter is very obscure—still wanders and is foolish, as we see, until it attains and perceives wisdom, and this perhaps is itself true religion. I am not dismissing you to idle fables, am I? I am not forcing you to believe anything rashly, am I? I simply say that our soul, immersed and entangled in error and foolishness, is seeking the way of truth, if there is any. Pardon me, if this is not true in your case, and, I beg of you, share with me your wisdom. But, if you recognize in yourself what I say, then, I pray you, let us seek truth together.

(15) Suppose that up to the present we have not listened to the proponent of any religion. Lo, we have entered on a new task and a new business. We have to seek out, I suppose the professors of this belief, if it exists. Suppose that we have found some holding to one opinion, others to another, and, in the diversity of their opinions, each seeking to draw everyone to his own side. But among these, let us suppose, certain ones are preeminent because of the celebrity of their fame and because they have taken possession of almost all peoples. Whether they have the truth is a great question. But would they not have to be investigated first so that, as long as we are in error, in that we are mere human beings, we may seem to err with the human race itself?

(16) But among a certain few there is truth. You now know, therefore, what it is, if you know among whom it is. Did I not say to you a little while ago that we should make our search as if entirely uninformed? But, if you infer from

the very force of truth that a few have it, but you know not who they are, what then? If those few who know the truth are such as to hold the multitude by their authority, whence could that small number, set apart in that multitude, release itself and, as it were, filter through?[1] Do we not see how few attain to great eloquence, while throughout the world the rhetorical schools are noisy with throngs of young men? Is it that all those who wish to develop into orators of value are terrified by the multitude of the unlearned and think they should vigorously apply themselves to the orations of Caecilius or of Erucius rather than to those of Tully?[2] The models that all make for are those that have been confirmed by the authority of their forefathers. The crowds of the unlettered work to learn the very same things which have been accepted by the few wise men as the things necessary to learn; very few succeed, fewer actually plead, and still fewer become famous. But what if the true religion be some such thing? What if the multitude of the unlearned frequent churches? Still there is no proof that, therefore, no one has been made perfect by those mysteries. And yet, if so few were eager for eloquence as the few that are eloquent, never would our parents have thought that we should be entrusted to such masters. Since we have been invited to these studies by the multitude (which, in large number, is ignorant), so that we might become enamored of what few can attain, why are we unwilling that our case be similar in religion, which, perchance, we are rejecting at great risk to our soul? For, if the truest and most sincere worship of God, even though it exists

1 The interpretation here adopted of this difficult passage is largely based on that of D. Bassi (transl. 46 n.1, 48 n.1).

2 In comparison with Cicero (Tully) the two orators here named had small reputation. For Erucius, see Quintilian, *Inst. Orat.* 8.3.22; for Caecilius (Q. Caecilus Metellus), Cicero, *Brutus*, 21.18 and Horace *Satires* 2.1.67.

only among a few, still exists among those with whom the multitude, however entangled in lusts and far removed from pure understanding, is in agreement—and who can doubt that this is possible?—I ask, if anyone should accuse us of rashness and foolishness in that we do not carefully search out among its own teachers that which it is a matter of great interest to us to find, what could we reply? That the multitude deterred me? Why did it not deter me from the study of the liberal arts, which scarcely contribute anything to this present life? Why not from the search for money? Why not from attaining honor? Why not, finally, from securing and maintaining good health, and, last of all, why not from the very pursuit of happiness? Yet, these are interests in which all are busy, though few excel.

(17) But those seemed to be absurd statements. According to whose assertion? According, of course, to that of those who are our enemies for whatever cause or reason—and this is not now the question—yet enemies still. Whenever I read, I learned through myself. Is this true? Without being imbued with some poetic training, you would not venture to take up Terentianus Maurus without a teacher.[3] Asper, Cornutus, Donatus, and countless others are required so that any poet can be understood whose verses are seen even to capture the applause of the theater. But, against books which, however they may be, are reported by the acknowledgment of almost the entire human race to be holy and full of divine things, you yet launch your attack without a guide, and you dare to

3 The four authors mentioned here would have been well known to St. Augustine the rhetorician. Of Terentianus Maurus (end of 2nd cent. B. C.) there survives a manual on prosody and metrics. Of about the same period is Asper, commentator on Terence, Sallust, and Virgil, while the Stoic Cornutus (1st cent. A. D.), who taught the poets Lucan and Persius, was also a commentator on Virgil. Donatus (4th cent. A. D.), a teacher of St. Jerome, wrote authoritatively on grammar and commented on Terence and Virgil.

pass sentence upon them without a teacher! And, if anything appears there which seems absurd, you do not accuse your own dullness and your own intellect, corrupted, like that of all the foolish, by the filth of this world, but rather those books which, perhaps, are simply unintelligible to such minds as yours. You should seek out someone both good and learned, or one who would be considered such by common consent, that through his teachings you might become better and more learned by his instruction. Such a one was not easily found? Let toil, then, be expended upon the search. There was no one in the land in which you lived? What purpose should more profitably send you traveling? He was in perfect hiding on the continent, or else did not exist? A sea voyage should then be taken. If he were not to be found on the nearby shores across the sea, you should go on even to those lands in which the deeds contained in those books are said to have taken place. What have we done of this kind, Honoratus? And yet what was perchance (for I am still speaking as though it were a matter of doubt) the holiest of religions, whose renown has taken possession of the entire world, has been condemned by the arbitrary judgment of us miserable boys. What if those matters which are seen to offend some ignorant souls in these same Scriptures were put there for this purpose, that when there should be read matters abhorrent to the feelings of ordinary men, not to speak of the prudent and holy, we should much more studiously look for an inner meaning? Do you not see how men try to interpret the Catamite of the Bucolics from whose mind passed all thought of the rough shepherd?[4] And how they insist that the boy Alexis, on whom Plato is also said to have written an amatory poem,[5]

4 Virgil, *Eclogues* 2.

5 For amatory verses on Alexis attributed to Plato, see J. M. Edmonds, *Elegy and Iambus* (Loeb Classical Library) II (London-New York 1931) 8-9.

has some great significance or other which escapes the understanding of the unlettered?—and all this when no sacrilege is involved in holding a very fertile poet as author of lascivious songs.

(18) But, actually, were we recalled and prohibited from investigating, either by the sanction of some law, or the power of our adversaries, or the base character of consecrated persons or a shameful report, or the newness of the institution, or a secret promise? By none of these. All the divine and human laws permit one to seek out the Catholic faith. To hold and exercise it is certainly permitted by human law, even if there is, as long as we err, a doubt concerning one divine law. No enemy terrifies us in our weakness—(although, if truth and the salvation of the soul, diligently sought after, have not been there found where this can be done with safety, they ought to be pursued at any risk); all ranks of dignities and powers are devoted to the service of this divine worship; eminently honorable and distinguished is the name of religion. What hinders one, then, from examining thoroughly and investigating in a devout and careful inquiry whether this is that which necessarily but few know and guard in all its integrity, even if the good will of all people conspires in its favor?

(19) Since all this is so, suppose that, as I have said, we are now for the first time trying to find the religion to which we should surrender our souls to be cleansed and renewed. Undoubtedly, we would have to begin with the Catholic Church, for there are now more Christians than there are Jews and pagans combined. But of these same Christians, although there are many heresies, and all wish to appear Catholic and call the others, themselves excepted, heretics, there is one Church, as all grant. If one considers the entire world, this Church embraces a larger proportion of the common peo-

ple, and, as those who know affirm, is also more sincere in truth than all the others. But the question about truth is another question. What is sufficient for those in search of it is that there is one Catholic Church to which different heresies give different names, since they are all called by their own distinctive titles which they dare not deny. From this, with judges who are hindered by no favors passing judgment, it can be understood to which is to be attributed the name Catholic which all seek to gain. But, that no one may think that this is to be made the subject of loquacious or superfluous discussion, there is certainly one Church in which, in a certain way, human laws themselves are also Christian. I do not want any decision to be made from this in advance, but I do judge this a very opportune point at which to begin the investigation. For the fact that the true worship of God, relying on no strength of its own, should seem to have to be supported by those whom it ought to support should not be a matter for fear. But certainly it will be a matter of perfect happiness if truth can be found there where it can with greatest security be both searched for and held; if it cannot, then, at length, it should be approached and examined thoroughly elsewhere at any peril whatsoever.

Chapter 8

(20) Now that these principles have been established, which, as I think, are so just that I ought to win this case with you in the face of any adversary, let me relate to you, as best I can, the method I used in seeking true religion in the spirit in which I have just explained it should be sought. For as I left you and crossed the sea, now delaying, now hesitating, as to what I should hold and what I should discard (for my vacillation kept ever increasing from day to day from the time

that I heard that man[1] who, as you know, had been promised at his coming as one sent from heaven to solve all our difficulties, and found him, except for a certain eloquence, just like the others), I planned and deliberated much, now that I am established in Italy, not as to whether I should remain in that sect into which I now regretted having fallen, but in what way the truth had to be found—that truth for which I longed with sighs to no one better known than to you. Often it seemed to me that it could not be found, and the mightly billows of my thoughts were carried on to favor the Academics. Often again, to the utmost of my capacity, gazing into the human mind, so full of life, so keen in perception, and so discerning I thought that the truth lay in no wise hidden except in the way it should be sought, and that this same way would have to be taken from some divine authority. It remained to find out what that authority was, since in such great dissensions every one promised that he would deliver it. Thus there grew up before me a forest yielding no way of escape and into which I was loath to force my way; amid these circumstances my mind was unceasingly disturbed with the desire of finding truth. I kept turning away more and more from those whom I had already determined to abandon. In such perils there remained no other alternative than to implore the help of Divine Providence with tears and piteous supplications, and this I did unremittingly. And now some disputations of the Bishop of Milan[2] had almost moved me to wish to inquire, not without some hope, into many things concerning the Old Testament itself, on which, as you know, we used to invoke curses as it had been ill commended to us. And I had determined to be a catechumen in

1 Undoubtedly the Manichaean bishop and doctor, Faustus, with whom St. Augustine deals in *Conf.* 5.3 ff. (in 5.5 the followers of Faustus are said to regard him as The Holy Spirit of God), and against whom he published a tremendous work in 33 books (his *Contra Faustum*).

2 St. Ambrose. See *Conf.* 5.13-14; 6.3.

the Church to which my parents had committed me until I should either find what I wanted or convince myself that the search need not be made. Had there been one who could teach me at that time, he would have found me very ready and docile. In this and similar ways let there be a care for your soul. Long have you also seen yourself affected,[3] and if now you think you have been tormented enough, and you wish to put an end to sufferings of this kind, follow the path of Catholic teaching which has come down to us from the apostles through Christ Himself, and will continue hence to posterity.

Chapter 9

(21) You say that this is ridiculous, whereas all profess to hold and teach this doctrine. All heretics profess it, I cannot deny, but so as to promise those whom they entice that they will give them a reason for things that are very obscure. And they especially accuse the Catholic Church that it commands its adherents to believe, while they boast that they do not impose the yoke of believing on their followers, but rather reveal the source of their teaching. What, you say, could have been said which would more redound to their praise? But this is not so. For they do this not through any endowment of strength, but to conciliate a certain large group under the name of reason. At this promise, the human soul naturally rejoices, and without considering its own strength and health, by trying to get the food of the strong, which is unwisely prescribed except for the strong, it rushes right in to the poisons of the deceivers. For unless those things are believed, which later, if he has succeeded and been worthy, each one attains to and

---

3 For this clause and the foregoing sentence the Maurist text provides basis for a somewhat smoother rendering: 'If you have long seen yourself also in this position, affected by a like care for your soul, and if you now think . . .'

perceives, and without a certain weighty power of authority, true religion cannot at all be rightly entered upon.

(22) But you ask, perhaps, for some explanation on this very point which would convince you that you ought not be taught first by reason and only then by faith. This can easily be done if only you are fair. But so as to do it with advantage, I wish you to reply to me as though I were questioning you. First of all, tell me why you think one should not believe. Because, you say, credulity itself, from which the credulous get their name, seems to me to be somewhat of a fault; otherwise we would not be in the habit of bringing up this term as a matter of reproach. For, if a suspicious man is at fault in that he suspects what has not been ascertained, how much more the credulous soul, who differs from the suspicious man in this, that the one allows some doubt in matters unknown to him; the other, none. But you know that we are not wont to call a man even curious without some reproach, but we call one studious even with praise. Therefore, please note what seems to you to be the distinction even between these two. You will surely answer that though each is moved by an intense desire to know, still, the curious man inquires into things which have no reference to him at all, while the studious man, on the contrary, investigates what concerns himself. Now we do not deny that to a man belong his wife and children, and their welfare. And if someone living in a foreign country should carefully question all newcomers as to the health and well-being of his wife and children, such a one would surely be influenced by an intense desire to know; yet we do not call studious this man whose desire of knowing is both very great and directed toward matters which most especially concern him. Therefore, you now understand that your definition of a studious person has this weakness: while every studious soul does indeed wish to

know those matters which refer to himself, still, not everyone who does this should be called studious, but rather he who with utmost zeal seeks that which tends to the liberal cultivation and enrichment of the mind. Yet we may rightly call him one who studies, especially if we add what he studies to hear. For we can call him even studious of his own [family], if he loves only his own [relatives]; yet, unless we make some addition, we do not think him worthy of the name studious. And I would not call a man studious of hearing who was eager to hear how his own family were, unless, in his joy at the good report, he wished to hear it again and again; but even if he wished to hear it only once, I would call him one who studies. Turn now to the curious person and tell me—if anyone should listen willingly to a tale which would be of no value to him at all, that is, one relating to matters of no concern to him, and did this in no offensive way nor often, but very rarely and moderately, either at a dinner or in some other group or meeting—would he seem to you to be curious? I think not, but in listening willingly he would surely seem to have some care for that matter. Therefore, the definition of a curious person also has to be corrected. For why also should not he who at some time suspects something be unworthy of the name suspicious, and, similarly, he who at some time believes something be undeserving of the name credulous? And so, just as there is a great difference between one who studies something and one who is absolutely studious, and again, between one who has some care for a thing and one who is curious, so likewise is there a difference between one who believes and one who is credulous.

Chapter 10

(23) But now consider, you will say, whether in religion we ought to believe. For even if we concede that it is one thing to believe, another to be credulous, it does not follow

that there is no fault in believing in religious matters. What if it be a fault to believe and to be credulous, as it is to be drunk and to be a drunkard? One who holds this view as certain, it seems to me, could have no friend. For, if it is base to believe anything, either he acts basely who believes a friend, or, in not believing a friend at all, I do not see how he can call either him or himself a friend. Here you will perhaps say: I grant that at times we have to believe something; now, explain how in religion it is not base to believe before one knows. I shall do so, if I can. Therefore, I ask you which you consider the more serious fault: to transmit religion to one unworthy or to believe what is said by those who transmit it? If you do not understand whom I am speaking of as unworthy, I mean one who approaches it with hypocrisy in his heart. You grant, as I think, that it is much more blameworthy to reveal whatever sacred secrets there are to such a man than to believe religious men who make some affirmation about religion itself. For no other answer would be becoming to you. So now, suppose that he is present who is going to transmit religion to you; how will you convince him that you approach with the right spirit, and that there is no guile or deceit in you as far as this matter is concerned? You will say with your own good conscience that there is no deceit in you, and you will assert this with what words you can, but still with words. For as a man you would not be able to reveal to a man the inner recesses of your soul so as to be completely known. But if he said: Yes, I believe you; is it not fairer that you also believe me, if I hold any truth, since you are about to receive and I am about to bestow a benefit on you?—what answer shall we give, save that you must believe?

(24) But, you say, would it not be better for you to give me the reason so that I might follow, wherever it should lead, without any rashness? Perhaps it would be. Since it is so im-

portant that you must come to the knowledge of God by reason, do you think that all men are capable of grasping the reasons by which the human mind is led to understand the divine, or are many capable, or just a few? A few I think, you say. Do you believe that you belong to this number? It is not my place, you say, to answer this. Therefore, you think he should believe you in this, also. And this, of course, he does. Please remember that he has already twice believed you when you said something uncertain, and that you are willing not even once to believe him when he advises you on religious matters. But suppose that it is so, and that you are approaching with the right attitude to receive religion, and so are one of the few men capable of understanding the reasons by which the divine power is known with certainty—what then? Do you think that the rest of men, who have not been endowed with so serene a nature, should be denied religion? Or should they be brought gradually by certain steps to those innermost mysteries? You see clearly which way is the more religious. For neither can it seem to you that any man whatever, in his eagerness for so great a thing, should in any way be deserted or rejected. But you will agree, will you not, that unless he first believes that he will arrive at the [goal] which he has set for himself, and shows the mind of a suppliant, obeying certain important and necessary precepts, and completely purging himself by a certain way of life, he will not in any other way attain to that which is pure truth? Surely you agree. What then about those (and I now believe that you belong to this class) who can very easily, with sure reasoning, accept the divine mysteries? Will it hinder them at all if they come the way which those who believe first of all come? I think not. But still, you say, what need is there for them to delay? Because, if by so doing they will in no way harm themselves, yet they will harm others by their example. For there is scarcely anyone who has a just estimate of his own powers. He who thinks too little of himself should be roused, while he who thinks too much should be checked, the former that he may not be crushed by despair, the latter that he may not be carried on headlong in his boldness. And this is easily done even if those who are strong enough to fly are forced for a little while, in order not to incite anyone to danger, to walk on a way that is also safe for others. This is the foresight of true religion; this has been divinely commmanded; this has been handed down to our blessed forefathers; this has been kept even to our own day. To desire to pervert and disturb it is nothing else than to seek a sacrilegious way to the true religion. As to those who do this, even if their desires are granted, they cannot arrive whither they intend. For, whatever kind of excellent ability they may have, unless God is present, they creep along the ground. And He is then present when those who tend toward God have at heart the interests of human society. No surer way to heaven can be found than this step. And I, indeed, cannot resist this reasoning, for how can I say that we should believe nothing without knowledge? For there is also no friendship at all unless something is believed which cannot be demonstrated by positive reasoning. Masters, without any fault on their part, often believe the stewards in their service. But in religion what can be more unjust than that the ministers of God should be willing to believe us when we promise sincerity, while we are unwilling to believe them when they issue precepts? Lastly, what can be a more healthful way than first to become fitted for the reception of truth by believing those things which have been divinely appointed for preparing and cultivating the mind in advance? Or, if you are already perfectly fitted, [what can be more healthful than] to go the round-about way where it is safest to enter, rather than to be a source of danger to yourself and an example of rashness to others?

Chapter 11

(25) Therefore, it now remains to consider in what way these men are not to be followed who promise to guide us by means of reason. For we have already said how we can, without fault, follow those who order us to believe; but to these sponsors of reason some men think that they can come, not only without censure, but even with some measure of praise. But this is not so, for there are [only] two [classes of] persons in religion who are praiseworthy:[1] the one consists of those who

1 Cf. *Retract.* 1.14.2; 'I also said, "There are two classes . . . sure to arrive." In these words of mine, if those "who have already found," whom we have declared to be "already in actual possession," are understood to be most blessed in the sense that they are so, not in this life, but in that which we hope for and to which we aim by the way of faith, the sense is interpreted without error. For they should be judged to have found the object of their search who are already in that place in which we desire to arrive, by seeking and believing, that is, by keeping the way of faith. But, if they are thought to be or to have been most blessed in this life, this does not seem to me to be true: not that absolutely no truth can be found in this life which the mind can discern unless it be accepted on faith, but because, whatever it is, it is not so great as to make us most blessed. For what the Apostle says: "We see now through a glass in a dark manner:" and, "now I know in part" (1 Cor. 13.12) cannot be discerned by the mind; it is seen clearly, but does not yet make us most blessed. That makes men blessed which, he says, we shall know "then face to face," and which "then I shall know even as I am known" (*ibid.*). Those who have found this object should be said to be in possession of the beatitude to which leads the way of faith we keep, and whither, by believing, we desire to arrive. But the great question is who are those most blessed who are already in possession of that to which our way leads. There is no question as to the holy angels—they are surely there. But there is a question as to whether we can go so far as to say that saintly men, now departed, stand in that possession. They have already been divested of the corruptible body, which weighs down the soul; but they still await, these also, the redemption of their own bodies, and their flesh rests in hope, and is not yet glorified with the incorruption that is to come. But whether they can, nevertheless, contemplate truth with the eyes of the heart, "face to face," as it is said, cannot be discussed here for lack of space. To the same beatitude, should likewise be referred my words "for the understanding of deep and honorable, nay even divine matters is a most blessed thing." For whatever can be known in this life, however much it be, is not yet perfect beatitude, since what remains unknown is by far an incomparably larger amount.'

have already found out, and whom one necessarily judges most blessed; the other, of those who are seeking very studiously and in the most correct way. The first kind, then, is already in actual possession, while the other kind, is on the way, by which, finally one is most sure to arrrive. There are three other kinds of men, definitely worthy of censure and aversion. One consists of those who have opinions, that is, those who think that they know what they do not know; another is made up of those who realize that they do not know, but do not seek in such a way as to find; the third, of those who neither think they know nor wish to seek. There are likewise three things bordering on each other, as it were, in the minds of men which are worthy of distinction: understanding, belief, and opinion. And if these are considered separately, the first is always without fault; the second is at times faulty; and the third is never without fault. For the understanding of deep and honorable, nay even divine, matters is a most blessed thing.[2] The understanding of superfluous things, however, is not harmful, but perhaps the learning was harmful in that it took up the time of necessary matters. And as to harmful matters themselves, the misery is not in the failure to understand them, but in the doing or suffering them. For, if someone should understand how an enemy can be slain without any danger to himself, he is not guilty through the understanding itself, but through the evil desire. And, if this desire is absent, what can be said to be more innocent? But belief is then blameworthy, either when something is believed about God which is unworthy of Him, or when, in the case of man, such belief is too readily held. But in other matters, if anyone believes something, but with the understanding that he does not know it, there is no fault. For I believe that wicked conspirators were once put to death

2 For the author's remarks on this sentence, see the end of the preceding note.

through the valor of Cicero, and yet, I not only do not know this, but I even know for sure that there is no way in which I can know it. But opinion is very base for two reasons: both in that he who has convinced himself that he already knows cannot learn (even if it were possible for the thing to be learned), and the very rashness is of itself a sign of a mind ill disposed. For, even if anyone thinks he knows that fact which I mentioned about Cicero, although nothing prevents him from learning it (for the matter itself cannot be held through knowledge), still, because he does not understand that there is much difference between grasping something by the sure reason of the mind,[3] which we call understanding, and entrusting it, with profit, to tradition or writing for posterity to believe, he surely errs; and no error is without its baseness. What we understand, accordingly, we owe to reason; what we believe, to authority; and what we have an opinion on, to error. But everyone who understands also believes, and everyone who has an opinion believes, too; but not everyone who believes understands, and no one who merely has an opinion understands. Therefore, if these three capabilities be referred to the five kinds of men which we have mentioned previously, that is, the two classes deserving approval (which we put first), and the other three faulty, we find that the first class, consisting of the blessed, believes truth itself, but the second, made up

3 Cf. *Retract.* 1.14.3: 'And my statement "there is much difference between grasping something by the sure reason of the mind, which we call understanding, and entrusting it, with profit, to tradition or writing for posterity to believe," and a little later, "what we understand, accordingly, we owe to reason, what we believe to authority" is not to be so taken that, in an ordinary conversation, we should fear to say we *know* what we believe on the authority of suitable witnesses. Strictly speaking, to be sure, we say we *know* only that which we grasp with the firm reason of the mind. But when we use words according to their common usage, just as even divine Scripture does, we should not hesitate to say that we *know* both what we perceive with our bodily senses and what we believe on the evidence of reliable witnesses, provided however we are aware of the distinction between the two.'

of those who seek after and love truth, believes authority; in both these classes, belief is praiseworthy. In the first of the faulty kinds, that is, in those who think they know what they do not know, there is surely faulty credulity. The other two objectionable kinds believe nothing, that is, those who seek truth with no hope of finding it, and those who do not seek it at all. And this is true only of things which refer to some system of knowledge. For in other activities of life, I truly know not how a man can believe nothing. Although even among those who say that in practice they follow the more probable, they yet prefer to seem unable to know rather than unable to believe. For who does not believe what he approves of? Or how is it that what they follow, if it is not approved of, is probable? Truth, therefore, has two kinds of adversaries: the one consisting of those who oppose only knowledge, not faith; the other, of those who reject both; yet I truly do not know whether they can be found in the [normal] activities of man. We have said this in order to understand that, by retaining our faith in those things which we do not yet grasp, we have been set free from the rashness of such as have opinions. For, those who say that we are to believe nothing, except what we know, are on their guard against the one name of opinion, which, one must admit, is a low and wretched one. But, if they consider carefully that there is a very great difference between, on the one hand, thinking one knows and, on the other, believing, under the influence of some authority, what one realizes he does not know, they would surely avoid errors and the charge of inhumanity and pride.

Chapter 12

(26) For, I ask, if what is not known need not be believed, how are children to be subject to their parents? And how are

they to love with mutual affection those whom they do not believe to be their own parents? For this cannot in any way be known through reason, but is believed of the father on the authority of the mother; but, as to the mother herself, it is not she, for the most part, that is believed, but midwives, nurses, and servants. For cannot she from whom a son can be stolen and another substituted, having been deceived herself, deceive others? Yet we believe, and we believe without any doubt, what we admit we cannot know. For who would not see that, unless this were so, filial devotion, the most sacred bond of the human race, would be violated by a most grievous sin of pride? For who, no matter how crazy he were, should think one ought to be blamed for fulfilling his duties to those whom he believed to be his parents, even though they were not? Who, on the other hand, has not judged that man deserving of exile who, perhaps, loved his real parents very little, lest he might love counterfeit parents? Many examples can be cited which show that absolutely nothing would remain intact in human society if we should determine to believe only what we can grasp by perception.

(27) But, now, listen to something I trust you will more easily accept. When the matter at stake is religion, that is, the worship and knowledge of God, those men are less to be followed who forbid us to believe and readily promise reason. For no one is in doubt that all men are either fools or wise.[1]

1 Cf. *Retract.* 1.14.4: 'Likewise, my statement, "No one is in doubt that all men are either fools or wise men" may appear to contradict what is read in the third book of *De libero arbitrio,* "as though human nature admits of no middle state between folly and wisdom." "But that statement was made in relation to a question as to whether the first man was made wise or foolish or neither; we could in no way call him a fool since he was created faultless, and folly is a serious fault; and how we could call wise a man who could be seduced was not clear. And so, for brevity's sake, I decided to say "as though human nature admits of no middle state between folly and wisdom." I was thinking of infants; though we confess that they bear original sin, yet strictly we

Now, I call wise not the gifted and witty, but those in whom there is, in as far as it can be in man, a knowledge, grasped with surety, both of man and of God, and a life and habits in accord with this knowledge. But others, whatever may be their skills or lack of skills, whether their way of life is approved of or not, I would count in the number of the fools. Since this is so, what man of average intelligence has not clearly seen that it will be more useful and healthful for the fools to obey the precepts of the wise than to live according to their own judgment? For, every deed, if it is not rightly done, is a sin; nor can one in any way do rightly what does not proceed from right reason. Moreover, right reason is virtue itself. For, to what human being is virtue readily at hand save to the wise man? The wise man alone, therefore, does not sin. And every fool, then, sins save in those acts in which he obeys the wise man. From right reason, then, such acts spring, nor is a fool to be considered, so to say, master of his own deed, since he is, as it were, the instrument and agency of the wise man. Therefore, if it is better for all men not to sin than to sin, surely all fools would live better lives if they were subservient to the wise. And, if no one doubts that this is true in matters of lesser import, as, for instance, in buying or tilling a field, in marrying a wife, in acknowledging[2] and bringing up children, and even in the control of household property, it is all the more true in religion. In the case of human events, fine distinctions can be made more readily than in the case of divine; and in things

can not call them either wise or foolish, since they do not yet use their free will either for good or for evil. But in the present passage I said that all men are either wise or foolish, wishing those to be understood who already have the use of reason (by which they are distinguished from cattle) so as to be men; just as we say that all men wish to be happy. Are we to fear that in this statement, so true and obvious, children (who have not yet the power to desire this) will be included?

2 This meaning for *suscipere* ('lift up') is based on the Roman practice of *susceptio,* by which a father acknowledged a child as his own by lifting it up.

more sacred and extraordinary, we sin so much the more impiously and dangerously in that we owe them greater service and devotion. You see, therefore, that nothing remains to us, as long as we are fools, if our hearts are set on a good and religious life, except to seek out the wise; by obeying them, we can become less conscious of and eventually escape altogether the foolishness which dominates us as long as it remains within us.

Chapter 13

(28) Here, again, a very difficult question arises. For how will we fools be able to find a wise man? Even if only a few dare to claim this title openly, yet many do so indirectly by so differing among themselves on those very things in the knowledge of which wisdom consists, that either none of them is necessarily wise, or but one. But when the fool tries to find out who that one is, I do not at all see how he can clearly distinguish and know him. For there are no signs whatever by which one can recognize something, unless he knows the thing itself of which these are the signs. And, of course, the fool does not know wisdom. For, though one is allowed in the case of gold and silver and other things of that kind to recognize them, at sight, without possessing them, not so can wisdom be seen by the mental eye of one who lacks it. Whatever we touch by bodily sense is offered to us from without, and that is why we can distinguish with our eyes things foreign to us, though we ourselves possess nothing of them or of their kind. But what is grasped with the intellect is within the mind, and having it is equivalent to seeing. But the fool lacks wisdom; accordingly, he does not know wisdom, nor can he see it with his eyes, for he cannot see it without possessing it, nor can he have it and be a fool. He does not, therefore, know it, and, not knowing it, he cannot recognize it elsewhere. Accordingly

as long as anyone is a fool, he cannot be completely sure of finding a wise man through whom, if he obey him, he can be freed from so grevious an evil as foolishness.

(29) For this immense difficulty in our search for religion, then, only God can supply the remedy. And, unless we believe that He exists and assists human souls, we ought not even look for the true religion itself. For what, I pray, do we desire to investigate with such great effort? What do we wish to reach? At what do we want to arrive? Is it to that which we believe does not exist and does not pertain to us? Nothing is more perverse than such an attitude. Though you would not be so bold as to ask me a favor (at least you would do so impudently), unless you believed that I would grant it, yet you come asking to find a religion, while at the same time you think that either God does not exist, or, if He does exist, that He has no care of us. What if the matter is so important that it cannot be found unless it be sought out diligently, and that with all our might? What if the extreme difficulty of finding is an exercise for the mind of the inquirer, leading to the full grasp and diffusion of the discovery? For what is more joyful and familiar to our eyes than the light of day? And yet, after prolonged darkness men cannot suffer or endure it. What is more beneficial than food and drink to a body worn out with illness? But we see that convalescents are restrained and checked so that they may not venture to give themselves over to the full plates of the healthy, and thus use food itself in such a way as to fall back into the disease which was depriving them of it. I am speaking of convalescents. Again, as to the sick themselves, do we not urge them to take something? In this, surely, they would not obey us at so great discomfort if they did not believe that they were going to recover. When, then, will you give yourself to this burdensome and laborious investigation? When will you ven-

ture to impose on yourself as much care and concern as the matter deserves, if you do not believe that the object of your search exists? Rightly, then, has it been set down by the majestic teaching of Catholicism that prospective converts should be convinced of [the value of] faith before all else.

Chapter 14

(30) And so (for our discussion is, indeed, about those who wish to be called Christians) what reason, I pray, does that heretic advance? Why should he recall me from believing as though it were a rash act? If he commands me to believe nothing, then I do not believe that this true religion itself anywhere exists in human life. And, when I do not believe that it exists, I do not search for it. But he, as I think, intends to point it out to the inquirer, for it has been written:[1] 'he that seeketh, findeth.' I would not come, therefore, to a man who forbids me to believe, if I did not believe something. Is there any greater insanity than that I should displease him by faith alone, which rests on no knowledge, when faith alone led me to him?

(31) Again, what about the fact that all heretics urge us to believe in Christ? Could they be in a more self-contradictory position? There is here a twofold way in which they should be pressed. First, they should be asked where is the reason which they kept promising? Where their rebuke to rashness? Where their assurance of knowledge? For if it is base to believe any one without reason, what are you waiting for? What are you busy about? That I may believe someone without reason so that I can more easily be influenced by your reason? Or is it that your reason will build a strong superstructure on a foundation of rashness? I say this according to

1 Matt. 7.8.

those whom I displease by believing. For I not only judge it most healthful to believe before using reason (since one is unfitted to comprehend reason), and, with faith itself, to prepare the ground to receive the seeds of truth, but I believe that such is the way, generally, by which safety can alone return to sick souls. Since this seems to them a matter for ridicule and one of utter rashness, surely they are impudent in suggesting that we believe in Christ! Next, I confess that I already believed in Christ and accepted what He said as true, even when my belief was unsupported by reason. Is this the first principle by which you will guide me, O heretic? Let me consider with myself a little in what men I believed concerning Him (since Christ Himself as He willed to appear to men I did not see, He who is said to have been seen even by the eyes of the common crowds), so that, already equipped with such faith, I now draw near to you. I see that I have believed no one except the affirmed opinion and the widespread report of peoples and nations, and that the mysteries of the Catholic Church have everywhere taken possession of these peoples. Why, then, should I not most preferably seek among them, with all diligence, for Christ's teachings, since it was under the influence of their authority that I already believed that Christ had taught something profitable? Will it be from you that I am to receive a better explanation of what He said, when I would have no belief in His existence, past or present, if it had been you who had commended this doctrine to my belief? In this matter, as I said, I believed a report which had the strength of numbers, agreement, and antiquity. And everyone knows that you, so few in number, so confused, and so new, offer nothing that has the dignity of authority. What, then, is that violent insanity of yours? Believe them that you must believe in Christ, and learn of us what He said. Why, I ask you? For, if they failed and could not teach me anything, I could much more easily convince myself that it was not necessary to believe in Christ than that I could learn anything about Him save from those through whom my faith in Him had come. O tremendous confidence! Or rather, tremendous folly! I teach you the precepts of Christ in whom you believe. What if I did not believe in Him? You could not, could you, teach me anything about Him? But, he [the man] says,[2] it is proper for you to believe. You do not mean that I should believe in Him on your recommendation, do you? No, he says, for we guide by reason those who believe in Him. Why, then, should I believe in Him? Because the report is well founded. Has this come about through you or through others? Through others, he says. Shall I, then, believe in them so as to be a pupil of yours? Perhaps I ought to, had not these men warned me especially not to approach you at all. For they say that your doctrine is a dangerous one. You will reply: they are liars. How, then, shall I believe them about Christ whom they have not seen, and yet not believe them about you, whom they are unwilling to see? Believe that which is written, he says. But in the case of all writing that presents something new or unheard of, or that is commended by a few, without the support of reason, credence is given not to it but to those who bring it forward. Therefore, if, few and unknown as you are, you bring forward these writings, one is not inclined to believe them. Likewise, too, contrary to your promise, you are exacting faith by a command rather than by using reason. Again, you will call me back to the large numbers and the judgment of many. Restrain, I pray you, your stubborn persistence and that, I know not what,

2 In the remainder of this paragraph, St. Augustine sometimes puts the argument of his opponent in the third person, using *inquit*, though at times he continues to use the second person. The apparent confusion disappears if one recognizes that both the second person and third person refer to the same opponent, the heretic.

untamed desire of handing down your name; rather, urge me to seek the chief men of this multitude, and that with the utmost labor and toil, so that I may learn something from them about those writings but for whose existence I should not know that I had to learn at all. Do not return into your hiding places, and do not lay snares in the name of truth which you are trying to take away from those whose authority you yourself acknowledge.

(32) But, if they say that we are not even to believe in Christ, unless they can give a reason that cannot be doubted, then they are not Christians. This is what certain pagans say against us, foolishly indeed, but not at variance with themselves or inconsistently. But who can bear to have these men profess to belong to Christ when they contend that nothing should be believed without their showing to fools a complete disclosure of reason as it concerns God. But we see that He Himself, so far as that history teaches which they themselves acknowledge, desired nothing more or more strongly than to be believed; they, on the other hand, with whom He had to deal, were not yet fit to receive the secrets of God. For what other purpose had His miracles, so numerous and so stupendous? He Himself said that He worked them for no other reason than that He might be believed. By faith He guided fools; you guide them by reason. He cried out to be believed; you cry out against it. He praised those who believed in Him; you revile them. Either He turned water into wine[3]—not to mention other miracles—while men could imitate Him in no such prodigy (though they could follow Him in His teaching), or that statement of His is to be considered of no value:[4] 'You believe in God, believe also in me,' or that man is to be accused of rashness who did not wish Him to come to

3 John 2.7-9.
4 John 14.1.

his home, but believed that the illness of his son would go away at His command alone.[5] Therefore, applying the medicine which was to heal the most corrupt customs, through His miracles He gained authority, through His authority He won faith, through faith He drew the multitude, through the multitude He got possession of antiquity, and through antiquity He strengthened religion. And this in no way can be torn asunder, either by the most foolish novelty of heretics, working through fraud, or even by the inveterate error of nations, violently struggling against it.

Chapter 15

(33) Therefore, even if I cannot teach, yet I do not cease to admonish. Since many wish to seem wise, and it is not easy for fools to recognize whether or not they are wise, I bid you pray to God with full intention and all prayers, with groans and even with tears, if possible, to free you from the evil of error, if your heart is set on a happy life. And you will find this more easily, if you willingly obey His precepts, the commands which He willed to strengthen by such weighty authority as that of the Catholic Church. Since a wise man is so closely united to God in mind that nothing intervening can separate him, for God is truth and one is not at all wise unless his mind is in contact with truth—we cannot deny that there is between the foolishness of man and the very pure truth of God a certain mean, the wisdom of man. For the wise man imitates God to the extent of his endowment. But for the fool there is nothing closer for him to imitate sanely than a wise man. And since it is not easy to recognize him through reason, as has been said, it was necessary to present certain miracles to the very eyes (which fools

5 Matt. 8.8; Luke 7.6-7.

use much more readily, than they do their minds), so that, moved by authority, men's lives and habits might first be purged, and thus become amenable to the acceptance of reason. Since, then, it had to be that man be imitated, and yet that hope be not placed in him, what could have been done more indulgently and generously by Divine Providence than that the very Wisdom of God, pure, eternal, unchangeable, to whom we needs must cling, should deign to take upon Himself manhood? And His purpose was not only to do that which would invite us to follow God, but also to suffer that which was deterring us from following God. Since no one can attain the surest and most supreme Good, without loving it perfectly and completely (and this is not possible as long as there persists any fear of bodily or chance ills), He won our love by His wondrous birth and His miracles, and He banished fear by His death and resurrection. But in all other things He showed Himself such (and it would be tedious to pursue this in detail) as to enable us to see how far divine mercy could be extended and to what heights human weakness could be elevated.

Chapter 16

(34) This is, believe me, the healthiest authority; this is the first way of uplifting our souls from their dwelling on earth; this is conversion to the true God from the love of this world. It is authority alone that moves fools to hasten on to wisdom. So long as we cannot understand pure truth, it is indeed wretched to be deceived by authority. But surely it is more wretched to be unmoved by authority. For, if the Providence of God does not preside over human affairs, there is no point in busying one's self about religion. But if both the outward appearance of all things (and they surely must be believed to come from some spring of purest beauty) and some, I

know not what, inner conscience exhorts all better souls, both publicly and privately as it were, that God is to be sought and served, we must not give up hope that God has established some authority, on which, if we rely, just as on a sure step, we will be raised up to God. But, laying aside reason, which in its purity is very difficult, as we have said, for fools to understand, this authority moves us in two ways, that is, by miracles, and by the crowds who follow it. No one of these is necessary to the wise man. Who denies the fact? But this is now our concern—that we be able to be wise, that is, to cling to truth. Surely, the sordid soul cannot do this. And the sordidness of the soul, to sum it up briefly, is love of anything whatsoever save the soul and God; in so far as anyone is more completely freed from these vices, he will the more easily gaze on truth. But it is surely perverse and preposterous to wish, then, to see truth in order to purge out the soul, since it is purged out for this very purpose that one may see. And for a man that cannot see the truth, authority is at hand to make him fit for this, and to allow him to purge himself. And no one doubts, as I said before, that authority prevails, partly through miracles, partly through the crowds that accept it. And I call a miracle anything which appears arduous or unusual, beyond the expectation or abilities of the one who marvels at it; of which kind there is nothing better suited for the people and in general for fools than what affects the senses. Such acts, again, are divided into two classes: there are certain ones which only evoke wonder, and there are certain others which win great favor and good will. For, if anyone should see a man flying, in that the act would yield no advantage to the spectator beyond the sight itself, he would only marvel. But if anyone, afflicted by a serious and hopeless disease, should, at a command, at once regain his health, love for the one who healed him will transcend his wonder at the cure. Such were the miracles wrought at that time when God appeared (so far as sufficed for His purpose) to men as the True Man. The sick were healed. The lepers were cleansed. To the lame power to walk was restored; to the blind, sight; and to the deaf, their hearing. Men of that day saw water changed into wine, five thousand fed to satiety with five loaves, seas traversed by foot, and dead men arise. So, certain miracles had regard for the body, by a more apparent benefit, certain others for the soul by a more hidden token, and all of them for men, in bearing witness to His majesty. Thus, divine authority then turned the wandering souls of men to itself. Why, you ask, do such things not occur now? Because they would not move people, unless they were miraculous, and, if they were customary, they would not be miraculous.[1] For consider the changes of day and night, the very constant order of heavenly bodies, the fourfold change of the seasons, the fall of leaves and their return to the trees the following spring, the infinite power in seeds, the beauty of light, and the varieties of colors, sounds, smells, and tastes; and then give me a man who sees and experiences these things for the first time, with whom we can still talk—he is amazed and overwhelmed at these miracles. But we have little respect for all these things, not because of the ease with which we know them (for what is more obscure than their causes?) but surely because we constantly experience them. Those miracles were wrought, then, very opportunely, so that authority might effectively influence the habits of the multitude, which, through the miracles, had

1 Cf. *Retract.* 1.14.5: 'In another place when I had mentioned the works which Jesus Christ did when He was here in the flesh, I went on to say, "Why, you ask, don't such things occur now?" And I replied, "Because they would not move people unless they were miraculous; and if they were customary, they would not be miraculous." I said this because such great miracles are no longer worked, nor all kinds—not because none at all are worked even now.'

been brought together, and then (after witnessing them) were sent out far and wide.

Chapter 17

(35)) But habits of any kind are so strong in their possession of the minds of men that, even in the case of those that are evil (and these usually come from the dominant passions), we can more quickly condemn and detest them than we can abandon or change them. Do you think that there has been little regard for men, in that not only many learned men maintain in argument but also a multitude of unlearned men and women among them and such different classes of people both believe and assert that one should worship as God nothing earthly, nothing fiery, nothing which can touch the bodily senses, but that He can be reached only by the intellect? And what about the fact that self-restraint even leads to a very slim diet of bread and water? that fasting lasts not for the day only, but for several days in succession? that chastity is carried even to a rejection of marriage and a family? that patience endures even to the setting at naught of crosses and flames? that generosity leads even to the distribution of family estates to the poor? and that, lastly, contempt for everything of this world stretches out even to a desire for death? Few practice these [heroic virtues], and fewer practice them well and wisely. And yet, [when they are practiced], nations approve, nations applaud, nations favor, and, finally, nations love such men. And, not without lifting up their minds to God or without certain sparks of virtue, nations acknowledge that it is due to their own weakness that they cannot do these things. This is the work of Divine Providence, achieved through the prophecies of the prophets, through the humanity and teaching of Christ, through the journeys of the apostles, through the sufferings, the crosses, the blood and the death of the martyrs, through the admirable lives of the saints, and in all these, at opportune times, through miracles worthy of such great deeds and virtues. When, then, we see so much help on God's part, so much progress and such fruit, shall we hesitate to bury ourselves in the bosom of that Church? For starting from the apostolic chair down through successions of bishops, even unto the open confession of all mankind, it has possessed the crown of authority. And the heretics who lurked around her in vain were condemned, in part by the judgment of the people themselves, in part by the weighty decisions of the councils, and also in part, by majestic miracles. To be unwilling to grant this Church the first place is surely the mark either of the height of impiety or of inconsiderate arrogance. For, if souls have no sure way to wisdom and health unless faith first prepares them for reason, in what else does ingratitude for divine help and assistance consist than in the wish to resist an authority endowed with so mighty a force? And if any system of thought, however lowly and easy, needs a teacher or a master if it is to be understood, what is more indicative of rash pride, in all its fullness, than to refuse to learn the books of the sacred mysteries from their own interpreters and to venture to condemn them unknown?

Chapter 18

(36) Therefore, if either our reasoning or our speech has moved you at all, and if you have a real interest in your own welfare, as I believe you have, I would like you to listen to me, and to entrust yourself with devout faith, eager hope, and simple charity to the good teachers of Catholic Christianity, and not to stop praying to God Himself, by whose goodness alone we were created, by whose justice we are punished, and by whose mercy we are set free. Thus, you will have the teachings and disputations of men who were both learned and

truly Christian, books also and calm thoughts, too, whereby you may easily find what you seek. But abandon completely those long-winded and wretched men (what gentler phrase might I have used?) who in their intensive search for the source of evil find nothing but evil. And in this inquiry they do indeed often stir up their listeners to ask questions, but, when they have them fully roused, they so teach them that it would be better to sleep forever than in this way to be awake. They make them frantic instead of drowsy; between these sicknesses, each of which is generally fatal, there is still this difference, that the drowsy die without violence to others, but the frantic are an object of dread to many in sound health and most of all to those who wish to succor them. For God is not the author of evil; He has never repented of any of His actions; He is not troubled by any stormy disturbance of the soul; His kingdom is not a little portion of the earth; He does not approve of nor does He command any sin or wickedness; and He never deceives. For these notions, and others similar to them, disturbed us as they brandished them before us in their mightly attacks and falsely charged that this was the teaching of the Old Testament; all of which is utterly false. And so I grant that they were right in censuring these notions. What then have I learned? What do you think except that when those notions are attacked, the Catholic system of teaching is not. And so I hold what truth I had learned from them; what I had considered false, I reject. But the Catholic Church taught me many other things, also, to which those men, bloodless of body but heavy of mind, cannot aspire, that is, such truths as: God is not corporeal; no part of Him can be seen with the eyes of man; He cannot in any way either in His substance or in His nature suffer violence or change, and He is neither a composite being nor one that has been made. And if you grant me these truths (for we cannot think otherwise about God), all their contrivances have been overturned. God did not beget or create evil; neither is there nor has there ever been any nature or substance which God did not beget or make; and yet nevertheless He frees us from evil. How all this comes about is proved by arguments so compelling that no one can possibly doubt, above all you and men like you, if to a good disposition are added faithful devotion and a certain quiet of mind, without which there can be no understanding whatever of such great matters. And here there is no talk out of thin air,[1] based on some Persian tale or other to which it is sufficient to lend an ear and a mind by no means subtle, but absolutely childish. Far indeed, far different is the truth, not as the Manichaeans say in their folly. Since this discourse, however, has gone much further than I intended, let us end the book here. And in it, I want you to remember, I have not yet begun to refute the Manichaeans; I have not yet attacked their triflings, nor have I revealed anything of importance about the Catholic Church itself. I only wished to take from you, if I could, the false notion about true Christians which was taught to us out of malice or ignorance, and to rouse you up to learn certain great and divine truths. Let this volume, therefore, be what it is. And when your soul becomes calmer, I shall perhaps be more ready to discuss other things.[2] AMEN.

1 The literal expression here used ('a tale from smoke') may be based on some now undocumented proverb similar to that in which 'selling empty smoke' meant making empty promises (e.g. Martial 4.5.7). The Persian origin of Manichaeism is alluded to in the following phrase.

2 Cf. *Retract. 1.14.6*: 'But the end of the book reads: "But since this discourse . . . other things." I did not say this as though I had not yet written anything against the Manichaeans, or committed anything about the Catholic doctrine to writing, since so many volumes, issued previously, bear witness to the fact that I had not been silent on either topic. But in the book written to him, I had not yet begun to refute the Manichaeans, I had not yet attacked their triflings, nor had I revealed anything important about the Catholic Church itself, because I hoped, that after this start, I should write him what had here not been written.'

ON FAITH IN THINGS UNSEEN

(*De fide rerum quae non videntur*)

Translated

by

ROY J. DEFERRARI, Ph.D., L.L.D., L.H.D.
The Catholic University of America

and

MARY FRANCIS McDONALD, O.P., Ph.D
Mt. St. Mary, Newburgh, N. Y.

INTRODUCTION

Although *On Faith in Things Unseen* is one of St. Augustine's minor writings, its finished style shows the masterful construction, lucid presentation of ideas, and beauty of expression so characteristic of most of what he wrote. It is also a typical example of St. Augustine's apologetical style of argument and his appeal to prophecy.

Because of its omission from the *Retractationes* and the *Indiculum* of Possidius, *On Faith in Things Unseen* long was considered spurious. The Louvain theologians had relegated this work to the place of a supplement, in their edition of St. Augustine, basing this censure on the opinion of Erasmus, who had even believed it to be a writing of Hugh of St. Victor. The Benedictine editors refuted this conjecture in stating that one manuscript of the work, that of the *Codex Gemmeticensis*,[1] was discovered which antedated Hugh of St. Victor and which made formal mention of St. Augustine as author. Moreover, the matter treated and the discourse are characteristic, not of Hugh, but of Augustine. A comparison of the content of this work with St. Augustine's treatment of the same matters in his other writings reveals marked similarity in ideas and their actual expression.

Finally, and the Benedictine editors remark that 'this must have escaped Erasmus' notice,' St. Augustine himself testi-

1 From the abbey of Jumièges, now preserved in the Municipal Library of Rouen, MS A.286 (472).

fies that this is his work in *Epistola* 231, to Count Darius, with these words: 'I also sent you other books, though you did not ask for them, that I might not do only what you asked; [they are] *On Faith in Things Unseen, On Patience, On Continence, On Providence,* and a large one, *Faith, Hope, and Charity.*'

On Faith in Things Unseen is generally considered to have been written after the year 399. Before that year, in which the Emperor Honorius passed laws against idolatry, St. Augustine's reference (7.10) to the abandonment of false gods, the conversion of their temples to other uses, and the extirpation of pagan rites and customs, would have had little point. On the other hand, in this work the author quoted Holy Scripture not acording to the Vulgate, but from the Old Latin versions. This proves that it was not written in the latter part of his life, when he began to adopt St. Jerome's translation of the Bible.

Because of the phrase, 'my dearly beloved' (8.11), it is probable that the work was preached as a sermon. Its purpose is to refute that crass empiricism which would admit no faith in the truths of revelation because they cannot be 'seen,' that is, perceived by our sensory experience.

Chapters 1-2 (sects. 1-4) present St. Augustine's philosophical argument for the necessity of admitting the reality of things unseen in everyday human relations. He shows that our experience of love, friendship, and other values is not based on what we perceive by the senses, but on an interior act, an immediate vision of our mind. This quality of the human mind, by which we grasp, and give assent to, intelligible truths, axioms, and values, elsewhere plays an important role in Augustine's theory of knowledge, ever since he wrote his *Answer to Skeptics* (*Contra Academicos*). He was to develop this theory fully in the ninth book of his great work, *The Trinity*.[2]

In chapters 3-4 (sects. 5-7) Augustine proceeds to the demonstration of theological faith. He takes up the further objections of empiricists, namely that mental knowledge of things unseen is always based on inference from outward signs and indications. But, in the case of supranatural faith, such signs and indications are given in the marks of holiness of the Church, visible here and now, as they have been foretold in Scripture.

Furthermore, from this demonstration of things present and visible (the Church) we are entitled to conclude also to the truth of the invisible mysteries of faith, past (regarding Christ) and future (regarding the Last Judgment), as predicted in the Old Testament. The Jews, who have these books, yet in their blindness do not believe, are being preserved by God as a permanent exhortation to Christians to be strong in the faith. Finally, the visible victory of the Gospel over the pagan world would not have been possible unless we believe the invisible mystery: that Christ is God who became man.

Like other sermons of St. Augustine,[3] *On Faith in Things Unseen* abounds in certain rhetorical figures, especially in compound sentences whose parts are parallel in structure but opposite in meaning (antithetical parison); and in clauses with the same verbal ending (antistrophe, homoioteleuton). Not all these fine points of style could be retained in translation without doing violence to the English language.

---

2 For the early beginnings of his doctrine, see J. Geyser, in M. Grabmann and J. Mausbach, *Aurelius Augustinus* (Köln 1930) 63-86. A brief explanation on *De Trinitate* 9 appears in V. J. Bourke, *Augustine's Quest of Wisdom* (Milwaukee 1945) 210 f.

3 Cf. E. Norden, *Die antike Kunstprosa* (3rd ed. Leipzig 1918) 2.616 f., 622 f.

In the absence of a more recent edition of *On Faith in Things Unseen,* the text used has been that of the Benedictines of St. Maur (3rd Venetian reprint 1797) tome 11, and Migne, *Patrologia Latina* 40.171-80. As to the Scriptural passages, the differences between the Old Latin text quoted by St. Augustine and the Vulgate are relatively unimportant for the purpose of the present translation; the Douay version of the Vulgate has therefore been adopted.

SELECT BIBLIOGRAPHY

Texts:

Benedictines of Saint Maur, Tome II (3rd Venetian reprint 1797).

J. P. Migne, *Patrologia Latina* 40, 171-80.

Secondary Works:

V. J. Bourke, *Augustine's Quest of Wisdom* (Milwaukee 1945).

J. Geyser, *Die erkenntnistheoretischen Anschauungen Augustins zu Beginn seiner schriftstellerischen Tätigkeit* in Grabmann-Mausbach, *Aurelius Augustinus* (Köln, 1930)

CONTENTS

ON FAITH IN THINGS UNSEEN

Chapter 1

THERE ARE SOME who think that the Christian religion ought to be ridiculed rather than upheld. The reason for this is that in it, not the thing which may be seen is set forth, but faith in things which are not seen is imposed upon men. For the sake of refuting those who, prudent in their own opinion, seem to be opposed to believing what they cannot see, we surely have not the power to present to the eyes of men the divine truths which we believe. Yet, we do show the minds of men that even those things which are not seen ought to be believed. Now, as regards those whom folly has made so servile to the eyes of the body that they do not think they ought to believe anything which they do not perceive through those eyes, they ought, in the first place, to be reminded of how many things there are which cannot be seen with such eyes—things which they not only believe, but also actually know.

These things are innumerable in our mind itself, whose nature is invisible—to say nothing of other things, like the very faith by which we believe, or the thought process by which we know either that we believe something or that we do not believe it, although it may be entirely outside the realm of those eyes. What is there so bare, so clear, what so certain to the interior vision of our minds? How, therefore, must we not believe what we do not see with our bodily eyes, when we perceive beyond any doubt either that we believe or do not believe where we cannot employ the eyes of the body?

(2) But, they say, we have no need to learn through the eyes of the body those things which are in the mind, since by the mind itself we can perceive them. Moreover, what you say we should believe you neither show us exteriorly, that we may acquire knowledge of them through our bodily eyes, nor are they within the mind, that we may perceive them by thought. It is, they say, just as if a man were ordered to believe, if only he could see the object of belief presented before him. Therefore, surely we ought to believe some temporal things also, which we do not see, that we may also deserve to see the eternal things which we believe.

But, whoever you are who will not believe except what you see, with your bodily eyes you surely see bodies present to you; your affections and thoughts present to you, because they are in your own mind, you see with that mind. Tell me, I ask you, with what eyes do you see your friend's will toward you? For, no will can be seen with bodily eyes. Or, indeed, do you also see in your mind that which is taking place in the mind of another? But, if you do not see it, how do you, on your part, requite his loving kindness, if you do not believe what you cannot see?

Or, perhaps you will say that you see the will of another through his deeds? Then you will see acts and hear words, but of your friend's will you will believe that which cannot be seen or heard. The will is not color or figure that may be impressed upon the eyes; nor is it a sound or formula that may strike upon the ears; nor, indeed, is it yours to be felt by the affection of your heart. It follows, therefore, that, although it is not seen or heard or grasped inwardly by you, it is believed. Otherwise, your life would be left barren of any friendship, or love bestowed upon you would not be paid back by you in turn.

What, then, becomes of that statement of yours that you

ought to believe only what you see either exteriorly with the body or interiorly with the mind? Lo, verily, out of your heart you believe in a heart that is not yours, and you place faith where you do not focus the glance of either your body or your mind. You discern your friend's countenance by means of your body; you discern your faith by means of your mind; but your friend's faith is not appreciated by you, unless there is in you a reciprocating faith, by which you may believe what you do not see in him. It certainly is possible, too, for a man to deceive by feigning kindness and by cloaking malice. He even may not plan to do harm—still, by expecting some advantage from you, he simulates love because he does not possess it.

(3) But, you say that you believe in a friend whose heart you cannot see because you have tested him in your trials and learned of what mind he was toward you in your dangers when he did not fail you. Does it seem to you, then, that we ought to desire affliction so that the love of our friends toward us may be proved? For, no one will be happy with the surest of friends unless through adversity he has been unhappy; so that, indeed, he may not enjoy the love of another by experience unless he is tortured with grief and fear. And how is it possible, then, for the sake of having true friends, to desire such happiness, which only unhappiness can prove, and not, rather, to fear it? It is true that we can have a friend even in prosperity, but he is proved more surely in adversity.

Chapter 2

But, surely, to prove your friend you would not submit yourself to your dangers if you did not believe. And since you thus submit yourself that you may prove him, you believe before you prove. Certainly, if we ought not to believe in things not seen, we still believe in the hearts of friends though these hearts be not yet truly tried; when we have proved them as good by our misfortunes, we still believe their kindness toward us rather than see it. It is only because our faith is so great that we decide, not inconsistently, that we see with its eyes, as it were, what we believe, since we ought to believe for this reason that we cannot see.

(4) If this faith in human affairs is removed, who will not mark how great will be their disorder and what dreadful confusion will follow? For, who will be cherished by anyone in mutual charity, since love itself is invisible, if what I do not see I ought not to believe? Friendship, then, will wholly perish, since it rests upon nothing more than mutual love. What of this will one be able to receive from another, if it shall be believed that nothing of it can be shown? Furthermore, when friendship perishes, neither the bonds of marriage nor of relationship and affinity will be retained in the mind, because in these, also, there surely is a friendly spirit of harmony. Then a husband and wife will not be able to have mutual affection, since they do not believe that there is any love, inasmuch as love cannot be seen. Nor will they desire to have children, for they do not believe that the children will return their love.[1] And, if children should be born and grow up, the parents themselves will love their own much less, and they will not see love for themselves in their children's hearts because love is invisible—if things unseen are believed, not by praiseworthy faith but by blameworthy rashness.

What shall I say, now, of the other relationships—of brothers, sisters, sons-in-law, fathers-in-law, and of those joined by any sort of blood-relationship or affinity—if charity is

1 *quos reddituros esse non credunt*: The MSS. vary here, some reading *credituros*; others, *reddituros*. The meaning is clear whether we say, 'that the children believe them in turn' or 'return [love] to them.'

uncertain and good will suspected; both the will of parents by their children and the children's feelings, likewise, by their parents; and, if due kindness is not rendered, because it is not thought to be due, since that which is not seen in another is believed not to exist? Furthermore, this caution is not appropriate, but rather odious, when we do not believe that we are loved because we do not see the love of those who love us, and when we, on our part, do not return love to others because we think we do not owe them mutual love. To such a degree are human affairs disturbed, if we should not believe what we do not see, that they would be completely overturned if we should refuse belief to all the inner dispositions[2] of men which we cannot see with certainty.

I will not mention how much those, who rebuke us for believing what we do not see, themselves believe of rumor, or history, or about places where they themselves have never been; nor how in these instances they do not say: 'We do not believe because we have not seen.' Because, if they say this, they are compelled to admit that they are uncertain about their own parents. For, even on this point they have believed by reports of others—who, in turn, are unable to demonstrate the fact because the event is already in the past. Men retain no consciousness of that time, and yet, without any hesitation they give agreement to what others say about it. Yet, if this should not be done, a faithless lack of reverence toward parents would necessarily follow, while a rashness in placing belief in those things which we can not see is seemingly avoided.

Chapter 3

Therefore, when we do not believe what we cannot see,

2 Here, as elsewhere, Augustine uses the term *voluntas* (will), with the connotation of good will, affection, disposition.

concord will perish and human society itself will not stand firm. How much more, then, ought faith to be placed in divine things, even if they are not seen. If this faith is not applied, it is not the friendship of some men which is violated, but the very essence of religion itself, so that the very depth of misery results.

(5) But, you will say, although I am not able to see the kindness of a friendly person toward me, I am able, nevertheless, to trace it by many indications; whereas you, on the contrary, can show no evidence of those things not seen which you wish us to believe. Meanwhile [we reply], it is no little matter that you admit that some things, even some not seen, ought to be believed through the clearness of certain manifestations. Thus, it is also established that not all things which are not seen ought not to be believed, and the statement which holds that we should not believe the things which we do not see lies convicted and rejected.

They are very much in error who think that we believe in Christ without any proofs of Christ. For, what evidences are more clear than those which have been foretold and fulfilled? Moreover, those of you who think that there are no evidences which you have not seen whereby you ought to believe in Christ, mark well the things that you see. The Church herself addresses you with the voice of maternal affection:

'I, whose success and growth throughout the whole world astonish you, was not always such as you now behold me. But, "In thy seed shall all the nations of the earth be blessed."[1] When God blessed Abraham, He gave promise of me; for, over all nations in the blessing of Christ am I poured forth. The record of succeeding generations testifies that Christ is the seed of Abraham. To consider this briefly: Abraham

1 Gen. 22.18.

begot Isaac, Isaac begot Jacob, Jacob begot twelve sons, from whom originated the people of Israel. In fact, Jacob himself was called Israel. Among these twelve sons he begot Juda, whence comes the name of the Jews from whom was born the Virgin Mary who brought forth Christ. And, lo, in Christ, that is, in the seed of Abraham, you see and marvel that all nations are blessed. Do you still fear to believe in Him whom you ought rather fear not to believe?

'Or do you hesitate or refuse to believe His birth of a virgin, when you ought rather to believe that thus it was fitting for God to be born man? Learn that this, too, was foretold by the Prophet: "Behold, a virgin shall conceive, and bear a son, and his name shall be called Emmanuel, which is interpreted, God with us."[2] You will not doubt, therefore, the motherhood of a virgin if you want to believe the nativity of a God, who does not relinquish the government of the universe and comes in flesh among men; who bestows fecundity on His mother,[3] yet does not diminish her integrity.

'Thus, it was necessary for Him to be born as a man, though as God He always was, that by this birth He might become God to us. Hence, the Prophet again speaks concerning Him: "Thy throne, O God, is forever and ever, the scepter of thy kingdom is a scepter of uprightness. Thou hast loved justice and hated iniquity: therefore, God, thy God, hath anointed thee with the oil of gladness above thy fellows.'[4] This is the spiritual anointing whereby God anointed God, that is, the Father anointed the Son; whence we know that He was called Christ from that chrism, that is, from the anointing. I am the Church about which it is said to Him in the same psalm (and what was yet to be is declared before-

2 Isa. 7.14.
3 *matri fecunditatem afferentem*: i.e., God (the Holy Spirit) bestows fecundity on Mary who thus becomes His (the Son's) mother.
4 Ps. 44.7-8.

hand as if it had been); "The queen stood on thy right hand, in gilded clothing; surrounded with variety,"[5] that is, clothed in the mystery of wisdom,[6] decorated with a variety of tongues. Then it is said to me: "Hearken, O daughter, and see, and incline thy ear: and forget thy people and thy father's house. For the king has greatly desired thy beauty, for he is the Lord thy God. And the daughters of Tyre shall adore him with gifts, yea, all the rich among the people shall entreat thy countenance. All the glory of the king's daughter is within, in golden borders, clothed round about with varieties. After her shall virgins be brought to the king: her neighbors shall be brought to thee. They shall be brought with gladness and rejoicing: they shall be brought into the temple of the king. Instead of thy fathers, sons are born to thee: thou shalt make them princes over all the earth. They shall remember thy name throughout all generations. Therefore shall people praise thee forever; yea, forever and ever." '[7]

(6) If you do not see this queen fruitful even now in royal offspring;

If she, to whom was said,[8] 'Hearken, O daughter, and see,' does not see fulfilled what she heard promised to her;

If she, to whom was said, 'Forget thy people and thy

5 Ps. 44.10.

6 *in sacramento sapientiae*: The medieval schoolmen already knew (cf. St. Thomas, *Sum. theol.* 3.60.1) that the Fathers at times used the the term *sacramentum*, not in its technical meaning (sacrament), but in the broader sense, of any *sacrum secretum* (holy mystery). Cf. A. Michel, 'Sacrements,' DThC 14.1 (1939) 485 ff. In his *Enarrationes in Psalmos*, St. Augustine interprets the same passage (Ps. 44.10) almost by the same words: the 'vestments' of the Church are *'sacramenta doctrinae in lingus omnibus variis'* (*PL* 36.509). See also ch. 7, *sacramentum amoris* (mystery of love).

7 Ps. 10.11-18.

8 The following is a detailed allegorical exposition of the preceding quotation from Ps. 44.11-18. Many years later, Augustine took up this interpretation, though in a more elaborate way, in his *Enarr. in Psalm.* (*PL* 36.510-14).

father's house,' does not put aside the rites of former religions of the universe;

If she, to whom was said, 'The king has greatly desired thy beauty, for he is the Lord, thy God,' does not everywhere confess the Lord Christ;

If she does not behold the peoples of the nations pour forth prayers to Christ and offer gifts to Him, about whom was said to her, 'Him shall the daughters of Tyre adore with gifts';

If the pride of the wealthy even be not put aside, and if they do not implore aid from the Church, to whom was said, 'All the rich among the peoples shall entreat thy countenance';

If He does not recognize the daughters of the king to whom she was commanded to say, 'Our Father who art in heaven';[9]

If she, about whom was said, 'All the glory of the king's daughter is within,' is not renewed in her saints in the interior man from day to day,[10]—though she also strikes deeply the eyes of those outside the fold by the shining renown of her preachers,[11] in their diversity of tongues, as 'in golden borders and clothed round about with varieties';

If, then, she is not afterwards made known by her odor of goodness in whatever place she is;

And, moreover, if consecrated virgins are not led to Christ, of whom is said and to whom is said, 'After her shall virgins be brought to the king: her neighbors shall be brought to thee'—and lest they shall seem to be led like captives into some prison, he says, 'They shall be brought with gladness

9 Matt. 7.9.

10 Cf. 2 Cor. 4.16.

11 The MSS. read: *quamvis et oculos extraneorum fulgentes fama praedicatorum suorum . . . perstringat;* the Benedictine edition keeps *oculos fulgentes* (she also strikes the shining eyes . . .), but suggests that perhaps *fulgente fama* should be read. We have followed this emendation.

and rejoicing: they shall be brought into the temple of the king';

If she does not bring forth sons from whom she may have fathers, so to speak, whom she will establish everywhere as guides for herself, to whom it is said, 'Instead of fathers, sons are born to thee: thou shalt make them princes over all the earth,' and to whose prayers she will commend herself as their mother: for she has been placed before them, yet subject to them, whence it is subjoined, 'They shall remember thy name throughout all generations';

If it is not on account of the preaching of these same fathers, wherein they have been mindful of her name without ceasing, that such great multitudes have been assembled within her, to whom is said, 'Therefore shall people praise thee forever; yea forever and ever'; and if they do not confess to her unendingly in their own tongues the praises of grace;

Chapter 4

If, finally, these things are not so clearly made manifest that the eyes of enemies discover no place toward which they may turn aside, where they are not struck by the same clearness that they are forced thereby openly to make confession:

Then, perhaps you speak rightly when you say that no proofs are pointed out to you whereby you may place belief even in things which you do not see! But, if these things which you do see have been long ago prophesied and are now so manifestly fulfilled; if the very truth makes itself clear to you by antecedent and subsequent effects, that you may believe the things which you do not see, then, O remnant of infidelity, blush with shame at those which you see.

(7) 'Give heed unto me,' the Church says to you, 'give heed unto me whom you see, even though you are unwilling to see. For, those who were believers at that time in the land of Juda learned of the marvelous Birth of Christ of a virgin, learned of His Passion, Resurrection and Ascension, and being present there learned all His divine words and the deeds firsthand. These things you have not seen: therefore, you refuse to believe them. Look upon these things, therefore; direct your attention to them; reflect upon the things which you behold, which are not narrated to you as of the past, nor foretold to you as of the future, but are clearly demonstrated to you as present.'

Now, does this seem vain or unsubstantial to you, and do you think that it is either a little or no divine miracle that all mankind runs its course in the name of One Crucified? You have not seen what was predicted and fulfilled concerning the human nativity of Christ, 'Behold a virgin shall conceive and bear a son,'[1] but you do see what was predicted and is fulfilled with regard to the word of God to Abraham, 'In thy seed shall all nations of the earth be blessed.'[2]

You have not seen what was foretold about the miracles of Christ, 'Come and behold ye the works of the Lord! What wonders he hath done upon the earth,'[3] but you do see that which was foretold, 'The Lord hath said to me: Thou art my son, this day have I begotten thee. Ask of me and I will give thee the Gentiles for thine inheritance, and the utmost parts of the earth for thy possession.'[4]

You have not seen what was foretold and accomplished concerning the passion of Christ, 'They have dug my hands and my feet. They have numbered all my bones, and they

1 Isa. 7.14.
2 Gen. 22.18.
3 Ps. 45.9.
4 Ps. 2.7-8.

have looked and stared upon me. They parted my garments amongst them: and upon my vesture they cast lots,'[5] but you do see what was prophesied in the same psalm and is now manifestly fulfilled, 'all the ends of the earth shall remember, and shall be converted to the Lord: and all the kindreds of the Gentiles shall adore in his sight. For the kingdom is the Lord's; and he shall have dominion over the nations.'[6]

Nor have you seen what was predicted and fulfilled about the Resurrection of Christ in the verses where the Psalmist, in the name of Christ, speaks of his betrayer and persecutors: 'They went out and spoke together to the same purpose: all my enemies whispered together against me: they devised evils against me. They determined against me an unjust word.'[7] And in this, to prove that they accomplished nothing by killing Him, He adds that He will rise again, saying, 'Shall he that sleepeth rise again no more?'[8] And then, a little further on, concerning His very betrayer, He spoke through the mouth of the same Prophet, what is also written in the Gospel, 'He who ate my bread, hath greatly supplanted me,'[9] that is, has trampled upon me. And He straightway added, 'But thou, O Lord, have mercy on me and raise me up again: and I will requite them.'[10] This has been entirely fulfilled; Christ slept and awakened again, that is, He arose—He who says by the same Prophet in another psalm, 'I have slept and have taken my rest: and I have risen up because the Lord hath protected me.'[11]

Truly, this you have not seen, but you do see His Church,

---

5 Ps. 21.17-19.
6 Ps. 21.28-29.
7 Ps. 40.7-9.
8 Ps. 40.9.
9 Ps. 40.10; John 13.18.
10 Ps. 40.11.
11 Ps. 3.6.

of which in a similar manner it was said and brought to completion, 'O Lord, my God, to thee the Gentiles shall come from the ends of the earth, and shall say: surely our fathers have possessed lies, a vanity which hath not profited them.'[12] This, indeed, you do behold, whether you wish to or not, even if as yet you think that there is, or has been, some usefulness in idols; however, certainly you have heard the numerous people of the nations say, after they abandoned or rejected or shattered these vanities to pieces, 'Surely our fathers have possessed lies, a vanity which hath not profited them. Shall a man make gods unto himself, and they are no gods?'[13]

And neither will you believe that it was foretold that these nations would come[14] to some place of God, as it has been said, 'To thee the Gentiles shall come from the ends of the earth.'[15] Understand, if you can, that it is unto the God of the Christians, who is supreme and the true God, that the people of these nations come, not by walking, but by believing. For, this same announcement has been made in these words by another Prophet: 'The Lord shall be terrible upon them, and shall consume all the gods of the earth: and they shall adore him every man from his own place, all the islands of the Gentiles.'[16] One says, 'To thee the Gentiles shall come from the ends of the earth'; the other, 'They shall adore him every man from his own place.' Therefore, they will not be required to withdraw from their own place in coming to Him, because they will find Him in whom they believe in their own hearts.

12 Jer. 16.19.
13 Jer. 16.19-20.
14 *gentes praedictas fuisse venturas*: Another rendering would be: 'that the aforesaid nations were to come . . . .' Both constructions leave grammatical uneasiness.
15 Jer. 16.19-20.
16 Soph. 2.11.

You have not seen what was foretold and fulfilled concerning the Ascension of Christ, 'Be thou exalted, O God, above the heavens,'[17] but that which necessarily results therefrom, 'And thy glory over all the earth'[18] you do see. Now, then, all those things already accomplished and transacted concerning Christ you have not witnessed, but you may not deny that you do see the things which are taking place here and now in the Church. We make clear to you that these two kinds of events have been prophesied. But, we are not able to point out for your sight that both of them have been fulfilled, because we have not the power to recall to sight what is past.

Chapter 5

(8) But, just as by means of tokens or marks which we do see we believe the good will[1] of our friends which we do not see, so the Church, which is now visible, is a token of all those past things and a harbinger of future things which are invisible to us, but which are pointed out in the very writings in which she herself is foretold. For, when prediction was made of the past things which can no longer be seen, and of the present things which can be seen, but not all,[2] at that time, none of them could be seen. Then, things predicted began to happen, from those which have been accomplished up to those which are now taking place; thus, the things which were related concerning Christ and the

17 Ps. 107.6.
18 *Ibid.*

1 See above ch. 2, n.2.
2 The MSS read: . . . *quae nunc possunt videri, omnia cum praenuntiarentur*, 'For when prediction was made of all these things, the past ones which can no longer be seen, and the present ones which can now be seen.' We have preferred the Benedictine emendation: *quae nec* possunt videri omnia, cum praenuntiarentur.

Church have come to pass, according to their preordained succession. And to this order belong the prophecies which similarly have been made concerning things to come: the day of judgment, the resurrection of the dead, the eternal punishment of the wicked with Satan, and the eternal reward of the just with Christ. Why, then, should we not believe those earliest and latest things which we do not see, when, as witnesses for both, we have things between them which we do see, and when in the books of the Prophets we hear, or read for ourselves, that the first and the middle and the last were all predicted before they took place? Unless, perhaps, unbelieving men think that those books were fashioned by the Christians in order that the things which they already believed might have greater authority and influence, if they should be considered to have been promised before actually taking place.

Chapter 6

(9) If they suspect this, let them search through the books of our opponents, the Jews. There they may read these things which we have mentioned, the prophecies made concerning the Christ, in whom we believe, and the Church, which we behold from the difficult beginnings of the faith[1] up to the everlasting happiness of the Kingdom. When they read, let them not wonder that the Jews, whose scriptures these are, do not understand because of the darkness of enmity. For, it was proclaimed beforehand by the very same prophets that they would not understand, because it was necessary for other things to be fulfilled, and by a hidden and just decree of God, for due punishment to be paid in accord-

1 *ab initio laborioso fidei*: Some MSS. add *quam tenemus* (which we hold), and some read, *ab in. laboriosae fidei* (quam ten.) 'from the beginnings of the difficult faith [which we hold].'

ance with their merits. For, indeed, He whom they crucified, He to whom they gave gall and vinegar—although He was hanging on the cross—He said to the Father, for the sake of those whom He would have led from the darkness into the light, 'Father, forgive them, for they know not what they do." But, for the sake of the others whom He was to abandon for more hidden causes, He said long before through the Prophet, 'And they gave me gall for my food, and in my thirst they gave me vinegar to drink. Let their table become as a snare before them, and a recompense, and a stumbling block. Let their eyes be darkened that they see not; and their back bend thou down always.'[3] Therefore, they roam about anywhere and everywhere, their darkened eyes a most remarkable proof for our cause, so that through them our arguments are upheld at the very time that this same people is rejected.

Therefore, it was appointed, lest these arguments should thus be lost, that this same sect should not be as nothing; but it was scattered over the earth so that, by carrying about with it the prophecies of grace conferred upon us, it might everywhere be beneficial to us for a more firm convincing of unbelievers.[4] Accept that which I am saying in the manner in which it was prophesied: 'Slay them not, lest at any time my people forget thy law. Scatter them by thy power.'[5] They have not been killed, therefore, for this reason, that they have not forgotten what things were read and heard among them. For if they should forget entirely the Sacred Scriptures,

2 Luke 23.34.
3 Ps. 68.22-24.
4 Cf. Rom. 11.15,30,32. The mystery of the preservation of the Jews made St. Paul exclaim: 'O the depth of the riches of the wisdom and of the knowledge of God! How incomprehensible are his judgments, and how unsearchable his ways' (*ibid.* 33).
5 Ps. 58.12.

although they do not comprehend them, they would be killed according to the Jewish rite itself, because, when the Jews knew nothing of the Law and the Prophets, they could be of no avail whatsoever. For this reason they have not been exterminated, but dispersed; although they themselves do not possess the faith whence they might be saved, they still retain in memory that whereby we are aided. They are our supporters in their books, our enemies in their hearts, our witnesses in their scrolls.

Chapter 7

(10) Even if no testimonies concerning Christ and the Church had appeared in advance, ought not the unexpected illumination of the human race by divine brightness move every one to believe, when we behold false gods abandoned; their images everywhere dashed to pieces; their temples razed or converted to other uses; so many vain rites rooted out from the most inveterate human traditions; and the one true God called upon by all classes of people? And this was brought about by one Man, who was derided by men, seized, bound, scourged, struck,[1] condemned, crucified, and put to death. For His disciples He chose men who were ignorant, inexperienced—fishermen and publicans—through whom His authority should be preserved; men whom He chose as witnesses of His Resurrection and Ascension. And this they have declared that they saw for themselves, and, filled with the Holy Spirit, they have proclaimed the Gospel in all tongues, even those they had never learned. Of those who heard them, some believed; some, not believing, violently withstood their preaching.

1 Editors insert *exspoliatum* (stripped) in place of the *expalmatum* of the MSS. The latter word was familiar to St. Augustine.

Accordingly, the faithful have been struggling, even to the death, for the sake of the truth, not by returning evil for evil, but by bearing evil patiently; they have been the victors, not by killing, but by dying. In such a way, then, has the world been changed to this religion; thus have the hearts of all been converted, men and women, young and old, learned and ignorant, wise and simple, mighty and weak, rich and poor, renowned and lowly. And this Church, spread throughout all nations, has so flourished that even now no sect contrary to the Catholic faith, no kind of error, arises which is so much in opposition to the Christian faith that it does not affect and strive to boast in the name of Christ. Indeed, such error would not be permitted to sweep over the earth, were it not for the fact that the very contradiction fosters sound discipline. [2]

How would the Crucified have been able to accomplish so much, had He not been God who became man, even if such things had not been foretold through the Prophets? Since however, so great a mystery of love did have its prophets and heralds going before, through whose inspired words it has been announced, and since it did come to pass exactly as it was foretold, who is so foolish as to say that the Apostles lied about Christ whom they preached as having come—just as the Prophets long before had predicted that He would come, and at the same time had made known future truths concerning the Apostles, too? Certainly, it was about them that they had said: 'There are no speeches nor languages, where their voices are not heard. Their sound hath gone forth into all the earth: and their words unto the ends of the world.'[3] And, surely, this we see fulfilled now in the world, although we have not yet seen Christ in the flesh. Who,

2 Cf. 1 Cor. 11.19.
3 Ps. 18.4-5.

therefore, except a man blinded by extreme foolishness, or hard and unyielding with a strange stubbornness, will not place faith in the sacred writings which have foretold the faith of the whole world?

Chapter 8

(11) But, my dearly beloved, you who have this faith or who have but newly received it, cherish it, and let it increase within you. For, just as the temporal things predicted so long before[1] have come to pass, so also will the eternal verities that have been promised come about. Let not the vain pagans deceive you, nor faithless Jews, nor deceitful heretics, nor those evil Christians who are in the Catholic Church itself, so much the more harmful because they are enemies within. And, lest the weak become upset for this reason, divine prophecy has not passed over it in silence, for, as a spouse speaking to his beloved in the Canticle of Canticles, Christ speaks to His Church: 'As a lily among thorns,' He says, 'so is my love among the daughters.'[2] He did not say 'in the midst of outsiders,' but 'in the midst of daughters.'

'He that hath ears to hear, let him hear.'[3] While the net which is cast into the sea and gathers together all kinds of fishes, as the Holy Gospel tells us, is being dragged toward the shore—that is, the end of the world—let him separate himself from the bad fishes, in heart, not in body, by changing his evil ways, not by breaking the holy net; lest those who are now seen to be the elect be reckoned among the reprobate and find not life, but eternal punishment, when the great dividing on that eternal shore shall begin.[4]

---

1 *temporalia tanto ante praedictas.* Several MSS. read: *temporalia tanta praedicta,* 'so many [or: such great] temporal things predicted.'
2 Cant. 2.2.
3 Matt. 13.19.
4 Cf. Matt. 13.47-50.

INDEX

INDEX

www.ingramcontent.com/pod-product-compliance
Lightning Source LLC
Chambersburg PA
CBHW020515110726
47899CB00004B/1123
* 9 7 8 0 8 1 3 2 1 3 1 9 4 *